Beginning Sensor Networks with Arduino and Raspberry Pi

Charles Bell

Apress·

Beginning Sensor Networks with Arduino and Raspberry Pi

Copyright © 2013 by Charles Bell

ISBN-13 (pbk): 978-1-4302-5824-7

ISBN-13 (electronic): 978-1-4302-5825-4

President and Publisher: Paul Manning
Lead Editor: Michelle Lowman
Developmental Editor: Tom Welsh
Technical Reviewer: Andrew Morgan
Editorial Board: Steve Anglin, Mark Beckner, Ewan Buckingham, Gary Cornell, Louise Corrigan, James DeWolf, Jonathan Gennick, Jonathan Hassell, Robert Hutchinson, Michelle Lowman, James Markham, Matthew Moodie, Jeff Olson, Jeffrey Pepper, Douglas Pundick, Ben Renow-Clarke, Dominic Shakeshaft, Gwenan Spearing, Matt Wade, Steve Weiss, Tom Welsh
Coordinating Editor: Jill Balzano
Copy Editor: Tiffany Taylor
Compositor: SPi Global
Indexer: SPi Global
Artist: SPi Global
Cover Designer: Anna Ishchenko

Distributed to the book trade worldwide by Springer Science+Business Media New York, 233 Spring Street, 6th Floor, New York, NY 10013. Phone 1-800-SPRINGER, fax (201) 348-4505, e-mail orders-ny@springer-sbm.com, or visit www.springeronline.com. Apress Media, LLC is a California LLC and the sole member (owner) is Springer Science + Business Media Finance Inc (SSBM Finance Inc). SSBM Finance Inc is a Delaware corporation.

For information on translations, please e-mail rights@apress.com, or visit www.apress.com.

Apress and friends of ED books may be purchased in bulk for academic, corporate, or promotional use. eBook versions and licenses are also available for most titles. For more information, reference our Special Bulk Sales–eBook Licensing web page at www.apress.com/bulk-sales.

Any source code or other supplementary materials referenced by the author in this text is available to readers at www.apress.com. For detailed information about how to locate your book's source code, go to www.apress.com/source-code/ .

I dedicate this book to my loving wife, Annette.

—Dr. Bell

Contents at a Glance

Contents

About the Author

Dr. Charles A. Bell conducts research in emerging technologies. He is a member of the Oracle MySQL Development team and is the team lead for the MySQL Utilities team. He lives in a small town in rural Virginia with his loving wife. He received his Doctor of Philosophy in Engineering from Virginia Commonwealth University in 2005. Dr. Bell is an expert in the database field and has extensive knowledge and experience in software development and systems engineering. His research interests include microcontrollers, three-dimensional printing, database systems, software engineering, and sensor networks. He spends his limited free time as a practicing Maker focusing on microcontroller projects and refinement of three-dimensional printers.Dr. Bell maintains a blog on his research projects and many other interests. You can find his blog at `http://drcharlesbell.blogspot.com/` .

About the Technical Reviewer

Andrew Morgan is currently a product manager with Oracle Corporation, responsible for MySQL's High Availability solutions, including replication and MySQL Cluster—this gives him lots of opportunity to travel to present at conferences or meet customers, and his record is five continents, seven countries, and nine cities within a week. He first combined his interest in the Raspberry Pi and MySQL when back in 2012 he decided to find out what it would take to get MySQL Cluster (the super-tough, hugely scalable, telco-grade database) running on the humble Pi (http://www.clusterdb.com/mysql-cluster/mysql-cluster-running-on-raspberry-pi/). Earlier in his career, he worked on telecoms software development at Nortel. Andrew holds a BSc in Computer Science from the University of Warwick. You can read Andrew's blog at www.clusterdb.com or follow him on Twitter @andrewmorgan.

Acknowledgments

I would like to thank all of the many talented and energetic professionals at Apress. I appreciate the understanding and patience of my managing editor, Michelle Lowman, coordinating editor, Jill Balzano, and development editor, Tom Welsh. Each was instrumental in the success of this project. I appreciate their encouragement and guidance. I would also like to thank the small army of publishing professionals at Apress for making me look so good in print. Thank you all very much!

I'd like to especially thank the technical reviewer and my colleague, Andrew, at Oracle for his patience, insight, and impressive attention to detail. Most importantly, I want to thank my wife, Annette, for her unending patience and understanding during the many hours I spent hunched over my laptop or conducting experiments on the dining table.

Introduction

The world of microcontrollers and increasingly capable and popular small computing platforms is enabling many more people to learn, experience, and complete projects that would previously have required dedicated (and expensive) hardware. Rather than purchase a commercial or made-for-consumers kit, enterprising developers can now build their own solutions to meet their needs. Sensor networks are just one example of how these small, powerful, and inexpensive components have made it possible for anyone with a moderate skill set to build their own sensor network.

This book presents a beginner's guide to sensor networks. I cover topics including what types of sensors exist, how they communicate their values (observations or events), how they can be used in Arduino and Raspberry Pi projects, and how to build your own home temperature sensor network.

I also include an introduction to the MySQL database server and how you can connect to, store, and retrieve data. Why, I even show you how to do it directly from an Arduino!

Who This Book Is For

I have written this book with a wide variety of readers in mind. It is intended for anyone who wants to get started building their own sensor networks or those who want to learn how to use components, devices, and sensors with an Arduino or Raspberry Pi.

Whether you have already been working with sensor networks, or maybe have taken an introductory electronics course, or even have read a good Apress book on the Arduino or Raspberry Pi, you will get a lot out of this book. Best of all, if you ever wanted to know how to combine sensors, Arduinos, XBee, MySQL, and Raspberry Pi to form a cohesive solution, this book is just what you need!

Most importantly, I wrote this book to meet my own needs. Although there are some excellent books on the Arduino, Raspberry Pi, sensors, and MySQL, I could not find a single reference that showed how to put all of these together. That is, until now.

About the Projects

There are nine chapters, seven of which include projects that demonstrate and teach key concepts of building sensor networks. Depending on your skill level with the chapter topic, you may find some of the projects easier to complete than others. It is my hope that you find the projects challenging and enlightening (but, more importantly, informative) so that you can complete your own sensor network projects.

In this section, I present some guidance on how best to succeed and get the most out of the projects.

Strategies

I have tried to construct the projects so that the majority of readers can accomplish them with little difficulty. If you encounter topics that you are very familiar with, I recommend working through the projects anyway instead of simply reading or skipping through the instructions. This is because some of the later projects build on the earlier projects.

On the other hand, if you encounter topics that you are unfamiliar with, I recommend reading through the chapter or section completely at least once before attempting the project. Take some time to fully absorb the material, and pay particular attention to the numerous links, tips, and cautionary portions. Some of those are pure gold for beginners.

Perhaps the most significant advice I can offer when approaching the projects is to attempt them one at a time. By completing the projects one at a time, you gain knowledge that you can build on for future projects. It also helps your establish a pace to work through the book. Although some accomplished readers can probably complete all the projects in a weekend, I recommend working through the book at a pace best suited for your availability (and enjoyment).

With some exceptions, the earlier chapters are independent and can be tackled in any order. This is especially true for the Arduino (Chapter 4) and Raspberry Pi (Chapter 5) chapters. Regardless, it is a good idea to read the book and work on the projects in order.

Tips for Buying Hardware

The hardware list for this book contains a number of common components such as temperature sensors, breadboards, jumper wires, and resistors. Most of these items can be found in electronics stores that stock supplies for electronics enthusiasts. The list also includes a number of specialized components such as XBee modules, XBee adapters, XBee shields, Arduino boards, and Raspberry Pi boards.

Each chapter has a list of the components used at the end of the chapter. In some cases, you reuse the hardware from previous chapters. I include a separate list for these items. I have placed the component lists at the end of each chapter to encourage you to read the chapter before attempting the projects.

The lists include the name of each component and at least one link to an online vendor that stocks the component. In addition, I include the quantity needed for the chapter and an estimated cost. If you add up all the components needed and sum the estimated cost, the total may be a significant investment for some readers.

The following sections are for anyone looking to save a little on the cost of completing the projects in this book or wanting to build up their own inventory of sensor network hardware on a budget.

Buy Only What You Need When You Need It

One way to mitigate a significant initial investment in hardware is to pace your buying. If you follow my advice and work on one project at a time, you can purchase only the hardware needed for that project. This will allow you to spread the cost over however long you plan to work through the book.

However, if you are buying your hardware from an online retailer, you may want to balance ordering the hardware for one project at a time against the potentially higher total shipping cost for multiple orders.

As mentioned, the more common electronics like LEDs, breadboards, and so on, can be found in traditional brick-and-mortar stores, but the cost may be a little higher. Once again, the cost of shipping to your location may dictate whether it would be cheaper to buy the higher-priced items from a local electronics shop versus an online retailer.

Online Auctions

One possible way to save money is to buy your components at a discount on online auction sites. In many cases, the components are the very same ones listed. In other cases, the components may be from vendors that specialize in making less-expensive alternatives. I have had a lot of success in buying quality hardware from online auction sites (namely eBay).

If you are not in a hurry and have time to wait for auctions to close and the subsequent shipping times, you can sometimes find major components like Arduinos, shields, power supplies, and the like at a reduced price by bidding for them. For example, open source hardware manufacturers sometimes offer their products via auctions or at special pricing for quantities. I have found a number of Arduino clones and shields at nearly half the cost of the same boards found on other sites or in electronics stores.

Hey, Buddy, Can You Spare an Arduino?

Another possible way to save some money on the hardware is to borrow it from your friends! If you have friends who are electronics, Arduino, or Raspberry Pi enthusiasts, chances are they have many of the components you need. Just be sure you return the components in working order![1]

A NOTE ABOUT NEWER ARDUINO BOARDS

The projects in this book are designed for a current, readily available version of the Arduino. The projects can be completed with the Duemilanove or Uno boards without modification. Although you can use the Leonardo (see specific notes in the chapters about the differences), you should consider the newer boards carefully before buying.

Some newer boards may require additional changes or extra steps to use. For example, the Due is perfectly suitable and an excellent choice for projects that require larger sketches; but you must use the newest beta version of the Arduino IDE, which may require slight changes to your sketch. There are a couple of other things unique to the Due, but I highlight these in the chapters. Finally, you can use the Yún, but you would be using only the Arduino side of the board so this may not be a cost-effective solution.

Downloading the Code

The code for the examples shown in this book is available on the Apress web site, www.apress.com. A link can be found on the book's information page under the Source Code/Downloads tab. This tab is located underneath the Related Titles section of the page.

Reporting Errata

Should you find a mistake in this book, please report it through the Errata tab on the book's page at www.apress.com. You will find any previously confirmed errata in the same place.

---

[1]And replace the components you implode, explode, or otherwise turn into silicon slag. Hey, it happens.

■ ■ ■

## CHAPTER 1

Introduction to Sensor Networks

Sensor networks are no longer expensive industrial constructs. You can build a simple sensor network from easily procured, low-cost hardware. All you need are some simple sensors and a microcontroller or computer with input/output capabilities. Yes, your Arduino and Raspberry Pi are ideal platforms for building sensor networks. If you've worked with either platform and have ever wanted to monitor your garden pond, track movement in your home or office, monitor the temperature in your house, monitor the environment, or even build a low-cost security system, you're halfway there!

As inviting and easy as that sounds, don't start warming up the soldering iron just yet. There are a lot of things you need to know about sensor networks. It's not quite as simple as plugging things together and turning them on. If you want to build a reliable and informative sensor network, you need to know how such networks are constructed.

In this chapter, we will explore sensor networks through a brief description of what they are and how they are constructed. We will also examine the components that make up a sensor network including an overview of sensors; the types of sensors available and the things that they can sense.

Anatomy of a Sensor Network

Sensor networks are everywhere. They're normally thought of as complicated monitoring systems for manufacturing and medical applications. However, they aren't always complicated, and they're all around you.

In this section, we will examine the building blocks of a sensor network and how they're connected (logically). First, let's look at some examples of sensor networks in an effort to visualize the components.

Examples of Sensor Networks

Although some of these examples may not be as familiar to you as others, it's a good idea as you read through these examples to try and imagine the components of the application. Visualize the sensors themselves—where they're placed and what data they may be reading and sending to another part of the network for processing and recording.

Automotive

Almost every modern automobile has a network of sophisticated sensors that monitor the performance of the engine and its subsystems. Some cars have additional sensors for monitoring external air temperature, tire pressure, and even proximity to objects and other vehicles.

If you take a late-model car in for service and get a chance to look in the garage area, you may notice several machines that resemble computer terminals on wheels (the newest ones are handheld units). These systems are diagnostic machines designed to connect to your car and read all the data the sensors and computer have stored. Some manufacturers use the industry standard interface called *on-board diagnostics* (OBD).[1] There are several versions of this interface and its protocols; most dealerships have equipment that supports all the latest protocols.

Some manufacturers use their own proprietary diagnostic systems, but many use the same connector as OBD-II. For example, Porsche uses what it calls *Porsche Integrated Workshop Information System* (PIWIS). While PIWIS uses the same connector as OBD-II, Porsche implemented a proprietary system to read and alter the data.

Interestingly, while manufacturers that use proprietary diagnostic systems require you to service your car at an authorized dealer, some enterprising technologists have created compatible systems. In the case of Porsche, Durametric (www.durametric.com/default.aspx) manufactures a host of products that enable basic maintenance features like fault and service-reminder reset and even advanced troubleshooting features for many Porsche models. Figure 1-1 shows one of the screens of the Durametric software reading the sensor data from a Porsche Cayman.

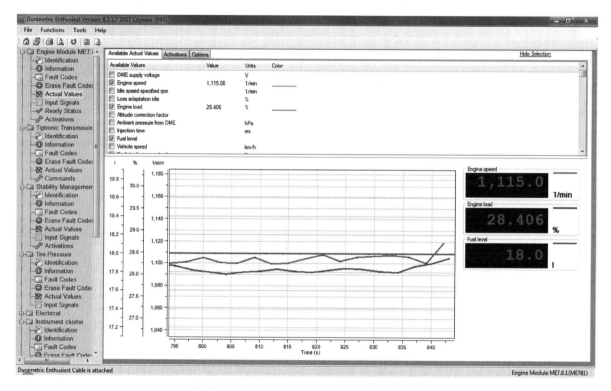

Figure 1-1. *Porsche diagnostic data from Durametric*

Notice the level of detail displayed. The image shows three metrics in the trace, but if you look at the top of the screen you will see many more metrics that can be monitored. The data shown in the graph was gathered in real time and displayed using the sophisticated sensor networks Porsche employs.

The use of sensors in automobiles has begun to spill over into related machinery such as motorcycles, boats, and even the venerable farm tractor. Many modern farm machines such as combines have sophisticated sensors that enable autopilot mode.[2]

---

[1] http://en.wikipedia.org/wiki/On-board_diagnostics

[2] It may be hard to imagine a 46,000-pound machine that resembles a medieval torture device being driven by a computer, but it's true. Some of the most expensive combines have more sophisticated technology than your favorite sports sedan.

Environment

The environment is on many peoples' minds, and many scientists are actively monitoring it. Motives for monitoring the environment range from checking a specific area or room for gases and tracking the area's temperature and humidity; to monitoring and reporting anomalies for sensitive equipment, such as running chemical analyses for clean rooms. Examples of environment sensor networks include those used to monitor air pollution, detect and track forest fires, detect landslides, provide earthquake early warnings, and provide industrial and structural monitoring.

Sensor networks are ideal for all forms of environmental monitoring. Due to the sensors' small size, low energy requirements, and low cost, implementers can install them at sites or at specific stations or machines for precise reporting. For example, a clean-room environment often requires very precise temperature and humidity control as well as extremely low levels of contaminants (loose particles floating in the air). Sensors can be used to measure these observations at key locations (windows, doors, air vents, and so on); the data is sent to a computer that records it and generates threshold alerts. Most sophisticated clean rooms tie the filtration, heat, and cooling systems into the same computer system (through the use of their own sensors) to control the environment based on the data collected from the sensor network.

Environmental sensors aren't limited to temperature, humidity, dew point, and air quality. Sensors for monitoring electromagnetic interference and radio frequencies may be used in hospitals to protect patients who rely on sensitive electronic medical equipment. Sensors for monitoring water purity, oxygen level, and contaminants may be used in fish farms to maximize crop yield.

Scientists and industrial engineers aren't the only ones who build environmental sensor networks. You can build your own using relatively low-cost sensors. In their book *Environmental Monitoring with Arduino: Building Simple Devices to Collect Data About the World Around Us* (Make, 2012), Emily Gertz and Patrick Di Justo show how to build simple sensor networks to monitor noise, water purity, and, of course, weather.

If this sounds too good to be true, consider for the moment your average home heating, ventilation, and cooling system (HVAC). It has a very simple sensor network, often in the form of a single sensor for ambient temperature (the thermostat on the wall) that feeds data to a control board that turns on the mechanisms to pump gases through the system and the fan to move air. Some modern HVACs use additional sensors to monitor air quality and engage additional active electronic filters[3] or to divert heat and cooling to areas where it's needed most.

IS A THERMOSTAT REALLY A SENSOR NODE?

If you've ever been in a home with a thermostat that used a sliding or rotating arm to set the desired temperature, it's likely you've encountered a simple sensor node. Older thermostats use a combination of a temperature-sensitive coil and a tilt switch mounted to it. This coil is in turn mounted to a plate that can be tilted one way or the other to adjust the desired temperature. As the room temperature changes, the coil expands or contracts, reorienting the tilt switch. Once the coil expands or contracts so that the tilt switch disengages, the flow of voltage to the HVAC unit ceases, thereby turning off the unit.

Some manufactures are creating increasingly sophisticated thermostats. Some are even capable of recording data and predicting trends. For example, the Nest Learning Thermostat (www.nest.com/living-with-nest/) can detect when someone is at home and can be accessed remotely via the Internet.

---

[3]Electronic filters are an absolute necessity for those of us with allergies living in areas with a high concentration of pollutants, both natural and manmade.

Atmospheric

Closely related to environmental monitoring is atmospheric monitoring: a sensor network designed to monitor air quality. Atmospheric monitoring is a form of environment monitoring, but there is a great deal more emphasis on studying the atmosphere. The obvious reason is that mammals simply can't survive without air (at least, not for long).

As in environment sensor networks, there are specialized sensors to measure all forms of air quality including free gases, particle contamination, smoke, humidity, and so on. Other motivations for building atmospheric sensor networks include measuring pollution from factories and automobiles, ensuring clean drinking water from water treatment plants, and measuring the effects of aerosols.

Fortunately for the hobbyist and aspiring atmospheric scientist, gas sensors are plentiful, and many are inexpensive. Better still, many example projects available on the Internet demonstrate how to construct atmospheric sensor networks.

ENVIRONMENT VS. ATMOSPHERE: WHAT'S THE DIFFERENCE?

If you're wondering what the difference is between environment and atmosphere, you aren't alone. Simply stated, *environment* is an aggregate of things around a subject (a person, an object, or an event) that influences the subject. Thus, it can be all the things around you including the ambient temperature, moisture content, and so on.

Atmosphere (literally, air) refers to the collection of gases that fills the spaces around objects. In essence, atmosphere is one of the elements in an environment. Scientists have defined many layers of atmosphere surrounding planet Earth. Most atmospheric sensors are designed to measure the unique gases for a specific level. The lower atmosphere where we live is called the *troposphere*.

Like the environmental monitoring sensor networks discussed earlier, you can build your own atmospheric sensor network. In their book *Atmospheric Monitoring With Arduino: Building Simple Devices to Collect Data About the Environment* (Make, 2012), Emily Gertz and Patrick Di Justo also show how to build simple sensor networks that measure gases such as butane and methane, light wavelengths, ozone, and more.

Security

Some of the most popular and prolific sensor networks are those used for security and surveillance. You may not think of security systems as sensor networks, but let's consider what is involved in a typical home or office security system.

A basic security system is designed to record and alert whenever a door or window is opened. The sensors in such a network are switches (the simplest of all sensors) that detect when a door or window is opened or closed. A central processor or microcontroller can be used to monitor the sensors and take action: for example, generating a signal with a buzzer or bell.

A surveillance system includes more than just a set of switches. Typically, such a system includes video sensors (cameras) and even audio sensors (microphones). The system may also include some form of monitor that records the data and enables users to view that data (see when doors were opened, listen to audio, and view video).

Most home surveillance systems include a digital video recorder (DVR) and one or more cameras. The system I use in my own home includes four cameras with audio. The system allows me to record data from the sensors programmatically and to view the video in real time. Figure 1-2 shows a typical and affordable home surveillance system from Harbor Freight (www.harborfreight.com).

Figure 1-2. *Security sensor network: home surveillance system from Harbor Freight*

Surveillance systems used in businesses are similar to home surveillance systems but typically include additional sensors and data tracking such as employee badging, equipment monitoring, and integration, along with offsite support services such as night watchmen and data archiving.

Although they aren't as inexpensive as temperature, humidity, light, or gas sensors, microphones and cameras are becoming cheaper. You can find these sensors at electronics stores such as Adafruit Industries. For example, Adafruit has a camera (http://adafruit.com/products/397) that you can connect to your Arduino or Raspberry Pi to record images and low-frame-rate video (see Figure 1-3).

Figure 1-3. *Camera sensor from Adafruit Industries (courtesy of Adafruit)*

Many security sensor networks are available for the consumer. They range from simple audio/visual monitoring to remote monitored systems that integrate into your home, tracking everything from movement to portal breaches, and even temperature and lighting.

SENSOR NETWORKS AND THE INTERNET

A growing community of enthusiasts are generating interest in what is called the *Internet of Things* (IOT). This phrase refers to the recent explosion of network-aware devices that can send data to other resources, thereby virtualizing the effects of the devices on users and their experience. The IOT therefore is about how these devices relate to the human experience. Sensor networks play a prominent part in the IOT, and several books have been written on the topic, including the following:

- *Building Internet of Things with the Arduino* by Charalampos Doukas (CreateSpace Independent Publishing Platform, 2012)

- *Architecting the Internet of Things* by Dieter Uckelmann, Mark Harrison, and Florian Michahelles (Springer, 2011)

- *Getting Started with the Internet of Things: Connecting Sensors and Microcontrollers to the Cloud* by Cuno Pfister (O'Reilly, 2011)

If you're interested in learning more about the IOT and how sensor networks are used, check out some of these titles.

The Topology of a Sensor Network

Now that you've seen a few examples, let's discuss the components of a sensor network: in this case, a garden pond monitoring system. Specifically, the system monitors the health of a fishpond. Thus, the system is an environmental sensor network.

The motivation is to ensure a safe environment for the fish. This means the water temperature should be within tolerance for the species of fish, the water depth should be maintained to avoid over- or under-filling, and the oxygen level of the water should be monitored to ensure that there is sufficient oxygen for the fish to survive.

Most pond owners have learned to build their ponds with the cycle of life in mind, to be sure the pond can sustain its environment. However, things can go wrong. The introduction of another species (like amphibians[4] or the dreaded algae infestation) can cause an imbalance that could threaten your prized Koi. Having the ability to detect when an imbalance begins can make the solutions much easier to implement.

Figure 1-4 shows a simple drawing depicting the sensors and their placement. In this system, there are three sensors, a monitoring control or recording system, and a communication medium—a way for the sensors to send their data to the monitor. Let's begin by discussing the sensors.

---

[4]Each pond I've built has eventually given birth to frogs. Where do they all come from?

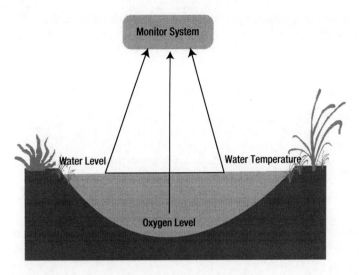

Figure 1-4. *Typical fishpond monitoring system*

If I were to build this system, I would use sensors that operate on low voltage so that I could use battery or solar to power them. Most sensors are discrete components that take voltage in and produce either digital or analog data. They require another component to read the data and send it to the pond-monitoring control system. If you're thinking this would be a good use for an Arduino, you're right! The Arduino is an excellent platform for reading data from one or more sensors and sending it to another system for processing. Some enterprising Arduino enthusiasts have built monitoring systems using only a single Arduino and multiple sensors.

Let's assume for this example that the pond-monitoring system is a computer with an Arduino attached to it so that you can record, view, or access the data remotely. You now have the sensors connected to an Arduino (called a *sensor node*) and the pond-monitoring system connected to another Arduino (called the *aggregator node*). What is missing is how to get the data from the sensor node to the aggregate node.

There are many ways to get two Arduino to communicate or share data, but this book limits the discussion to media that permit long-distance communication—wired or wireless. Wired communication in this case can be via an Ethernet shield (a special daughter board designed to sit on top of the Arduino) or a wireless fidelity (WiFi) shield fitted to each Arduino.

As you can see, many levels of hardware and protocols are involved in building sensor networks. Now that you have a general idea of what the major components are, let's examine the communication media and then discuss the types of sensor nodes.

Communication Media

Now that you understand the topology of a sensor network, let's consider how sensors communicate their data to the other nodes in the network. They do so through two basic forms of network communication: wired and wireless.

Wired Networks

Wired networks can take several forms. All involve some form of hardware designed to permit electrical signals[5] to be sent from one device to another via a wire or cable. Thus, sensor networks that employ wired communication must also add network hardware to the nodes in the network.

---

[5]There is a special form of wired network that uses optical signals. The cables are made from glass fibers that use light waves instead of electrical signals.

As I mentioned earlier, you can use an Arduino with an Ethernet shield to connect the sensor node(s) to the aggregate or data-collection nodes. If your sensors were hosted with Raspberry Pi computers, you would already have the necessary hardware to connect two Raspberry Pi computers—they all have RJ-45 LAN ports.

Of course, using wired Ethernet isn't as simple as plugging a cable in to two devices. Unless you use a crossover cable, you need some form of Ethernet switch to connect the devices. A detailed discussion of Ethernet networks and hardware is beyond the scope of this book, but it's a viable communication medium for sensor networks.

Wireless Networks

A more popular and more versatile medium is wireless communication. In this case, you use a wireless device such as a WiFi shield for each Arduino or WiFi adapters for Raspberry Pi computers. Like wired Ethernet, wireless Ethernet (WiFi) requires the addition of a wireless router. However, WiFi has a much shorter maximum distance, so it may not be suitable for some networks.

But you have another form of wireless at your disposal. You can use XBee wireless modules instead of Ethernet (WiFi). XBee provides a specialized, lightweight protocol that is ideal for use in sensor nodes and small microcontrollers and embedded systems. The rest of this book uses XBee modules for the communication mechanism of the example sensor network projects.

One of the features of XBee modules is that they are low power and can be placed into a periodic sleep mode to conserve power. However, the best feature is that XBee modules can be connected directly to sensors, allowing you to build even lighter weight (and cheaper) sensor nodes. XBee modules are discussed in more detail in Chapter 2.

Hybrid Networks

Some sophisticated sensor networks require the mixing of both communication media. For example, an industrial sensor network may collect data using sensor nodes installed in many different buildings or rooms. You may want to isolate the sensor networks into subsystems because each area may require a different form of sensor network. In this case, it may be better to use wireless for certain segments in which the use of wired networks is difficult (for example, a sensor on a moving industrial robot) and wired Ethernet to link the subsystems to a central data-recording or -monitoring system.

Types of Sensor Nodes

Sensor nodes are composed of one or more sensors (although this book uses only one sensor per node) and a communication device to transmit the data. As mentioned, the communication device can be a microcontroller like an Arduino, an embedded system, or even a small-footprint computer like a Raspberry Pi. Typically, sensor nodes are designed for unattended operation; they're sometimes installed on mobile objects or in locations where wired communication is impractical. In these situations, sensor nodes can be designed to operate without being tethered to a power or communication source.

Logically, sensor nodes can be classified into different types based on how they're used. The following sections detail type of sensor node used in this book. It helps to think of the sensor nodes by role so that you can design and plan the sensor network using logical building blocks.

Basic Sensor Nodes

At the lowest (or *leaf*) level of the sensor network is a basic sensor node. This is the type of node described thus far—it has a single sensor and a communication mechanism. These nodes don't store or manipulate the captured data in any way—they simply pass the data to another node in the network.

Data Nodes

The next type of node is a data node. Data nodes are sensor nodes that store data. These nodes may send the data to another node, but typically they're devices that send the data to a storage mechanism such as a data card; to a database via a computer; or directly to a visual output device like an LCD screen, panel meter, or LED indicators.

Data nodes require a device that can do a bit more than simply pass the data to another node. They need to be able to record or present the data. This is an excellent use for a microcontroller, as you'll see in later chapters. Digi, the makers of the XBee, has dedicated sensor nodes that measure temperature, humidity, and light information and transmit the data on the network. Where is the fun in that? In this book, you build your own sensor nodes.

Data nodes can be used to form autonomous or unattended sensor networks that record data for later archiving. Returning to the fishpond example, many commercial pond-monitoring systems employ self-contained sensor devices with multiple sensors that send data to a data node; the user can visit the data node and read the data for use in analysis on a computer.

Aggregator Nodes

Another type of node is an aggregate node. These nodes typically employ a communication device and a recording device (or gateway) and no sensors. They're used to collect data from one or more data or sensor nodes. In the examples discussed thus far, the monitoring system would have one or more aggregator nodes to read the data from the sensors. Figure 1-5 shows how each type of nodes would be used in a fictional sensor network.

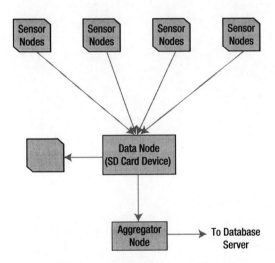

Figure 1-5. *Types of nodes in a sensor network*

For the more general case, the diagram should probably show multiple data nodes (so that the aggregator node is actually aggregating stuff).

In this example, several sensor nodes at the top send data wirelessly to a data node in the middle. The data node collects the data and saves it to a secure digital card, which then sends the data to an aggregator node that communicates with a database server via a wired computer network to store the data. Mixing data nodes with aggregator nodes ensures that you won't lose any data if your aggregator node fails or the recording and monitoring system fails or goes offline.

Now that you understand the types of nodes in a sensor network, let's examine sensors: how they can measure data, and examples of sensors available for building low-cost sensor networks.

Sensors

With all this talk of sensors and what sensor networks are and how they communicate data, you may be wondering what exactly sensors are and what makes them sense. This section and its subsections answer those questions and more. Let's begin with the definition of a sensor.

A *sensor* is a device that measures phenomena of the physical world. These phenomena can be things you see, like light, gases, water vapor, and so on. They can also be things you feel, like temperature, electricity,[6] water, wind, and so on. Humans have senses that act like sensors, allowing us to experience the world around us. However, there are some things your sensors can't see or feel, such as radiation, radio waves, voltage, and amperage. Upon measuring these phenomena, it's the sensors' job to convey a measurement in the form of either a voltage representation or a number.

There are many forms of sensors. They're typically low-cost devices designed for a single purpose and with a limited capability for processing. Most simple sensors are discrete components; even those that have more sophisticated parts can be treated as separate components. Sensors are either analog or digital and are typically designed to measure only one thing. But an increasing number of sensor modules are designed to measure a set of related phenomena, such as the USB Weather Board from SparkFun Electronics (`www.sparkfun.com/products/10586`) (see Figure 1-6).

Figure 1-6. *USB Weather Board (courtesy of SparkFun and Juan Pena)*

Notice the blue module with *XBee* written on it. This is a wireless module that permits the sensor board to send its data to another node or multiple nodes. The XBee is discussed in more detail in Chapter 2.

The following sections examine how sensors measure data, how to store that data, and examples of some common sensors.

---

[6]Shocking, isn't it?

How Sensors Measure

Sensors are electronic devices that generate a voltage based on the unique properties of their chemical and mechanical construction. They don't actually manipulate the phenomena they're designed to measure. Rather, sensors sample some physical variable and turn it into a proportional electric signal (voltage, current, digital, and so on).

For example, a humidity sensor measures the concentration of water (moisture) in the air. Humidity sensors react to these phenomena and generate a voltage that the microcontroller or similar device can then read and use to calculate a value on a scale. A basic, low-cost humidity sensor is the DHT-22 available from most electronic stores (see Figure 1-7).

Figure 1-7. *DHT-22 humidity sensor (courtesy of Adafruit)*

The DHT-22 is designed to measure temperature as well as humidity. It generates a digital signal on the output (data pin). Although simple to use, it's a bit slow and should be used to track data at a reasonably slow rate (no more frequently than about once every 3 or 4 seconds).

When this sensor generates data, that data is transmitted as a series of high (interpreted as a 1) and low (interpreted as a 0) voltages that the microcontroller can read and use to form a value. In this case, the microcontroller reads a value 40 bits in length (40 pulses of high or low voltage)—that is, 5 bytes—from the sensor and places it in a program variable. The first two bytes are the value for humidity, the second two are for temperature, and the fifth byte is the checksum value to ensure an accurate read. Fortunately, all this hard work is done for you in the form of a special library designed for the DHT-22 and similar sensors. Let's see how this works in practice.

Listing 1-1 shows an excerpt from the DHT library provided by Adafruit for the Arduino platform. You can find this library at `https://github.com/adafruit/DHT-sensor-library`. The listing shows the method used to read the humidity from the DHT-22 sensor library on the Arduino.

Listing 1-1. Reading Temperature and Humidity with a DHT-22

```
// Read data from a DHT-22 sensor using the DHT library.
void loop() {
  float humidity = dht.readHumidity();
  float temperature = dht.readTemperature();
```

```
  // Make sure they are numbers or fail.
  if (isnan(temperature) || isnan(humidity)) {
    Serial.println("ERROR: DHT values are not numbers!");
  } else {
    Serial.print("Temperature (C): ");
    Serial.print(temperature);
    Serial.print("Humidity: ");
    Serial.print(humidity);
  }
}
```

Notice that the DHT library provides methods to make it very easy to read the temperature (in Celsius) and humidity and display those values.[7] Yes, it's that easy! If you'd like to experiment with the DHT-22, there is an excellent tutorial on Adafruit's site (http://learn.adafruit.com/dht).

Recall that the DHT-22 produces a digital value. Not all sensors do this; some generate a voltage range instead. These are called *analog sensors*. Let's take a moment to understand the differences. This will become essential information as you plan and build your sensor nodes.

Analog Sensors

Analog sensors are devices that generate a voltage range, typically between 0 and 5 volts. An analog-to-digital circuit is needed to convert the voltage to a number. Most microcontrollers have this feature built in, and the Arduino is a fine example. The Arduino has a limited set of pins that operate on analog data and incorporate analog to digital (A/D) conversion circuits.

But it isn't that simple (is it ever?). Analog sensors work like resistors and, when connected to microcontrollers, often require another resistor to "pull up" or "pull down" the voltage to avoid spurious changes in voltage known as *floating*. This is because voltage flowing through resistors is continuous in both time and amplitude. Thus, even when the sensor isn't generating a value or measurement, there is still a flow of voltage through the sensor that can cause spurious readings. Your projects require a clear distinction between OFF (zero voltage) or ON (positive voltage). Pull-up and pull-down resistors ensure that you have one of these two states. It's the responsibility of the A/D converter to take the voltage read from the sensor and convert it to a value that can be interpreted as data.

WHAT IS A RESISTOR?

A *resistor* is one of the standard building blocks of electronics. Its job is to impede current and impose a reduction in voltage (which is converted to heat). Its effect, known as *resistance*, is measured in ohms. A resistor can be used to reduce voltage to other components, limiting frequency response, or protect sensitive components from over voltage.

When a resistor is used to pull up voltage (by attaching one end to positive voltage) or pull down voltage (by attaching one end to ground) (resistors are bidirectional), it eliminates the possibility of the voltage floating in an indeterminate state. Thus a pull-up resistor ensures that the stable state is positive voltage, and a pull-down resistor ensures that the stable state is zero voltage (ground).

An excellent getting-to-know-electronics book is the *Encyclopedia of Electronic Components* by Charles Platt (O'Reilly, 2012).

---

[7]Using the serial monitor feature of the Arduino IDE. See Chapter 3 for details on how to use the serial monitor.

When sampled (when a value is read from a sensor), the voltage read must be interpreted as a value in the range specified for the given sensor. Remember that a value of, say, 2 volts from one analog sensor may not mean the same thing as 2 volts from another analog sensor. Each sensor's data sheet shows you how to interpret these values.

When you use a microcontroller like the Arduino, the A/D converters conveniently change the voltage into a value that uses 10 bits, resulting in an integer value between 0 and 1,023. For example, a sensor may measure phenomena in a range consisting of 200 points on a scale. The lowest value typically represents 0 and the highest 1,023. The Arduino in this case can be programmed to convert the value read from the A/D converter into a value on the sensor's scale.

As you can see, working with analog sensors is a lot more complicated than using the DHT-22 digital sensor from the previous section. With a little practice, you will find that most analog sensors aren't difficult to use once you understand how to attach them to a microcontroller and how to interpret their voltage on the scale in which the sensor is calibrated to work.

Digital Sensors

Digital sensors like the DHT-22 are designed to produce a string of bits using serial transmission (one bit at a time). However, some digital sensors produce data via parallel transmission (one or more bytes[8] at a time). As described previously, the bits are represented as voltage, where high voltage (say, 5 volts) or ON is 1 and low voltage (0 or even -5 volts) or OFF is 0. These sequences of ON and OFF values are called *discrete values* because the sensor is producing one or the other in pulses—it's either ON or OFF.

Digital sensors can be sampled more frequently than analog signals because they generate the data more quickly and because no additional circuitry is needed to read the values (such as A/D converters and logic or software to convert the values to a scale). As a result, digital sensors are generally more accurate and reliable than analog sensors. But the accuracy of a digital sensor is directly proportional to the number of bits it uses for sampling data.

The most common form of digital sensor is the pushbutton or switch. What, a button is a sensor? Why, yes, it's a sensor. Consider for a moment the sensor attached to a window in a home security system. It's a simple switch that is closed when the window is closed and open when the window is open. When the switch is wired into a circuit, the flow of current is constant and unbroken (measuring positive volts using a pull-up resistor) when the window is closed and the switch is closed, but the current is broken (measuring zero volts) when the window and switch is open. This is the most basic of ON and OFF sensors.

Most digital sensors are actually small circuits of several components designed to generate digital data. Unlike analog sensors, reading their data is easy because the values can be used directly without conversion (except to other scales or units of measure). Some may suggest this is more difficult than using analog sensors, but that depends on your point of view. An electronics enthusiast would see working with analog sensors as easier, whereas a programmer would think digital sensors are simpler to use.

So, what do you do with the data once it's measured? The following section briefly describes some aspects of sensor data and considerations for storing that data.

Storing Sensor Data

Storing sensor data depends on how the data is interpreted and ultimately how it will be used. If you plan to use a computer—or, better, a database—to store the data, you should store it in a way that makes sense.

For example, storing a sequence of voltages from an analog signal may be considered preserving the data in its purest form, but without context or an A/D converter, the data may be meaningless. Storing the digital conversion of the voltage may not be wise either, because you have to remember the scale and range in order to derive the values intended to be represented. Thus it makes much more sense to store the resulting conversion to scale. Fortunately, when you're using digital sensors, the only thing you need to remember is what unit of measure is being used (Celsius, Fahrenheit, feet, meters, and so on). Therefore, it's best to save the final form of the measurement.

---

[8]This depends on the width of the parallel buffer. An 8-bit buffer can communicate 1 byte at a time, a 16-bit buffer can communicate 2 bytes at a time, and so on.

But where do you store this information? Commercial sensor networks store the data in an embedded database or file-storage device, transmit it to another system for storage, or store it on removable digital media. Older sensor networks (like a polygraph or EKG machine) store the data as hard copy using graphs (making them very obsolete).

There are a number of simple storage devices and technologies you can use to build your own sensor networks, ranging from local devices for the Arduino to modern hard drives on the Raspberry Pi. These storage mechanisms are listed here and discussed in more detail when this book examines the types of hardware used and application of technologies in building sensor networks:

- Hard-copy printer

- Secure digital card

- USB hard drive

- Web server

- Database server (MySQL)

Now let's take a look at some of the sensors available and the types of phenomena they measure.

Examples of Sensors

All sensor networks begin with one sensor and a means to read and interpret the data. This chapter has presented a lot of information about sensors. You may be thinking of all manner of useful things you can measure in your home or office, or even in your yard or surroundings. You may want to measure the temperature changes in your new sun room, detect when the mail carrier has tossed the latest circular in your mailbox, or perhaps keep a log of how many times your dog uses his doggy door. I hope that by now you can see these are just the tip of the iceberg when it comes to imagining what you can measure. You should be thinking about what kind of sensor network you want to build; you can use this book as a means to learn how to build it.

What types of sensors are available? The following list describes some of the more popular sensors and what they measure. This is just a sampling of what is available. Perusing the catalogs of online electronics vendors like Mouser Electronics (`www.mouser.com`), SparkFun Electronics (`www.sparkfun.com`), and Adafruit Industries (`http://adafruit.com/`) will reveal many more examples:

- *Accelerometers*: These sensors measure motion or movement of the sensor or whatever it's attached to. They're designed to sense motion (velocity, inclination, vibration, and so on) on several axes. Some include gyroscopic features. Most are digital sensors. A Wii Nunchuck (or WiiChuck) contains a sophisticated accelerometer for tracking movement. Aha: now you know the secret of those funny little thingamabobs that came with your Wii.

- *Audio sensors*: Perhaps this is obvious, but microphones are used to measure sound. Most are analog, but some of the better security and surveillance sensors have digital variants for higher compression of transmitted data.

- *Barcode readers*: These sensors are designed to read barcodes. Most often, barcode readers generate digital data representing the numeric equivalent of a barcode. Such sensors are often used in inventory-tracking systems to track equipment through a plant or during transport. They're plentiful, and many are economically priced, enabling you to incorporate them into your own projects.

- *RFID sensors*: Radio frequency identification uses a passive device (sometimes called an *RFID tag*) to communicate data using radio frequencies through electromagnetic induction. For example, an RFID tag can be a credit-card-sized plastic card, a label, or something similar that contains a special antenna, typically in the form of a coil, thin wire, or foil layer that is tuned to a specific frequency. When the tag is placed in close proximity to the reader, the reader emits a radio signal; the tag can use the electromagnet energy to transmit a nonvolatile message embedded in the antenna, in the form of radio signals which is then converted to an alphanumeric string.[9]

- *Biometric sensors*: A sensor that reads fingerprints, irises, or palm prints contains a special sensor designed to recognize patterns. Given the uniqueness inherit in patterns such as fingerprints and palm prints, they make excellent components for a secure access system. Most biometric sensors produce a block of digital data that represents the fingerprint or palm print.

- *Capacitive sensors*: A special application of capacitive sensors, pulse sensors are designed to measure your pulse rate and typically use a fingertip for the sensing site. Special devices known as pulse oximeters (called *pulse-ox* by some medical professionals) measure pulse rate with a capacitive sensor and determine the oxygen content of blood with a light sensor. If you own modern electronic devices, you may have encountered touch-sensitive buttons that use special capacitive sensors to detect touch and pressure.

- *Coin sensors*: This is one of the most unusual types of sensors.[10] These devices are like the coin slots on a typical vending machine. Like their commercial equivalent, they can be calibrated to sense when a certain size of coin is inserted. Although not as sophisticated as commercial units that can distinguish fake coins from real ones, coin sensors can be used to add a new dimension to your projects. Imagine a coin-operated WiFi station. Now, that should keep the kids from spending too much time on the Internet!

- *Current sensors*: These are designed to measure voltage and amperage. Some are designed to measure change, whereas others measure load.

- *Flex/Force sensors:* Resistance sensors measure flexes in a piece of material or the force or impact of pressure on the sensor. Flex sensors may be useful for measuring torsional effects or as a means to measure finger movements (like in a Nintendo Power Glove). Flex-sensor resistance increases when the sensor is flexed.

- *Gas sensors*: There are a great many types of gas sensors. Some measure potentially harmful gases such as LPG and methane and other gases such as hydrogen, oxygen, and so on. Other gas sensors are combined with light sensors to sense smoke or pollutants in the air. The next time you hear that telltale and often annoying low-battery warning beep[11] from your smoke detector, think about what that device contains. Why, it's a sensor node!

- *Light sensors*: Sensors that measure the intensity or lack of light are special types of resistors: light-dependent resistors (LDRs), sometimes called photo resistors or photocells. Thus, they're analog by nature. If you own a Mac laptop, chances are you've seen a photo resistor in action when your illuminated keyboard turns itself on in low light. Special forms of light sensors can detect other light spectrums such as infrared (as in older TV remotes).

- *Liquid-flow sensors*: These sensors resemble valves and are placed in-line in plumbing systems. They measure the flow of liquid as it passes through. Basic flow sensors use a spinning wheel and a magnet to generate a Hall effect (rapid ON/OFF sequences whose frequency equates to how much water has passed).

---

[9]http://en.wikipedia.org/wiki/Radio-frequency_identification
[10]www.sparkfun.com/products/11719
[11]I for one can never tell which detector is beeping, so I replace the batteries in all of them.

- *Liquid-level sensors*: A special resistive solid-state device can be used to measure the relative height of a body of water. One example generates low resistance when the water level is high and higher resistance when the level is low.

- *Location sensors*: Modern smartphones have GPS sensors for sensing location, and of course GPS devices use the GPS technology to help you navigate. Fortunately, GPS sensors are available in low-cost forms, enabling you to add location sensing to your sensor network. GPS sensors generate digital data in the form of longitude and latitude, but some can also sense altitude.

- *Magnetic-stripe readers*: These sensors read data from magnetic stripes (like that on a credit card) and return the digital form of the alphanumeric data (the actual strings).

- *Magnetometers*: These sensors measure orientation via the strength of magnetic fields. A compass is a sensor for finding magnetic north. Some magnetometers offer multiple axes to allow even finer detection of magnetic fields.

- *Proximity sensors*: Often thought of as distance sensors, proximity sensors use infrared or sound waves to detect distance or the range to/from an object. Made popular by low-cost robotics kits, the Parallax Ultrasonic Sensor uses sound waves to measure distance by sensing the amount of time between pulse sent and pulse received (the echo). For approximate distance measuring,[12] it's a simple math problem to convert the time to distance. How cool is that?

- *Radiation sensors*: Among the more serious sensors are those that detect radiation. This can also be electromagnetic radiation (there are sensors for that too), but a Geiger counter uses radiation sensors to detect harmful ionizing. In fact, it's possible to build your very own Geiger counter using a sensor and an Arduino (and a few electronic components).

- *Speed sensors*: Similar to flow sensors, simple speed sensors like those found on many bicycles use a magnet and a reed switch to generate a Hall effect. The frequency combined with the circumference of the wheel can be used to calculate speed and, over time, distance traveled. Yes, a bicycle computer is yet another example of a simple sensor network: the speed sensor on the wheel and fork provides the data for the monitor on your handlebars.

- *Switches and pushbuttons*: These are the most basic of digital sensors used to detect if something is set (ON) or reset (OFF).

- *Tilt switches*: These sensors can detect when a device is tilted one way or another. Although very simple, they can be useful for low-cost motion-detection sensors. They are digital and are essentially switches.

- *Touch sensors*: The touch-sensitive membranes formed into keypads, keyboards, pointing devices, and the like are an interesting form of sensor. You can use touch-sensitive devices like these for sensor networks that need to collect data from humans.

- *Video sensors*: As mentioned previously, it's possible to obtain very small video sensors that use cameras and circuitry to capture images and transmit them as digital data.

- *Weather sensors*: Sensors for temperature, barometric pressure, rain fall, humidity, wind speed, and so on are all classified as weather sensors. Most generate digital data and can be combined to create comprehensive environmental sensor networks. Yes, it's possible to build your own weather station from about a dozen inexpensive sensors, an Arduino (or a Raspberry Pi), and a bit of programming to interpret and combine the data.

---

[12]Accuracy may depend on environmental variables such as elevation, temperature, and so on.

Summary

Sensors are everywhere. They're in your office, your car, and even your home. Most of the sensors you encounter are discrete, like a smoke detector or thermostat. Sometimes they're part of a much larger collection of sensors designed to realize some feature, such as the sensors in your car that keep your speed constant when you set the cruise control.

Now that you've learned more about the types of sensors and the data they communicate, you've probably started to think of some cool projects to build. This book will prepare you to realize those projects. This chapter examined what sensor networks are, how they're constructed, how they communicate, and how sensors work. You even saw a bit of code!

The next chapter focuses on the communication medium used in this book, by diving into a short tutorial of the XBee wireless module. You see how to set up and configure these devices for use in transmitting sensor data to data and aggregate nodes.

CHAPTER 2

■ ■ ■

Tiny Talking Modules: An Introduction to XBee Wireless Modules

The application of sensor networks often precludes the use of wired sensors. Although it's possible to use wired sensors installed in a controlled environment that supports a cable plant, you seldom have this luxury. Sometimes you can connect some parts of a sensor network to a wired network, but the sensors are located in areas where running wires is impractical. Thus, most sensor networks require using wireless technology to transmit data from the sensors to other nodes in the network.

There are many forms of wireless communication. This book uses one of the easiest: the XBee wireless module from Digi. In this chapter, you explore the basics of using the XBee modules, from choosing a module to configuring it for use with a microcontroller, and finally to creating a simple network.

What Is an XBee?

An XBee is a self-contained, modular, cost-effective component that uses radio frequency (RF) to exchange data between XBee modules. XBee modules transmit on 2.4 GHz or long-range 900 MHz and have their own network protocols.

The XBee module itself is very small—about the size of a large postage stamp—making it easy to incorporate in small projects like sensor nodes. The modules are also low power and can use a special sleep mode to further reduce power consumption.

Although the XBee isn't a microcontroller, it does have a limited amount of processing power that you can use to control the module. One of these features, the sleep mode, can help extend battery life for battery-powered (or solar-powered) sensor nodes. You can also instruct the XBee module to monitor its data pins and transmit the data read to another XBee module. Aha! So you can use XBee modules to link a sensor node to a data-aggregator node.

While the XBee can be used to read sensor data, its limited processing power may mean it is not suitable for all sensor nodes. For example, sensors that require algorithms to interpret or extrapolate meaningful data may not be suited for using an XBee alone. You may need to use a microcontroller or computer to perform the additional calculations.

■ **Note** To configure an XBee module, you must use a Windows machine. This is because the Digi configuration tool, X-CTU, is only available on Windows. Fortunately, it works well in a Windows virtual machine (VM).

The following sections explore how to get started using XBee modules, beginning with how to choose an XBee module. I encourage you to read through the chapter before embarking on the project. I list the materials needed to complete this chapter's projects before the chapter summary.

XBee Primer

This section describes the types of XBee modules available, how to choose modules for your project, and how to configure them. I have kept this section short and terse, while providing enough information to explain what XBee modules you will be using and why.

Choosing XBee Modules

If you visit the Digi web site for its XBee line of wireless modules (`www.digi.com/products/wireless-wired-embedded-solutions/zigbee-rf-modules/zigbee-mesh-module/`), you will see a list of modules to choose. There are modules that support proprietary (Digi) protocols, WiFi (UART or SPI to 802.11 b/g/n), and ZigBee[1] and 802.15.4 protocols. So how do you know which to choose?

Some of the most popular XBee modules are those that support the ZigBee protocol. You will be using these modules for the projects in this book. If you click the link for the ZigBee modules, you will find there are more choices based on application. There are XBee modules that support the ZigBee feature set, ZigBee embedded surface mount modules, and 802.15.4[2] protocols. This book uses the modules that support the ZigBee Pro feature set.

OK, WHAT'S A ZIGBEE?

ZigBee is an open standard for network communication based on the IEEE 802 standard. The protocol supports the formation of mesh networks that can automatically configure (via the coordinator and router roles), heal broken links, and allow transmission of data over longer ranges using intermediate nodes (data is passed through the mesh from node to node). Despite the name, ZigBee is not owned by Digi, nor is it limited to the similarly named XBee module.

If you click the link for the ZigBee PRO modules (`www.digi.com/products/wireless-wired-embedded-solutions/zigbee-rf-modules/zigbee-mesh-module/xbee-zb-module`), you will see that there are two types of XBee ZigBee modules (commonly named XBee-ZB[3])—standard and PRO. The standard module is just called XBee-ZB, while the PRO modules are called XBee-PRO ZB. The PRO modules have more power and a longer range than the standard modules (300 feet versus 133 feet). As you can imagine, the PRO modules are more expensive. They also have additional features such as internal memory for more complex applications. To keep costs to a minimum, this book uses the standard XBee-ZB modules.

Although you won't find them on the Digi web site, there are several iterations (called *series*) of XBee-ZB modules. Series 1 modules use an older chipset that supports point-to-point communication.[4] Series 2 and 2.5 have a newer chipset that supports several forms of communication, including mesh networks. You will use series 2 modules for this book.

---

[1]ZigBee is based on the 802.15.4 protocol that provides power management, addressing, and error control, as well as networking features.
[2]For more information, see `http://en.wikipedia.org/wiki/IEEE_802.15.4`.
[3]A registered trademark of Digi International.
[4]Sometimes called cable replacement because it effectively links two devices together without a cable.

But you're not done yet. You also have to choose the antenna type you want to use. There are five antenna options for the PRO module and four for the standard modules. Figure 2-1 depicts each type available for the XBee-ZB modules. The following list describes each in more detail:

- *Whip or wire antenna*: A simple solution consisting of a single wire soldered onto the XBee module. These tend to be the cheaper of the antenna options because they do not require any additional hardware to use. They also provide omnidirectional signals, which means they send (radiate) approximately the same signal strength in all directions. This is the module you would use when building sensor nodes whose orientation is unknown and whose antenna wire can be exposed (not enclosed in a case). The wire antenna is not durable and can be easily broken if flexed too often. See the sidebar "Dude! You Broke It!"

- *Chip*: These modules have the antenna mounted as a discrete component on the module. This provides an option without any protrusions, but it does have a limitation. The signal is transmitted in a rough pattern that resembles a heart shape, which means the signal is attenuated in many directions (not omnidirectional). However, because the chip antenna is nearly flush, it makes a good choice for any sensor that will be placed (or worn) in a small space. It's a good alternative to the whip antenna.

- *U.FL*: This option has a very small connector that requires an adapter cable (called a *pigtail*) to permit the connection to an external antenna. These antennas have the advantage that the XBee module can be enclosed in a casing (even metal) and the antenna mounted to the exterior of the case. These modules tend to cost a few dollars more and require the purchase of the pigtail as well as the antenna.

- *RPSMA*: Like the U.FL option, this one provides for an external antenna; but it uses the much larger RPSMA connector. You can mount a swivel antenna to the connector directly, but the risk of stress on the antenna is too great. Thus, you should use an extension cable and mount the antenna externally. Like the U.FL option, these modules cost a bit more and require the purchase of an antenna.

- *PCB*: The antenna is printed or embedded as a wire trace onto the module itself. This type of module is similar to the chip antenna and may be a bit less expensive to manufacture. Currently, only the PRO modules are available with this antenna option.

RPSMA

PCB

WHIP

CHIP

U.FL

Figure 2-1. *XBee module antenna options*

DUDE! YOU BROKE IT!

If you are like me and move your electronics from location to location for trade shows, conferences, and so on, be aware that the whip antenna is misnamed. The small wire protruding from the module is not durable and in fact is very fragile.

You get four or maybe six chances to bend the antenna, so take care to orient the antenna to its 90-degree position (straight up) and leave it there! Flexing the antenna one too many times will result in a broken XBee module.[5]

If you discovered this the hard way, like I did, you can solder a replacement antenna using a bit of stranded wire of the same gauge and length. Soldering the old antenna back in place by stripping a bit of the insulation is another option, but that does change its radiation properties slightly.

Now you know that there are many types of XBee modules and that this book's projects are limited to the XBee-ZB series 2 modules, I can discuss how to communicate with the modules.

Interacting with an XBee-ZB Module

When you examine the XBee module, the first thing you notice is that the pin layout is much smaller than that of a typical discrete component designed for breadboard use. Furthermore, you cannot connect your computer directly to the XBee. You need a USB adapter to mount the XBee to allow communication with the module. Fortunately, several variants are available. You use the USB adapter to configure the module.

---

[5]Don't crack that whip! Don't even go there. Bend once and leave it!

You can use a USB dongle like the XBee Explorer dongle from SparkFun Electronics (www.sparkfun.com/products/9819). This option allows you to mount the XBee module in the headers (the two rows of 10-pin connectors) on the PCB and plug the entire unit into your USB port. Since it is only a bit larger than the XBee module itself and has no need for a cable, it may be the best choice for using your XBee in remote locations.

Figure 2-2 shows the XBee Explorer dongle without the XBee module. It accepts series 1, 2, and 2.5 standard or PRO models.

Figure 2-2. *XBee Explorer dongle (courtesy of SparkFun)*

Notice the white outline of the XBee module on the right side of the PCB. This indicates the correct orientation of the module on the board. Be sure to check pin alignment before inserting it into your USB port.

A similar option is the XBee Explorer USB, also from SparkFun (www.sparkfun.com/products/8687). Instead of being made as a dongle, it is a separate PCB base unit with a mini-USB connector. It also supports series 1, 2, and 2.5 standard or PRO modules. It requires a USB-to–mini USB cable. Figure 2-3 shows the XBee Explorer USB unit.

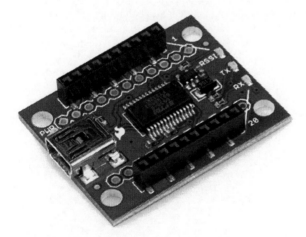

Figure 2-3. *XBee Explorer USB (courtesy of SparkFun)*

Both options from SparkFun include the mounting holes for headers that can be used with breadboards, giving you access to all the pins of the XBee module. Although they do not come with the pins soldered in place, the pins are easy to add if you so desire. You will see in later chapters where this would be helpful.

A lower-cost option is the XBee Adapter kit from Adafruit (`www.adafruit.com/products/126`). Like most kits from Adafruit, some assembly is required, but the directions on the product site are impeccable and very detailed. This option is less expensive because it does not include the USB controller circuitry. Rather, it is designed to be used with a Future Technology Devices International (FTDI) cable, also available from Adafruit (`www.adafruit.com/products/70`).[6] This cable requires software drivers that are available via the FTDI driver page (`www.ftdichip.com/Drivers/VCP.htm`).

Like the SparkFun options, it works with series 1 and 2 standard or PRO modules, and you can solder on breadboard-friendly headers and use the module as a breakout board. Figure 2-4 shows an assembled XBee Adapter kit. Be sure to orient the FTDI cable as shown in the figure.

Figure 2-4. *XBee Adapter kit (courtesy of Adafruit)*

Before using the Adafruit XBee Adapter with the FTDI cable, you must download and install the drivers from `www.ftdichip.com/Drivers/VCP.htm`. These drivers permit the FTDI chipset to appear and behave as a normal USB serial port. Click the VCP Drivers link to the left, choose the link that matches your operating system and architecture, and download the driver. You may need to unzip the driver; then install it. Once installed, your FTDI device will appear as a USB COM port.

Digi also produces an XBee development kit that contains two XBee standard modules, two XBee PRO modules, and four USB interface boards. It also includes all the cables you need to get started. Although the cost is rather intimidating ($299.00 suggested retail), it does provide a one-stop shopping option for those looking for maximum practicality and no assembly (other than plugging the modules into the interface boards). Figure 2-5 shows the Digi ZigBee Development Kit (`www.digi.com/products/model?mid=3681`).

---

[6]If you plan to use Arduino clones that also require a FTDI cable, such as the Sippino from SpikenzieLabs (`www.spikenzielabs.com`), the cost of the FTDI cable is less because you can use the one cable for all of your FTDI components.

Figure 2-5. *Digi ZigBee Development Kit*

While there are other options available from many vendors, including older serial interface modules, these are among the best and easiest-to-use options I have found for working with XBee modules. When you get to the point where we are using XBee modules with Arduino, you'll see an example of an XBee shield that enables direct connection of the XBee to the Arduino pins.

WHAT IS A SHIELD?

A shield is a PCB designed to mount on top of an Arduino by connecting to the headers on the Arduino. Shields are used to extend the hardware features of the Arduino. There are shields for controlling LCDs, Ethernet, XBees, and much more.

Pin Layout

If you look at the XBee module, you will see a total of 20 pins. If you view the module from the top (the side with the antenna), the pins are labeled 1–10 starting on the upper left and 11–20 starting from the lower right. Thus pin 1 is in the upper left, and pin 20 is in the upper right. But what do all these things do?

You will be exploring these pins in more detail in later chapters, but for now (if you are curious), Table 2-1 depicts the pin layout for a typical XBee module. In this case, I am presenting the pin layout of an XBee-ZB series 2 module.

Table 2-1. *XBee Pin Layout*

Pin	Name	Description	Direction	Default
1	VCC	Power supply	N/A	N/A
2	DOUT	UART data out	OUT	OUT
3	DIN/CONFIG	UART data in	IN	IN
4	DIO12	Digital I/O 12	BOTH	DISABLED
5	RESET	Module reset	BOTH	Open collector with pullup
6	RSSI PWM/DIO10	RX signal strength, digital I/O 10	BOTH	OUT
7	DIO11	Digital I/O 11	BOTH	IN
8	Reserved	No connection	NA	DISABLED
9	DTR/SLEEP_RQ/DIO08	Sleep control, digital I/O 8	BOTH	IN
10	GND	Ground	N/A	N/A
11	DIO4	Digital I/O 4	BOTH	DISABLED
12	CTS/DIO7	Clear to send, digital I/O 7	BOTH	OUT
13	ON/SLEEP	Status, digital I/O 9	OUT	OUT
14	VREF	No connection	IN	N/A
15	ASSOCIATE/DIO5	Associated indicator, digital I/O 5	BOTH	OUT
16	RTS/DIO6	Request to send, digital I/O 6	BOTH	IN
17	AD3/DIO3	Analog I/O 3, digital I/O 3	BOTH	DISABLED
18	AD2/DIO2	Analog I/O 2, digital I/O 2	BOTH	DISABLED
19	AD1/DIO1	Analog I/O 1, digital I/O 1	BOTH	DISABLED
20	ADO/DIO0	Analog I/O 0, digital I/O 0	BOTH	DISABLED

To find more information about the XBee module hardware, see the datasheet from Digi at http://ftp1.digi.com/support/documentation/90000976_G.pdf.

In the next section, you will see how to get started configuring the modules for use in your projects.

Configuring Modules

Configuring XBee modules is not very difficult. Because you are using ZigBee modules, you need to set the address for each module, choose a role to perform in the network, and configure your modules to interface with whatever sensor or microcontroller you are using to process the sensor data. Let's begin by discussing ZigBee addressing.

CAN SENSORS BE CONNECTED DIRECTLY TO THE XBEE?

The XBee module can read sensor data via its I/O ports. However, not all sensors can be connected directly to an XBee module. If the sensor requires direct I/O using special communication protocols, you need a microcontroller to read the sensor data and then send it to the XBee for transmission. You will see this in action when you explore using a DHT-22 temperature sensor in the next chapter.

Addresses

The XBee modules are branded with a specific serial number or address located on the bottom of the module. This is a little inconvenient given that you normally cannot see the back of the module when it is mounted. However, you can find the address using either the Digi configuration application or a simple serial terminal application.

Figure 2-6 shows the underside of an XBee module. Notice the numbers printed under the model number. You use these together to form a 64-bit address unique to each XBee module. This is referred to by many publications as the *radio address*.

Figure 2-6. *XBee address printed on the back of the module*

■ **Note** It is common to see the XBee referred to as either a *module* or a *radio*. These terms are often interchanged. I refer to the XBee in general terms with *module*, and with *radio* when referring to the transmit and receive capabilities of the radio itself.

The radio's address is used to target messages for delivery. In many ways, it is similar to an IP address, but in this case it is a specific radio address.

Along with the specific 64-bit radio address, ZigBee networks use a 16-bit address within each network that is assigned to each radio. In addition, you can assign a short text string to identify each radio. Along with that, there is a personal area network (PAN) address that can be used to logically group the radios in a network. Finally, all radios must be transmitting and receiving on the same channel (frequency). To recap, when an XBee radio wants to send a message to another radio, it must use the same channel and set the destination PAN and a specific 16-bit radio address. You see these options in action in the following sections.

ZigBee Networks

Like Ethernet networks, ZigBee networks are based on a predefined network stack where each layer in the stack is responsible for a specific transformation of the data messages. Also like other networks, ZigBee networks support message routing, ad hoc network creation, and self-healing mesh topologies. Thus, the radio address and the PAN address are needed to support these features.

Support for mesh topologies is made possible with the addition of different roles that each node (radio) can perform in the network. The following list describes each role in more detail, starting from the most complex.

- *Coordinator*: A single coordinator is needed for each network. This node is responsible for administering addresses and forming and managing the network. All other nodes search for the coordinator and exchange handshake information at startup.

- *Router*: A node that is configured as a router is designed to pass on (*route*) information to other radios. Routers enable the healing of mesh networks by joining networks and exchanging messages from other nodes. Routers are typically powered with reliable sources because they must be dependable. Thus, a data-aggregation node would be a good choice for the router radio mode.

- *End device*: An end device is a node that sends or receives information to the router nodes and the coordinator. It has an advantage in that less processing is going on, so power consumption is lower. End devices support a sleep mode to reduce power requirements still further. Most of your sensor nodes will be configured as end devices.

You can configure your XBee modules in any way you want, provided you have at least one coordinator in the network. To form a mesh, simply employ several routers, where one or more end devices exchange messages and the routers exchange messages with a coordinator. Figure 2-7 shows a typical mesh network.

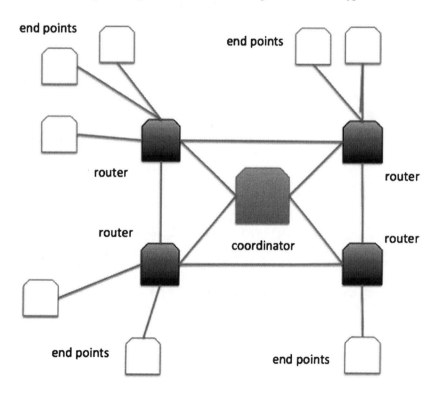

Figure 2-7. *ZigBee mesh network*

■ **Tip** Configuring XBee modules can sometimes go wrong. When this happens, the issue can be very frustrating to diagnose and correct. I include a troubleshooting section at the end of this chapter that will help you solve many of the common things that can go wonky and drive you batty. If you get stuck, check out the troubleshooting section.

Updating Firmware

The first thing you should do when starting to configure XBee modules is to load the latest version of the firmware and set the role. *Firmware* in this case refers to the program for the XBee's embedded microcontroller. You should only need to change the firmware if any of your modules are using an older version or if you want to experiment with different configurations. Digi makes this easy by providing a nice configuration application named X-CTU.

Loading firmware can only be done with the X-CTU application. Sadly, it runs only on Windows. Fortunately, it's used only once in a while, for loading the firmware and setting the ZigBee role. All other operations that you encounter in this book—and for most projects—can be achieved with the AT command via a simple serial terminal application. You can download the latest version of the X-CTU software from the following URL:

`www.digi.com/support/productdetail?pid=4624&osvid=0&type=utilities`

If you use only a Mac or Linux machine, you may want to consider either borrowing a friend's Windows laptop or running a Windows virtual machine using Oracle's VirtualBox (`www.virtualbox.org/`) software. Of course, you need a valid Windows license to install the virtual machine. Again, you are not likely to need this software more than once or twice while setting up your modules—only when you need to install or update the firmware or change the role of a module.

When you install the software, you have the option to download the latest firmware updates. Depending on the speed of your Internet connection, this step could take some time to run. If you elect to skip this step, you can do it from within the software.

■ **Note** If you are running Windows 7 or earlier, you may need to download and install the Digi drivers from `www.digi.com/support/productdetail?pid=4624&osvid=0&type=utilities`.

Once the software is installed and you launch the X-CTU software, you need to connect to your XBee module. To connect to the XBee, simply insert the XBee module into the adapter and connect it to your computer. You should see the power LED glow.

The default serial connection parameters are 9600 baud, no flow control, 8 bits, no parity, and 1 stop bit (also written as 96008N1). If you find your XBee won't communicate, chances are it is operating at a different baud rate. If you change the baud rate, you should change it for all modules.

The software has several tabs, including a PC Settings tab for configuring the serial settings. You also see a Range Test tab and a Terminal tab. For all the adapters listed here, the default values are fine. Figure 2-8 shows the PC Settings page.

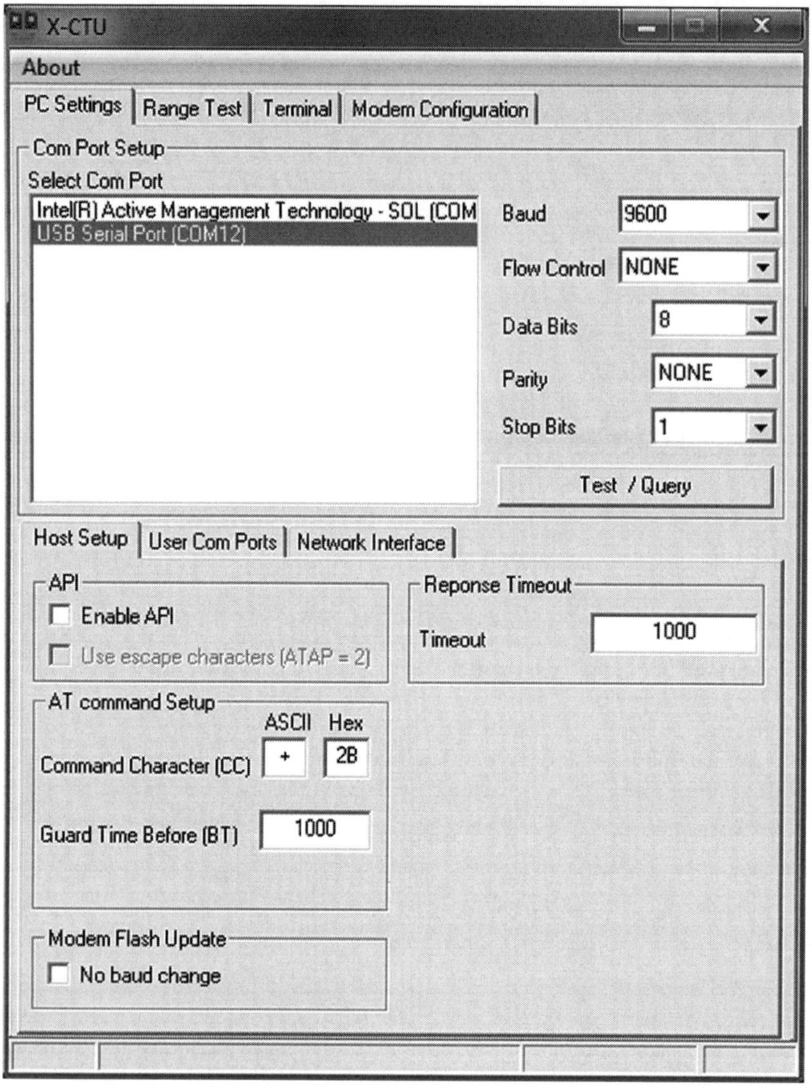

Figure 2-8. X-CTU PC Settings page

If you do not see your serial port in the Select Com Port list, you may need to restart the application. For example, you should see something like USB Serial Port (COM12). If you do not see an entry, exit the application, check the USB adapter to ensure that it is getting power, and verify that you have the proper drivers loaded (hint: the FTDI cable requires special drivers—see the Adafruit product page for more information).

Select the port for your module, and click the Test/Query button to ensure that you're connected. You should see a pop-up dialog with messages indicating that communication with the modem was successful. Click OK to close the dialog.

Once you have connected to the module, you can use the Modem Configuration tab. Click the tab, and click the Read button to read the module's current configuration. Figure 2-9 shows the Modem Configuration page after reading the configuration of an XBee module.

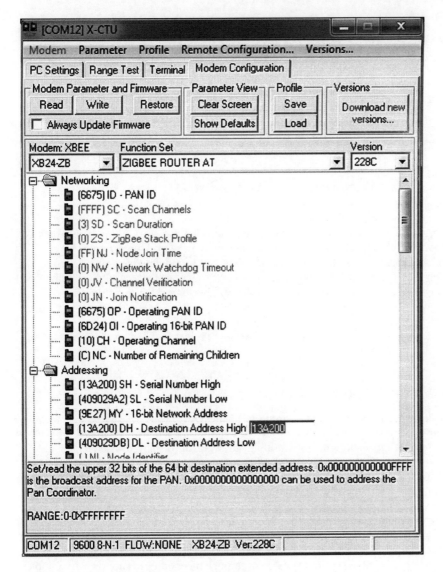

Figure 2-9. X-CTU Modem Configuration page

■ **Note**   If you elect to load the 2.5 version of the firmware, the screen may be slightly different and have 2.5-specific entries. The entries discussed here apply to both series 2 and series 2.5 firmware versions.

Notice the drop-down lists above the list containing the module settings. The Modem drop-down selects the model for the modem (the module). If you are working with a new module, you may need to change this setting to match your module. The series 2 XBee standard modules' model number is XB24-ZB. The PRO series 2 are designated as XBP24-ZB. The Function Set drop-down allows you to set the role for the module. In this case, you are using the ZigBee router role using the AT firmware. Finally, the Version drop-down lets you choose the version of the role, if applicable.

AT VS. API

XBee modules communicate in one of two ways: AT or API. AT means the module accepts AT commands via its local serial connection and displays information in a human-readable format using a derivative of the Hayes modem command set. API means the module is configured to send and receive data via its protocol stack. Thus, when you want to communicate with a module to configure it, you use the AT method. The API method is used throughout the rest of this book.

■ **Note** All modules must use the same communication firmware (AT or API) and version for their roles.

If you want to change the role, set the drop-down lists accordingly and then click the Write button. This writes a new copy of the firmware to the module. If you had a previous version, this action overwrites the current settings.

As mentioned earlier, you can also change the settings for all values that have user-defined options. These are usually shown in green. Clicking one opens a text box that allows you to change the value. For example, you may want to set the PAN address, destination address, and node identifier. If you click a value that takes a text string, like the node identifier, you must click Set, enter the new value, and then click OK. As in the firmware upload process, to save the settings, click the Write button and wait while the module is configured.

Now that you have seen how to manage the XBee module's firmware and role, let's look at an easier (and Mac and Linux friendly) way to set the user-defined values.

Changing Settings with a Terminal Application

Most of the settings for an XBee module can be changed using a terminal application. If you have a Windows machine and are running the X-CTU software, you can use the terminal feature (click the Terminal tab after connecting). It has one interesting feature that some terminal applications do not: the ability to switch the display to hexadecimal. This could be handy if you are trying to debug messages.

If you use your own terminal application, like CoolTerm for Mac OS X, you need to turn on some features in the settings or options for the connection. Ensure that local echo is turned on so you can see the commands you are typing; and you may need to turn on CRLF to make the response from the XBee appear on a new line.

The XBee module has two modes: command and transparent. Command mode is initiated with a special command, +++, where the module sends a response back via the serial connection. Transparent mode is the default mode: the module sends data to the radio destination specified. In other words, use command mode when you want to talk to the module and transparent mode when you want to talk via or through the module to another. For example, sending data via the XBee to another XBee uses transparent mode.

Thus, to configure your XBee modules after loading the correct firmware, you open a terminal application and issue the appropriate command. Table 2-2 shows some of the more common AT commands you use to configure XBee modules.

Table 2-2. *Common XBee AT Commands*

Command	Description	Use	Response
+++	Enter command mode	Put the module in command mode.	OK
ATCN	Exit command mode	Return to transparent mode.	OK
AT	Attention	Check to see if the module is available.	OK
ATWR	Save	Write settings to firmware.	OK
ATID	PAN ID	Display the PAN ID.	PAN ID
ATID nnnn	PAN ID	Change the PAN ID.	OK
ATSH	64-bit serial high	Display the high part of the 64-bit serial number.	Address
ATSL	64-bit serial low	Display the low part of the 64-bit serial number.	Address
ATDH	64-bit destination high	Display the high part of the 64-bit destination address.	Address
ATDH nnnn	64-bit destination high	Set the high part of the 64-bit destination address.	OK
ATDL	64-bit destination low	Display the low part of the 64-bit destination address.	Address
ATDL nnnn	64-bit destination low	Set the low part of the 64-bit destination address.	OK
ATMY	16-bit address	Display the 16-bit address assigned by the coordinator.	Address
ATNI	Node ID	Display the text string node identifier.	id
ATNI text	Node ID	Set the text string node identifier.	OK
ATRE	Reset	Reset the XBee to factory defaults.	OK

Some commands require a value for setting variables. Omitting the variable results in displaying the current value. All commands except +++ require you to press Enter to execute. If you press the +++ command and nothing happens, try it again, waiting a second or two between each attempt. You can also try typing a little faster (or a little slower) until the command-mode switch takes effect.

■ **Tip** All numeric values are entered as hexadecimal values.

To demonstrate how these commands work, let's connect a module that has been loaded with the ZigBee ROUTER AT firmware. Figure 2-10 shows a typical configuration session starting with connecting to the module and displaying its values and then exiting command mode using CoolTerm on Mac OS X.

■ **Note** The first time you run the ATDH, ATDL, or ATMY command without a parameter, you may see a result of 0. This indicates the value has not been set.

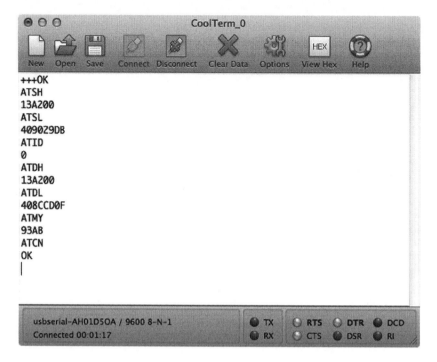

Figure 2-10. *Getting information about a module with a terminal*

■ **Tip**   When in command mode, you have only 10 seconds to enter a command before the module returns to transparent mode. If this happens, you see no response when entering commands. Simply issue the +++ command again, and reissue the command.

Next, Figure 2-11 shows a session where you set the destination address (the XBee to which you want to connect) and its PAN ID using X-CTU on Windows (it does not matter which terminal application you use).

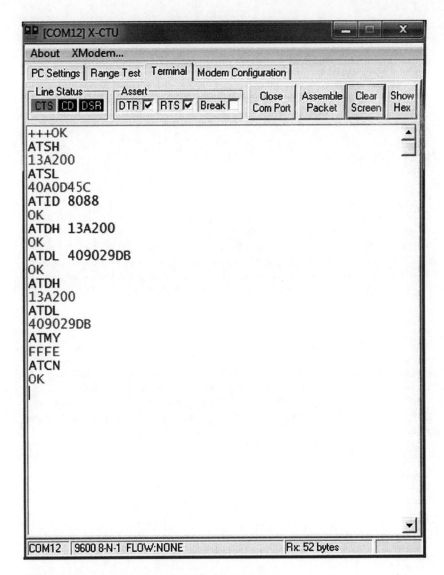

Figure 2-11. *Configuring a module with a terminal*

Now that you know the types of modules you need to form wireless networks using the ZigBee protocol and how to configure them, you can start building wireless networks. The next section explains how to create the most basic of XBee project: the "Hello, World!" XBee equivalent.

For More Information

If you would like to learn more about the XBee modules and how they communicate, an excellent resource is the Digi web site (www.digi.com). You can also search on Google for "XBee" and "ZigBee" to find a number of blogs, how-to pages, and more that will help by presenting different projects and solutions solved using the XBee-ZB modules.

There are also a number of excellent books that you can refer to for additional information, project ideas, and more. I list two of the better titles here:

- *Building Wireless Sensor Networks: with ZigBee, XBee, Arduino, and Processing*, by Robert Faludi (O'Reilly, 2010), ISBN 978-0596807733

- *The Hands-on XBEE Lab Manual: Experiments that Teach you XBEE Wireless Communications*, by Jon Titus (Newnes, 2012), ISBN 978-0123914040

An XBee Wireless Chat Room

For this example, you need two XBee modules, two USB adapters and required cables, and either one or two computers. You can use one computer and a terminal application that allows for multiple windows, each connected to a different USB serial port. You can also use one computer with a terminal application in the host OS and another in a virtual machine. For demonstration purposes, I will use two computers.

This project is a sort of "Hello, World!" test for the XBee. Rather than writing a simple program to print the messages, you will use two XBee modules configured as a simple point-to-point network with one coordinator and one router. You'll set both modules to use AT firmware so you can demonstrate the transparent mode and see the messages you are passing in clear text. This is what will make the chat work. What is typed on one computer will appear on another. Cool, eh?

Loading the Firmware for the Modules

The first thing you need to do is to load the firmware for each module. Recall that you use the X-CTU application to load the firmware. Recall also that the version number for the roles chosen must match. For the XBee modules I used in writing this chapter, the version number for a coordinator is 20A7. The first two digits are the role, and the last two digits are the version. It is not critical if your modules have a version other than A7, as long as they both have the same. The following are some of the major roles and their values:

- 20xx, coordinator, AT/transparent operation

- 21xx, coordinator, API operation

- 22xx, router, AT/transparent operation

- 23xx, router, API operation

- 28xx, end device, AT/transparent operation

- 29xx, end device, API operation

Use the X-CTU application to configure the first XBee module as the COORDINATOR AT function set. First connect to the module, and then read its configuration by clicking the Read button on the Modem Configuration page. Although you could also set the variables for the destination address, PAN ID, and the like with the X-CTU application, you'll wait and use a terminal application instead.

Figure 2-12 shows the X-CTU application settings used to load the firmware. When your selections are correct, click the Write button to write the firmware for the coordinator. This goes through a series of steps to program the module (called a *modem* in X-CTU), set the AT commands, and verify the process.

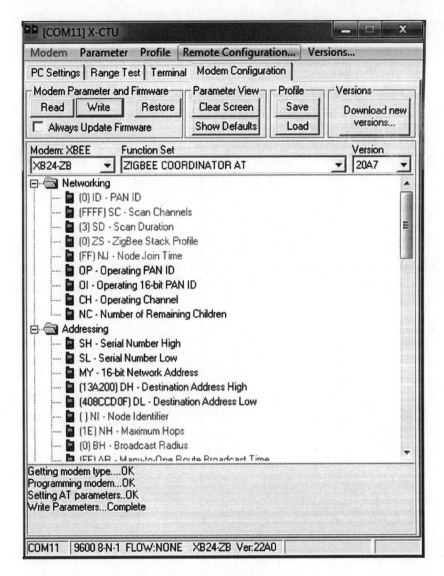

Figure 2-12. *Loading firmware for the coordinator*

When the write process is done, disconnect the coordinator and place a small piece of colored tape on the module so you know it is the coordinator. It isn't critical for now, but later on it would be handy to know which is the coordinator. Now follow the same steps for the router. Figure 2-13 shows the settings for the router.

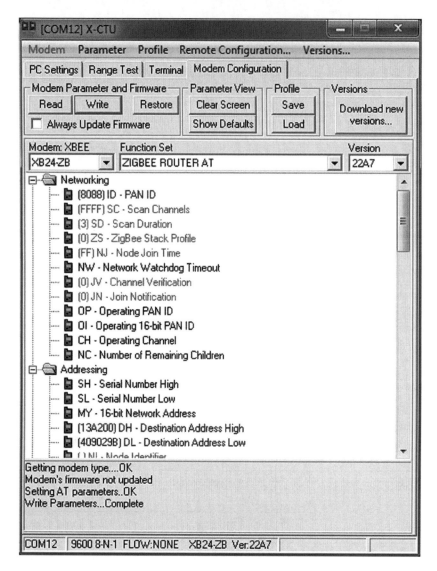

Figure 2-13. *Loading firmware for the router*

Capturing Serial Numbers

Recall that XBee radios require the 64-bit address (serial number) of the destination radio to send data. You need to record these before you begin the project. Take a moment to record the 64-bit serial numbers for each of your XBee modules.

If you have inserted your XBee modules into their adapters, you can use a terminal application to query the modules for the address using the ATSH and ATSL commands. Do that now, and write the information in Table 2-3.[7] There are spaces for additional information that you will be using, so refer to this table as you proceed with the project.

---

[7]If you prefer not to write in your book, take a piece of paper and make a chart like Table 2-3 to store the information. If the paper is thin, you can fold it and use it as a bookmark.

Table 2-3. *XBee Configuration Data*

Role	Serial High	Serial Low	PAN ID	Node ID
Coordinator AT				
Router AT				

Configuring the Coordinator

To configure the coordinator, connect the USB adapter and launch your terminal application. You want to set the destination address of this radio (the coordinator) to the serial number of the other radio (the router). Thus, you set the destination address on the coordinator to the address of the router.

You must also choose a PAN ID to use on the network. Let's use the iconic 8088.[8] In this case, it does not matter what you use as long as all modules on the network have the same PAN ID and the value is in the range 0000–FFFF (hexadecimal). Also set the Node ID to COORDINATOR to make it easier to identify. Figure 2-14 shows the configuration session for the coordinator.

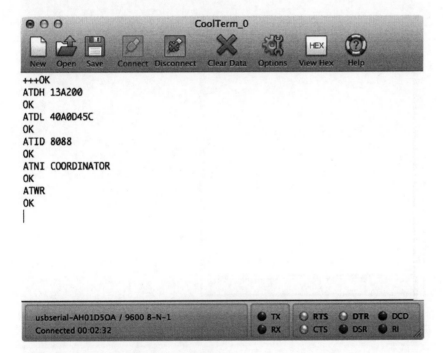

Figure 2-14. *Configuring the coordinator*

Configuring the Router

To configure the router, connect the USB adapter and launch your terminal application. You want to set the destination address of this radio (router) to the serial number of the other radio (coordinator).

Like the coordinator, you set the PAN ID to 8088. Also set the Node ID to ROUTER to make it easier to identify. Figure 2-15 shows the configuration session for the router.

---

[8]Does that number mean anything to you? Hint: IBM PC.

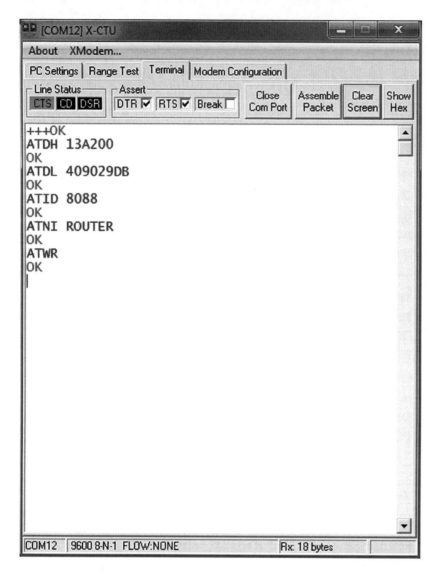

Figure 2-15. *Configuring the router*

Let the Chat Begin

That's it: you are ready to start the chat session. All you need to do now is return the modules to transparent mode by either using the ATCN command or simply waiting 10 seconds. Ready? If your terminal provides a `clear` function, clear the screen in both terminals and then try typing something in one terminal and see what happens.

If your configurations worked, you should see text from one terminal appear in the other and vice versa. If you do, congratulations—you have just set up your first XBee network (albeit a very simple point-to-point network). Figure 2-16 shows the results of the test I ran from my PC using X-CTU. This terminal feature is nice in that it color-codes the messages. The red text is text received, and the blue is text sent.

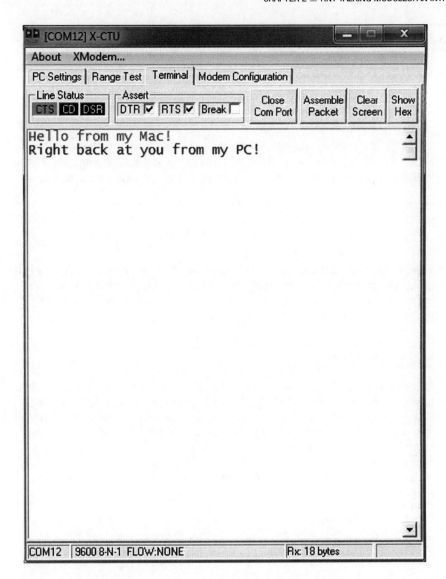

Figure 2-16. *Successful chat*

For bonus points, unplug your USB adapters and switch them from one computer to the other; then restart your terminal programs. Notice anything special? That's a trick question, because you should see the chat example working as before. It matters not which is the coordinator in this case; and because you wrote the values to the XBee nonvolatile memory, the modules "remember" their settings even if unplugged. Very nice, eh?

IS POINT-TO-POINT GOOD ENOUGH?

You may be wondering if you can use point-to-point networking in sensor networks. The short answer is that in some cases you can. For example, if you have a small number of nodes that are unlikely to be taken offline, you may be able to form a network with point-to-point networks. In this case, you would be forming a star topology network.

However, there are limitations, such as the fact that if a node in the middle goes down, it orphans all the nodes on one side of the node from the other. You also cannot form multiple-point connections, and broadcasting may require extra programming to accomplish. For these reasons and more, sophisticated sensor networks can benefit from using a mesh topology.

For More Fun

If you'd like experiment more with point-to-point networks and the AT firmware using the chat example, try adding a third XBee to the network. Connect it to your router node, and type some data. Where does it appear: the coordinator or the router? Try it again, connecting the new module to the coordinator. Does the text appear where you expect it? Hint: make the new module a router as well, and set its destination address to the first router.

Building an XBee-ZB Mesh Network

Now that you know what an XBee module is, how to select models for use in your projects, and how to configure them for sending and receiving data in a point-to-point network, let's look at something a bit more complicated and more in line with sensor networks. In this project, you configure three XBee modules: one as a coordinator, another as a router, and the last as an end device. However, instead of the AT firmware, you use the API firmware that is required for forming mesh networks. The goal isn't to explore the API firmware in depth; rather, it is to see how the XBee modules can be used to transmit the data through the network.

Recall that the API firmware is designed to implement the full ZigBee protocol, meaning the data messages are encapsulated inside a packet layered with headers. In other words, messages are transmitted as binary data rather than text as you saw with the AT firmware.

There is a lot to the API firmware and the ZigBee protocol. Fortunately, you do not have to get too far into the specifics in order to use it. However, it does help to know how the packets are formed so that you can diagnose and debug your data messages. I shall present some of the frequently encountered packets as you progress through the book.

If you would like to know more about the ZigBee protocol and its many packet formats (called *frame types*), see one of the following resources:

- *Building Wireless Sensor Networks: with ZigBee, XBee, Arduino, and Processing*, by Robert Faludi (O'Reilly, 2010), ISBN 978-0596807733

- "XBee/XBee-PRO ZB RF Modules," Digi International, 2011, http://ftp1.digi.com/support/documentation/90000976_H.pdf

- ZigBee Wireless Standard, Digi International, www.digi.com/technology/rf-articles/wireless-zigbee

- Digi API Frame Maker, Digi International, http://ftp1.digi.com/support/utilities/digi_apiframes2.htm

Loading the Firmware for the Modules

The first thing you need to do is to load the firmware for each module using the X-CTU application. Start by loading the ROUTER API function set on one module, and set it aside. Then load another module with the ROUTER API function set, and set it aside. Finally, load the last module with the COORDINATOR API function set.

Configuring the XBee Modules

Each module should be reset with the factory defaults. You can do this with the X-CTU application on the Modem Configuration page. Click the Restore button to set the factory defaults, and then click Write. That is all you need to do!

But what about all those addresses and PAN IDs and stuff? Simply put, you don't need them. The modules will automatically connect to the coordinator (or router), and the coordinator will assign the 16-bit addresses to each module. Clearly, this is a lot easier to configure than the AT point-to-point mode.

Although that is true, it is also much harder to experiment using the API firmware. Recall that the API firmware transmits and receives data messages in binary form. In order to see this network in action, you need to form special packets called *transmission request packets*.

Forming Test Messages

The test message is a simple numeric value embedded in a packet called a transmit request packet. (It's called a *transmit request frame* in some of the documentation.) The packet requires a very specific format.

If you have ever worked with low-level data packets like those encountered in Ethernet networks (TCP packets) or other communication protocols like the MySQL client protocol, you are already familiar with the basic concepts. However, if you haven't, the layout of the data may seem strange. Table 2-4 shows the layout of an example transmission request packet. It's described in more detail later.

Table 2-4. *Transmission Request Packet*

Field	Offset	Example	Description
Delimiter	0	7E	Start of packet delimiter
Length	1	00 10	Bytes between length and checksum
API Command	3	10	Request transmission
Frame ID	4	01	UART data frame
Destination Address 64-bit	5	00 00 00 00 00 00 00 00	64-bit address of coordinator
Destination Address 16-bit	13	00 00	16-bit destination address
Radius	15	00	Maximum number of hops
Options	16	00	Options
RFData	17	99 99	Data payload
Checksum	19	BC	0xFF minus sum of bytes in packet

The important parts of this packet are the length, addresses, and data payload. These are the parts you would most likely want to change. In this case, the 64-bit address is the default address for the coordinator. The coordinator gets this address using the default settings. The same is true for the 16-bit address. The example makes a payload of hexadecimal 99 99 (39321 in decimal). Because you use only 2 bytes for this, the length (the length in bytes of all parts of the packet following the length part, up to but not including the checksum part) is 16 (1+1+8+2+1+1+2). The checksum is calculated as 0xFF minus the 8-bit sum of the bytes between the length and the checksum.

Sound complicated? It can be. Fortunately, you do not need to do this manually very often. In fact, the XBee itself will build these packets for you when you use it to send data. The libraries you use to talk to the XBee from the Arduino and Raspberry Pi will also make life much easier for you.

So what do you do for this project? Do you create the packets yourself? If you are concerned about counting bytes and figuring out the checksum, fear not. Digi has a web site that will make your experience with this project a happy one. Take a moment and go to http://ftp1.digi.com/support/utilities/digi_apiframes2.htm.

This web site, called the Digi API Frame Maker, lets you explore the various API packet (frame) types and construct sample packets. Try it out. Go to the site, choose 0x10 Transmit Request from the drop-down list, and plug in the data from Table 2-4. Notice the two calculated fields marked with ###: when you click the Build Packet button, the Packet box fills with the sample packet. If you have entered the data using the example values in Table 2-4, you see the following packet information:

```
7E 00 10 10 01 00 00 00 00 00 00 00 00 00 00 00 00 00 99 99 BC
```

You can use this sample packet to test sending data from the end device. Let's create two more sample data packets. This time, create one with a payload of 77 77. Next, create one with a payload of 88 88, but make it a broadcast packet by setting the 64-bit address to 00 00 00 00 00 00 FF FF. The following shows each of these packets:

```
7E 00 10 10 01 00 00 00 00 00 00 00 00 00 00 00 00 00 77 77 00
7E 00 10 10 01 00 00 00 00 00 00 FF FF 00 00 00 00 88 88 E0
```

Take a moment to open a text editor, copy each of these packets into it, and save it as a text file. You should copy this file to every computer you plan to use to run the project.

Testing the Network

Now it is time to power up your XBee modules. Start with the coordinator, then the first router, and finally the second router. You need to connect terminal applications to the router and end device. For this project, you need to enter and display information in hexadecimal form. For example, the X-CTU application allows you to create a packet and send it as a group.

Once you have all the modules connected to a terminal application, activate the hexadecimal display on each. For this example, I used two computers (you can use three or as few as one). The coordinator is connected to a Mac running CoolTerm, the router is connected to a Windows 7 virtual machine running X-CTU, and the end device is connected to a Windows 7 laptop running X-CTU.

You should give the modules five to ten minutes to self configure before proceeding. How do you know everything is working? Well, it's not easy. If a module is running in X-CTU, you can use the Modem Configuration tab to read the values and determine if the module has joined the network: you can tell once the 16-bit address is set (MY). There are also commands you can use to test the network join status, but that is a more advanced topic.

OK, so you've waited, and everything should be working. Let's find out. On the end device, click the Assemble Packet button, selecting Hex as the display mode, copy and paste the transmit request packet with the 99 99 data payload into the dialog, and click Send Data. Figure 2-17 shows the Assemble Packet dialog.

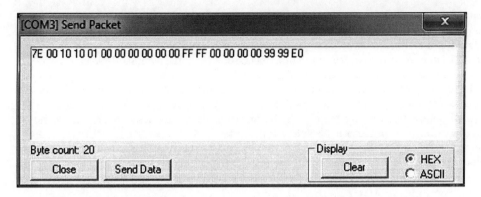

Figure 2-17. *Assemble Packet dialog*

Send the same packet several times, and observe what happens at the end device. Figure 2-18 shows the results of entering the command (and a few others).

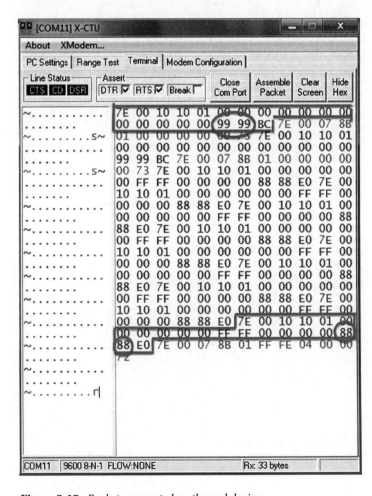

Figure 2-18. *Packets generated on the end device*

Notice the box around the first packet sent (in blue text). This is the command you entered. Following that is the response from the coordinator. Notice in the packet sent the values that are set. If you do not see a response from the coordinator, try the command several times. It may take a few tries to get the coordinator to respond. Normally, once it responds the first time, it will continue to respond to commands. Notice that I sent the command twice.

Also, take a look at the response packet. It starts with the delimiter, followed by two bytes for length and frame type = 8B. Return to the Digi API Frame Maker web site, and create a packet named 0x8B Tx Status. After the frame ID (01), you see the 16-bit address of the sender (00 00—the coordinator) and a status value of 00, which means success. This is how you can tell which module acknowledged (received) the data packet. Cool, eh? Keep that web site handy. It will save you a lot of flipping through the manuals to find the packet layout.

Now switch to the router, and enter the command with the 77 77 data payload. Figure 2-19 shows the results of this command (and other commands). I will let you observe the data packet sent and the response.

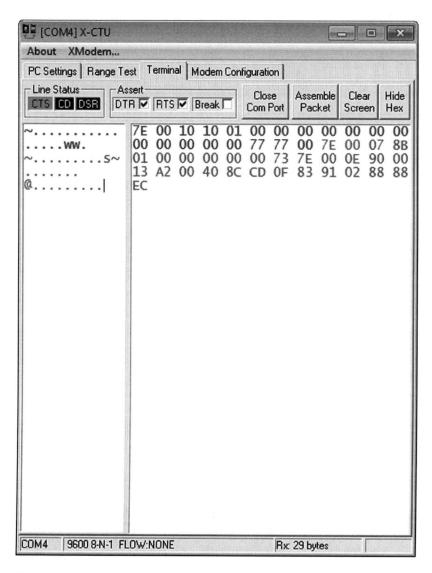

Figure 2-19. *Packets generated on the router*

Return to the end device, and enter the broadcast transmit request packet (the one with 88 88 and address 00 00 00 00 00 00 FF FF). Send it a few times, and then switch to the coordinator and see what is going on there. Now look at Figure 2-18 again. Notice the last command entered and its response. You should see something similar (hint: look at highlighted lines).

What about the router? Shouldn't it get the broadcast too? Examine Figure 2-19 again. Notice the last packet received (hint: it begins with 7E). This is a receive packet (frame type 90). Go to the Digi API Frame Maker, and select this packet type. Notice that in the fourth byte you see the sender's 64-bit address of 00 13 A2 00 40 8C CD 0F and its 16-bit address 83 91. If you wrote down the addresses of all your XBee modules (you did, didn't you?), you know this is the end device. This demonstrates yet another way to diagnose sent messages.

Next let's check the coordinator. You expect to see the data message sent from the end device (99 99), one sent from the router (77 77), and the broadcast message (88 88) also sent from the end device. Figure 2-20 shows the messages on the coordinator. Depending on the order in which you connected your devices, you could see them in a slightly different order here. What is important is that you see all three packets.

Figure 2-20. *Packets received on the coordinator*

I have highlighted the starts of packets and the data payload for you. Look at the first message. It shows a data payload of 77 77, as you sent, but it also contains the 64-bit and 16-bit addresses of the sender. Compare that to your XBees and ensure that it is indeed the router (00 13 A2 00 04 8C CC AA / D8 B6).

Now look at the message sent from the end device (not the broadcast). Can you find the sender's address? Does it match your end device? It does! With these examples, you can see how to determine from where a data message was sent.

If you were wondering how the mesh could automatically configure and heal itself and not lose what came from where, wonder no longer. If you think about it, that is a nice feature—you always know where your sensor data was generated. A short bit of programming is all you need to translate those addresses into something more readable, like Office Temperature Sensor or Outside Temperature.

What about that broadcast message? In Figure 2-20, you see the broadcast was indeed sent to the coordinator. I leave the diagnostics to you to determine whether the sender's address is correct. A broadcast message might be handy for sending power-down or sleep-mode commands to all of your sensor nodes or perhaps a command to send to all of your data-aggregate nodes to save their data to the media they are using.

So, you have seen how messages can be sent from one module to the coordinator directly and how broadcast messages can be sent to all modules. If you were able to duplicate or perform similar operations on your own XBee modules, congratulations! You now have a very simple wireless mesh network.

Although this project did not contain any sensor nodes, if you consider the end device as the sensor node and the keyboard as the sensor sending data, you can see how a typical sensor network will perform. In this case, the end device sends its data packet to the coordinator by default and can broadcast data if needed. Sending all data to the coordinator is also a clue as to how a data-aggregate node may be configured with an XBee module. You build on this premise in upcoming chapters.

For More Fun

If you'd like some more practice creating test packets, try sending a network node-detection command from the router and see what you get. Hint: you want an AT command packet (frame), and use the ND command.

Component Shopping List

You need a number of components to complete the projects in this chapter. Table 2-5 lists them.

Table 2-5. *Components Needed*

Item	Vendors	Est. Cost USD	Qty Needed
XBee-ZB (ZB) Series 2 or 2.5	www.sparkfun.com	$25.00	3
	www.adafruit.com		
	www.makershed.com		
XBee Explorer Dongle	www.sparkfun.com/products/9819	$24.95	1**
XBee Explorer USB	www.sparkfun.com/products/8687	$24.95	1**
USB-to–mini USB cable for use with the XBee Explorer USB	www.sparkfun.com/products/11301	$3.95	1 for each USB explorer
XBee Adapter Kit	www.adafruit.com/products/126	$10.00	1**
FTDI cable for use with the XBee Adapter Kit	www.adafruit.com/products/70	$20.00	1***

** You need only three of any of the USB adapters.
*** One needed for each XBee Adapter Kit.

Be sure to get the correct cables. Also remember that you need three matching XBee-ZB modules. The adapter boards need not be the same, but you should have three of them.

```
CABLE TROUBLE SOLUTION
```

If you are like me and have many USB projects, one of the first frustrations you may encounter is the seeming randomness of choice of USB connectors. It seems like every time I buy a new component, it takes a different USB cable. Rather than carry a set of cables in my kit, I've found a solution from SparkFun that has made my life much easier. The USB Cerberus cable (www.sparkfun.com/products/11515) includes a standard USB A-type male connector on one end and a set of three common connectors on the other (B, mini-B, and micro-B). I recommend buying one for each of your electronics kits.

Another frustration concerns powering devices with USB hubs and the like. Once again, I used to carry around a bunch of power cables to power all of my components. In this case, SparkFun comes to the rescue again with its Hydra power cable (sparkfun.com/products/11579). This cable has a standard USB A-type connector on one end and a set of three connectors on the other (barrel plug for Arduino, JST, and alligator clips). Very cool.

Troubleshooting Tips and Common Issues

If you encounter problems getting either of the chapter projects working, don't feel bad, and don't give up! Despite their diminutive size and powerful feature sets, these little pests can cause you a lot of grief if they are not configured correctly. This section explores some best practices for solving some of the more common problems.

Things to Check

The following is a list of tips for helping you determine what is wrong and how to fix it:

- *Cabling*: It may sound silly, but check to ensure that all of your modules are powered correctly—either by the host microcontroller or USB adapter. You'd be surprised how easy it is to tell your OS to eject a USB dongle. If this happens, it is likely your adapter may have all its power LEDs lit but the terminal cannot connect. Try removing the cable and reinserting it. Also check the serial port, because some operating systems may reassign the serial port if moved from one port to another.

- *Is it plugged in?* You should also check that the module is plugged into its socket in the proper orientation and no pins are skipped (misaligned).

- *Serial settings*: Check your baud rate. If you've changed it on the XBee, your terminal application may not have saved the setting. If you want to change the setting, be sure to set it the same for all of your XBee modules as well as your terminal applications.

- *AT address*: If you are building point-to-point systems with the AT firmware, be sure to check your addresses! Remember that the destination address needs to point to the address of the module where you wish to send data (ATDH/ATDL). Be sure to use the ATWR command to save the values.

- *Version*: Always make sure the version you use for the firmware is the same on all modules. Some versions are incompatible with others. It is best to always use the same version.

- *Is the XBee dead?* If your XBee module cannot be read by your terminal application or it stops responding to X-CTU, you may have encountered what some refer to as *bricking*, which makes the module worthless except as a doorstop or brick. If this happens, try resetting the module. If your adapter does not have a reset button (only a few do), you can connect the adapter and then gently (very gently) remove the module and reinsert it. When the module starts responding, reload the firmware. For extreme cases, see www.instructables.com/id/Restoring-your-broken-XBee/.

- *Old values keep coming back*: If you change your settings in the AT firmware but the old values keep coming back even after you use ATWR, use the reset command (ATRE) to return all values to their factory defaults.

Common Issues

The following are some of the more common scenarios you may encounter and what to do about them:

- *AT commands don't work*: If the +++ command won't wake up the module, make sure the module has the AT firmware loaded. I fussed for nearly 15 minutes with what I thought was a dead module, only to discover it was loaded with the API firmware.

- *Strange errors in AT mode*: Make sure your modules are configured with the same version of the AT firmware. You can use the ATVR command to check each module.

- *Settings go missing or revert*: One of the most common errors is making all of your settings and failing to write the values with ATWR. You need to use this command to save the values. The XBee modules may not work until you have done this and returned to transparent mode.

- *Inability to use Backspace*: It can be very frustrating to try to enter commands with values using the AT firmware because the Backspace key doesn't work in most terminal applications. When you make a mistake, press Enter and try the command again. Always check the setting with the command's display option (the command with no value).

- *API firmware doesn't work*: If you are sure you have all of your modules configured for the same version of the API firmware, try unplugging all the modules and plugging the coordinator in first followed by the routers and then your end devices. It may take as long as ten minutes for the coordinator to join all the nodes to the network.

You can also visit Robert Faludi's web page for common XBee mistakes (www.faludi.com/projects/common-xbee-mistakes/). He lists a lot of things that go wrong when you are unfamiliar with XBees and how to configure them. As he states, they aren't as unreliable or quirky as they seem to be. Most quirks are a result of user error. Sadly, it isn't always obvious that that is the case.

Finally, use the Digi web site and its knowledgebase (www.digi.com/support/kbase/). There is a wealth of information out there. Chances are, someone has had a similar problem, and a simple search of the knowledgebase and forums may reveal the solution.

Summary

In this chapter, we covered a lot of ground. You were introduced to the XBee-ZB module and the ZigBee protocol, and you experimented with the AT and API firmware. You also learned a great deal about the XBee and its many features. Although it seems like I discussed a lot, the truth is that you have only just begun learning about the XBee and how to use it in your sensor networks.

I will be returning to the XBee topic throughout the rest of this book. Chapter 3 explores how to host sensors with an Arduino microcontroller, and Chapter 4 examines how to host sensors with a Raspberry Pi. If you enjoyed the projects in this chapter, the projects in the next chapter are likely to be even more enjoyable because you get to see a real sensor in action.[9]

---

[9] I must concede that you have already seen a sensor at work—you! As part of the experiment in the projects, you typed commands and entered data packets that simulated sensor data. Did you sense that?

CHAPTER 3

■ ■ ■

Arduino-Based Sensor Nodes

One of the greatest advances in physical computing has been the proliferation of microcontrollers. A microcontroller consists of a processor with a small instruction set,[1] memory, and programmable input/output circuitry contained on a single chip. Microcontrollers are usually packaged with supporting circuitry and connections on a small printed circuit board.

Microcontrollers are used in embedded systems where small software programs can be tailored to control and monitor hardware devices, making them ideal for use in sensor networks. One of the most successful and most popular microcontrollers is the Arduino platform.

In this chapter, you explore the Arduino platform with the goal of using the Arduino to manage sensor nodes. You see a short tutorial on the Arduino and several projects to help get you started working with the Arduino.

What Is an Arduino?

The Arduino is an open source hardware prototyping platform supported by an open source software environment. It was first introduced in 2005 and was designed with the goal of making the hardware and software easy to use and available to the widest audience possible. Thus, you do not have to be an electronics expert to use the Arduino.

The original target audience included artists and hobbyists who needed a microcontroller to make their designs and creations more interesting. However, given its ease of use and versatility, the Arduino has quickly become the choice for a wider audience and a wider variety of projects.

This means you can use the Arduino for all manner of projects from reacting to environmental conditions to controlling complex robotic functions. The Arduino has also made learning electronics easier through practical applications.

Another aspect that has helped the rapid adoption of the Arduino platform is the growing community of contributors to a wealth of information made available through the official Arduino web site (http://arduino.cc/en/). When you visit the web site, you find an excellent "getting started" tutorial as well as a list of helpful project ideas and a full reference guide to the C-like language for writing the code to control the Arduino (called a *sketch*).

Arduino also provides an integrated development environment called the Arduino IDE. The IDE runs on your computer (called the *host*), where you can write and compile sketches and then upload them to the Arduino via USB connections. The IDE is available for Linux, Mac, and Windows. It is designed around a text editor especially designed for writing code and a set of limited functions designed to support compilation and loading of sketches.

Sketches are written in a special format consisting of only two required methods—one that executes when the Arduino is reset or powered on and another that executes continuously. Thus, your initialization code goes in setup() and your code to control the Arduino goes in loop(). The language is C-like, and you may define your own variables and functions. For a complete guide to writing sketches, see http://arduino.cc/en/Tutorial/Sketch.

---

[1] Meaning it is designed for a small, specific set of functionality.

You can expand the functionality of sketches and provide for reuse by writing libraries that encapsulate certain features such as networking, using memory cards, connecting to databases, doing mathematics, and the like. Many such libraries are included with the IDE. There are also some libraries written by others and contributed to Arduino.cc through open source agreements—some of which have been bundled with the IDE.

The Arduino supports a number of analog and digital *pins* that you can use to connect to various devices and components and interact with them. The mainstream boards have specific pin layouts, or *headers*, that allow the use of expansion boards called *shields*. Shields let you add additional hardware capabilities such as Ethernet, Bluetooth, and XBee support to your Arduino. The physical layout of the Arduino and the shield allow you to stack shields. Thus, you can have an Ethernet shield as well as an XBee shield, because each uses different I/O pins. You learn the use of the pins and shields as you explore the application of Arduino to sensor networks.

The next sections examine the various Arduino boards and briefly describe their capabilities. I list the boards by when they became available, starting with the most recent models. Many more boards and variants are available, and a few new ones are likely to be out by the time this book is printed, but these are the ones that are typically used in a sensor network project.

Arduino Models

A growing number of Arduino boards are available. Some are configured for special applications, whereas others are designed with different processors and memory configurations. Some boards are considered official Arduino boards because they are branded and endorsed by Arduino.cc. Because the Arduino is open source and, more specifically, licensed using a Creative Commons Attribution Share-Alike license, anyone can build Arduino-compatible boards (often called Arduino *clones*). However, you must follow the rules and guidelines set forth by Arduino.cc.[2] This section examines some of the more popular Arduino branded boards.

The basic layout of an Arduino board consists of a USB connection, a power connector, a reset switch, LEDs for power and serial communication, and a standard spaced set of headers for attaching shields. The official boards sport a distinctive blue-colored PCB with white lettering. With the exception of one model, all the official boards can be mounted in a chassis (they have holes in the PCB for mounting screws). The exception is an Arduino designed for mounting on a breadboard.

Leonardo

The Leonardo board represents a bold leap forward for the Arduino platform. Although it supports the standard header layout, ensuring the continued use of shields, it also includes a USB controller that allows the board to appear as a USB device to the host computer. The board uses a newer ATmega32u4 processor with 20 digital I/O pins, of which 12 can be used as analog pins and 7 can be used as a pulse-width modulation (PWM) output. It has 32KB of flash memory and 2.5KB of SRAM.

The Leonardo has more digital pins than its predecessor but continues to support most shields. The USB connection uses a smaller USB connector. The board is also available with and without headers. Figure 3-1 depicts an official Leonardo board. Details and a full datasheet can be found at http://arduino.cc/en/Main/ArduinoBoardLeonardo.

---

[2]For a complete description of the Arduino.cc license policies and more information about building and selling your own Arduino-compatible board, see http://arduino.cc/en/Main/FAQ.

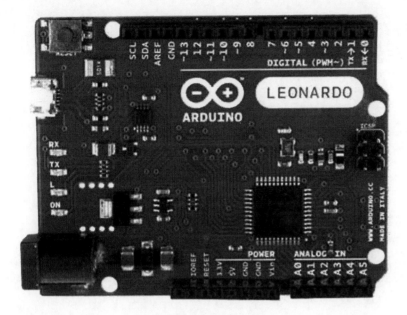

Figure 3-1. *Arduino Leonardo (courtesy of Arduino.cc)*

Uno

The Uno board is the first standard Arduino board featuring an ATmega328 processor; 14 digital I/O pins, of which 6 can be used as PWM output; and 6 analog input pins. The Uno board has 32KB of flash memory and 2KB of SRAM.

The Uno is available either as a surface-mount device (SMD) or a standard IC socket. The IC socket version allows you to exchange processors, should you desire to use an external IC programmer to build custom solutions. Details and a full datasheet are available at `http://arduino.cc/en/Main/ArduinoBoardUno`. It has a standard USB type B connector and supports all shields. Figure 3-2 depicts the Arduino Uno revision 3 board.

Figure 3-2. *Arduino Uno (courtesy of Arduino.cc)*

53

Due

The Arduino Due is a new, larger, and faster board based on the Atmel SAM3X8E ARM Cortex-M3 processor. The processor is a 32-bit processor, and the board supports a massive 54 digital I/O ports, of which 14 can be used for PWM output; 12 analog inputs; and 4 UART chips (serial ports); as well as 2 digital-to-analog (DAC) and 2 two-wire interface (TWI) pins. The new processor offers several advantages:

- 32-bit registers
- DMA controller (allows CPU-independent memory tasks)
- 512KB flash memory
- 96KB SRAM
- 84MHz clock

The Due has the larger form factor (called the *mega footprint*)[3] but still supports the use of standard shields as well as mega format shields. The new board has one distinct limitation: unlike other boards that can accept up to 5V on the I/O pins, the Due is limited to 3.3V on the I/O pins.

The Arduino Due is intended to be used for projects that require more processing power, more memory, and more I/O pins. Despite the significant capabilities of the new board it remains open source and comparable in price to its predecessors. Look to the Due for your projects that require the maximum hardware performance. Figure 3-3 shows an Arduino Due board.

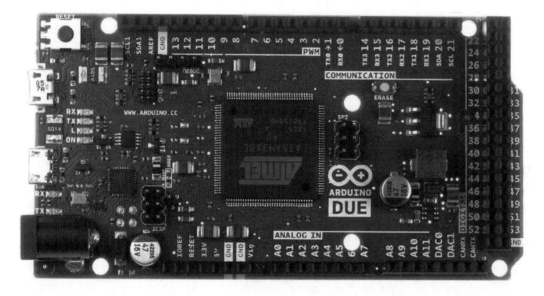

Figure 3-3. *Arduino Due (courtesy of Arduino.cc)*

---

[3]Compare Figures 3-2 and 3-3. Notice how much larger the Due is than the Uno. If you choose to incorporate a Due, Mega, or similar board, you may have to set aside more room to mount the board.

Mega 2560

The Arduino Mega 2560 is an older form of the Due. It is based on the ATmega2560 processor (hence the name). Like the Due, the board supports a massive 54 digital I/O ports, of which 14 can be used as PWM output; 16 analog inputs; and 4 UARTs (hardware serial ports). It uses a 16MHz clock and has 256KB of flash memory.

The Mega 2560 is essentially a larger form of the standard Arduino (Uno, Duemilanove, etc.) and supports the standard shields. Figure 3-4 shows the Arduino Mega 2560 board.

Figure 3-4. *Arduino Mega (courtesy of Arduino.cc)*

Interestingly, the Arduino Mega 256 is the board of choice for Prusa Mendel and similar 3D printers that require the use of a controller board named RepRap Arduino Mega Pololu Shield (RAMPS).

Mini

The Arduino Mini is a small form-factor board designed for use with breadboards. Thus, it has all its pins arranged in male headers that plug directly into a standard breadboard. It is based on the ATmega328 processor (older models use the ATmega168) and has 14 digital I/O pins, of which 6 can be used as PWM output, and 8 analog inputs. The Mini has 32KB of flash memory and uses a 16MHz clock.

Unlike other Arduino boards, the Mini does not have a USB connector. To connect to and program the Mini, you must use a USB Serial adapter or RS232-to-TTL serial adapter. Figure 3-5 shows the Arduino Mini.

Figure 3-5. *Arduino Mini (courtesy of Arduino.cc)*

■ **Note** The Mini has a limitation with regard to input voltage. You should avoid voltages over 9V.

Micro

The Arduino Micro is a special form of the new Leonardo board and uses the same ATmega32u4 processor with 20 digital I/O pins, of which 12 can be used as analog pins and 7 can be used as PWM output. It has 32KB of flash memory and 2.5KB of SRAM.

The Micro was made for use on breadboards in the same way as the Mini but in a newer, updated form. But unlike the Mini, the Micro is a full-featured board complete with USB connector. And like the Leonardo, it has built-in USB communication, allowing the board to connect to a computer as a mouse or keyboard. Figure 3-6 shows the Arduino Micro board.

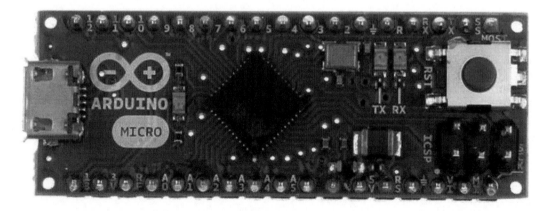

Figure 3-6. *Arduino Micro (courtesy of Arduino.cc)*

Although branded as an official Arduino board, the Arduino Micro is produced in cooperation with Adafruit.

Nano

The Arduino Nano is an older form of the Arduino Micro. In this case, it is based on the functionality of the Duemilanove[4] and has the ATmega328 processor (older models use the ATmega168) and 14 digital I/O pins, of which 6 can be used as PWM output, and 8 analog inputs. The mini has 32KB of flash memory and uses a 16MHz clock.

Like the Micro, it has all the features needed for connecting to and programming via a USB connection. Figure 3-7 shows an Arduino Nano board.

Figure 3-7. *Arduino Nano (courtesy of Arduino.cc)*

Arduino Clones

A growing number of Arduino boards are available from a large number of sources. Because the Arduino is open hardware, it is not unusual or the least bit illicit to find Arduino boards made by vendors all over the world.

Although some would insist the only real Arduinos are those branded as such, the truth of the matter is that as long as the build quality is sound and the components are of high quality, the choice of using a branded versus a copy, hence clone, is one of personal preference. I have sampled Arduino boards from a number of sources, and with few exceptions they all perform their intended functions superbly.

Except for the Arduino Mini, the Arduino clone boards have a greater variety of hardware configurations. Some Arduinos are designed for use in embedded systems or on breadboards, and some are designed for prototyping. I examine a number of the more popular clone boards in the following sections.

Arduino Pro

The Arduino Pro is manufactured by SparkFun (`www.sparkfun.com/`). It is based on the ATmega328 processor (older models use the ATmega168) and has 14 digital I/O pins, of which 6 can be used as PWM output, and 8 analog inputs. The Pro has 32KB of flash memory and 2KB of SRAM, and it uses a 16MHz clock.

The Arduino Pro has a footprint similar to the Uno but does not come with headers. However, it can support standard shields if headers are added. This makes the Arduino Pro ideal for use in semi-permanent installations where the pins can be soldered to the components or circuitry. Figure 3-8 shows an Arduino Pro board.

---

[4]Which means "2009" in Italian.

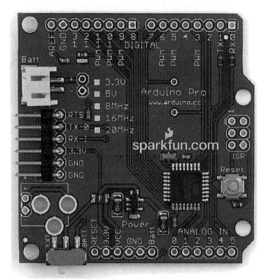

Figure 3-8. *Arduino Pro (courtesy of Arduino.cc)*

Also, the Pro does not include a USB connector and therefore must be connected to and programmed with an FTDI cable or similar breakout board. It comes as either a 3.3V model with an 8MHz clock or a 5V model with a 16MHz clock. Because it is intended for permanent installation, it also provides a connector for battery power.

Arduino Pro Mini

The Arduino Pro Mini is another board from SparkFun. It is based on the ATmega168 processor (older models use the ATmega168) and has 14 digital I/O pins, of which 6 can be used as PWM output, and 8 analog inputs. The Pro Mini has 16KB of flash memory and 1KB of SRAM, and it uses a 16MHz clock.

The Arduino Pro Mini is modeled on the Arduino Mini and is also intended for use on breadboards but does not come with headers. This makes the Arduino Pro Mini ideal for use in semi-permanent installations where the pins can be soldered to the components or circuitry and space is a premium. Figure 3-9 shows an Arduino Pro Mini board.

Figure 3-9. *Arduino Pro Mini (courtesy of Arduino.cc)*

Also, the Pro Mini does not include a USB connector and therefore must be connected to and programmed with a FTDI cable or similar breakout board. It comes as either a 3.3V model with a 8MHz clock or a 5V model with a 16MHz clock.

Fio

The Arduino Fio is yet another board made by SparkFun. It was designed for use in wireless projects. It is based on the ATmega328P processor with 14 digital I/O pins, of which 6 can be used as PWM outputs, and 8 analog pins. It has 32KB of flash memory and 2KB of SRAM.

The Fio requires a 3.3V power supply, which allows for use with a lithium polymer (LiPo) battery which can be recharged via the USB connector on the board.

Its wireless pedigree can be seen in the XBee socket on the bottom of the board. Although the USB connection lets you recharge the battery, you must use an FTDI cable or breakout adapter to connect to and program the Fio. Similar to the Pro models, the Fio does not come with headers, allowing the board to be used in semi-permanent installations where connections are soldered in place. Figure 3-10 shows an Arduino Fio board.

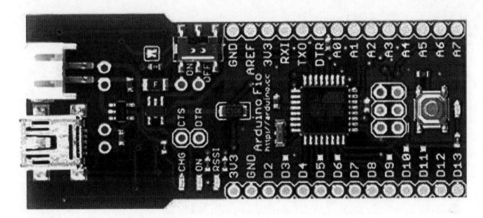

Figure 3-10. *Arduino Fio (courtesy of Arduino.cc)*

Seeeduino

The Seeeduino is an Arduino clone made by Seeed Studio (www.seeedstudio.com). It is based on the ATmega328P processor and has 14 digital I/O pins, of which 6 can be used as PWM outputs, and 8 analog pins. It has 32KB of flash memory and 2KB of SRAM.

The board has a footprint similar to the Arduino Uno and supports all standard headers. It supports a number of enhancements such as I2C and serial Grove connectors and a mini USB connector, and it uses SMD components. It is also a striking red color with yellow headers. Figure 3-11 shows a Seeeduino board.

Figure 3-11. *Seeeduino (courtesy of Seeed Studio)*

Sippino

The Sippino from SpikenzieLabs (`www.spikenzielabs.com`) is designed to be used on a solder-less breadboard. It costs less because it has fewer components and a much smaller footprint. Fortunately, SpikenzieLabs also provides a special adapter called a shield dock that allows you to use a Sippino with standard Arduino shields.

It is based on the ATmega328 processor and has 14 digital I/O pins, of which 6 can be used as PWM output, and 6 analog input pins. The Sippino board has 32KB of flash memory and 2KB of SRAM.

The Sippino does not have a USB connection, so you have to use an FTDI cable to program it. The good news is you need only one cable no matter how many Sippinos you have in your project. I have a number of Sippinos and use them in many of my Arduino projects where space is at a premium. Figure 3-12 shows a Sippino mounted on a breadboard.

Figure 3-12. *Sippino (courtesy of SpikenzieLabs)*

The shield dock is an amazing add-on that lets you use the Sippino as if it were a standard Uno or Duemilanove. Figure 3-13 shows a Sippino mounted on a shield dock.

Figure 3-13. *Sippino on a shield dock (courtesy of SpikenzieLabs)*

Prototino

The Prototino is another product of SpikenzieLabs. It has the same components as the Sippino, but instead of a breadboard-friendly layout, it is mounted on a PCB that includes a full prototyping area. Like the Sippino, it is based on the ATmega328 processor and has 14 digital I/O pins, of which 6 can be used as PWM output, and 6 analog input pins. The Prototino board has 32KB of flash memory and 2KB of SRAM.

The Prototino is ideal for building solutions that have supporting components and circuitry. In some ways it is similar to the Nano, Mini, and similar boards in that you can use it for permanent installations. But unlike those boards (and even the Arduino Pro), the Prototino provides a space for you to add your components directly to the board. I have used a number of Prototino boards for projects where I have added the components to the Prototino and install it in the chassis. This allowed me to create a solution using a single board and even build several copies quickly and easily.

Like the Sippino, the Prototino does not have a USB connection, so you have to use an FTDI cable to program it. Figure 3-14 shows a Prototino board.

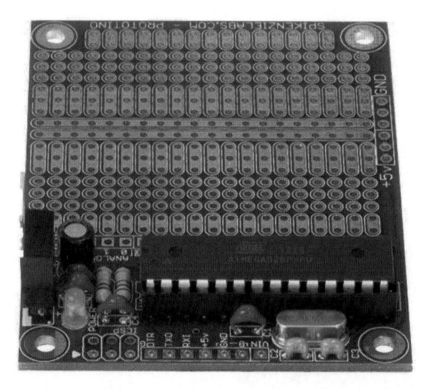

Figure 3-14. *Prototino (courtesy of SpikenzieLabs)*

┌──┐
THERE IS EVEN ONE MADE OF PAPER
└──┘

Every now and then you encounter something mundane that's made truly interesting by a change in medium. Such is the case of the PAPERduino created by Guilherme Martins. The PAPERduino is a minimal Arduino that uses a paper template in place of the PCB. All you need to do is download and print out the templates, purchase a small list of commonly available discrete components, and follow the connection diagram printed on the template to solder the components to short lengths of wire. You can find out more by visiting the following web site: http://lab.guilhermemartins.net/2009/05/06/paperduino-prints/.

So, Which Do I Buy?

If you're wondering which Arduino to buy, the answer depends on what you want to do. For most of the projects in this book, any Arduino Uno or similar clone that supports the standard shield headers is fine. You need not buy the larger Due or its predecessors, since the added memory and I/O pins aren't needed.

I use the Arduino Uno as the basis for all the projects in this book. Although you can use an older board without issues, there are some issues with using the newer Leonardo board. I point these out as you encounter them. Most issues have to do with the relocated pins on the Leonardo board. For example, the SPI header pins (at upper left in Figure 3-2) have been moved on the Leonardo.

If you want to save some money, you can build all the Arduino projects in this book with the older Arduino Duemilanove board. If you look around, you may find these boards at bargain prices. There are also a lot of Duemilanove clones. In fact, a quick search on eBay shows about a dozen examples for around $15.00 USD as compared to $30.00 or more for an Uno or a Leonardo.

For future projects, there are some things you should consider before choosing the Arduino. For example, if your project is largely based on a breadboard or you want to keep the physical size of the project to a minimum, and you aren't going to use any shields, the Arduino Mini may be the better choice. Conversely, if you plan to do a lot of programming to implement complex algorithms for manipulating or analyzing data, you may want to consider the Due for its added processing power and memory.

The bottom line is that most of the time your choice will be based on physical characteristics (size, shield support, and so on) and seldom on processing power or memory. SparkFun has an excellent buyer's guide in which you can see the pros and cons of each choice. See www.sparkfun.com/pages/arduino_guide for more details.

Where to Buy

Due to the popularity of the Arduino platform, many vendors sell Arduino and Arduino clone boards, shields, and accessories. The Arduino.cc web site (http://arduino.cc/en/Main/Buy) also has a page devoted to approved distributors. If none of the resources listed here are available to you, you may want to check this page for a retailer near you.

Online Retailers

There are a growing number of online retailers where you can buy Arduino boards and accessories. The following lists a few of the more popular sites.

- *SparkFun*: From discrete components to the company's own branded Arduino clones and shields, SparkFun has just about anything you could possibly want for the Arduino platform. www.sparkfun.com/

- *Adafruit*: Carries a growing array of components, gadgets, and more. It has a growing number of products for the electronics hobbyist, including a full line of Arduino products. Adafruit also has an outstanding documentation library and wiki to support all the products it sells. www.adafruit.com/

- *Maker Shed*: The front store for MAKE Magazine and the Maker movement, Maker Shed has many products for the Arduino platform, including a growing number of custom project kits. From building your own bass guitar to building a robot, this store will tell you it has a lot to offer. www.makershed.com

You can also visit the manufacturers of some of the clone boards. The following are the leading clone manufacturers and links to their storefronts:

- *SpikenzieLabs*: www.spikenzielabs.com/

- *Seeed Studio*: www.seeedstudio.com/

Retail Stores (USA)

There are also brick-and-mortar stores that carry Arduino products. Although there aren't as many as there are online retailers, and their inventories are typically limited, if you need a new Arduino board quickly you can find them at the following retailers. You may find additional retailers in your area. Look for popular hobby electronic stores:

- *Radio Shack*: Most stores are independently owned, but most carry a modest array of Arduino boards, shields, and accessories, including Arduino-branded products as well as popular clone products. www.radioshack.com/

- *Fry's*: An electronics superstore with a huge inventory of electronics, components, microcontrollers, computer parts, and more. If you have never had the chance to visit a Fry's store, you should be prepared to spend some time there. Fry's carries Arduino-branded boards, shields, and accessories as well as products from Parallax, SparkFun, and many more. http://frys.com/

- *Micro Center*: Micro Center is similar to Fry's, offering a huge inventory of products. However, most Micro Center stores have a smaller inventory of electronic components than Fry's. www.microcenter.com/

Now that you have a better understanding of the hardware details and the variety of Arduino boards available, let's dive in to how to use and program the Arduino. The next section provides a tutorial for installing the Arduino programming environment and programming the Arduino. Later sections present projects to build your skills for developing sensor networks.

Arduino Tutorial

This section is a short tutorial on getting started using an Arduino. It covers obtaining and installing the IDE and writing a sample sketch. Rather than duplicate the excellent works that precede this book, I cover the highlights and refer readers who are less familiar with the Arduino to online resources and other books that offer a much deeper introduction. Also, the Arduino IDE has many sample sketches that you can use to explore the Arduino on your own. Most have corresponding tutorials on the Arduino.cc site.

Learning Resources

A lot of information is available about the Arduino platform. If you are just getting started with the Arduino, Apress offers an impressive array of books covering all manner of topics concerning the Arduino, ranging from getting started using the microcontroller to learning the details of its design and implementation. The following is a list of the more popular books:

- *Beginning Arduino* by Michael McRoberts (Apress, 2010)

- *Practical Arduino: Cool Projects for Open Source Hardware (Technology in Action)* by Jonathan Oxer and Hugh Blemings (Apress, 2009)

- *Arduino Internals* by Dale Wheat (Apress, 2011)

There are also some excellent online resources for learning more about the Arduino, the Arduino libraries, and sample projects. The following are some of the best:

- *Arduino.cc*: `http://arduino.cc/en/`

- *Adafruit tutorials*: `http://learn.adafruit.com/`

- *Make tutorials*: `http://makezine.com/category/electronics/arduino/`

The Arduino IDE

The Arduino IDE is available for download for the Mac, Linux (32- and 64-bit versions), and Windows platforms. You can download the IDE from `http://arduino.cc/en/Main/Software`. There are links for each platform as well as a link to the source code if you need to compile the IDE for a different platform.

Installing the IDE is straightforward. I omit the actual steps of installing the IDE for brevity, but if you require a walkthrough of installing the IDE you can see the Getting Started link on the download page or read more in *Beginning Arduino* by Michael McRoberts (Apress, 2010).

Once the IDE launches, you see a simple interface with a text editor area (a white background by default), a message area beneath the editor (a black background by default), and a simple button bar at the top. The buttons are (from left to right) Compile, Compile and Upload, New, Open, and Save. There is also a button to the right that opens the serial monitor. You use the serial monitor to view messages from the Arduino sent (or printed) via the Serial library. You see this in action in your first project. Figure 3-15 shows the Arduino IDE

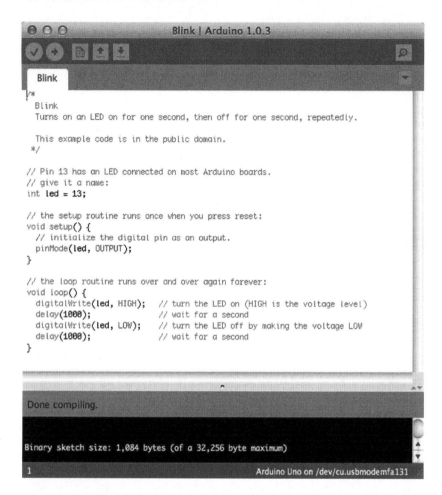

Figure 3-15. *The Arduino IDE*

Notice that in Figure 3-15 you see a sample sketch (called blink) and the result of a successful compile operation. Notice also at the bottom that it tells you that you are programming an Arduino Uno board on a specific serial port.

Due to the differences in processor and supporting architecture, there are some differences in how the compiler builds the program (and how the IDE uploads it). Thus, one of the first things you should do when you start the IDE is choose your board from the Tools ➤ Board menu. Figure 3-16 shows a sample of selecting the board on the Mac.

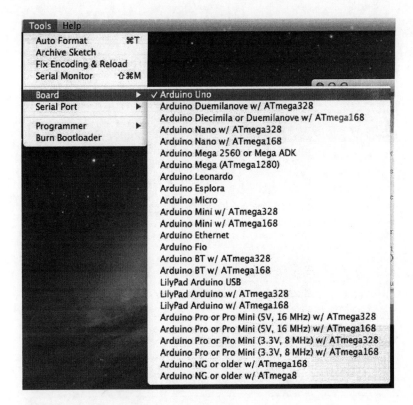

Figure 3-16. *Choosing the Arduino board*

Notice the number of boards available. Be sure to choose the one that matches your board. If you are using a clone board, check the manufacturer's site for the recommended setting to use. If you choose the wrong board, you typically get an error during upload, but it may not be obvious that you've chosen the wrong board. Because I have so many different boards, I've made it a habit to choose the board each time I launch the IDE.

The next thing you need to do is choose the serial port to which the Arduino board is connected. To connect to the board, use the Tools ➤ Serial Port menu option. Figure 3-17 shows an example on the Mac. In this case, no serial ports are listed. This can happen if you haven't plugged your Arduino in to the computer's USB ports (or hub), you had it plugged in but disconnected it at some point, or you have not loaded the drivers for the Arduino (Windows). Typically, this can be remedied by simply unplugging the Arduino and plugging it back in and waiting until the computer recognizes the port.

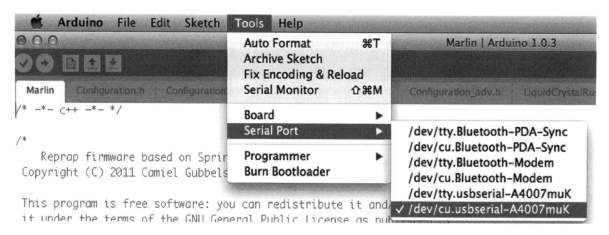

Figure 3-17. *Choosing the serial port*

■ **Note**   If you use a Mac, it doesn't matter which port you choose: either the one that starts with tty or the one that starts with cu will work.

■ **Tip**   See http://arduino.cc/en/Guide/Howto if you need help installing the drivers on Windows.

OK, now that you have your Arduino IDE installed, you can connect your Arduino and set the board and serial port. You see the LEDs on the Arduino illuminate. This is because the Arduino is getting power from the USB. Thus, you do not need to provide an external power supply when the Arduino is connected to your computer. Next, you dive into a simple project to demonstrate the Arduino IDE and learn how basic sketches are built, compiled, and uploaded.

Project: Hardware "Hello, World!"

The ubiquitous "Hello, World!" project for the Arduino is the blinking light. The project uses an LED, a breadboard, and some jumper wires. The Arduino turns on and off through the course of the loop() iteration. That's a fine project for getting started, but it does not relate to how sensors could be used.

Thus, in this section, you expand on the blinking light project by adding a sensor. In this case, you still keep things simple by using what is arguably the most basic of sensors: a pushbutton. The goal is to illuminate the LED whenever the button is pushed.

Hardware Connections

Let's begin by assembling an Arduino. Be sure to disconnect (power down) the Arduino first. You can use any Arduino variant that has I/O pins. Place one LED and one pushbutton in the breadboard. Wire the 5V pin to the breadboard power rail and the ground pin to the ground rail, and place the pushbutton in the center of the breadboard. Place the LED to one side of the breadboard, as shown in Figure 3-18.

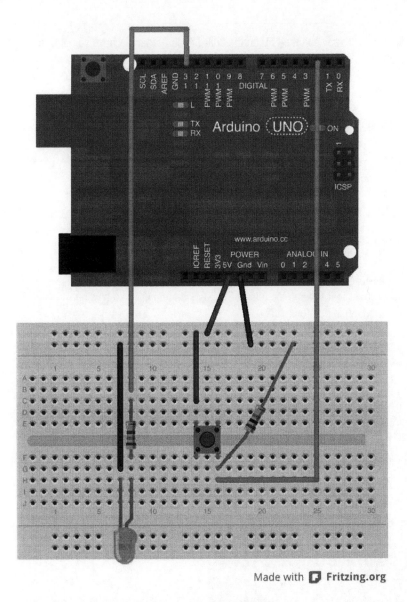

Made with **⚡ Fritzing.org**

Figure 3-18. *Diagram of an LED with a pushbutton*

You're almost there. Now wire a jumper from the power rail to one side of the pushbutton, and wire the other side of the pushbutton to (DIGITAL) pin 2 on the Arduino (located on the side with the USB connector). Next, wire the LED to ground on the breadboard and a 150-Ohm resistor (colors: brown, green, brown, gold). The other side of the resistor should be wired to pin 13 on the Arduino. You also need a resistor to pull the button low when the button is not pressed. Place a 10K Ohm resistor (colors: brown, black, orange, gold) on the side of the button with the wire to pin 2 and ground.

The longest side of the LED is the positive side. The positive side should be the one connected to the resistor. It doesn't matter which direction you connect the resistor; it is used to limit the current to the LED. Check the drawing again to ensure that you have a similar setup.

■ **Tip** If you power on your shiny new Arduino, you may see the LED on the board flash. This is because some Arduino boards come with the blink sketch preloaded.

■ **Note** Most Arduino boards have an LED connected to pin 13. You reuse the pin to demonstrate how to use analog output. Thus, you may see a small LED near pin 13 illuminate at the same time as the LED on the breadboard.

COOL GADGET

One of the coolest gadgets for working with the Arduino is the Arduino mounting plate from Adafruit (www.adafruit.com/products/275).

This small acrylic plate has space for a half-sized breadboard and an Arduino. It even has mounting holes for bolting the Arduino to the plate and small rubber feet to keep the plate off the work surface. The following illustration (courtesy of Adafruit) shows the mounting plate in action.

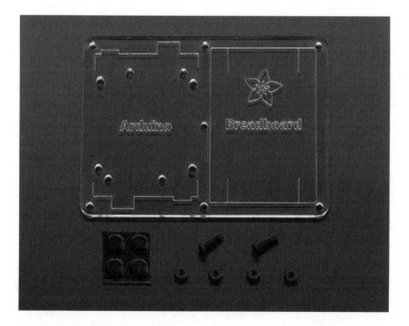

Although you can make your own Arduino mounting plate from Lexan or Plexiglas (I have), the Adafruit product is just a notch better than what you can make yourself. For about $5.00 USD, you can keep your Arduino and breadboard together and avoid scratches on your table (from the sharp prongs on the bottom of the Arduino)—and, better still, avoid the nasty side effects of accidentally placing a powered Arduino on a conductive surface (never a good idea).

Writing the Sketch

The sketch you need for this project uses two I/O pins on the Arduino: one output and one input. The output pin will be used to illuminate the LED, and the input pin will detect the pushbutton engagement. You connect positive voltage to one side of the pushbutton and the other side to the input pin. When you detect voltage on the input pin, you tell the Arduino processor to send positive voltage to the output pin. In this case, the positive side of the LED is connected to the output pin.

As you see in the drawing in Figure 3-18, the input pin is pin 2 and the output pin is pin 13. Let's use a variable to store these numbers so you do not have to worry about repeating the hard-coded numbers (and risk getting them wrong). Use the pinMode() method to set the mode of each pin (INPUT, OUTPUT). You place the variable statements before the setup() method and set the pinMode() calls in the setup() method, as follows:

```
int led = 13;      // LED on pin 13
int button = 2;    // button on pin 2

void setup() {
  pinMode(led, OUTPUT);
  pinMode(button, INPUT);
}
```

In the loop() method, you place code to detect the button press. Use the digitalRead() method to read the status of the pin (LOW or HIGH), where LOW means there is no voltage on the pin and HIGH means positive voltage is detected on the pin.

You also place in the **loop()** method the code to turn on the LED when the input pin state is HIGH. In this case, you use the digitalWrite() method to set the output pin to HIGH when the input pin state is HIGH and similarly set the output pin to LOW when the input pin state is LOW. The following shows the statements needed:

```
void loop() {
  int state = digitalRead(button);
  if (state == HIGH) {
    digitalWrite(led, HIGH);
  }
  else {
    digitalWrite(led, LOW);
  }
}
```

Now let's see the entire sketch, complete with proper documentation. Listing 3-1 shows the completed sketch.

Listing 3-1. Simple Sensor Sketch

```
/*
  Simple Sensor - Beginning Sensor Networks

  For this sketch, we explore a simple sensor (a pushbutton) and a simple
  response to sensor input (a LED). When the sensor is activated (the
  button is pushed), the LED is illuminated.
*/

int led = 13;      // LED on pin 13
int button = 2;    // button on pin 2
```

```
// the setup routine runs once when you press reset:
void setup() {
  // initialize pin 13 as an output.
  pinMode(led, OUTPUT);
  pinMode(button, INPUT);
}

// the loop routine runs over and over again forever:
void loop() {
  // read the state of the sensor
  int state = digitalRead(button);

  // if sensor engaged (button is pressed), turn on LED
  if (state == HIGH) {
    digitalWrite(led, HIGH);
  }
  // else turn off LED
  else {
    digitalWrite(led, LOW);
  }
}
```

When you've entered the sketch as written, you are ready to compile and run it.

■ **Tip** Want to avoid typing all this by hand? You can find the source code on the Apress site for this book. See http://apress.com/9781430258247.

Compiling and Uploading

Once you have the sketch written, test the compilation using the Compile button in the upper-left corner of the IDE. Fix any compilation errors that appear in the message window. Typical errors include misspellings or case changes (the compiler is case sensitive) for variables or methods.

After you have fixed any compilation errors, click the Upload button. The IDE compiles the sketch and uploads the compiled sketch to the Arduino board. You can track the progress via the progress bar at lower right, above the message window. When the compiled sketch is uploaded, the progress bar disappears.

Testing the Sensor

Once the upload is complete, what do you see on your Arduino? If you've done everything right, the answer is nothing. It's just staring back at you with that one dark LED—almost mockingly. Now, press the pushbutton. Did the LED illuminate? If so, congratulations: you're an Arduino programmer!

If the LED did not illuminate, hold the button down for a second or two. If that does not work, check all of your connections to make sure you are plugged in to the correct runs on the breadboard and that your LED is properly seated with the longer leg connected to the resistor, which is connected to pin 13.

On the other hand, if the LED stays illuminated, try reorienting your pushbutton 90 degrees. You may have set the pushbutton in the wrong orientation.

Try out the project a few times until the elation passes. If you're an old hand at Arduino, that may be a very short period. If this is all new to you, go ahead and push that button and bask in the glory of having built your first sensor node!

The next section examines a more complicated sensor node, using a temperature and humidity sensor that sends digital data. As you will see, there is a lot more to do.

Hosting Sensors with Arduino

The digital and analog pins of the Arduino make it an ideal platform for hosting sensors. Since most sensors need very little in the way of supporting components, you can often host multiple sensors on one Arduino. For example, it is possible to host a temperature sensor or even multiple temperature sensors, barometric, humidity, and so on, for sampling weather conditions from a given site.

SparkFun and Adafruit have excellent web sites that provide a great deal of information about the products they sell. Often the sensor product page includes links to examples and more information about using the sensor. If you are new to electronics, you should stick to sensors that provide examples of their use. It may sound like cheating, but unless you have a good knowledge of electronics, using a sensor incorrectly can get expensive as you burn your way through a few destroyed components before you get it right.

However, when there is another sensor you want to use, you should examine its data sheet. Most manufacturers and vendors supply the data sheet via a link on the product page. The data sheet provides all the information you need to use the sensor but may not have an actual example of its use. If you are familiar with electronics, this is all you are likely to need.

If you are more of a hobbyist or novice at electronics, check the wikis and forums on Arduino.cc, SparkFun, and Adafruit. These sites have a wealth of information and a great many examples, complete with sample code. If you cannot find any examples, you can try googling for one. Use terms like "Arduino <sensor name> example". If you cannot find any examples and are not an experienced electronics technician, you might want to reconsider using the sensor.

Another thing to consider is how you connect the sensor to the Arduino. Recall that there are a number of different physical layouts, depending on the Arduino you choose. Thus, you should be familiar with the pin layout of your Arduino when planning your Arduino-hosted sensor nodes. If you are hosting a single sensor with your Arduino, this may not be an issue. By way of example, Figure 3-19 shows an Arduino Leonardo board with the I/O pins highlighted. If you look carefully at your Arduino board, you see abbreviated text next to each pin to indicate its purpose. Some smaller-form-factor Arduino boards may not have room for the labels. In this case, consult the vendor's product page and print it out for future reference.

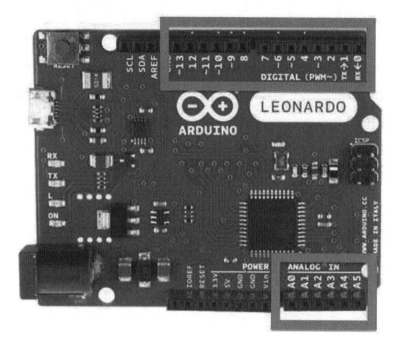

Figure 3-19. *Identifying the I/O pins on an Arduino board*

Now let's put the knowledge you've gained from learning about the Arduino to use in building a sensor node with an Arduino and a sensor.

Project: Building an Arduino Temperature Sensor

In this project, you build a more sophisticated Arduino hosted sensor node. This project not only demonstrates how to host sensors with an Arduino but also provides an example of why you need a microcontroller to host certain types of sensors. In this case, the DHT22 sensor is a digital sensor that has its own protocol, which requires a bit of logic to interpret correctly, thereby making it more complicated to use with an XBee.[5] Later, you see an example of a simple analog sensor that you can connect directly to an XBee module.

This project uses a DHT22 temperature and humidity sensor connected to the Arduino via a breadboard. The DHT22 is a simple digital sensor that produces digital signals. It requires a single resistor to pull up from the data pin to voltage. *Pull up* in this case makes sure the data value is "pulled up" to the voltage level to ensure a valid logic level on the wire.

Let's jump right in and connect the hardware.

■ **Note**   This example was adapted from an example on the Adafruit web site (`http://learn.adafruit.com/dht`).

---

[5]At least, I have not found anyone who has done this successfully.

Hardware Setup

The hardware required for this project includes an Arduino, a DHT22 humidity and temperature sensor, a breadboard, a 4.7K Ohm resistor (colors: yellow, purple, red, gold), and breadboard jumper wires.

■ **Tip**   If you get stuck or want more information, there is an excellent tutorial on Adafruit's web site.

Begin by placing your Arduino next to a breadboard. Plug the DHT22 sensor in to one side of the breadboard, as shown in Figure 3-20. Please refer to this figure often and double-check your connections before powering on your Arduino (or connecting it to your laptop). You want to avoid accidental experiments in electrical chaos theory.

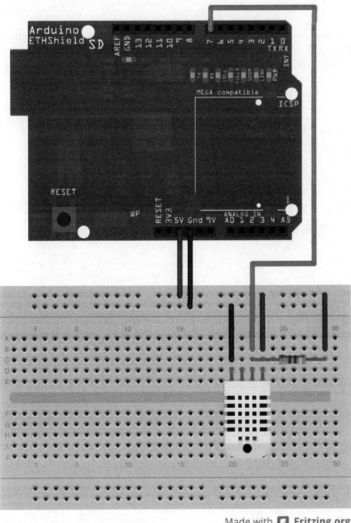

Figure 3-20. Wiring the DHT22

Next, connect the power from the Arduino to the breadboard. Use one jumper wire to connect the 5V pin on the Arduino to the breadboard power rail and another for the ground (GND) pin on the Arduino to the ground rail on the breadboard. With these wires in place, you are ready to wire the sensor. You use three of the four pins, as shown in Table 3-1.

Table 3-1. *DHT22 Connections*

Pin	Connected to
1	+5V, 4.7K resistor between the power supply and the data pin (strong pullup)
2	Pin 7 on Arduino, 4.7K resistor
3	No connection
4	Ground

Next, connect the ground and power of the sensor to the breadboard power and ground rails. Then connect one wire from the data pin on the sensor to pin 7 of the Arduino. There is one last connection: you use a pull-up resistor of 4.7K Ohm connected to the data wire and the power rail of the breadboard.

Software Setup

To use the DHT22 with an Arduino, you need to have the latest DHT22 library. You can find the library at `https://github.com/ringerc/Arduino-DHT22`. You must download the library and place it in your Arduino libraries folder.

■ **Tip** The Arduino libraries folder is generally found in your documents folder. See `http://arduino.cc/en/Guide/Libraries` for more information concerning your platform. For example, on Windows, the folder is named `libraries` versus `Libraries`.

To download the library, click the Download ZIP button, save the file, and then unzip it. The folder that is created has an unusual name: `Arduino-DHT22-master`. You must rename it to something like `DHT22` to remove the dashes so the Arduino environment won't complain. If your Arduino environment is running when you copy the folder, you need to restart it for the Arduino environment to read the new library.

Now that you have the hardware configured and the DHT22 library set up, let's write some code!

Writing the Sketch

Recall that I mentioned the DHT22 has its own protocol for communicating data. It uses a number of different values as the first byte sent, in what is referred to as an *error code*. Several types of errors can occur, including the trivial case where there is no error. Table 3-2 lists the various error codes and their meanings (what action you should take).

Table 3-2. *DHT22 Error Codes*

Error Code	Cause or Recommended Action
DHT_ERROR_CHECKSUM	Checksum failed. Could indicate read/send errors. Values read may not be accurate.
DHT_BUS_HUNG	Error reading from sensor. Try again at the next cycle.
DHT_ERROR_NOT_PRESENT	Cannot communicate with the sensor. Check the wiring.
DHT_ERROR_ACK_TOO_LONG	Too long between data sent and acknowledgement. Try again at the next cycle.
DHT_ERROR_SYNC_TIMEOUT	Synchronization failure during read. Try again at the next cycle.
DHT_ERROR_DATA_TIMEOUT	Timeout sending data. Try again at the next cycle.
DHT_ERROR_TOOQUICK	Wait at least 2 seconds between reads.
DHT_ERROR_NONE	No error. Read values.

As you can see in the table, most error conditions are related to read errors. The DHT22 is a rather slow device, so you should not try to read values more often than every 2 minutes. Also, some of the errors can have additional data that you can read. For example, the checksum error still contains the values sent, but they may be invalid.

I mentioned that the DHT22 sensor had its own protocol. What you see in Table 3-2 is only a small part of that protocol: the part you must include in your sketch. However, there is much more going on in the DHT library. If you are curious, open the DHT library with your Arduino IDE and explore the methods. Only then will you get a taste of what the protocol for reading from the sensor is really like.

What you have so far is the need to read from the sensor and interpret its error code. To do this, you use a switch statement (a shorter form of if/else if). To make the code easier to read and easier to maintain, place this code in a separate function called read_data(). Listing 3-2 shows the completed method.

Listing 3-2. The read_data() Method

```
void read_data() {
  DHT22_ERROR_t errorCode;

  errorCode = myDHT22.readData();
  switch(errorCode)
  {
    case DHT_ERROR_NONE:
      char buf[128];
      sprintf(buf, "%hi.%01hi, %i.%01i",
                  myDHT22.getTemperatureCInt()/10,
                  abs(myDHT22.getTemperatureCInt()%10),
                  myDHT22.getHumidityInt()/10,
                  myDHT22.getHumidityInt()%10);
      Serial.print("Data read:");
      Serial.print(buf);
      break;
    case DHT_ERROR_CHECKSUM:
      Serial.print("check sum error ");
      Serial.print(myDHT22.getTemperatureC());
      Serial.print("C ");
      Serial.print(myDHT22.getHumidity());
      Serial.println("%");
      break;
```

```
      case DHT_BUS_HUNG:
        Serial.println("BUS Hung ");
        break;
      case DHT_ERROR_NOT_PRESENT:
        Serial.println("Not Present ");
        break;
      case DHT_ERROR_ACK_TOO_LONG:
        Serial.println("ACK time out ");
        break;
      case DHT_ERROR_SYNC_TIMEOUT:
        Serial.println("Sync Timeout ");
        break;
      case DHT_ERROR_DATA_TIMEOUT:
        Serial.println("Data Timeout ");
        break;
      case DHT_ERROR_TOOQUICK:
        Serial.println("Polled too quick ");
        break;
    }
}
```

Notice at the top of the method that you call the DHT library method read_data(). You instantiate an object named myDHT22 in the preamble of the sketch. Following that, you use a switch statement and include each of the error codes, taking specific action for each. In the case of the DHT_ERROR_NONE (no error) result, you format the data for sending to the serial monitor.

The serial monitor is a special window (dialog) that you can use to send messages from your sketch. In Listing 3-2, every call to Serial.print() and Serial.println() results in a message being shown in the serial monitor. You can open the serial monitor after a sketch is uploaded by clicking the button at upper right in the Arduino IDE sketch window.

Notice for the DHT_ERROR_NONE case that you simply build a string from a static buffer of size 128 using the sprintf()[6] method to format and populate the values for display. Once you have all the code entered into your Arduino environment and your Arduino is ready to go, it is time to try it out.

■ **Caution** Watch out for array sizes! If you intend to save character string data returned by sensor nodes, be sure your data will fit into memory (buf).

I mentioned needing to instantiate an object in the preamble. You also need to include the DHT library and supporting files. The following shows the statements needed. Here you include the SPI and DHT22 library header files, define the data pin for the sensor as pin 7 on the Arduino, add a delay constant of 5 seconds, and instantiate an instance of the DHT class:

```
#include <SPI.h>
#include <DHT22.h>
#define DHT22_PIN 7        // DHT2 data is on pin 7
#define read_delay 5000    // 5 seconds
DHT22 myDHT22(DHT22_PIN); // DHT22 instance
```

---

[6]A very commonly used method. See the sprintf() documentation at www.cplusplus.com/reference/cstdio/sprintf/ for more details.

The setup() method is where you initiate the serial monitor. The workings of the sketch in the loop() method are also simplistic. Here you wait for the delay period defined and then read the data by calling your read_data() method. Recall that the Arduino will execute these two statements until it is powered down. Listing 3-3 shows the completed sketch.

Listing 3-3. Completed Sketch: Reading a DHT-22 Sensor

```
/*
  Sensor Networks Example Arduino Hosted Sensor Node

  This sensor node uses a DHT22 sensor to read temperature and humidity
  printing the results in the serial monitor.

*/
#include <SPI.h>
#include <DHT22.h>

#define DHT22_PIN 7        // DHT2 data is on pin 7

#define read_delay 5000    // 5 seconds

DHT22 myDHT22(DHT22_PIN); // DHT22 instance

void read_data() {
  DHT22_ERROR_t errorCode;

  errorCode = myDHT22.readData();
  switch(errorCode)
  {
    case DHT_ERROR_NONE:
      char buf[128];
      sprintf(buf, "%hi.%01hi, %i.%01i\n",
                  myDHT22.getTemperatureCInt()/10,
                  abs(myDHT22.getTemperatureCInt()%10),
                  myDHT22.getHumidityInt()/10,
                  myDHT22.getHumidityInt()%10);
      Serial.print("Data read:");
      Serial.print(buf);
      break;
    case DHT_ERROR_CHECKSUM:
      Serial.print("check sum error ");
      Serial.print(myDHT22.getTemperatureC());
      Serial.print("C ");
      Serial.print(myDHT22.getHumidity());
      Serial.println("%");
      break;
    case DHT_BUS_HUNG:
      Serial.println("BUS Hung ");
      break;
    case DHT_ERROR_NOT_PRESENT:
      Serial.println("Not Present ");
      break;
```

```
      case DHT_ERROR_ACK_TOO_LONG:
        Serial.println("ACK time out ");
        break;
      case DHT_ERROR_SYNC_TIMEOUT:
        Serial.println("Sync Timeout ");
        break;
      case DHT_ERROR_DATA_TIMEOUT:
        Serial.println("Data Timeout ");
        break;
      case DHT_ERROR_TOOQUICK:
        Serial.println("Polled too quick ");
        break;
    }
}

void setup() {
  Serial.begin(115200);   // Set the serial port speed
}

void loop() {
  delay(read_delay);
  read_data();
}
```

Open a new Arduino sketch by clicking the New menu button or by choosing File ⌧ New. Now you can compile, upload, and test the project.

Test Execution

Executing the sketch means uploading it to your Arduino and watching it run. If you haven't connected your Arduino, you can do that now.

I like to begin by compiling the sketch. Click the check mark on the left side of the Arduino application, and observe the output in the message screen at the bottom. If you see errors, fix them and retry the compile. Common errors include missing the DHT22 library (which may require restarting the Arduino application), typing errors, syntax errors, and the like. Once everything compiles correctly, you are ready to upload your sketch by clicking the Upload button on the toolbar.

Right after the upload completes, open the serial monitor by clicking the button at right on the toolbar. Observe the Arduino messages. Figure 3-21 shows the typical output you should see.

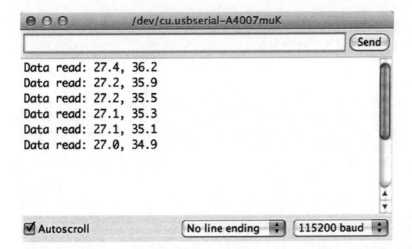

Figure 3-21. Serial monitor output for the DHT22 sensor project

If you see similar output, congratulations! You have just built your first Arduino-hosted sensor node. This is an important step in building your sensor network, as you now have the tools needed to start building more sophisticated, wireless sensor nodes and aggregate nodes for recording sensor data.

Let's take the Arduino sensor experience one step further and add XBee modules to enable the sensor to be placed away from the Arduino. This effectively demonstrates how an Arduino can remotely host a number of sensor nodes and thus become an aggregate node in a sensor network.

Project: Using an Arduino as a Data Collector for XBee Sensor Nodes

This project combines what you have learned about the Arduino in this chapter and the XBee in Chapter 2. More specifically, you use an Arduino and a remote sensor that connects the sensor with the Arduino using XBee modules. But first, let's build the XBee sensor node and test it with your laptop before you build the Arduino component.

XBee Sensor Node

The XBee sensor node is a single XBee module with a simple sensor connected to one of the analog input pins. For this project, you tell the XBee to send data using short time periods; but for a real project, you would want to consider using a slower sampling rate or perhaps using sleep mode, in which the XBee sleeps for some time then sends data, and repeats. We set the sampling rate when we configure the XBee module later in this chapter. For now, let's let the XBee send samples more frequently so you can see something happening.[7]

The XBee has a really nifty feature for monitoring battery power. You can tell the XBee to send the current supply power as part of the data packet. In this case, it sends whatever voltage is being supplied to the XBee. This is really neat because it allows you to build in to your solution a trigger to remind you to change the batteries in your sensor node(s). If you have a home or apartment with smoke detectors, you may have already experienced a similar circuit. For those of us with homes that have multiple smoke detectors, it can be somewhat of a "Where's Waldo?" game to find the detector that is chirping! This is why whenever six months go by or the first detector starts chirping, I change the batteries in all of them.

---

[7]It can sometimes be maddening to wait for an XBee that has an extended sleep cycle. It is best to not use sleep while you are prototyping the solution.

Hardware Setup

To keep the project easy to build, you use a breadboard for the sensor node. Once you have built a few sensor nodes, you can move them to PCB breadboards for semi-permanent installation or perhaps design and build your own custom PCB for your sensor nodes.

The hardware for the XBee sensor node consists of a breadboard, a breadboard power supply, a TMP36 temperature sensor, and a 0.10μF capacitor. You also need an XBee explorer board and a set of male headers (0.1" spacing for breadboards) like those available from Adafruit or SparkFun. Figure 3-22 shows the SparkFun regulated explorer board. The regulated board is a bit more expensive, but it has power regulation built in so if you accidentally connect 5V it won't fry your XBee. As an owner of a now completely useless XBee (it's not even big enough to use as a coaster), I can tell you that it is worth the extra cost.

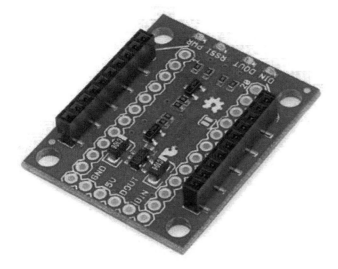

Figure 3-22. *SparkFun regulated XBee explorer (courtesy of SparkFun)*

■ **Note**   Most breakout boards do not come with the breadboard headers installed. You have to solder them yourself, get someone to do it for you, or, with some careful shopping, find another board that is already assembled.

Once you have the components assembled, plug them in to your breadboard as shown in Figure 3-23. Be sure to set the breadboard power supply to 3.3V.

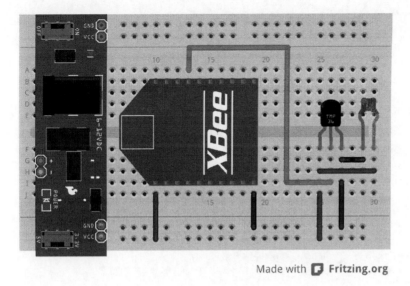

Made with ■ Fritzing.org

Figure 3-23. *XBee temperature sensor node*

There is no need to install the XBee module just yet. You need to configure its settings. You do that in the next section.

It is important to note that the drawing shows positive power going to pin 1 of the XBee. Be sure to check the pins on your breakout board to be certain you are connecting to the right pin. For example, the SparkFun regulated explorer input voltage is not on pin 1.

■ **Note** The breadboard power supply can be any 6V to 12V power supply. The 9V wall wart that most use to power their Arduino will do nicely.

Notice that you also connect your data line from the TMP36 to pin 17 (analog 3) on the XBee, and you connect ground to the ground pin on the breakout board (or explorer). Be sure to orient the TMP36 with the flat side as shown in the drawing. That is, with the flat side facing you, pin 1 is on the left and is to be connected to input power, the middle pin is data, and pin 3 is to be connected to ground. You can place the capacitor in either orientation, but be sure it is connected to pin 1 and 3 of the TMP36.

■ **Caution** If your breakout board power supply allows for multiple settings, make sure it is set on 3.3V! More than that may do harm to your XBee. Can you guess how I figured that out?

ALTERNATIVE TO A BREADBOARD POWER SUPPLY

If you plan to make a few XBee sensor nodes for semi-permanent installation, you may not want to use a breadboard. Rather, you may want to use a PCB breadboard and solder your XBee breakout board, sensor, and supporting electronics in place. In this case, a breadboard power supply might not be convenient. Similarly, if you want to keep costs down, you can build a basic power supply from a few parts that can accept up to 12V and still regulate the power to your XBee at 3.3V.

All you need are a 7833-voltage regulator, a 1μF capacitor, a 10μF, and a 2-terminal terminal block (or similar power connector). In total, you should be able to buy these components for a few dollars even at an electronics retail store—and less from an electronics online store. Arranging the circuit is easy. The following picture shows the components wired to a breadboard.

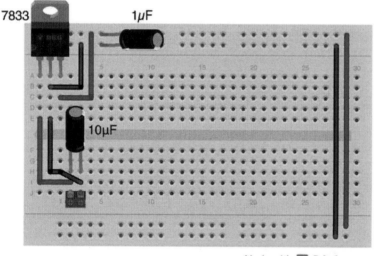

Made with ▄ **Fritzing.org**

You need only a little imagination and some wire to transfer the circuit to a PCB breadboard. Notice the orientation of the capacitors—keep the white strip on the negative side!

■ **Caution** Be sure to double-check your wiring before powering on the sensor node.

Configuring the XBee

The XBee module you use on the XBee sensor node is either an end device or a router with API firmware. You use the X-CTU application to connect to the XBee with a USB adapter. From the Modem Configuration tab, you can load the firmware as well as make modifications to the AT parameters.

In this case, you want the XBee module to send data every 15 seconds (15,000 milliseconds), read data on analog line 3, and send you the reference voltage. Thus, in the X-CTU application, you want to change the corresponding values using hexadecimal numbers. Table 3-3 shows the values you need to change. Recall that all values are entered in hexadecimal and that you can change the value in X-CTU by first clicking the row that corresponds to the setting.

Table 3-3. *XBee Options and Values*

Section	Parameter	Description	Value
I/O Settings	D3: AD3/DIO3 Configuration	Trigger analog or digital data recording	2 - ADC
I/O Settings | I/O Sampling	IR: I/O Sampling Rate	Time to wait to send data	3A98
I/O Settings | I/O Sampling	V+: Supply Voltage Threshold	Supply voltage	FFFF

Open the X-CTU application on your Windows machine, and load the API firmware for an XBee module. You can use one of the modules you used in Chapter 2, provided you don't use the coordinator. You will use that module to test the XBee sensor node. Change the settings as shown, and then click Write to save the settings to the XBee module.

Testing the XBee Sensor Node

To test the XBee sensor node, you use your XBee coordinator with API firmware installed on the USB adapter. Do this first so the coordinator can be up and running when you start the XBee sensor node. Plug it in to your computer, and open a terminal application with the display set to show hexadecimal values.

Next, connect your power supply to your XBee sensor node. It will take a few moments for the XBee to connect to the coordinator and join the network. Once it does, you start to see the coordinator receiving data, as shown in Figure 3-24.

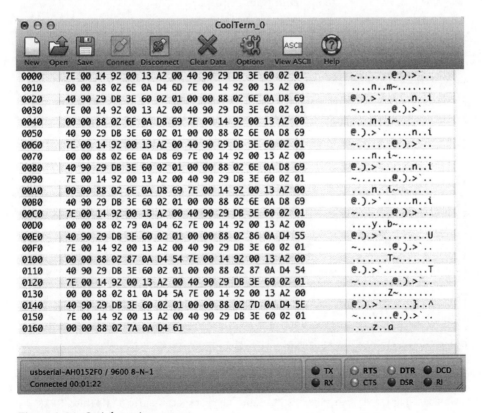

Figure 3-24. *Serial monitor output*

You should see an I/O data sample receive (Rx) Indicator packet. Notice in the image that the first row begins with 7E (hex). This is the start-of-packet delimiter. Search ahead until you find the next 7E value. The values from the start delimiter to the value before the next start delimiter make up the data packet from the XBee temperature sensor node. Table 3-4 decodes the first sample packet in the example.

Table 3-4. *IO Data Sample Rx Indicator Packet*

Value	Field Name	Notes
7E	Start delimiter	
00 14	Packet length	20 bytes to checksum
92	Frame type	I/O Data Sample Rx Indicator
00 13 A2 00 40 90 29 DB	64-bit address	Address of XBee sensor node
3E 60	16-bit address	
02	Options	
01	Number of samples	1 data sample
00 00	Digital mask	Digital pins that have data
88	Analog mask	Analog pins that have data
02 6E	Sample	Temperature from sensor
0A D4	Supply voltage	
93	Checksum	

■ **Note**   If you used the newer version 2.5 firmware, you may see slightly different codes for the options byte, but the important ones to look for are sample and voltage values.

This data packet represents the data sent from the XBee. In this case, you set the XBee to send any value from the analog pin 3 every 15 seconds. You also set the option to send the value of the supply voltage. Notice the value for the analog mask: the value 88 in hexadecimal is converted to 1000 1000 in binary. The first part of the byte is an indicator that the supply voltage is also included in the data packet. The second part of the byte indicates that AD3 (pin 3) was the source of the sample. If you were sampling multiple sensors, the mask would have the bits for the data pin set or 0001 for pin 0, 0010 for pin 1, and 0100 for pin 2.

From the table, you see there is indeed one data sample with a value of 02 6E (hex, 622 decimal). The value is 622 because this is the voltage in millivolts read from the sensor. To calculate the temperature, you must use the following formula:

```
temp =  ((sample * 1200/1024) - 500)/10
```

Thus, you have ((622 * 1200/2400)-500)/10 = 22.89 degrees Celsius. The supply voltage is a similar formula:

```
voltage = (sample * 1200/1024)/1000
```

Here you convert the data read to volts rather than millivolts. Thus, the data packet contained 0A D4 (hex, 2772), and the voltage read is 3.24 volts. If you are powering an XBee sensor from a battery, you can use this value to determine when you need to change or charge the battery.

Take a few moments to study the other samples in the example and check the data samples for the temperature read. Once you are convinced your XBee sensor node is sending similar data, you can conclude that the sensor node is working correctly. Now that you have a working, tested sensor node, let's set up your Arduino to receive the information remotely.

Arduino with XBee Shield

You can use an Arduino to read the data from the XBee sensor node. This gives you an example of using an Arduino as a data aggregator (collector) of sensor data from XBee sensor nodes. Let's set up an Arduino with an XBee. This project demonstrates using an Arduino to receive data via XBee, but you can also send data via XBee.

Hardware Setup

The sample setup in this section uses a typical Arduino (Uno, Leonardo, etc.) that supports standard shields. Although it is not expressly necessary to use a shield designed to accept an XBee module, most XBee shields are designed to make the use of the XBee easier. In other words, you don't have to worry about how to wire the XBee to the Arduino. Figure 3-25 shows an Arduino with an XBee shield from SparkFun.

Figure 3-25. *Arduino XBee shield (courtesy of SparkFun)*

I use this shield to demonstrate how to communicate with an XBee module. If you decide to use another shield, be sure to check that shield's documentation for examples of how to use it and compare it with the code in this project. Make the appropriate modifications (hardware connections and changes to the sketch) so that your project will work correctly with your shield.

The shield lets you choose to communicate with the Arduino with the onboard serial circuitry (UART[8]) for the Arduino via digital pins 0 and 1. But these are also the pins used when communicating with the Arduino via USB from the Arduino IDE. Fortunately, the SparkFun XBee shield has a small switch that allows you to choose to use pins 2 and 3 instead. You use this option so that you can write a script to read data from the shield via the XBee and still connect to the Arduino IDE and use the serial monitor. But there is a catch: only one UART is available. You must use the software serial library to simulate a second serial connection. The software serial library is included in the Arduino IDE. You see how to do this in the "Software Setup" section.

■ **Tip** If you are using a different XBee shield, you should consult the documentation on the shield and use the pins as instructed. Some shields are hard wired.

If you do not want to use a shield, you can wire your XBee to an Arduino as you did earlier. In this case, you use an XBee breakout board from SparkFun to mate to a breadboard. Figure 3-26 shows the wiring diagram for wiring the XBee regulated explorer breakout board to an Arduino. Notice that you use the 5V pin from the Arduino. If you are using a nonregulated breakout board, you should use the 3.3V pin instead. Always double-check the maximum voltage of any component you use before powering on the project.

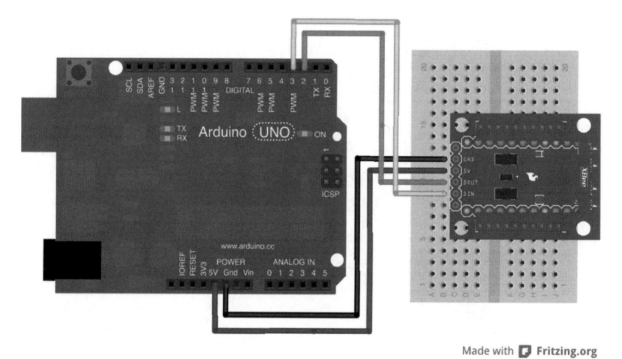

Made with ⬛ **Fritzing.org**

Figure 3-26. *Connecting an XBee to an Arduino via a SparkFun XBee breakout board*

---

[8]http://en.wikipedia.org/wiki/Universal_asynchronous_receiver/transmitter

▓ **Note**   Either of these methods will work for this project.

Whichever method you choose, take the XBee coordinator module off your USB adapter and insert it into the XBee shield or the XBee regulated explorer breakout board. Now that the hardware is ready, let's set up your Arduino environment and write a sketch to read the data from the XBee sensor node.

Software Setup

The XBee communicates via a serial connection. Although you can write your own communication statements to communicate with an XBee, there is an easier way. Andrew Rapp has written a library that encapsulates communication with an XBee module. The library is called XBee Arduino and can be found at http://code.google.com/p/xbee-arduino/.

To get started, download version 0.4 of the XBee library, unzip it, and copy it to your Arduino library folder. You can find the name of the library by checking the options for your Arduino IDE. You can determine where this is by examining the preferences for the Arduino environment, as shown in Figure 3-27. For example, my sketches folder on my Mac is /Users/cbell/Documents/Arduino. Thus, I copied the XBee library to a folder named /Users/cbell/Documents/Arduino/Libraries/XBee.

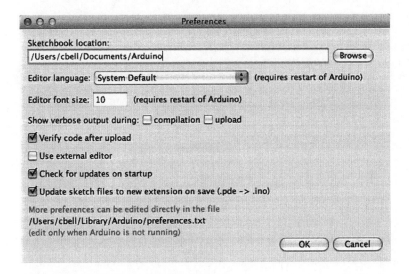

Figure 3-27. *Arduino Preferences dialog*

▓ **Tip**   If you copy a library to your libraries folder while the Arduino application is running, you must restart the application to detect the new library.

Once the library is installed and you have restarted your Arduino IDE, you can write the script to read the data from the XBee. The library has classes for each of the popular XBee data packets to send and receive data to or from an XBee. This project uses the IO sample class because you know that is the only packet we are interested in using in this project.

You need to create several parts of the sketch. Using the XBee library is easier than writing your own communication methods, but the library has certain setup steps and methods you need to use to read the data packet.

To begin, let's include the library headers for the XBee and software serial libraries. Recall that the software serial library is part of the Arduino IDE:

```
#include <XBee.h>
#include <SoftwareSerial.h>
```

Now you must define the pins you use to communicate to the XBee module. You use the serial monitor as an output device, so you need to use alternative pins. In this case, you use pins 2 and 3 for the receive and transmit connections. You need to define these and initialize the software serial library and use that to communicate to the XBee. The following shows the definitions needed:

```
uint8_t recv = 2;
uint8_t trans = 3;
SoftwareSerial soft_serial(recv, trans);
```

Next, you must instantiate the XBee library and helper classes. In this case, you need the helper class for the I/O data sample packet:

```
XBee xbee = XBee();
ZBRxIoSampleResponse ioSample = ZBRxIoSampleResponse();
```

Now we are ready to write the startup code. For this project, you must initiate the software serial library and pass that to the XBee library for use in communicating with the XBee module. You also need to initialize the default serial class so that you can use print() statements to display the data read in a later portion of the code. Listing 3-4 shows the complete setup() method.

Listing 3-4. Arduino XBee setup() Method

```
void setup() {
  Serial.begin(9600);
  while (!Serial);   // Leonardo boards need to wait for Serial to start
  soft_serial.begin(9600);
  xbee.setSerial(soft_serial);
}
```

Notice the line with the while loop. You need to add this for use on Leonardo boards. If you omit this and run the sketch on a Leonardo board, the XBee may fail to work. Add this loop to allow the Leonardo time to start the Serial instance.

Now let's code the methods you use to read the data from the packet. You learn how to read the packet from the XBee a bit later. First, let's examine how to get the source address for the data packet. Listing 3-5 shows the code for doing so.

Listing 3-5. Arduino XBee get_address() Method

```
void get_address(ZBRxIoSampleResponse *ioSample) {
  Serial.print("Received data from address: ");
  Serial.print(ioSample->getRemoteAddress64().getMsb(), HEX);
  Serial.print(ioSample->getRemoteAddress64().getLsb(), HEX);
  Serial.println("");
}
```

Notice that you simply use the ioSample class instance and call the method getRemoteAddress64().getMsb(). Actually, this is a call to a subclass (RemoteAddress64) and its method getMsb(). This returns the most significant byte (high 16 bits) of the 64-bit address. You do the same for the least significant bit with the getRemoteAddress64().getLsb() call. You then print these values, specifying that you want to print them in hexadecimal. If you were reading data from multiple XBee nodes, it would be handy to apply a name to each address, such as "bedroom" or "living room". I leave that for you as an exercise.

Next you want to read the data payload. In this case, you want to read the temperature data sent to the XBee coordinator from the XBee sensor node. Listing 3-6 shows the code needed to do this. You use the formulas discussed previously to convert the millivolt value read by the sensor to temperature in Celsius and then convert that to Fahrenheit.

Listing 3-6. Arduino XBee get_temperature() Method

```
void get_temperature(ZBRxIoSampleResponse *ioSample) {
  float adc_data = ioSample->getAnalog(3);

  Serial.print("Temperature is ");
  float temperatureC = ((adc_data * 1200.0 / 1024.0) - 500.0) / 10.0;
  Serial.print(temperatureC);
  Serial.print("c, ");
  float temperatureF = ((temperatureC * 9.0)/5.0) + 32.0;
  Serial.print(temperatureF);
  Serial.println("f");
}
```

Finally, you need to read the supply voltage from the data packet. In this case, the supply voltage appears after the data samples. Because you know there is only one data sample (via the analog sample mask), you know that the analog voltage appears right before the checksum. Sadly, there is no method currently to fetch that information from the I/O sample packet in the XBee library. However, all is not lost, because the author of the library stores the data in an array and has supplied a subclass for you to use to fetch the raw data. In this case, you want bytes 17 (most significant byte) and 18 (least significant byte) from the data. You know these are the indexes needed by counting from the byte following the frame type starting from zero. See Table 3-4 for details.

Like the temperature data, you must convert the value read to volts using the formula discussed previously. Listing 3-7 shows the code needed to read, convert, and display the supply voltage for the XBee sensor node. Notice that you shift the most significant byte 8 bits so that you can preserve the 16-byte floating-point value.

Listing 3-7. Arduino XBee get_supply_voltage() Method

```
void get_supply_voltage() {
  Serial.print("Supply voltage is ");
  int ref = xbee.getResponse().getFrameData()[17] << 8;
  ref += xbee.getResponse().getFrameData()[18];
  float volts = (float(ref) * float(1200.0 / 1024.0))/1000.0;
  Serial.print(" = ");
  Serial.print(volts);
  Serial.println(" volts.");
}
```

Take some time to examine the calculations. In this example, you convert the voltage read and sent by the XBee sensor node to Celsius and then again to Fahrenheit. You also convert the supply voltage to volts for easier reading. All these values are sent to the serial monitor for feedback during testing.

Once you have those methods implemented, you place the code to read the data from the XBee in the loop()
method, calling these methods to decipher the data and print it to the serial monitor.

Because this loop() method is called repeatedly, you use the XBee class method to read the packet and then
determine if the packet is the I/O data sample packet. If it is, you read the data from the packet. If it is not, you add
some simple error handling so that the Arduino can continue to read data rather than stop. Listing 3-8 shows the
completed loop() method.

Listing 3-8. Arduino XBee loop() Method

```
void loop() {
  xbee.readPacket();

  if (xbee.getResponse().isAvailable()) {

    if (xbee.getResponse().getApiId() == ZB_IO_SAMPLE_RESPONSE) {
      xbee.getResponse().getZBRxIoSampleResponse(ioSample);

      // Read and display data
      get_address(&ioSample);
      get_temperature(&ioSample);
      get_supply_voltage();
    }
    else {
      Serial.print("Expected I/O Sample, but got ");
      Serial.print(xbee.getResponse().getApiId(), HEX);
    }
  } else if (xbee.getResponse().isError()) {
    Serial.print("Error reading packet.  Error code: ");
    Serial.println(xbee.getResponse().getErrorCode());
  }
}
```

Notice that in the code you check to see whether the packet is available; if it is, you read it. If the packet read is the
right frame type, in this case ZB_IO_SAMPLE_RESPONSE, you read the data from the packet and display it. If it isn't the
right packet, you print out to the serial monitor the frame type of the packet received. If there is an error reading the
packet, you capture that in the last else and display the error to the serial monitor.

Notice the contents of the block of code for the ZB_IO_SAMPLE_RESPONSE condition. You begin by initializing the
I/O data sample class with the data read, then read the address of the XBee that sent the packet, and then perform the
calculations for temperature and reference voltage.

Once you understand the code so far, start a new file and type the information into your new sketch window.
Listing 3-9 shows the completed sketch for the Arduino XBee receiver project. This code is also available on the Apress
site at the source code link for this book.

Listing 3-9. Arduino XBee Receiver

```
/**
  Sensor Networks Example Arduino Receiver Node

  This project demonstrates how to receive sensor data from
  an XBee sensor node. It uses an Arduino with an XBee shield
  with an XBee coordinator installed.
```

```
  Note: This sketch was adapted from the examples in the XBee
  library created by Andrew Rapp.
*/

#include <XBee.h>
#include <SoftwareSerial.h>

// Setup pin definitions for XBee shield
uint8_t recv = 2;
uint8_t trans = 3;
SoftwareSerial soft_serial(recv, trans);

// Instantiate an instance of the XBee library
XBee xbee = XBee();

// Instantiate an instance of the IO sample class
ZBRxIoSampleResponse ioSample = ZBRxIoSampleResponse();

void setup() {
  Serial.begin(9600);
  while (!Serial);    // Leonardo boards need to wait for Serial to start
  soft_serial.begin(9600);
  xbee.setSerial(soft_serial);
}

// Get address and print it
void get_address(ZBRxIoSampleResponse *ioSample) {
  Serial.print("Received data from address: ");
  Serial.print(ioSample->getRemoteAddress64().getMsb(), HEX);
  Serial.print(ioSample->getRemoteAddress64().getLsb(), HEX);
  Serial.println("");
}

// Get temperature and print it
void get_temperature(ZBRxIoSampleResponse *ioSample) {
  float adc_data = ioSample->getAnalog(3);

  Serial.print("Temperature is ");
  float temperatureC = ((adc_data * 1200.0 / 1024.0) - 500.0) / 10.0;
  Serial.print(temperatureC);
  Serial.print("c, ");
  float temperatureF = ((temperatureC * 9.0)/5.0) + 32.0;
  Serial.print(temperatureF);
  Serial.println("f");
}

// Get supply voltage and print it
void get_supply_voltage() {
  Serial.print("Supply voltage is ");
  int ref = xbee.getResponse().getFrameData()[17] << 8;
  ref += xbee.getResponse().getFrameData()[18];
```

```
  float volts = (float(ref) * float(1200.0 / 1024.0))/1000.0;
  Serial.print(" = ");
  Serial.print(volts);
  Serial.println(" volts.");
}

void loop() {
  //attempt to read a packet
  xbee.readPacket();

  if (xbee.getResponse().isAvailable()) {
    // got something

    if (xbee.getResponse().getApiId() == ZB_IO_SAMPLE_RESPONSE) {

      // Get the packet
      xbee.getResponse().getZBRxIoSampleResponse(ioSample);

      // Read and display data
      get_address(&ioSample);
      get_temperature(&ioSample);
      get_supply_voltage();
    }
    else {
      Serial.print("Expected I/O Sample, but got ");
      Serial.print(xbee.getResponse().getApiId(), HEX);
    }
  } else if (xbee.getResponse().isError()) {
    Serial.print("Error reading packet.  Error code: ");
    Serial.println(xbee.getResponse().getErrorCode());
  }
}
```

Take some time to ensure that the sketch compiles before you upload it to your Arduino. Remember, once the sketch is uploaded, it begins to run.

Testing the Final Project

To test the project, ensure that you start your Arduino first and then the XBee sensor node. Start the Arduino, upload the sketch, and then turn on the serial monitor. You should observe the link lights on the XBee regulated breakout board flicker as the XBee node is accepted by the coordinator on the Arduino and added to the network. Within about 5 seconds, the XBee sensor node begins sending data. When this occurs, the Arduino sketch should start printing statements to your serial monitor. Figure 3-28 shows an example of the output you should see in the serial monitor.

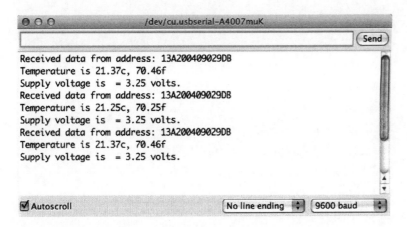

Figure 3-28. *Serial monitor output*

Did you see something similar? If so, you're doing great work and now have the rudimentary components to build sensor nodes and Arduino-based sensor data aggregators.

If you do not see any output in the serial monitor, do not panic. Instead, double-check that the XBee on your Arduino is plugged in correctly and that you are using the correct pins in the sketch that correspond to how the XBee shield you are using connects to the Arduino (not all shields use pins 2 and 3 like the SparkFun shield). Hint: check the documentation for your shield.

If all that is correct, make sure you are using the coordinator API firmware on the XBee connected to the Arduino and the router API firmware on the XBee sensor node. If you are still having issues, step back to the previous project to ensure that the sensor node is still working.

You can also try turning off both the Arduino and the XBee sensor node; then turn on the Arduino, wait about 10 seconds, and turn the XBee sensor node back on. Sometimes the handshake process and network join can stall, and nothing happens for a while. Turning an XBee off and back on in this order ensures that it will reattempt to configure.

On the other hand, maybe you are getting data, but it is not correct—the temperature read is far too low for the actual environment. I had this happen once when the wire I was using to connect to the data pin on the TMP36 was accidentally removed. The bottom line is, always check and recheck your wiring.

For More Fun

If you would like to expand the project, you can add a second XBee sensor node and modify the Arduino sketch to supply a location for each node. For example, you could label one node "office" and the other "kitchen". The sketch should record (write to the serial monitor) the location of the sensor along with the sensor data from the XBee.

Component Shopping List

A number of components are needed to complete the projects in this chapter. They are listed in Table 3-5.

Table 3-5. *Components Needed*

Item	Vendors	Est. Cost USD	Qty Needed
LED (any color)	www.sparkfun.com/products/9592	$0.35	1
Pushbutton (breadboard mount)	www.sparkfun.com/products/97	$0.35	1
Breadboard (not mini)	www.sparkfun.com/products/9567	$5.95	1
Breadboard jumper wires	www.sparkfun.com/products/8431	$3.95	1
DHT22	www.sparkfun.com/products/10167	$9.95	1
	www.adafruit.com/products/385		
150 Ohm resistor			1
4.7 K Ohm resistor (Resistor Kit)	www.sparkfun.com/products/10969	$7.95	1
10 K Ohm resistor (Resistor Kit)			1
Arduino XBee shield	www.sparkfun.com/products/10854	$24.95	1
XBee-ZB (ZB) series 2 or 2.5	www.sparkfun.com	$25.00	2
	www.adafruit.com		
	www.makershed.com		
TMP36 sensor	www.sparkfun.com/products/10988	$1.50	1
	www.adafruit.com/products/165		
Breadboard power supply	www.sparkfun.com/products/10804	$14.95	1
Wall power supply (6V–12V)	www.sparkfun.com/products/10273	$6.95	1
0.10μF capacitor	www.sparkfun.com/products/8375	$0.25	1
XBee regulated explorer with headers	www.sparkfun.com/products/11373	$9.95	1
Breakaway male headers (set)	www.sparkfun.com/products/11239	$9.95	1
	www.adafruit.com/products/392		
Arduino Uno (any that supports shields)	Various	$25.00 and up	1
SparkFun XBee shield	www.sparkfun.com/products/10854	$24.95	1
Soldering iron and solder			1

Summary

This chapter covered a lot of ground. You explored the Arduino platform, including the many forms available and how to write sketches (programs) to control the Arduino. I also showed you how to host sensors with the Arduino by using a temperature and humidity sensor.

You applied the information you learned about the XBee in Chapter 2 to create an XBee sensor node to read temperature data. You then set up an Arduino with an XBee coordinator to receive the sensor data from the XBee sensor node and display it in the serial monitor.

In the next chapter, you learn about the Raspberry Pi and discover how to use the I/O pins on the Raspberry Pi to read data from sensors.

CHAPTER 4

■ ■ ■

Raspberry Pi-based Sensor Nodes

Using microcontrollers to host sensors is an economical way to build a sensor network. But what do you do when you need more computational power than a microcontroller can provide? What if you need to convert the data to a different format, incorporate the data in an application, or print a hard copy of the sensor data? In these situations, you likely need a computer that has more processing power, can allow the use of common applications, permits the use of scripting languages, and affords access to peripherals.

Although personal computers are relatively inexpensive, there are distinct disadvantages to using them in your sensor networks—especially as sensor nodes. If the sensors are located in areas where mains power is unreliable or unavailable, or where there is a risk of overheating, or where there is simply no room to install a personal computer, you must either transmit the data to another node for processing or store it locally and process it later.

However, there is another limitation to using a personal computer as a sensor node: a personal computer has no general input/output (I/O) ports. You can purchase expansion cards for collecting data, but these are often built for use in server or desktop computers. If you consider the cost of the computer and the data-collection card, the cost of the sensor node becomes uneconomical.

So what do you do in these cases? If only there were a low-cost computer with sufficient processing power and memory, that used standard peripherals, supported programmable I/O ports,[1] and had a small form factor. That's exactly what the Raspberry Pi can do.

This chapter explores getting started with the Raspberry Pi, including how to use the system and how to read sensors using the I/O ports. You also explore a few types of sensors and examine the differences in how you read data from them.

What Is a Raspberry Pi?

The Raspberry Pi is a small, inexpensive personal computer. Although it lacks the capacity for memory expansion and can't accommodate on-board devices such as CD, DVD, and hard drives, it has everything a simple personal computer requires. That is, it has two USB ports, an Ethernet port, HDMI (and composite) video, and even an audio connector for sound.

The Raspberry Pi has an SD drive[2] that you can use to boot the computer into any of several Linux operating systems. All you need is an HDMI monitor (or DVI with an HDMI-to-DVI adapter), a USB keyboard and mouse, and a 5V power supply, and you're off and running.

---

[1]In this case, you require I/O ports that can be used as components in an electronic circuit and can be accessed (read from and written to) by programming libraries.
[2]Secure Digital (SD): a small removable memory drive the size of a postage stamp.
See http://en.wikipedia.org/wiki/Secure_Digital.

> ■ **Tip**   You can also power your Raspberry Pi using a USB port on your computer. In this case, you need a USB type A male to micro-USB type B male cable. Plug the type A side in to a USB port on your computer and the micro-USB type B side in to the Raspberry Pi power port.

The board is available in several versions and comes as a bare board costing as little as $35.00. It can be purchased online from electronics vendors such as SparkFun and Adafruit. Most vendors have a host of accessories that have been tested and verified to work with the Raspberry Pi. These include small monitors, miniature keyboards, and even cases for mounting the board.

In this section, you explore the origins of the Raspberry Pi, take a tour of the hardware connections, and discover what accessories are needed to get starting using the Raspberry Pi.

Noble Origins

The Raspberry Pi was designed to be a platform to explore topics in computer science. The designers saw the need to provide inexpensive, accessible computers that could be programmed to interact with hardware such as servo motors, display devices, and sensors. They also wanted to break the mold of having to spend hundreds of dollars on a personal computer, and thus make computers available to a much wider audience.

The designers observed a decline in the experience of students entering computer science curriculums. Instead of having some experience in programming or hardware, students are entering their academic years having little or no experience with working with computer systems, hardware, or programming. Rather, students are well versed in Internet technologies and applications. One of the contributing factors cited is the higher cost and greater sophistication of the personal computer, which means parents are reluctant to let their children experiment on the family PC.

This poses a challenge to academic institutions, which have to adjust their curriculums to make computer science palatable to students. They have had to abandon lower-level hardware and software topics due to students' lack of interest or ability. Students no longer wish to study the fundamentals of computer science such as assembly language, operating systems, theory of computation, and concurrent programming. Rather, they want to learn higher-level languages to develop applications and web services. Thus, some academic institutions are no longer offering courses in fundamental computer science.[3] This could lead to a loss of knowledge and skillsets in future generations of computer professionals.

To combat this trend, the designers of the Raspberry Pi felt that, equipped with the right platform, youth could return to experimenting with personal computers as in the days when PCs required a much greater commitment to learning the system and programming it in order to meet your needs. For example, the venerable Commodore 64, Amiga, and early Apple and IBM PC computers had very limited software offerings. Having owned a number of these machines, I was exposed to the wonder and discovery of programming at an early age.[4]

WHY IS IT CALLED RASPBERRY PI?

The name was partly derived from design committee contributions and partly chosen to continue a tradition of naming new computing platforms after fruit (think about it). The Pi portion comes from Python, because the designers intended Python to be the language of choice for programming the computer. However, other programming language choices are available.

---

[3]My alma mater has suffered a similar transition. I mourn for the loss of knowledge.
[4]My first real computer was an IBM PCjr. I followed it by building my own IBM PC AT computer, complete with a 10MB hard drive. Ah, those were the glory days of personal computers!

The Raspberry Pi is an attempt to provide an inexpensive platform that encourages experimentation. The following sections explore more about the Raspberry Pi, including the models available, required accessories, and where to buy the boards.

Models

There are currently two models of Raspberry Pi boards: Model A and Model B. The Model A board was the first mass-produced board and has 256MB of RAM, one USB port, and no Ethernet port. This was followed closely by the Model B board, which has 512MB of RAM, two USB ports, and an Ethernet port. Figure 4-1 shows the Model A board, and Figure 4-2 shows the Model B board.

Figure 4-1. *Raspberry Pi Model A (courtesy of the Raspberry Pi Foundation)*

Figure 4-2. *Raspberry Pi Model B (courtesy of the Raspberry Pi Foundation)*

WHAT HAPPENED TO THE $25 RASPBERRY PI?

If you have been following the release of the Raspberry Pi in various media, you have probably heard that the boards were priced at a mere $25.00. However, most retailers list the Raspberry Pi for $35.00 or more. Why is that?

The Model A was initially priced at $25.00, whereas the Model B cost a bit more at $35.00. However, due to supply and demand, you are likely to see average prices for either board (in the United States) at $40–50.00 at the time of writing.

You can often find the older Model A board at online retailers and auction sites for a bit less than the current Model B board. If you plan to use the Raspberry Pi for experimentation and do not need the extra memory, you can use a Model A board and a USB Ethernet module.

The examples in this chapter and the remaining chapters use the Model B variant.

A Tour of the Board

Not much larger than a deck of playing cards, the Raspberry Pi board contains a number of ports for connecting devices. This section presents a tour of the board. If you want to follow along with your board, hold it with the Raspberry Pi logo face up. I will work around the board clockwise. Figure 4-3 depicts a drawing of the board with all the major connectors labeled.

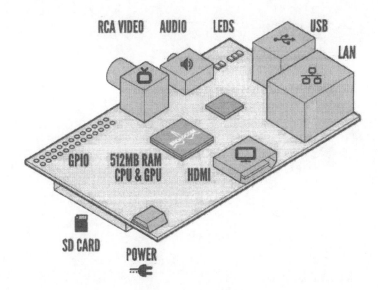

Figure 4-3. *Raspberry Pi Model B (courtesy of the Raspberry Pi Foundation and Paul Beech)*

In the center of the near side you see an HDMI connector. Directly opposite on the far side is an RCA connector. These are the two options[5] for connecting a monitor. You can use the RCA connector on one side to connect to a typical TV monitor (at very low resolution) or use the HDMI connector on the other side to connect to a high-resolution computer monitor or TV. For most uses, you will want to use the HDMI connector. If you have a DVI-enabled monitor, you can use an HDMI-to-DVI adapter.

On the left side are the micro-USB power connector on the top of the board and the SD card slot on the bottom. The power connector is known to be a bit fragile on some boards, so take care plugging and unplugging it. Be sure to avoid putting extra strain on this cable while using your Raspberry Pi.

Interestingly, most cases are not designed to protect the SD card. When installed, the SD card protrudes a few centimeters out of the board. For example, if you use a Pibow case, the SD card protrudes and can be subjected to strain if the board is knocked about. You can mitigate this risk by using Adafruit's low-profile microSD card adapter (www.adafruit.com/products/966), shown in Figure 4-4. The adapter permits the SD card to be flush or slightly inset in the case. Of course, this means you need a microSD card rather than an SD card, but fortunately these are plentiful.

---

[5]Actually, there is another video option on the board. The small ribbon cable connector on the left is a DSI video connector. To date, there are no examples using this connector for video, but it is an option for the adventurous. There is also a camera connector located behind the Ethernet port.

Figure 4-4. *Low-profile microSD adapter (courtesy of Adafruit)*

■ **Caution**   Because the board is small, it is tempting to use it in precarious places like a moving vehicle or on a messy desk. Ensure that your Raspberry Pi is in a secure location. The power, HDMI, and SD card slots seem to the most vulnerable connectors.

On the far side of the board is the general-purpose input/output (GPIO) header (a double row of 13 pins each), which can be used to attach to sensors and other devices. You work with this connector later in this chapter. To the right of the GPIO header is the aforementioned RCA connector, and to the right of that is the 3.5mm audio plug.

On the right side of the board are two USB connectors and the Ethernet connector. An external powered USB hub connected to the USB ports on the Raspberry Pi can power some boards, but it is recommended that you use a dedicated power supply connected to the micro-USB connector.

Take a moment to examine the top and bottom faces of the board. As you can see, components are mounted on both sides. This is a departure from most boards that have components on only one side. The primary reason the Raspberry Pi has components on both sides is that it uses multiple layers for trace runs. This permits the board to be much smaller and enables the use of both surfaces. This is probably the most compelling reason to consider using a case—to protect the components on the bottom of the board and thus avoid shorts and board failure.

Required Accessories

The Raspberry Pi is sold as a bare system board with no case, power supply, or peripherals. Depending on how you plan to use the Raspberry Pi, you need a few commonly available accessories. If you have been accumulating spares like me, a quick rummage through your stores may locate most of what you need.

If you want to use the Raspberry Pi in console mode (no graphical user interface), you need a USB power supply, a keyboard, and an HDMI monitor. The power supply should have a minimal rating of 700mA or greater. If you want to use the Raspberry Pi with a graphical user interface, you also need a pointing device (such as a mouse).

If you have to purchase these items, stick to the commonly available brands and models without extra features. For example, avoid the latest multifunction keyboard and mouse. Chances are, they require drivers that are not available for the various operating system choices for the Raspberry Pi.

You also must have an SD card. I recommend a 4GB or higher version. Recall that the SD is the only on-board storage medium available. You will need to put the operating system on the card, and any files you create will be stored on the card.

If you want to use sound in your applications, you also need a set of powered speakers that accept a standard 3.5mm audio jack. Finally, if you want to connect your Raspberry Pi to the Internet, you need an Ethernet cable.

HOW CAN I TELL IF MY DEVICE WILL WORK?

If you want to make sure your device will work with the Raspberry Pi, the simplest thing to do is try it! If you prefer not to take chances, you can check the Raspberry Pi hardware compatibility list at `http://elinux.org/RPi_VerifiedPeripherals`. This list contains many devices and commentary from various users in the community who have tested the devices. If you are just starting out with the Raspberry Pi, look for devices that require little or no extra configuration or drivers.

Recommended Accessories

I highly recommend at least adding small rubber or silicone self-adhesive bumpers to keep the board off your desk. On the bottom of the board are many sharp prongs that can come into contact with conductive materials; which can lead to shorts or, worse, a blown Raspberry Pi. These bumpers are available at most home-improvement and hardware stores.

If you plan to move the board from room to room or you want to ensure that your Raspberry Pi is well protected against accidental damage, you should consider purchasing a case to house the board. Many cases are available, ranging from simple snap-together models to models made from laser-cut acrylic or even milled aluminum. The following list includes several excellent choices, complete with vendor links.

Pi Tin

The Pi Tin from SparkFun is a basic, clear, two-piece case that snaps together. It uses light pipes to make reading the status LEDs easier and has cutouts for the GPIO header. It is inexpensive and an excellent choice for the budget minded. Figure 4-5 shows the Pi Tin from SparkFun: `www.sparkfun.com/products/11623`.

Figure 4-5. *Pi Tin (courtesy of SparkFun)*

Pi Box

The Pi Box from Adafruit is an example of a good acrylic case. It is made using acrylic plates that snap together. It has cutouts for ports. It is a bit more expensive than the basic two-piece cases, but it also looks better than others (this opinion is somewhat subjective, of course). It has two issues: the prongs that join the sides can break if you use too much force, and access to the GPIO header is limited. In fact, if your connector is too tall, the cable will not fit in the slot. Modifying the case is an option, but because it is acrylic, doing so may not be easy. Figure 4-6 shows the Pi Box from Adafruit: www.adafruit.com/products/859.

Figure 4-6. *Pi Box (courtesy of Adafruit)*

Pibow

The Pibow is available from Adafruit and comes in various colors. It is also made from pieces of acrylic, but they're arranged in a novel slice pattern. To assemble the Pibow, you place the Raspberry Pi on the bottom plate and stack the layers, finishing with a clear top plate. Key layers provide cutouts for all ports including the GPIO header. However, this case too has a very narrow slot, and some cables will not fit correctly. Four nylon fasteners secure the case as a unit. Once assembled, the case looks great and is very solid. Figure 4-7 shows the Pibow from Adafruit: www.adafruit.com/products/975.

Figure 4-7. *Pibow (courtesy of Adafruit)*

▥ **Tip**   If you plan to experiment with the GPIO pins or require access to the power test pins or the other ports located on the interior of the board, you may want to consider either using the self-adhesive bumper option or ordering a case that has an open top to make access easier. Some cases are prone to breakage if opened and closed frequently.

Aside from a case, you should also consider purchasing (or pulling from your spares) a powered USB hub. The USB hub power module should be 700–1000mA. A powered hub is required if you plan to use USB devices that draw a lot of power, such as a USB hard drive or a USB soft missile launcher.

Where to Buy

The Raspberry Pi has been available in Europe for some time. It is getting easier to find, but very few brick-and-mortar stores stock the Raspberry Pi. Fortunately, a number of online retailers stock it, as well as a host of accessories that are known to work with the Raspberry Pi. The following are some of the more popular online retailers with links to their Raspberry Pi catalog entry:

- *SparkFun:* www.sparkfun.com/categories/233

- *Adafruit:* www.adafruit.com/category/105

- *Maker Shed:* www.makershed.com/Raspberry_Pi_Boards_and_Accessories_s/227.htm

A RASPBERRY PI LAPTOP?

The Raspberry Pi has made a significant contribution to physical computing. Not only does it enable more sophisticated sensor nodes, but it also makes a decent lightweight general-purpose computer. With a proper monitor, mouse, and storage device, you can do most Internet and modest productivity tasks. In fact, some people have replaced their home desktop computer with a Raspberry Pi!

If you are like me and you need to be able to work from anywhere,[6] using a Raspberry Pi may not be very convenient, given that you must have a separate monitor and keyboard. Wouldn't it be great if you could take your Raspberry Pi with you? Well, now you can!

What you need is a surplus Atrix Lapdock from Motorola. Originally designed to allow the Aria phone to be used as a laptop, the Lapdock provides an 11.6" HDMI monitor, a USB keyboard, a mouse, a two-port USB hub, and speakers. More important, it is battery powered and can easily power the Raspberry Pi. The Lapdock has mini-HDMI and mini-USB ports that can be connected to the Raspberry Pi without modifying the Lapdock.

But there is a catch: you must purchase a mini-HDMI female-to-female adapter and a mini-HDMI male to HDMI male cable[7] and build your own Frankenstein USB cable from a micro-USB extension cable and a type A USB cable. The custom cable is needed to allow the Raspberry Pi to use the USB keyboard and mouse as well as power the board. The following figure shows how the cable is constructed. You can find a detailed tutorial video at www.adafruit.com/blog/2012/09/10/cables-adapters-for-the-atrix-raspberry-pi-laptop/.

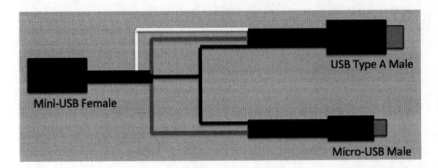

To build the cable, cut a normal USB type A connector from a standard USB cable,[8] bisect a standard micro-USB extension cable, and splice the wires as shown. You can abandon the wires in the ends that have no connections shown. The micro-USB male connector will be used to power the Raspberry Pi, and the USB type A male connector will provide connectivity to the Lapdock keyboard and mouse. Once you have this cable made, you're ready to go. For the best results, I recommend a sturdy case to mount your Raspberry Pi so as not to damage it during transport.

---

[6]Places like your couch, favorite recliner, patio, coffee bar, and so on.
[7]Be sure to select a cable that supports device sensing. If your Lapdock does not power on when the Raspberry Pi is connected, it is most likely the HDMI cable. Try another cable.
[8]Be sure to get permission before "borrowing" a cable from a friend or spouse—it won't be usable as a standard cable when you're finished modifying it.

To use the Raspberry Pi laptop, start by connecting the HDMI cable, then any peripherals (like a hard drive), and then the USB cable, and open the lid of the Lapdock. Within a few seconds, your new laptop is ready to go! The next figure shows the ports on the rear of the Lapdock under the folding door, and the one after that shows the laptop in action.

The best part of this project is the cost. You can find used and surplus Lapdocks on auction sites and similar electronics clearance stores. For example, on eBay the Lapdock is priced at about $60.00. You can also find the cables online or at most electronics stores. However, the female-to-female mini-HDMI adapter is a bit harder to find. I was able to purchase one on eBay from a dealer in China. Shipping was surprisingly fast, and the cost was reasonable. My cost for a mobile Raspberry Pi (not including the Raspberry Pi) was under $100.00.

The next section presents a short tutorial on getting started using the Raspberry Pi. If you have already learned how to use the Raspberry Pi, you can skip to the following section to begin learning how to connect sensors to your board.

Raspberry Pi Tutorial

The Raspberry Pi is a personal computer with a surprising amount of power and versatility. You may be tempted to consider it a toy or a severely limited platform, but that is far from the truth. With the addition of onboard peripherals like USB, Ethernet, and HDMI video, the Raspberry Pi has everything you need for a lightweight desktop computer. If you consider the addition of the GPIO header, the Raspberry Pi becomes more than a simple desktop computer and fulfills its role as a computing system designed to promote hardware experimentation.

The following sections present a short tutorial on getting started with your new Raspberry Pi, from a bare board to a fully operational platform. A number of excellent works cover this topic in much greater detail. If you find yourself stuck or wanting to know more about beginning to use the Raspberry Pi and more about the Raspbian operating system, see *Learn Raspberry Pi with Linux* by Peter Membrey and David Hows (Apress, 2012). If you want to know more about using the Raspberry Pi in hardware projects, an excellent resource is *Practical Raspberry Pi* by Brendan Horan (Apress, 2013).

Getting Started

As mentioned in the "Required Accessories" section, you need an SD card (or a microSD with the microSD adapter), a USB power supply rated at 700mA or better with a male micro-USB connector, a keyboard, a mouse (optional), and an HDMI monitor or a DVI monitor with an HDMI adapter. However, before you can plug these things in to your Raspberry Pi and bask in its brilliance, you need to create a boot image for your SD card.

Installing a Boot Image

The process of installing a boot image involves choosing an image, downloading it, and then copying it to your SD card. The following sections detail the steps involved.

Choosing the Image

The first thing you need to do is decide which operating system variant you want to use. There are several excellent choices, including the standard Raspbian "wheezy" variant. Each is available as a compressed file called an *image* or *card image*. You can find a list of recommended images along with links to download each on the Raspberry Pi foundation download page: `www.raspberrypi.org/downloads`. The following images are available at the site.

- *Raspbian wheezy:* The basic image. It is based on Debian and contains a graphical user interface (Lightweight X11 Desktop Environment [LXDE]), development tools and rudimentary multimedia features.

- *Soft-float Debian wheezy:* The image is similar to the Raspbian wheezy image, but uses a different application binary interface (ABI). It was created to be used with software packages like Oracle JVM, which don't support the ABI used by Raspbian wheezy.

- *Arch Linux ARM:* The image is based on Arch Linux, which provides a user experience intended for more advanced users. It is also optimized for fast booting.

If you are just starting with the Raspberry Pi, you should use the Raspbian image. This image is also recommended for the examples in this book.

There are a few other image choices, including a special variant of the Raspbian image from Adafruit. Adafruit calls their image "occidentals" and includes a number of applications and utilities preinstalled, including Wifi support and several utilities. Some Raspberry Pi examples—especially those from Adafruit—require the occidentals image. You can find out more about the image and download it at
`http://learn.adafruit.com/adafruit-raspberry-pi-educational-linux-distro/overview.`

Copying the Image to the SD Card

Once you select an image and download it, you first unzip the file and then copy it to your SD card. There are a variety of ways to do this. The following sections describe some simplified methods for a variety of platforms. You must have an SD card reader/writer connected to your computer. Some systems have SD card drives built in (Lenovo laptops, Apple laptops and desktops, and so on).

Windows

To create the SD card image on Windows, you can use the Win32 Disk Imager software from Launchpad (`https://launchpad.net/win32-image-writer`). Download this file, and install it on your system. Unzip the image if you haven't already, and then insert your SD card into your SD card reader/writer. Launch the Win32 Disk Imager application, select the image in the top box, and then click WRITE to copy the image to the SD.

■ **Caution**   The copy process overwrites anything already on the SD card, so be sure to copy those photos to your hard drive first!

Mac OS X

To create the SD card image on the Mac, download the image and unzip it. Insert your SD card into your SD card reader/writer. Be sure the card is formatted with FAT32. Next, open the System report (hint: use the Apple menu ➤ About this Mac).

Click the card reader if you have a built-in card reader, or navigate through the USB menu and find the SD card. Take note of the disk number. For example, it could be disk4.

Next, open the Disk Utility and unmount the SD card. You need to do this to allow the Disk Utility to mount and connect to the card. Now things get a bit messy. Open a terminal, and run the following command, substituting the disk number for *n* and the path and name of the image file for `<image_file>`:

```
sudo dd if=<image_file> of=/dev/diskn bs=1m
```

At this point, you should see the disk-drive indicator flash (if there is one), and you need to be patient. This step can run for some time with no user feedback. You will know it is complete when the command prompt is displayed again.

Linux

To create the SD card image using Linux, you need to know the device name for the SD card reader. Execute the following command to see the devices currently mounted:

```
df -h
```

Next, insert the SD card or connect a card reader, and wait for the system to recognize it. Run the command again:

```
df -h
```

Take a moment to examine the list and compare it to the first execution. The "extra" device is your SD card reader. Take note of the device name: for example, /dev/sdc1. The number is the partition number. So, /dev/sdc1 is partition 1, and the device is /dev/sdc. Next, unmount the device (I will use the previous example):

```
umount /dev/sdc1
```

Use the following command to write the image, substituting the device name for <device> and path and name of the image file for <image_file> (for example, /dev/sdc and my_image.img):

```
sudo dd bs=4M if=<image_file> of=<device>.
```

At this point, you should see the disk-drive indicator flash (if there is one), and you may need to be patient. This step can run for some time with no user feedback. You will know it is complete when the command prompt is displayed again.

Booting Up

To boot your Raspberry Pi, insert the SD card with the new image and plug in your peripherals. Wait to plug in the USB power last. Because the Raspberry Pi has no On/Off switch, it will start as soon as power is supplied. The system bootstraps and then starts loading the OS. You see a long list of statements that communicate the status of each subsystem as it is loaded. You don't have to try to read or even understand all the rows presented,[9] but you should pay attention to any errors or warnings. When the boot sequence is complete, you see a command prompt as shown in Figure 4-8.

---

[9]They go by so fast, it is unlikely you will be able to read them anyway. Basically, they're noise unless there is an error, and those usually appear in the last few lines displayed.

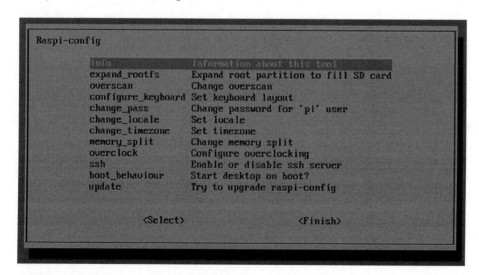

```
[   10.914711] bcm2835 ALSA chip created!
[ ok ] Activating lvm and md swap...done.
[....] Checking file systems...fsck from util-linux 2.20.1
done.
[ ok ] Mounting local filesystems...done.
[ ok ] Activating swapfile swap...done.
[ ok ] Cleaning up temporary files....
[ ok ] Setting kernel variables ...done.
[ ok ] Configuring network interfaces...done.
[ ok ] Cleaning up temporary files....
[ ok ] Setting up ALSA...done.
[info] Setting console screen modes.
[info] Skipping font and keymap setup (handled by console-setup).
[ ok ] Setting up console font and keymap...done.
[ ok ] Setting up X socket directories... /tmp/.X11-unix /tmp/.ICE-unix.
INIT: Entering runlevel: 2
[info] Using makefile-style concurrent boot in runlevel 2.
[ ok ] Network Interface Plugging Daemon...skip eth0...done.
[ ok ] Starting enhanced syslogd: rsyslogd.
[ ok ] Starting periodic command scheduler: cron.
[ ok ] Starting system message bus: dbus.
Starting dphys-swapfile swapfile setup ...
want /var/swap=100MByte, checking existing: keeping it
done.
[ ok ] Starting NTP server: ntpd.
[ ok ] Starting OpenBSD Secure Shell server: sshd.
My IP address is 10.0.1.50

Debian GNU/Linux 7.0 raspberrypi tty1

raspberrypi login: pi
Password:
Last login: Fri May 10 21:59:15 EDT 2013 on tty1
Linux raspberrypi 3.6.11+ #371 PREEMPT Thu Feb 7 16:31:35 GMT 2013 armv6l

The programs included with the Debian GNU/Linux system are free software;
the exact distribution terms for each program are described in the
individual files in /usr/share/doc/*/copyright.

Debian GNU/Linux comes with ABSOLUTELY NO WARRANTY, to the extent
permitted by applicable law.
pi@raspberrypi ~ $ fbgrab -c 1 start_screen.png
_
```

Figure 4-8. *Example boot sequence*[10]

You may be prompted to enter a username and password. The default user is simply *pi,* and the password is *raspberry* (no quotes, all lowercase). Enter that at the prompts, and the Raspberry Pi presents you with the configuration menu shown in Figure 4-9.

```
Raspi-config

      info                 Information about this tool
      expand_rootfs        Expand root partition to fill SD card
      overscan             Change overscan
      configure_keyboard   Set keyboard layout
      change_pass          Change password for 'pi' user
      change_locale        Set locale
      change_timezone      Set timezone
      memory_split         Change memory split
      overclock            Configure overclocking
      ssh                  Enable or disable ssh server
      boot_behaviour       Start desktop on boot?
      update               Try to upgrade raspi-config


            <Select>                       <Finish>
```

Figure 4-9. *Raspberry Pi configuration menu*

---

[10]Raspberry Pi images were generated with `fbgrab`. You can install it with `sudo apt-get install fbgrab`.

The configuration menu displays a list of common initial options you may want to set when using the Raspberry Pi. It is loaded on the first boot for convenience. You can navigate among the options using the up and down arrow keys and select the action buttons using the Tab key. The menu items are described briefly here:

- info: Show brief help about the Raspi-config menu.

- expand_rootfs: Use the full space on the SD card.

- Overscan: Change how the video signal is sent to the monitor/TV. Use this if your output image from the Raspberry Pi does not fill the available display area.

- configure_keyboard: Change keyboard mapping (country/language specific).

- change_pass: Change the password for the Pi user. Use this if your Raspberry Pi will be connected to a network and especially if it is accessible from the Internet.

- change_locale: Change the localization settings for the system. This sets country/language-specific display modes: for example, how time, currency, dates, and so on are displayed.

- change_timezone: Set the local time zone.

- memory_split: Change the memory settings for the system. Experts only. This is not needed for normal Raspberry Pi use.

- overclock: Change the CPU timing settings (also called *speed*) for the system. Experts only. This is not needed for normal Raspberry Pi use.

- ssh: Enable/disable the ssh server. If you want to be able to remotely log in to your Raspberry Pi, you should enable the ssh server.

- boot_behaviour: Enable/disable boot to the GUI windowing system.

- update: Retrieve the latest updates for the OS. The Raspberry Pi must be connected to the Internet for this to work.

▓ **Note**   Future releases of the configuration menu will include additional options. Once you have connected your Raspberry Pi to the Internet and executed the Update option, it is a good idea to check the menu for new options.

The first time you boot your system, you should use a few of these options. At a minimum, you should set the root file system to use the entire SD card space, change the keyboard setup, set your locale and time zone, and, if you want to be able to remotely log in, enable the ssh server.

When you first initialize an image on an SD card, the process does not use the entire space available. The expand_rootfs option does this for you. In some cases, the system will be rebooted when the operation is complete, so make sure you don't have other things running before executing this option.

Setting the keyboard, locale, and time zone enables you to use the Raspberry Pi in a manner you are used to with a PC. In particular, your keyboard will have the special symbols where you expect them; dates, time, and similar values will be displayed correctly; and your clock will be set the correct local time. These operations may not require a reboot. You should set these prior to using the Raspberry Pi in earnest.

On future boots, the system will start, and, once you are logged in, it will be in terminal mode (unless you selected the option to start in the windowing environment). From here, you can explore the system using command-line utilities or start the graphical user interface with startx. Take some time and explore the system before proceeding. If you want to restart the configuration session, use the command sudo raspi-config.

Once your Raspberry Pi is running and you have spent time exploring and learning the basics for system administration, you are ready to start experimenting with hardware. The next section explores how to connect your Raspberry Pi to a sensor and read the data generated.

SD CARD CORRUPTION

Imagine this scenario. You're working away on creating files, downloading documents, and so on. Your productivity is high, and you're enjoying your new low-cost, super-cool Raspberry Pi. Now imagine the power cable accidentally gets kicked out of the wall, and your Raspberry Pi loses power. No big deal, yes? Well, most of the time.

The SD card is not as robust as your hard drive. You may already know that it is unwise to power off a Linux system abruptly, because doing so can cause file corruption. Well, on the Raspberry Pi it can cause a complete loss of your disk image. Symptoms range from minor read errors to inability to boot or load the image on bootstrap. This can happen—and there have been reports from others that it has happened more than once.

That is not to say all SD cards are bad or that the Raspberry Pi has issues. The corruption on accidental power-off is a side effect of the type of media. Some have reported that certain SD cards are more prone to this than others. The best thing you can do to protect yourself is to use an SD card that is known to work with Raspberry Pi and be sure to power the system down with the `sudo shutdown -h now` command—and never, ever power off the system in any other manner.

You can also make a backup of your SD card. See `http://elinux.org/RPi_Beginners#Backup_your_SD_card` for more details.

GPIO Pin Mapping

The Raspberry Pi has a special hardware feature called the general-purpose I/O (GPIO) header. It is located in the upper-left portion of the board and resembles a floppy drive header.[11] The header consists of 2 rows of 13 male pins. Figure 4-10 shows the layout of the GPIO header of the Model B Raspberry Pi.

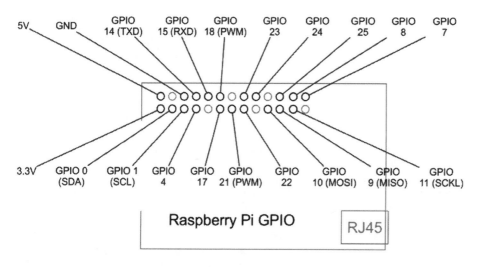

Figure 4-10. *GPIO pin assignments (courtesy of Adafruit)*

---

[11]What? Never heard of floppy drives? The original ones were indeed floppy. For bonus points, what was the storage capacity of the 8" dual-sided, double-density floppy medium?

All GPIO pins can be configured as either input (reading) or output (writing). The voltage read can be used for digital I/O. Specifically, when the voltage is less than 1.7V, the value is 0; greater than 1.7V is a value of 1. For output pins, you can set the voltage from 0 to 3.3V.

Notice that the pins are not named in order. For example, there are GPIO 0 and GPIO 1 but no GPIO 2 or GPIO 3. This naming may be a source of confusion because is doesn't follow what you would expect, nor does it mirror the neat layout of the Arduino. Thus, when working with the GPIO header you should check your pin choices carefully.

Also notice that some pins have two names. For example, GPIO 14 and GPIO 15 are also named TXD (transmit) and RXD (receive), respectively. These pins can be used for serial communication. GPIO 18 and GPIO 21 are labeled PWM (pulse wave modulation), which is used for powering LEDs, motors, and similar devices. GPIO 0 and GPIO 1 are also named SDA and SCL, respectively, and are used for I2C communication. I2C is a fast digital protocol that uses two wires (plus power and ground) to read data from circuits (or devices). Finally, GPIO 9, GPIO 10, and GPIO 11 are also named MISO, MOSI, and SCKL, respectively, and are used for SPI communication.

■ **Caution** All pins are limited to 3.3V. Attempting to send more than 3.3V will likely damage your Raspberry Pi. Always test your circuit for maximum voltage before connecting to your Raspberry Pi. You should also limit current to no more than 5mA.

If you want to ensure that you are protecting your Raspberry Pi from higher voltage and current, most expansion boards have additional circuitry for power protection. A number of expansion boards are available, including Gertboard (www.element14.com/community/docs/DOC-51726?ICID=raspberrypi-gert-banner) and Slice of PI/O (http://shop.ciseco.co.uk/k002-slice-of-pi-o/). This book does not cover the use of expansion boards, but you may want to consider using expansion boards if your sensors involve complex circuitry that requires more ports or additional features like motor controllers or relays.

Rather than expansion boards, here you use a simple prototyping board instead. The one I've chosen is called the Pi Cobbler Breakout board and is available from Adafruit (www.adafruit.com/products/914). It features a ribbon cable and a breadboard-compatible connector with the pins arranged in the same order as those on the Raspberry Pi. Figure 4-11 shows the Pi Cobbler connected to a Raspberry Pi. The board does not provide any additional functionality other than making it easier to work with GPIO by connecting the Raspberry Pi to a breadboard.

Figure 4-11. *Pi Cobbler Breakout board (courtesy of Adafruit)*

■ **Caution** Whenever you want to connect sensors or circuits to the GPIO header—either directly (not recommended) or via a breakout board (recommended)—you should first shut down your Raspberry Pi. This may sound inconvenient and even like a pain when you're working through a project, but it is the best method for ensuring that you do not accidentally short some pins or make the wrong connections.

I've found it best to make the connections with the Raspberry Pi powered off and to take a couple of passes verifying the connections are connected to the right pins. It is very easy to connect to the wrong pin—there are so many, and they are in close proximity. The odd arrangement of the pin numbers doesn't help, either. Properly admonished, let's jump into working with your Raspberry Pi GPIO and hook up some sensors!

An alternative form of the Pi Cobbler places the ribbon connector at a right angle to the breadboard connector, making it easier to see the pin labels. This version is called the Pi T-Cobbler (www.adafruit.com/products/1105). Figure 4-12 shows the Pi T-Cobbler.

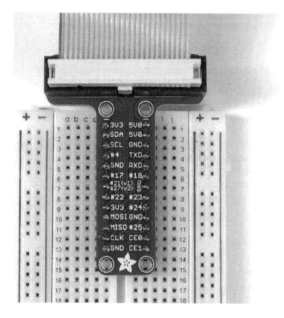

Figure 4-12. *Pi T-Cobbler Breakout board (courtesy of Adafruit)*

■ **Note** The Pi Cobbler and T-Cobbler come partially assembled. You need to solder (or have someone solder) the breadboard headers to the breakout board.

You can also find several variants on the Pi Cobbler and T-Cobbler on popular online auction and electronics discount sites. Whichever breakout board you choose, it will permit you to connect your Raspberry Pi to a breadboard, making experimentation with electronics (and sensors) much easier. It won't protect you against accidental power overload, so be mindful of that. The following projects use a breadboard; so if you have a Pi Cobbler, connect your Raspberry Pi to your breadboard.

Now that you know how to connect hardware to the GPIO pins, you need to know what software is required to allow you to write programs to read from and write to those pins.

Required Software

You need to install a number of software packages to work with the GPIO header. This section examines the required software for using the Python programming language. You can use C and Scratch language extensions, but Python is the best to learn because it is syntactically easy to read and easy to master. Also, the designers of the Raspberry Pi chose Python initially as its only language, so you are likely to find more examples on the Internet to which to refer for ideas and help.

PYTHON? ISN'T THAT A SNAKE?

The Python programming language is a high-level language designed to be as close to like reading English as possible while being simple, easy to learn, and very powerful. Pythonistas[12] will tell you the designers have indeed met these goals.

Python does not require a compilation step prior to being used. Rather, Python applications (whose file names end in .py) are interpreted on the fly. This is very powerful; but unless you use a Python development environment, some syntax errors will not be discovered until the application is executed. Fortunately, Python provides a robust exception-handling mechanism

If you have never used Python or you would like to know more about it, the following are few good books that introduce the language. A host of resources are also available on the Internet, including the Python documentation pages at www.python.org/doc/:

- *Programming the Raspberry Pi*, by Simon Monk (McGraw-Hill, 2013)

- *Beginning Python from Novice to Professional, 2nd Edition*, by Magnus Lie Hetland (Apress, 2008)

- *Python Cookbook*, by David Beazley and Brian K. Jones (O'Reilly Media, 2013)

Interestingly, Python was named after the British comedy troupe Monty Python and not the reptile. As you learn Python, you may encounter campy references to Monty Python episodes. Having a fondness for Monty Python, I find these references entertaining. Of course, your mileage may vary.

By default, the Raspbian wheezy image includes Python 2.7.3 and a host of supporting libraries. But it does not include everything you need. To fully access all the GPIO features, you also need the Raspberry Pi Python GPIO module (RPi.GPIO) for communicating with the GPIO pins, pySerial for connecting to serial devices, and python-smbus for accessing the I2C bus. If you use an expansion board, the manufacturer may also have special modules you need to install. No special modules are needed for the Pi Cobbler breakout board. If you are interested in writing games, you may also want to install the python-game package.

But first, you need some prerequisites. You must install additional Python modules using the following commands. Your Raspberry Pi needs to be connected to the Internet to execute these commands, because they download the modules from the Internet:

```
sudo apt-get update
sudo apt-get install python-dev
```

---

[12]Python experts often refer to themselves using this term. It is reserved for the most avid and experienced Python programmers.

To install the RPi.GPIO module, pySerial, and python-smbus modules, issue the following commands:

```
sudo apt-get install python-rpi.gpio
sudo apt-get install python-serial
wget http://sourceforge.net/projects/pyserial/files/latest/pyserial-2.5.tar.gz
tar -xvf pyserial-2.5.tar.gz
cd pyserial-2.5
sudo python ./setup.py install
cd ..
sudo apt-get install python-smbus
```

Now that you have the software loaded, it's time to experiment! If you haven't plugged in your breakout board, shut down your Raspberry Pi (using sudo shutdown -h now) and connect the breakout board, and then restart your Raspberry Pi. The next section explores a simple hardware project—the same project from Chapter 3, except this time you use a Raspberry Pi. This shows the applicability of the Raspberry Pi to physical computing.

Project: Hardware "Hello, World!"

As you did with the Arduino, you will build a "Hello, World!" project for the Raspberry Pi. This project uses an LED that the Raspberry Pi turns on and off through calls to a Python library function. That's a fine project for getting started, but it does not relate to how sensors could be used.

Thus, in this section, you expand on the LED project by adding a sensor. In this case, you still keep things simple by using what is arguably the most basic of sensors: a pushbutton. The goal is to illuminate the LED whenever the button is pushed.

Hardware Connections

Let's begin by assembling a Raspberry Pi, Pi Cobbler from Adafruit (optional), breadboard, one LED, and one pushbutton. You start with the Raspberry Pi powered down.

Plug the breakout board into the breadboard. Wire the 3.3V pin, *not the 5V pin*, to the breadboard power rail, the ground pin to the ground rail, and a loop around to the other side of the board. This connection provides power to the breakout board. Thus, you do not need a breadboard power supply.

Place the LED and pushbutton to one side of the breadboard, as shown in Figure 4-13. Remember, the longest leg on the LED is the positive side. Notice that I show the Raspberry Pi and the Pi Cobbler breakout board but not the cable to the Raspberry Pi, for brevity. The Raspberry Pi is connected via a ribbon cable to the Pi Cobbler. Be sure to align the cable so the colored stripe (indicating pin 1) is aligned with pin 1 on the connector. Do this for both the Raspberry Pi and the breakout board.

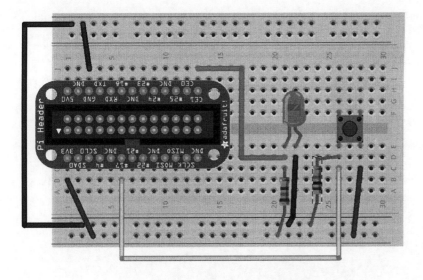

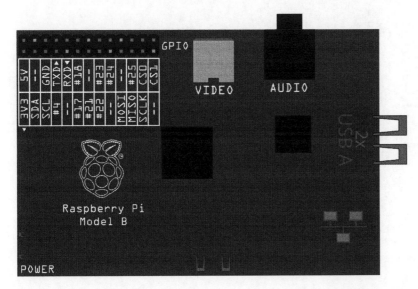

Made with 🟥 Fritzing.org

Figure 4-13. *Diagram of an LED with a pushbutton*

▨ **Caution**   Connecting the 5V pin to any other pin on the GPIO header can damage your Raspberry Pi. If you use a sensor that requires 5V input, be sure to double check that its maximum output is 3.3V or less.

You're almost there. Now wire a jumper from the power rail to one side of the pushbutton, and wire the other side of the pushbutton to pin GPIO 17 on the breakout board (pin #6 on the left side). Wire the LED to ground on the breadboard and a 150-Ohm resistor (colors: brown, green, brown, gold). The other side of the LED should be wired to pin GPIO 7 on the breakout board (see Figure 4-13).

You also need a resistor to pull the button LOW when the button is not pressed. Place a 10K Ohm resistor (colors: brown, black, orange, gold) on the side of the button with the wire to pin GPIO 17 and ground. The shortest side of the LED is the ground side. This side should be the one connected to the resistor. It does not matter which direction you connect the resistor. It is used to limit the current to the LED. Check the drawing again to ensure that you have a similar setup.

(ANOTHER) COOL GADGET

One of the coolest gadgets for working with the Raspberry Pi is the Raspberry Pi Dish mounting plate from Adafruit (www.adafruit.com/products/942). This small acrylic plate has space for a full-sized breadboard and a Raspberry Pi. It even has mounting holes for bolting the Raspberry Pi to the plate and small rubber feet to keep the plate off the work surface. The following figure shows the mounting plate in action.

Although you can make your own Raspberry Pi mounting plate from Lexan or Plexiglas, the Adafruit product is a notch better than what you can make yourself. For about $23.00, you can keep your Raspberry Pi and breadboard together and avoid scratches to your table and shorts caused by components on the bottom of the Raspberry Pi coming into contact with conductive material.

Writing the Script

The script you need for this project requires two pins: one output and one input. The output pin will illuminate the LED, and the input pin will detect the pushbutton engagement. You connect positive voltage to one side of the pushbutton and the other side to the input pin. When you detect voltage on the input pin, you tell the Raspberry Pi processor to send positive voltage to the output pin. In this case, the positive side of the LED is connected to the output pin.

Now, open a text editor with the following command to create a new Python module:

```
nano hello_raspi.py
```

When the editor opens, type the following code to set up the GPIO module and establish the pin assignments:

```
import RPi.GPIO as GPIO    # GPIO library
LED_PIN = 7
BUTTON_PIN = 17
GPIO.setmode(GPIO.BCM)
GPIO.setup(LED_PIN, GPIO.OUT)
GPIO.setup(BUTTON_PIN, GPIO.IN)
```

As you see in the drawing in Figure 4-13, the input pin is pin GPIO 17 and the output pin is pin GPIO 7. Let's use a variable to store these numbers so you do not have to worry about repeating the hard-coded numbers (and risk getting them wrong). Use the GPIO.setup() method to set the mode of each pin (GPIO.IN, GPIO.OUT).

You also need to place the code to turn on the LED when the input pin state is HIGH (==1). In this case, you use the GPIO.output() method to set the output pin to HIGH when the input pin state is HIGH (1) and similarly set the output pin to LOW when the input pin state is LOW (0). The following shows the statements needed:

```
GPIO.output(LED_PIN, GPIO.LOW)
while 1:
    if GPIO.input(BUTTON_PIN) == 1:
        GPIO.output(LED_PIN, GPIO.HIGH)
    else:
        GPIO.output(LED_PIN, GPIO.LOW)
```

■ **Tip**   Indentation is important in Python. Indented statements form a code block. For example, to execute multiple statements for an if statement, indent all the lines that you want to execute when the conditions are evaluated as true.

Now let's see the entire script in Listing 4-1, complete with proper documentation.

Listing 4-1. Simple Sensor Script

```
# RasPi Simple Sensor - Beginning Sensor Networks
#
# For this script, we explore a simple sensor (a pushbutton) and a simple
# response to sensor input (a LED). When the sensor is activated (the
# button is pushed), the LED is illuminated.

import RPi.GPIO as GPIO    # GPIO library

# Pin assignments
LED_PIN = 7
BUTTON_PIN = 17

# Setup GPIO module and pins
GPIO.setmode(GPIO.BCM)
GPIO.setup(LED_PIN, GPIO.OUT)
GPIO.setup(BUTTON_PIN, GPIO.IN)
```

```
# Set LED pin to OFF (no voltage)
GPIO.output(LED_PIN, GPIO.LOW)

# Loop forever
while 1:
    # Detect voltage on button pin
    if GPIO.input(BUTTON_PIN) == 1:
        # Turn on the LED
        GPIO.output(LED_PIN, GPIO.HIGH)
    else:
        # Turn off the LED
        GPIO.output(LED_PIN, GPIO.LOW)
```

Once you've entered the script as written, you are ready to run it. To run the Python script, launch it as follows:

```
python hello_raspi.py
```

Did you get an error about not having access to the GPIO library or /dev/mem? This is because the GPIO feature is restricted to root access only to protect the system. Accessing the GPIO library requires root access. Fortunately, you can amend the previous command with sudo, and all is well:

```
sudo python hello_raspi.py
```

Testing the Sensor

Once the script is started, what do you see on your Raspberry Pi? If you've done everything right, the answer is "Nothing." It's just staring back at you with that one dark LED—almost mockingly. Now, press the pushbutton. Did the LED illuminate? If so, congratulations: you're a Raspberry Pi Python GPIO programmer!

If the LED did not illuminate, hold the button down for a second or two. If that does not work, check all of your connections to make sure you are plugged in to the correct runs on the breadboard and that your LED is properly seated with the longer leg connected to the resistor and to pin GPIO 7.

On the other hand, if the LED stays illuminated, try reorienting your pushbutton 90 degrees. You may have set the pushbutton in the wrong orientation.

Try the project a few times until the elation passes. If you're an old hand at Raspberry Pi, that may be a very short period. If this is all new to you, go ahead and push that button and bask in the glory of having built your first sensor node!

Now, how do you stop it? Because you coded an endless loop (intentionally), you need to use Ctrl+C to cancel the script. This will not harm your Raspberry Pi or the GPIO or the circuitry.

The next section examines a more complicated sensor node using a temperature and humidity sensor.

For More Fun

To make the script a bit more user friendly, you can change the code to exit more gracefully. The following are some interesting suggestions:

- Loop for no more than 10,000 iterations. Hint: use a variable and increment it.

- Use a second LED, and set up the code to toggle both LEDs so that when the button is pressed, one illuminates and the other turns off.

- Use a second button so that when the second button is pressed, the loop terminates. Hint: use sys.exit() or break.

Hosting Sensors with Raspberry Pi

The GPIO pins of the Raspberry Pi make it an ideal platform for hosting sensors. Because most sensors need very little in the way of supporting components, you can often host multiple sensors on one Raspberry Pi. For example, it is possible to host a temperature sensor or even multiple temperature, barometric, humidity, and other sensors for sampling weather conditions from a given site.

ANALOG ONLY?

The Raspberry Pi GPIO pins do not support digital signals—they are all analog pins. This is one of the many small cost considerations that help keep the price down. To access digital signals, you need an analog-to-digital controller. If you encounter a situation in which you want to use a digital sensor, you can look at the 12-bit ADC - 4 Channel with Programmable Gain Amplifier from Adafruit (www.adafruit.com/products/1083).

As I discussed in Chapter 3, a host of sensors are available. SparkFun and Adafruit each have excellent web sites that provide a great deal of information about the products they sell. You can also Google for examples of using analog sensors with the Raspberry Pi.

Although this chapter demonstrates how to host sensors with the Raspberry Pi using a breakout board connected to a breadboard, the restriction of using analog only and 3.3V maximum voltage makes the Raspberry Pi less versatile than the Arduino. Add to that the fact that you must run Python scripts using root, and hosting sensors on a Raspberry Pi becomes a bit harder to do (but not overly so) and more cumbersome than doing so with an Arduino.

You can still connect sensors directly to the Raspberry Pi, as you see in the next section. However, you may want to consider using the Raspberry Pi as an aggregate node using an XBee connected to XBee-hosted sensors or even Arduino-hosted sensors. But first, let's see how to connect a sensor to the Raspberry Pi and read some data.

To make things easier, you use a project similar to the one you used in Chapter 3. More specifically, you build a sensor node with a Raspberry Pi and a single temperature sensor. Before you begin, let's discuss some safety factors related to working with the Raspberry Pi GPIO header.

Project: Building a Raspberry Temperature Sensor Node

The next project you explore is another temperature sensor example. This time, you use a temperature sensor that utilizes a special digital protocol to send. As mentioned previously, the Raspberry Pi does not have an analog-to-digital converter.

Although this may be yet another temperature sensor node, the project also gives you experience in reading digital sensors that use the one-wire protocol—which is built in to the Raspberry Pi GPIO. Specifically, you use the DS18B20 digital temperature sensor available from SparkFun and Adafruit.

In some respects, the hardware portion of this project is easier than the previous project because there are fewer parts; but the code is more complex. Let's begin with the hardware setup.

Hardware Setup

The hardware needed for this project is a breadboard, a breakout board for the Raspberry Pi (such as Pi Cobbler), a DS18B20 digital temperature sensor, a 4.7K Ohm resistor, and some jumper wires. Insert your breakout board into the breadboard, aligning pin 1 (3.3V) to position 1 on the breadboard. This will help you orient the pins more easily by using the numbers on the breadboard to quickly find the pins without counting (and miscounting) them. Figure 4-14 shows the correct orientation of the breakout board. I omit the ribbon cable for brevity.

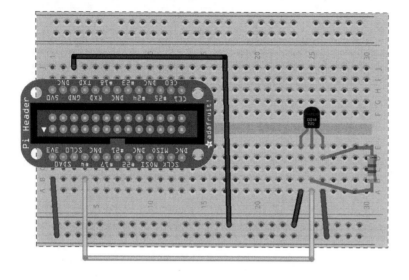

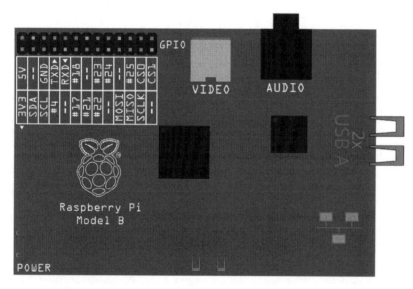

Made with ▣ Fritzing.org

Figure 4-14. Connecting a temperature sensor to a Raspberry Pi

Next, install the temperature sensor to the right of the breakout board with pin 1 to the left. If you hold the sensor such that the flat side is facing you, pin 1 is on the left of the flat side of the sensor. Connect the 4.7K Ohm resistor between pin 3 (right) and pin 2 (center).

Connect power from the breakout board to the power rail of the breadboard and ground from the breakout board to the ground rail of the breadboard, as shown in Figure 4-14. Next, connect power to pin 3 of the sensor and ground to pin 1. Finally, connect pin 2 of the sensor to GPIO 4. Why GPIO 4? Because the sensor is a digital sensor, and you can use the one-wire facility (because it uses only a single data wire) to read the data. Cool, eh?

WHAT ABOUT THE WATERPROOF VERSION?

If you have the waterproof version of the DS18B20 digital temperature sensor, the sensor has four wires. Typically the wires are colored red, black, white or yellow or orange, and copper or silver. The copper or silver wire is not used; it is part of the shielding. The red wire is connected to power, the black wire is connected to ground, and white or yellow or orange is the data wire. If your sensor has other color-coded wires, check with the vendor to make sure you know how each wire is labeled.

Testing the Hardware

Once you have double-checked your connections, go ahead and boot up your Raspberry Pi. Because the sensor uses the one-wire protocol to read data, you can use features built in to the Raspberry Pi to read data from the sensor. This isn't nearly as elegant as writing a Python script, but it will permit you to see that all is working correctly before you start programming.

You will use a special utility called modprobe. This utility loads (or unloads) modules into the Linux kernel. In the vernacular of other operating systems, it loads device drivers. The modprobe utility can do far more than just load modules (drivers); to learn more about it, see http://linux.die.net/man/8/modprobe.

The modules you want to load are named w1-gpio and w1-therm. The w1-gpio module registers and loads the new sensor connected to pin GPIO 4. The w1-therm module registers and loads a module that has support for temperature sensors.

When you use modprobe to load each of these modules (w1-gpio first), the Raspberry Pi enables data collection on pin GPIO 4 and reads data from the sensor and stores it in a file. The file is named starting with 28 and followed by a unique file name. If you had other sensors, there would be a file for each one.

The file contains the raw data read from the sensor. You can open this file and inspect its contents to see the raw data. Figure 4-15 shows the commands you use to load the modules and then inspect the file along with the output that shows the name of the file created.

```
pi@raspberrypi /sys/bus/w1/devices $ sudo modprobe w1-gpio
pi@raspberrypi /sys/bus/w1/devices $ sudo modprobe w1-therm
pi@raspberrypi /sys/bus/w1/devices $ cd /sys/bus/w1/devices/
pi@raspberrypi /sys/bus/w1/devices $ ls
28-0000043abfd1  w1_bus_master1
pi@raspberrypi /sys/bus/w1/devices $ cd 28-0000043abfd1
pi@raspberrypi /sys/bus/w1/devices/28-0000043abfd1 $ cat w1_slave
9f 01 4b 46 7f ff 01 10 40 : crc=40 YES
9f 01 4b 46 7f ff 01 10 40 t=25937
pi@raspberrypi /sys/bus/w1/devices/28-0000043abfd1 $ cat w1_slave
9f 01 4b 46 7f ff 01 10 40 : crc=40 YES
9f 01 4b 46 7f ff 01 10 40 t=25937
pi@raspberrypi /sys/bus/w1/devices/28-0000043abfd1 $ cat w1_slave
a2 01 4b 46 7f ff 0e 10 d8 : crc=d8 YES
a2 01 4b 46 7f ff 0e 10 d8 t=26125
pi@raspberrypi /sys/bus/w1/devices/28-0000043abfd1 $ cat w1_slave
a7 01 4b 46 7f ff 09 10 e0 : crc=e0 YES
a7 01 4b 46 7f ff 09 10 e0 t=26437
pi@raspberrypi /sys/bus/w1/devices/28-0000043abfd1 $ cat w1_slave
ac 01 4b 46 7f ff 04 10 86 : crc=86 YES
ac 01 4b 46 7f ff 04 10 86 t=26750
pi@raspberrypi /sys/bus/w1/devices/28-0000043abfd1 $ cat w1_slave
af 01 4b 46 7f ff 01 10 bc : crc=bc YES
af 01 4b 46 7f ff 01 10 bc t=26937
pi@raspberrypi /sys/bus/w1/devices/28-0000043abfd1 $ cat w1_slave
b1 01 4b 46 7f ff 0f 10 8d : crc=8d YES
b1 01 4b 46 7f ff 0f 10 8d t=27062
pi@raspberrypi /sys/bus/w1/devices/28-0000043abfd1 $ cat w1_slave
b1 01 4b 46 7f ff 0f 10 8d : crc=8d YES
b1 01 4b 46 7f ff 0f 10 8d t=27062
pi@raspberrypi /sys/bus/w1/devices/28-0000043abfd1 $
```

Figure 4-15. *Testing the temperature sensor hardware*

Notice that in the example I ran the cat[13] (concatenate and print) utility to print out the data in the file several times. I placed my hand over the sensor while running the utility in order to simulate an increase in temperature. Can you see how the values changed?

Software Setup

The software required for this project is already installed. You will write a short Python script to read the data from the sensor and display it to standard out (the terminal window). Begin by importing the required modules as shown below here:

```
import glob
import os
import time
```

Next, you use the Python module named os to make a system call to run the two modprobe commands from previous example. In this case, you use the os.system() method:

```
os.system('modprobe w1-gpio')
os.system('modprobe w1-therm')
```

---

[13]In case you were curious, there is no dog command.

Before you jump in to the code to read the file, let's make it easier by declaring a few variables to contain the directory and the file name. In this case, you don't know the file name, but you do know the directory. You can use the glob module to search for files matching a wildcard in a specific directory. You do so with the following code:

```
datadir = glob.glob('/sys/bus/w1/devices/28*')[0]
datafile = os.path.join(datadir, 'w1_slave')
```

Notice that you know the parent directory and the starting portion of the directory. The glob module does all the work for you. If there were multiple directories matching the wildcard, the call would return a list. In this case, you have only one sensor, so you can expect only one directory.

Now you are ready to read the data from the file. You can design your own code however you like, but I've elected to write two methods (defined with the def directive). I will use one method to open the file and read all the lines (data) in the file and another method to use the data read to calculate the temperature in Celsius and Fahrenheit. Let's look at the first method. I've named it read_data():

```
def read_data():
    f = open(datafile, 'r')
    lines = f.readlines()
    f.close()
    return lines
```

As you can see, it is very straightforward and reads like the steps you would imagine. Specifically, you open the file, read all the lines in the file, close the file, and return what you read.

Now let's look at the second method. I've named it get_temp():

```
def get_temp():
    temp_c = None
    temp_f = None
    lines = read_data()
    while not lines[0].strip().endswith('YES'):
        time.sleep(0.25)
        lines = read_data()

    pos = lines[1].find('t=')
    if pos != -1:
        temp_string = lines[1][ pos+2:]
        temp_c = float(temp_string) / 1000.00
        temp_f = temp_c * 9.00 / 5.00 + 32.00

    return temp_c, temp_f
```

This method has two parts. The first part reads the data from the file using the previous method and checks the first line (arrays and lists start with index 0 in Python) to see if the status is YES. If it isn't, you read the line from the file again and repeat until you find a file that has the correct, valid status.

The next part looks in the file for the data read. In this case, you look for a substring that starts with t= and then read the data after that and convert it to Celsius and Fahrenheit. You return those values for use in printing the data.

Let's put it all together. Listing 4-2 shows the completed script, including documentation. Open an editor, create a file named pi_temp.py, and enter the source code shown. Feel free to modify it to suit your mood or particular brand of humor.

Take some time to explore this completed code until you understand how it all works. There are several Pythonisms[14] in this file, so do not be intimidated if some of the code isn't clear right away. For example, look at the print statement in the next-to-last line. This statement could be written differently, but what is shown is the accepted standard most Python programmers adopt.

Listing 4-2. The pi_temp.py Script

```python
# RasPi Temperature Sensor - Beginning Sensor Networks
#
# For this script, we explore connecting a digital temperature sensor
# to the Raspberry Pi and reading the data. We display the temperature
# in Celsius and Fahrenheit.

# Import Python modules (always list in alphabetical order)
import glob
import os
import time

# Issue the modprobe statements to initialize the GPIO and
# temperature sensor modules
os.system('modprobe w1-gpio')
os.system('modprobe w1-therm')

# Use glob to search the file system for directories that match the prefix.
# Save the path to the directory.
datadir = glob.glob('/sys/bus/w1/devices/28*')[0]
# Create the full path to the file
datafile = os.path.join(datadir, 'w1_slave')

# Procedure for reading the raw data from the file.
# Open the file and read all of the lines then close it.
def read_data():
    f = open(datafile, 'r')
    lines = f.readlines()
    f.close()
    return lines

# Read the temperature and return the values found.
def get_temp():
    # Initialize the variables.
    temp_c = None
    temp_f = None
    lines = read_data()

    # If the end of the first line ends with something other than 'YES'
    # Try reading the file again until 'YES' is found.
```

---

[14]Meaning it is the preferred way. Sometimes code can be described as "pythonic," which also means it was written in the preferred Python style or with specific syntax. Learning to program Python with Pythonisms comes second to everyone who learns Python, but it is the mark of a true Pythonista to be able to know the difference.

```
    while not lines[0].strip().endswith('YES'):
        time.sleep(0.25)
        lines = read_data()

    # Search the second line for the data prefixed with 't='
    pos = lines[1].find('t=')

    # A return code of -1 means it wasn't found.
    if pos != -1:

        # Get the raw data located after the 't=' until the end of the line.
        temp_string = lines[1][ pos+2:]

        # Convert the scale for printing
        temp_c = float(temp_string) / 1000.00

        # Convert to Farenheit
        temp_f = temp_c * 9.00 / 5.00 + 32.00

    # Return the values read
    return temp_c, temp_f

# Main loop. Read data then sleep 1 second until cancelled with CTRL-C.
while True:
    temp_c, temp_f = get_temp()
    print("Temperature is {0} degrees Celsius, "
          "{1} degrees Fahrenheit.".format(temp_c, temp_f))
    time.sleep(1)
```

Take a few minutes to double-check your file to make sure you have typed all the statements correctly. If you have an editor on your desktop or laptop, you might want to use it to create and edit the file using the syntax-checking feature to catch any errors. The script won't run correctly on your desktop or laptop, but checking the syntax can be a big help.

Now that the software is written, let's see what it does.

Testing the Sensor

As in the previous project, you need to run the script as root using sudo python ./pi_temp.py. When you do so, you may not see any output right away, but within a second or two you should start seeing output like that shown in Figure 4-16.

```
pi@raspberrypi ~ $ sudo python ./pi_temp.py
Temperature is 25.812 degrees Celsius, 78.4616 degrees Fahrenheit.
Temperature is 25.812 degrees Celsius, 78.4616 degrees Fahrenheit.
Temperature is 25.812 degrees Celsius, 78.4616 degrees Fahrenheit.
Temperature is 25.812 degrees Celsius, 78.4616 degrees Fahrenheit.
Temperature is 25.875 degrees Celsius, 78.575 degrees Fahrenheit.
Temperature is 26.25 degrees Celsius, 79.25 degrees Fahrenheit.
Temperature is 26.75 degrees Celsius, 80.15 degrees Fahrenheit.
Temperature is 27.187 degrees Celsius, 80.9366 degrees Fahrenheit.
Temperature is 27.562 degrees Celsius, 81.6116 degrees Fahrenheit.
```

Figure 4-16. *Output of the temperature sensor script (*`pi_temp.py`*)*

If you get syntax errors, go back and check that you have entered every line exactly as shown in Listing 4-2. Python is really good at providing enough information to fix most syntax errors. If you encounter any, you see not only what the error is but also the line number of the file where the error occurs. Once you have fixed the error, try the script again until you see the correct output.

The next section explores a more complex project in which the Raspberry Pi communicates with a digital sensor that uses the I2C protocol.

For More Fun

To make this project a bit more fun, try connecting a second sensor (of the same type), and print out the data including the sensor from which the data was read. Hints: you can use the serial number embedded in the file to identify the sensor, and you should connect them in parallel. That is, each sensor connects to the same ground (pin 1) and power connections (pin 3). The data output (pin 2) of each sensor is wired to the same GPIO pin.

For extra-special fun, modify the code to detect when the sensor read has failed and print an appropriate error message. Can you spot where this is possible?[15] I'll give you a hint: what happens in the get_temp() method if t= is not found?

Project: Building a Raspberry Barometric Pressure Sensor Node

This project demonstrates how to use a different type of sensor—one that uses the I2C bus. For this, you need two wires to connect and facilities to communicate to the sensor. Fortunately, the Raspberry Pi has such a facility, but it takes a bit of work to make it available. You will use the BMP085 sensor module from SparkFun (www.sparkfun.com/products/11282) or Adafruit (www.adafruit.com/products/391). Figure 4-17 shows the module from SparkFun.

---

[15]Hardcore code junkies and hackers alike love this stuff.

Figure 4-17. *BMP085 I2C sensor (courtesy of SparkFun)*

The I2C feature is disabled by default on the Raspberry Pi. Before you look at the hardware setup for this project, let's enable the I2C feature. Begin by editing the modprobe blacklist configuration file. This file is used to tell modprobe which modules should be ignored when it's loading modules. The file is located in /etc/modprobe.d and is named raspi-blacklist.conf. Use the following command to edit the file with the nano console-based text editor:

```
sudo nano /etc/modprobe.d/raspi-blacklist.conf
```

Use the # symbol to comment out the line that contains the i2c-bcm2708 module. You can use the arrow keys to navigate; press Ctrl+X, reply Y, and press Enter to save the file. The resulting file should look like the following:

```
blacklist spi-bcm2708
#blacklist i2c-bcm2708
```

Next, you must add the I2C module to the list of modules loaded at boot time. To do this, you need to edit the /etc/modules file. Use the following command:

```
sudo nano /etc/modules
```

Add the line i2c-dev (no quotes) to the end of the file, and save it. The resulting file should look like this:

```
# /etc/modules: kernel modules to load at boot time.
#
# This file contains the names of kernel modules that should be loaded
# at boot time, one per line. Lines beginning with "#" are ignored.
# Parameters can be specified after the module name.

snd-bcm283
i2c-dev
```

Once the file is saved, reboot your Raspberry Pi. Watch for error messages during the boot process. If all is well, you will not see any errors concerning I2C, but you may see other status messages about I2C. These are fine. You are now ready to begin connecting the hardware.

The hardware portion of this project is easier than that in the previous project because there are fewer parts, but the code is more complex. Let's begin with the hardware setup.

Hardware Setup

The hardware needed for this project is a breadboard, a breakout board for the Raspberry Pi (such as Pi Cobbler), a BMP085 sensor module, and some jumper wires. Insert your breakout board into the breadboard, aligning pin 1 (3.3V) to position 1 on the breadboard.

Connect the 3.3V pin on the Raspberry Pi breakout board to power-on the sensor module. Connect the ground wire to the ground wire on the sensor. The I2C pins on the Raspberry Pi are pins GPIO 0 (SDA) and GPIO 1 (SCL). Connect wires from these pins to corresponding pins on the sensor module. Figure 4-18 shows the physical connections.

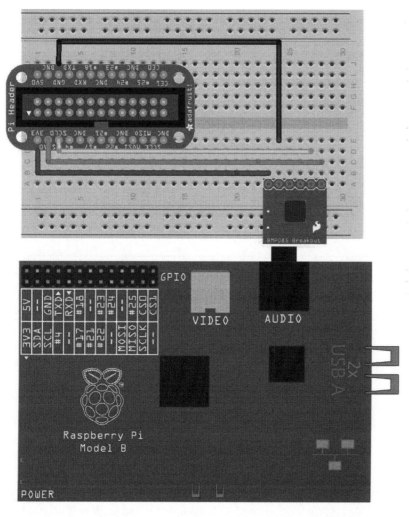

Figure 4-18. *Connecting the BMP085 sensor to a Raspberry Pi*

■ **Caution** Do not connect the 5V pin to the sensor module. This module operates on 3.3V and does not contain a regulator circuit. You will damage the sensor if you connect it to the 5V pin.

Testing the Hardware

Once you have double-checked your connections, go ahead and boot up your Raspberry Pi. When you have logged in, run the following command:

```
sudo i2cdetect -y 0
```

This command uses a utility to detect any sensors on the I2C bus. I say *sensors* because you can use the I2C protocol to connect multiple sensors. Each sensor has its own address. Figure 4-19 shows the output of running the command.

```
pi@raspberrypi ~ $ sudo i2cdetect -y 0
     0  1  2  3  4  5  6  7  8  9  a  b  c  d  e  f
00:          -- -- -- -- -- -- -- -- -- -- -- -- --
10: -- -- -- -- -- -- -- -- -- -- -- -- -- -- -- --
20: -- -- -- -- -- -- -- -- -- -- -- -- -- -- -- --
30: -- -- -- -- -- -- -- -- -- -- -- -- -- -- -- --
40: -- -- -- -- -- -- -- -- -- -- -- -- -- -- -- --
50: -- -- -- -- -- -- -- -- -- -- -- -- -- -- -- --
60: -- -- -- -- -- -- -- -- -- -- -- -- -- -- -- --
70: -- -- -- -- -- -- -- 77
pi@raspberrypi ~ $
```

Figure 4-19. Testing the barometric pressure sensor hardware

Notice in the example that the graph shows data in column 7 for row 70 and a value of 77. This means the sensor is at address 0x77 (in hexadecimal). If other sensors were installed, they would appear in the graph as well. Remember this address, because you need it for the code.

If you do not see any devices in the output from this command, try it with –y 1 and see if this produces any output. This tells the i2cdetect utility that your Raspberry Pi is a newer version:

```
sudo i2cdetect -y 1
```

Software Setup

The software required for this project is the smbus Python module that you loaded earlier and a special library designed to communicate with the BMP085. You need a special module because the I2C protocol is bidirectional, and most I2C components are designed to respond to one or more commands to evoke data generation. In this case, you need a Python module that supports the BMP085 sensor module as well as many other I2C modules.

133

This module is available from GitHub and was provided by the nice people at Adafruit. To download the module and install it, issue the following commands. If you already have `git` installed, you can skip the first command (it simply installs the `git` utility):

```
sudo apt-get install git
git clone http://github.com/adafruit/Adafruit-Raspberry-Pi-Python-Code.git cd Adafruit-Raspberry-Pi-Python-Code
cd Adafruit_BMP085
```

Because there is no install feature to this library, you must either alter your `PYTHONPATH` environment variable or execute your Python script from the source directory. In this case, do the latter, because it is easier. If you are Python and Linux savvy, you may want to install the code in your Python installation.

I2C SENSOR LIBRARIES

A number of I2C sensor modules are available. However, corresponding Python (or other language) libraries have not been built for all of them. You should research the availability of a library to support the sensor prior to deciding to use it in your network. If you are a programmer, you may be able to adapt existing code (libraries) to add support for the new sensor by examining the data sheet and writing appropriate commands to interact with the sensor.

You will use the `Adafruit_BMP085` code module to read data from the I2C bus. The Python module has support for a number of I2C modules, including the BMP085, and is based on the `Adafruit_I2C` module, which is also in this directory. To use the `Adafruit_BMP085` library, you import the class for the BMP085 module as follows:

```
from Adafruit_BMP085 import BMP085
```

Next, you need to initialize the class. In this case, you use the defaults and supply only the address for the module. You assign the instance to a variable so you can use it to make calls to the library later. Use the address you discovered from the `i2cdetect` utility:

```
bmp = BMP085(0x77)
```

Once that is done, you only need to read the values using the methods provided by the library and then print out the information. The major methods you use are shown here:

```
bmp.readTemperature()
bmp.readPressure()
bmp.readAltitude()
```

Now let's put it all together. Listing 4-3 shows the complete listing of the script. Open an editor, create a file named `pi_bmp085.py`, and enter the source code shown.

As you can see, with the help of the new library, your Python script becomes very short and very easy to write. This is a great example of how members of the Python community freely (well, most anyway) exchange ideas and share code for common and not-so-common tasks.

Listing 4-3. The pi_bmp085.py Script

```
# RasPi I2C Sensor - Beginning Sensor Networks
#
# For this script, we connect to and read data from an
# I2C sensor. We use the BMP085 sensor module from Adafruit
# or Sparkfun to read barometric pressure and altitude
# using the Adafruit I2C Python code.

import time

# Import the BMP085 class
from Adafruit_BMP085 import BMP085

# Instantiate an instance of the BMP085 class passing
# the address of the sensor as displayed by i2cdetect.
bmp085 = BMP085(0x77)

# Read data until cancelled
while True:
    try:
        # Read the data
        pressure = float(bmp085.readPressure()) / 100
        altitude = bmp085.readAltitude()

        # Display the data
        print("The barometric pressure at altitude {0:.2f} "
              "is {1:.2f} hPa.".format(pressure, altitude))

        # Wait for a bit to allow sensor to stabilize
        time.sleep(3)

    # Catch keyboard interrupt (CTRL-C) keypress
    except KeyboardInterrupt:
        break
```

Now that the software is written, let's see what it does.

Testing the Sensor

As in the previous project, you need to run the script as root using sudo python ./ pi_bmp085.py. When you do so, you may not see any output right away; but within a second or two you should start seeing output like that shown in Figure 4-20.

```
pi@raspberrypi ~/Adafruit-Raspberry-Pi-Python-Code/Adafruit_BMP085 $ sudo python ./pi_bmp085.py
The barometric pressure at altitude 1012.86 is 2.75 hPa.
The barometric pressure at altitude 1012.94 is 3.00 hPa.
The barometric pressure at altitude 1012.86 is 3.25 hPa.
The barometric pressure at altitude 1012.91 is 3.75 hPa.
The barometric pressure at altitude 1012.92 is 2.33 hPa.
The barometric pressure at altitude 1013.00 is 2.83 hPa.
The barometric pressure at altitude 1012.87 is 3.41 hPa.
The barometric pressure at altitude 1012.81 is 4.25 hPa.
The barometric pressure at altitude 1012.89 is 3.16 hPa.
```

Figure 4-20. *Output of the barometric pressure sensor script (*pi_bmp085.py*)*

If you encounter syntax errors such as "TypeError: 'int' object has no attribute '__getitem__'" while running your code, you may need to alter the Adafruit_I2C.py file to correct the problem. There is a method named getPiRevision() that returns a 0 or 1 depending on the revision number of your Raspberry Pi. Unfortunately, there have been several revisions since this code was written, and this method may not return the correct value. If you see the error, you can fix it by commenting out the return and replacing it with the known value for your Raspberry Pi:

```
def getPiRevision():
  "Gets the version number of the Raspberry Pi board"
  # Courtesy quick2wire-python-api
  # https://github.com/quick2wire/quick2wire-python-api
  try:
    with open('/proc/cpuinfo','r') as f:
      for line in f:
        if line.startswith('Revision'):
          #return 1 if line.rstrip()[-1] in ['1','2'] else 2
          return <NUM>
  except:
    return 0
```

In this case, replace <NUM> with 0 or 1, corresponding to the value you used for the i2cdetect utility. For example, a Raspberry Pi that I had exhibited this behavior, but I was able to see the I2C module by passing 0 to i2cdetect. Thus, I changed the code as follows:

```
if line.startswith('Revision'):
  #return 1 if line.rstrip()[-1] in ['1','2'] else 2
  return 0
```

The next section explores a more complex project in which the Raspberry Pi is a data collector (an aggregate node) hosting sensor data via an XBee wireless connection to a sensor node. You will reuse the sensor node created in Chapter 3. If you have not read through and succeeded in building the projects in Chapter 3, you may want to go back and complete the last project before proceeding.

For More Fun

The BMP085 sensor reads the barometric pressure, as you have seen, but it also reads temperature. Change the previous code to read the temperature data as well as the barometric pressure.

Project: Creating a Raspberry Pi Data Collector for XBee Sensor Nodes

This project combines what you have learned about the Raspberry Pi in this chapter and the XBee in Chapter 2 and the XBee sensor node from Chapter 3. More specifically, you use a Raspberry Pi and a remote sensor connecting the sensor with the Raspberry Pi using XBee modules. You know the basics from Chapter 3, so let's dive right in.

XBee Sensor Node

Follow the text from Chapter 3 to create the XBee sensor node. As a reminder, this node is constructed as shown in Figure 4-21.

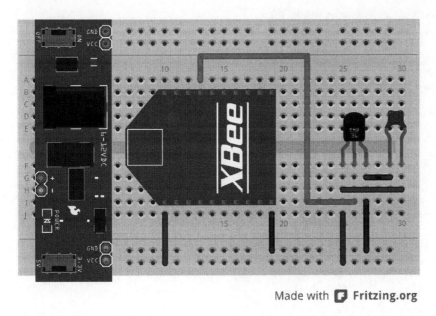

Made with **⚡ Fritzing.org**

Figure 4-21. *XBee sensor node*

Hardware

The hardware setup for this project is very easy. All you need to do is use the serial interface that is part of the GPIO header to connect to the XBee's serial interface. It's that easy! Do not power on your Raspberry Pi or sensor node until after all hardware connections are complete and verified correct. I will tell you when to power up later in this section.

You need a breadboard and an XBee breadboard adapter like the one you used in Chapter 3; plug it in to the breadboard. Then plug in your Raspberry Pi breadboard adapter. Now wire the 3.3V and ground to the pins on your XBee adapter. If you are using the XBee Explorer Regulated from SparkFun (`www.sparkfun.com/products/11373`), you can connect to the 5V power because the XBee Explorer can regulate the power (hence the name). The SparkFun board as shown has the serial interface pins arranged in a header on one side of the board. It also has onboard voltage regulation to protect the XBee in the event you accidentally connect the 5V pin instead of the 3.3V pin to the explorer.

■ **Note**   If you have soldered breadboard headers to the XBee adapter but have not soldered headers for the serial I/O header, take a moment to do that. You can connect the XBee via the other header, but the consolidated header makes it a bit easier.

Next, wire the TXD (output) pin GPIO 14 on the Raspberry Pi breadboard adapter to the DIN pin on the XBee explorer. Then wire the RXD (input) pin GPIO 15 on the Raspberry Pi breadboard adapter to the DOUT pin on the XBee explorer. Figure 4-22 shows the completed connections.

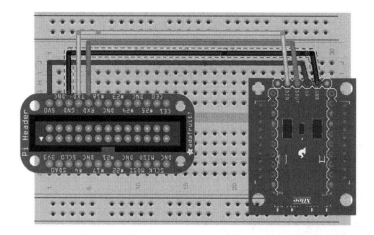

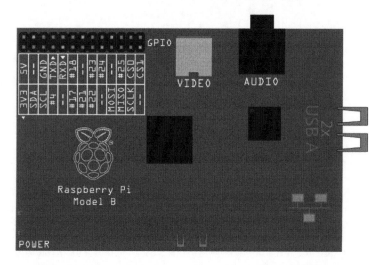

Made with 🅵 **Fritzing.org**

Figure 4-22. *Connecting an XBee to a Raspberry Pi*

If you are not using the SparkFun adapter, be sure to check the documentation on your adapter to make sure you are connecting the right pins. Take your coordinator XBee module and insert it into the XBee.

There is one more thing you need to do. The designers of the Raspberry Pi included the facility to connect a serial terminal to the Raspberry Pi at boot time. This terminal dominates the serial interface and as such will make strange commands to your XBee module. This won't harm the module, but it can cause the module to behave strangely.

Thus, you must turn off the boot terminal. In this case, you are looking for anything that references ttyAMA0 (the device file for the serial port). To do so, power on your Raspberry Pi, and edit the /boot/cmdline.txt file as follows. Remove any reference to ttyAMA0, and save the file:

```
sudo cp /boot/cmdline.txt /boot/cmdline.txt.bak
sudo nano /boot/cmdline.txt
```

Notice that you are making a backup of the file in case you alter it too much. If you have problems on reboot, try resetting the file.

Next, edit the /etc/inittab file, and remove references to the device file there:

```
sudo cp /etc/inittab /etc/inittab.bak
sudo nano /etc/inittab
```

Comment out the following or similar lines (those that reference ttyAMA0) using a # symbol, and save the file:

```
2:23:respawn:/sbin/getty -L ttyAMA0 115200 vt100
```

Once the files are edited, plug in your XBee module and reboot your Raspberry PI. You also need the XBee temperature sensor node you built in Chapter 3. When the Raspberry Pi has rebooted (without errors), turn on your XBee sensor node. After a few seconds you should see the data light blink on the nodes, indicating that data is being sent.

Software

Before you can write your script, you need to download and install a special library. The software needed for this project is a special Python module developed specifically to encapsulate (make it easy to use) the XBee protocols and frame-handling mechanisms. To install the module, issue the following commands:

```
wget https://python-xbee.googlecode.com/files/XBee-2.1.0.tar.gz
tar -xvf XBee-2.1.0.tar.gz
cd XBee-2.1.0
sudo python ./setup.py install
```

Once the library is installed, you can start using it. This library is based on the Python serial library. In fact, the classes exposed in the XBee library require an instance of a serial class as a parameter in the constructor (the __init__() method). Thus, you must import both the serial and xbee libraries as follows:

```
import serial
import xbee
```

Before you instantiate those classes, let's make some definitions to make maintenance easier and improve readability of the source code. In this case, you create a reference to the serial port and the baud rate:

```
SERIAL_PORT = '/dev/ttyAMA0'
BAUD_RATE = 9600
```

■ **Note** If you have changed the baud rate of your XBee module, you must use that rate here.

Now you can instantiate the classes. Pass the `tty` file you defined earlier to the serial class, and then pass the instance to the xbee class. Because you are using the ZigBee protocol, you must also use the specialized ZigBee class included in the xbee library:

```
ser_port = serial.Serial(SERIAL_PORT, BAUD_RATE)
xbee1 = xbee.zigbee.ZigBee(ser_port)
```

Once you have these classes instantiated, reading from the XBee module is easy. You simply call the `wait_read_frame()` method, which waits until a frame is received before returning. This way you do not have to write your own code to wait for packets. Cool, eh?

```
data_samples = xbee1.wait_read_frame()
```

That was easy. Now the hard part begins. The `wait_read_frame()` method returns a dictionary rather than a raw list of bytes or some other structure. Dictionaries make things easier because you can reference a portion of the data by using only a label. For example, the syntax `dictionary['first_word']` returns any value associated (stored with/at) label `first_word`.

Unfortunately, there is no documentation (that I could find) that describes the contents or layout of the dictionary returned. When this occurs, you can turn to your friend the *pretty print library*. You use it like this:

```
import pprint
data_samples = xbee1.wait_read_frame()
pprint.pprint(data_samples)
```

This prints the contents of the data sample frame in a human-readable format. Figure 4-23 shows what the output looks like. As you can see, the frame has a dictionary entry of `samples`, which is also a dictionary (a dictionary is indicated by the {} brackets). In that dictionary, you see the data samples returned. The first data sample is labeled `adc-3`, which corresponds to pin 3 of the data input on the XBee, and the supply voltage is labeled `adc-7`.

```
{'id' : 'rx_io_data_long_addr',
 'options': '\x01',
 'samples': [{'adc-3': 647, 'adc-7': 2776}],
 'source_addr': '>`',
 'source_addr_long': '\x00\x13\xa2\x000\x90)\xdb'}
```

Figure 4-23. *Sample printout of frame data from* `wait_read_frame()`

Now let's put all that together and see what the completed code looks like. Open an editor, create the file `pi_xbee.py`, and enter the code from Listing 4-4.

Listing 4-4. Reading Data from an XBee Module

```
# RasPi XBee Data Aggregator - Beginning Sensor Networks
#
# For this script, we read data from an XBee coordinator
# node whenever data is received from an XBee sensor node.
#
```

```
# The data read is from one sample (temperature from a
# TMP36 sensor and the supply voltage at the source.

#import pprint
import serial
import xbee

SERIAL_PORT = '/dev/ttyAMA0'
BAUD_RATE = 9600

# Instantiate an instance for the serial port
ser_port = serial.Serial(SERIAL_PORT, BAUD_RATE)

# Instantiate an instance of the ZigBee class
# and pass it an instance of the Serial class
xbee1 = xbee.zigbee.ZigBee(ser_port)

# Read and display temperature data
while True:
    try:
        # Read a data frame from the XBee
        data_samples = xbee1.wait_read_frame()
        #pprint.pprint(data_samples)

        # Get the address of the source XBee
        address = data_samples['source_addr_long']

        print("Reading from XBee:")
        samples = data_samples['samples'][0]

        # Calculate temperature in Celsius
        temp_c = ((samples['adc-3'] * 1200.0 / 1024.0) - 500.0) / 10.0

        # Calculate temperature in Fahrenheit
        temp_f = ((temp_c * 9.0) / 5.0) + 32.0

        # Display the temperature in Celsius and Fahrenheit
        print("  Temperature is {0} c, "
              "{1} f".format(temp_c, temp_f))

        # Calculate supply voltage
        volts = (float(samples['adc-7']) * (1200.0 / 1024.0)) / 1000.0

        # Display the supply voltage
        print("  Supply voltage = {0} volts.".format(volts))

    # Catch keyboard interrupt (CTRL-C) keypress
    except KeyboardInterrupt:
        break

# Close the port
ser_port.close()
```

Testing the Final Project

Now you can run your script and observe the output. Start the script with sudo python ./pi_xbee.py. Figure 4-24 shows sample output from the script. To see the data change, I simply touched the sensor (careful not to short the pins), allowing my body heat to increase the values read.

```
pi@raspberrypi ~ $ sudo python ./pi_xbee.py
Reading from XBee:
  Temperature is 25.703125 c, 78.265625 f
  Supply voltage = 3.2578125 volts.
Reading from XBee:
  Temperature is 25.703125 c, 78.265625 f
  Supply voltage = 3.2578125 volts.
Reading from XBee:
  Temperature is 25.703125 c, 78.265625 f
  Supply voltage = 3.2578125 volts.
Reading from XBee:
  Temperature is 26.7578125 c, 80.1640625 f
  Supply voltage = 3.2578125 volts.
Reading from XBee:
  Temperature is 26.171875 c, 79.109375 f
  Supply voltage = 3.2578125 volts.
Reading from XBee:
  Temperature is 25.9375 c, 78.6875 f
  Supply voltage = 3.2578125 volts.
```

Figure 4-24. *Output of the XBee aggregate node script (*pi_xbee.py*)*

Did you see something similar? If so, you're doing great work and now have the knowledge needed to build sensor nodes and Raspberry Pi-based sensor data aggregators.

If you do not see any data at all, go back to Chapter 3 and follow the troubleshooting tips from the last project in the chapter. You can always plug the coordinator module in to a USB explorer and use a terminal program on your personal computer to see if data is being received from the XBee sensor node.

___

■ **Tip** If you don't see any data, power off your sensor node and Raspberry Pi. Remove the coordinator module from the Raspberry Pi, plug it in to a USB XBee explorer, plug that in to your personal computer and connect a serial program to the port, and then power up your sensor node. After a few moments, you should see data being received on the coordinator node.

___

For More Fun

If you would like to expand the project, you can add a second XBee sensor node and modify the code to specify which node the data came from. For example, the script should record (write to standard output) the source of the data along with the sensor data from the XBee.

Component Shopping List

A number of components are needed to complete the projects in this chapter; they are listed in Table 4-1. Some of them, like the XBee modules and supporting hardware, are also included in the shopping list from Chapter 3. These are shown in Table 4-2.

Table 4-1. *Components Needed*

Item	Vendors	Est. Cost USD	Qty Needed
Raspberry Pi Model B		$35 and up[16]	1
HDMI or HDMI to DVI cable	Most online and retail stores	Varies	1
HDMI or DVI monitor	Most online and retail stores	Varies	1
USB keyboard	Most online and retail stores	Varies	1
USB Type A to micro-USB male	Most online and retail stores	Varies	1
SD card, 2GB or more	Most online and retail stores	Varies	1
Raspberry Pi breakout board	www.adafruit.com/products/914	$7.95	1
DS18B20 digital temperature sensor	www.sparkfun.com/products/245 www.adafruit.com/products/374	$4.95	1
Barometric pressure sensor	www.sparkfun.com/products/11282 www.adafruit.com/products/391	$19.95	1
XBee Explorer Regulated	www.sparkfun.com/products/11373	$9.95	2
Ethernet cable and Internet connection			1
Breadboard (not mini)	www.sparkfun.com/products/9567	$5.95	2

---

[16]I recommend shopping around to find the best deal. At the time of writing, demand for the Raspberry Pi is still greater than the supply, so the cost is a bit higher.

Table 4-2. *Components Reused From Chapter 3*

Item	Vendors	Est. Cost USD	Qty Needed
LED (any color)	www.sparkfun.com/products/9592	$0.35	1
Pushbutton (breadboard mount)	www.sparkfun.com/products/97	$0.35	1
Breadboard (not mini)	www.sparkfun.com/products/9567	$5.95	1
Breadboard jumper wires	www.sparkfun.com/products/8431	$3.95	1
4.7K Ohm resistor (Resistor Kit)	www.sparkfun.com/products/10969	$7.95	1
10K Ohm resistor (Resistor Kit)			1
XBee-ZB (ZB) Series 2 or 2.5	www.sparkfun.com www.adafruit.com www.makershed.com	$25.00	2
TMP36 sensor	www.sparkfun.com/products/10988 www.adafruit.com/products/165	$1.50	1
Breadboard power supply	www.sparkfun.com/products/10804	$14.95	1
Wall power supply (6V–12V)	www.sparkfun.com/products/10273	$6.95	1
0.10uF capacitor	www.sparkfun.com/products/8375	$0.25	1
XBee Explorer Regulated with headers	www.sparkfun.com/products/11373	$9.95	1
150 Ohm resistor			

Summary

In this chapter, you explored the origins of the Raspberry Pi, including a tour of the hardware and a list of the available operating systems. You discovered how to create an SD boot image and learned how to start using the Raspberry Pi.

You also discovered how to use the GPIO header to illuminate a LED, read data from sensors, and read data via an XBee from an XBee sensor node. By executing these projects, you have learned far more about the Raspberry Pi than most.

By now you should start to see the parts of building a sensor network coming together. You've explored XBee modules for wireless communication, host sensors with the Arduino and Raspberry Pi, and even how to build aggregate sensor nodes with both platforms. The next chapter examines some methods for what to do with the data that you collect. As you will see, a variety of methods are available.

CHAPTER 5

■ ■ ■

Where to Put It All: Storing Sensor Data

If you have had success with the projects thus far in the book, you have at your disposal several forms of sensor and data-aggregate nodes. In essence, you have the basic building blocks for constructing a sensor network to monitor and record temperature data. It would not take much more work to add nodes for other environmental sensors such as humidity or barometric pressure. Indeed, the basic sensor node you have built can host a variety of sensors.

If you have run the example projects and experimented with the challenges, no doubt you have noticed that a lot of data is being generated. What do you do with that data? Is it meaningful only at the instant it is generated, or do you think it is more likely that you would want to store the data and examine it later? For example, if you want to know the temperature range for your workshop on a monthly basis throughout the year, logically you need data from an entire year[1] to tabulate and average.

Arduino boards don't have built-in storage devices. Raspberry Pi boards come with a Secure Digital (SD) drive and can accept USB-based storage devices where you can store data, but what do you do with the data from your Arduino-based nodes?

This chapter examines the available storage methods and gives examples of how to store data using those methods. Sample projects are provided to illustrate the mechanisms and code, but I omit the sensor-specific code for brevity.

Storage Methods

Sensor data can come in several forms. Sensors can produce numeric data consisting of floating-point numbers or sometimes integers. Some sensors produce more complex information that is grouped together and may contain several forms of data. Knowing how to interpret the values read is often the hardest part of using a sensor. In fact, you saw this in a number of the sensor node examples. For example, the temperature sensors produced values that had to be converted to scale to be meaningful.

Although it is possible to store all the data as text, if you want to use the data in another application or consume it for use in a spreadsheet or statistical application, you may need to consider storing it either in binary form or in a text form that can be easily converted. For example, most spreadsheet applications can easily convert a text string like "123.45" to a float, but they may not be able to convert "12E236" to a float. On the other hand, if you plan to write addition code for your Arduino sketches or Raspberry Pi Python scripts to process the data, you may want to store the data in binary form to avoid having to write costly (and potentially slow) conversion routines.

But that is only part of the problem. Where you store the data is a greater concern. You want to store the data in the form you need but also in a location (on a device) that you can retrieve it from and that won't be erased when the host is rebooted. For example, storing data in main memory on an Arduino is not a good idea. Not only does it consume valuable program space, but it is volatile and will be erased when the Arduino is powered off.

---

[1]Or at least the data from the time period in question.

The Raspberry Pi offers a better option. You can easily create a file and store the data on the root partition or in your home directory on the SD card. This is nonvolatile and does not affect the operation of the Raspberry Pi operating system. The only drawback is that it has the potential to result in too little disk space if the data grows significantly. But the data would have to grow to nearly two gigabytes (for a 2GB SD card) before it would threaten the stability of the operating system (although that can happen).

So what are your options for storing data with Arduino? Are there any other possibilities with the Raspberry Pi? There are two types of storage to consider: local and remote. Local storage includes any method that results in the data being stored with the node: for example, storing data on the SD card on the Raspberry Pi. Remote storage includes any method where the data is stored on a device or medium that is not directly connected to the node: for example, storing data on a different node or even on a server connected to the Internet.

STORING DATE AND TIME WITH SAMPLES

Neither the Arduino nor the Raspberry Pi has a real-time clock (RTC) on board. If you want to store your sensor data locally, you have to either store the data with an approximate date and time stamp or use an RTC module to read an accurate date/time value.

Fortunately, there are RTC modules for use with an Arduino or the Raspberry Pi. If your Raspberry Pi is connected to the Internet and you have enabled the network time synchronization feature, you do not need the RTC module. However, if your Raspberry Pi is not connected to the Internet, and you want to store accurate time data, you should consider using the RTC module.

The following sections examine the various local and remote storage options available for the Arduino and Raspberry Pi.

Local Storage Options for the Arduino

Although it is true that the Arduino has no onboard storage devices,[2] there are two ways you can store data locally for the Arduino. You can store data in a special form of nonvolatile memory or on an SD card hosted via either a special SD card shield or an Ethernet shield (most Ethernet shields have a built-in SD card drive).

■ **Note** If you are truly inventive (or perhaps unable to resist a challenge), you can use some of the communication protocols to send data to other devices. For example, you could use the serial interface to write data to a serial device.

The following sections discuss each option in greater detail. Later sections present small projects you can use to learn how to use these devices for storing data.

Nonvolatile Memory

The most common form of nonvolatile memory available to the Arduino is electrically erasable programmable read-only memory (EEPROM—pronounced "e-e-prom" or "double-e prom"). EEPROMs are packaged as chips (integrated circuits). As the name suggests, data can be written to the chip and is readable even after a power cycle but can be erased or overwritten.

---

[2]Except for the new Arduino Yún, which has an SD drive and USB ports for connecting external devices. The Yún is sure to be a game changer for the Arduino world.

Most Arduino boards have a small EEPROM where the sketch is stored and read during power up. If you have ever wondered how the Arduino does that, now you know. You can write to the unused portion of this memory if you desire, but the amount of memory available is small (512KB). You can also use an EEPROM and wire it directly to the Arduino via the I2C protocol to overcome this limitation.

Writing to and reading from an EEPROM is supported via a special library that is included in the Arduino IDE. Due to the limited amount of memory available, storing data in the EEPROM memory is not ideal for most sensor nodes. You are likely to exceed the memory available if the data you are storing is large or there are many data items per sample.

You also have the issue of getting the data from the EEPROM for use in other applications. In this case, you would have to build not only a way to write the data but also a way to read the data and export it to some other medium (local or remote).

That is not to say that you should never use EEPROM to store data. Several possible reasons justify storing data in EEPROM. For example, if your sensor node is likely to be isolated, or connectivity to other nodes is limited, you may want to use an EEPROM to temporarily store data while the node is offline. In fact, you could build your sketch to detect when the node goes offline and switch to the EEPROM at that time. This way, your Arduino-based sensor node can continue to record sensor data. Once the node is back online, you can write your sketch to dump the contents of the EEPROM to another node (remote storage).

SD Card

You can also store (and retrieve) data on an SD card. The Arduino IDE has a library for interacting with an SD drive. In this case, you would use the library to access the SD drive via an SD shield or an Ethernet shield.

Storing data on an SD card is done via files. You open a file and write the data to it in whatever format is best for the next phase in your data analysis. Examples in the Arduino IDE and elsewhere demonstrate how to create a web server interface for your Arduino that displays the list of files available on the SD card.

Compared to EEPROMs, SD cards store many times more data. You can purchase high-density SD cards that exceed 128GB of storage space. That's a lot of sensor data!

You may choose to store data to an SD card in situations where your sensor node is designed as a remote sensor with no connectivity to other nodes, or you can use it as a backup-logging device in case your sensor node is disconnected or your data-aggregator node goes down. Because the card is removable and readable in other devices, you can read it on another device when you want to use the data.

Using an SD card means you can move the data from the sensor node to a computer simply by unplugging the card from the Arduino and plugging it in to the SD card reader in your computer.

Project: Saving Data in Nonvolatile Memory

Recall that you can use the local EEPROM on an Arduino to store data. There are some excellent examples in the Arduino IDE that I encourage you to experiment with at your leisure. They are located under the Examples menu under the EEPROM submenu. You need only an Arduino and your laptop to experiment with writing to and from the EEPROM on the Arduino.

Rather than rehash the example sketch for using the built-in EEPROM, this section outlines a project to use an external EEPROM to store data. Unlike the local EEPROM, which uses a dedicated library to interact with, an external EEPROM uses the I2C communication protocol.

Hardware Setup

The hardware for this project consists of a 24LC256 or 24LC512 EEPROM chip like those from SparkFun (www.sparkfun.com/products/525), a pushbutton, jumper wires, and an Arduino. Figure 5-1 shows a typical 24LC256 pin-mount EEPROM chip.

Figure 5-1. *I2C EEPROM chip (courtesy of SparkFun)*

The pushbutton will allow you to reset the memory on the chip. Doing so erases the data values stored, resetting the memory configuration for reuse. You will find this feature particularly handy when using the sketch for the first time, debugging problems, and reusing the chip once memory has been read and stored on another medium.

The chip communicates via an I2C bus. You can set the address for the chip by connecting ground or power to pins A0–A2, as shown in Figure 5-2. You can think of this as a binary number, where connecting ground to all three pins is the lowest address available (0x50) and power to all three pins is the highest address available (0x57). Table 5-1 shows the possible addresses and connections required. You use the lowest address (0x50) by connecting ground to all three pins.

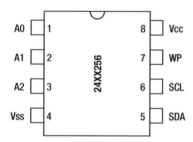

Figure 5-2. *Pinout of the I2C EEPROM*

Table 5-1. *Setting the Address of the I2C EEPROM*

Address	A0	A1	A2
0x50	Ground	Ground	Ground
0x51	Ground	Ground	+5V
0x52	Ground	+5V	Ground
0x53	Ground	+5V	+5V
0x54	+5V	Ground	Ground
0x55	+5V	Ground	+5V
0x56	+5V	+5V	Ground
0x57	+5V	+5V	+5V

Now that you understand how to address the chip, let's connect it to your Arduino. Begin by placing the chip in a breadboard with the half circle pointing to the right. This establishes pin 1 as the upper-right pin. Connect a ground wire to all four pins on the top side of the chip. These are pins 1–4, as shown in Figure 5-2.

Next, connect pin 5 (SDA) to pin 4 on the Arduino and pin 6 (SCL) to pin 5 on the Arduino. Connect a ground wire to pin 7. Then connect positive voltage (+5V) to pin 8. Finally, connect the pushbutton to pin 2 on one side and power on the other. Use a 10K Ohm resistor to pull the button HIGH (connect it to positive voltage) as you did in a previous project. See Figure 5-3 for a detailed wiring diagram. Be sure to double-check your connections.

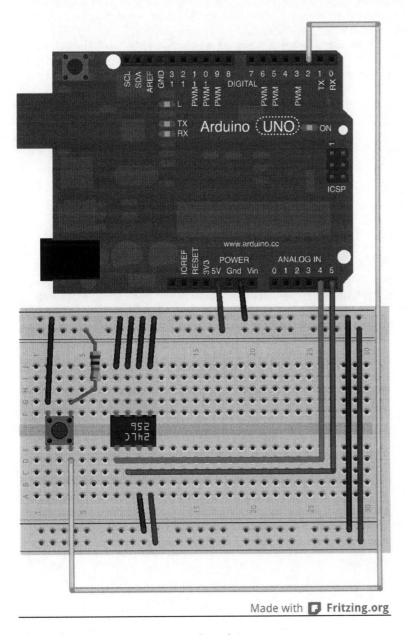

Figure 5-3. Wiring the EEPROM to the Arduino

■ **Note**   If you are using the Leonardo board, you need to use the SDC and SCL pins located near the USB port.

Software Setup

With the wiring in place, you are ready to start writing a sketch to read and write data. Rather than write a script to simply store data, in this example you write a sketch to let you write data to and read it from the chip. You also include a reset operation to allow you to overwrite any memory.

You add the read methods so that you can create additional sketches to read data, should you wish to review the data, move the chip (data) to another Arduino, or use another sketch to process the data.

Let's get started. You use the I2C library (called Wire) to interact with the EEPROM. Open a new sketch, and enter the following:

```
#include <Wire.h>

#define FIRST_SAMPLE 0x02  // First position of first sample
#define MEM_ADDR 0x50       // EEPROM address
#define BUTTON_PIN 0x02     // Button pin
#define EEPROM_SIZE 32768   // Size of 24LC256
#define SAMPLE_BYTES 2      // Size of sample in bytes

int next_index = 0;         // Address of first sample
```

These statements include the Wire library and define a number of constants you use in the sketch. Notice that you have an address for the first sample (the position in memory on the chip), the address for the chip, a pin for the pushbutton, the maximum size (for the 256 chip), and the number of bytes per sample.

You need a number of methods. You need the ability to write a single byte to memory, store a sample, read a byte, and read a sample. Let's look at the simplest forms of these methods—the read byte method:

■ **Note**   In the following code, `address` refers to the address of the EEPROM chip, and `index` is the location in memory that you want to access.

```
byte read_byte(int address, unsigned int index)  {
  byte data = 0xFF;

  Wire.beginTransmission(address);
  Wire.write((int)(index >> 8));    // MSB
  Wire.write((int)(index & 0xFF)); // LSB
  Wire.endTransmission();

  Wire.requestFrom(address,1);

  if (Wire.available()) {
    data = Wire.read();
  }
  return data;
}
```

Notice the process for communicating with the chip. First you start a transmission with the chip, send the address that you intend to read, and then end the transmission. The address is a two-byte value, and the statements show you how to manipulate the bytes to form a word (two bytes). The next method, requestFrom() tells the chip you want to read a single byte. If the chip is ready, you read the data. Finally, you return the value to the caller.

You use the same format for every operation you wish to use with the chip. Let's look at the write method to write a single byte to the chip:

```
void write_byte(int address, unsigned int index, byte data) {
  Wire.beginTransmission(address);
  Wire.write((int)(index >> 8));    // MSB
  Wire.write((int)(index & 0xFF)); // LSB
  Wire.write(data);
  Wire.endTransmission();

  delay(5);
}
```

Notice that you have the same setup—you begin the transmission and set the value at the index specified. What differs is that you send the data (write it) before you end the transmission.

But how do you know what is written to which address (or index)? Rather than just write data willy-nilly or in some illogical order, let's use the first byte at index 0 to store the number of data samples (or rows) and the second byte to store how many bytes each sample consumes (or columns). In this way, you make the data easier to read because it is uniform and easier to manage on a reboot.

In fact, let's add a new method to display the contents of the data in the EEPROM on startup. Recall for the Arduino that if you want to execute a method once at startup, you place it in the setup() method. The following shows how you can use the existing read method to read data from the EEPROM and display the information in the serial monitor.

This technique makes it easy to verify that the code is working by running the dump method on startup. In essence, you create a crude self-diagnostic mechanism that you can use to check the state of the data. If you see anything other than valid data at startup, you know something has gone wrong:

```
void setup(void) {
  int bytes_per_sample = SAMPLE_BYTES;
  byte buffer[SAMPLE_BYTES];

  Serial.begin(115200);
  Wire.begin();

  next_index = read_byte(MEM_ADDR, 0);
  bytes_per_sample = read_byte(MEM_ADDR, 1);
  ...
}
```

But wait! What does this code do if you encounter an uninitialized EEPROM? In that case, you can create a special method to initialize the EEPROM. The following shows the initialize() method:

```
void initialize(int address) {
  // Clear memory
  // NOTE: replace '10' with EEPROM_SIZE to erase all data
  for (int i = 0; i < 10; i++) {
    write_byte(address, i, 0xFF);
  }
  write_byte(address, 0, FIRST_SAMPLE);
  write_byte(address, 1, SAMPLE_BYTES);
```

```
  Serial.print("EEPROM at address 0x");
  Serial.print(address, HEX);
  Serial.println(" has been initialized.");
}
```

You use the `write_byte()` method to write 0 for the number of bytes and the constant defined earlier for the number of bytes per sample. The method begins by writing 0xff to the first 10 bytes to ensure that you have no data stored; then the number of bytes is written to index 0 and the number of bytes per sample to index 1. You add some `print` statements for feedback.

But how does this method get called? One way would be to put it in your `setup()` method as the first call after the call to initialize the Wire library, but that would mean you would have to comment out the other methods, load the sketch, execute it, remove the method, and reload. That seems like a lot of extra work. A better way is to trigger this method with a pushbutton. Code to do this is placed in the `loop()` method, as shown here:

```
if (digitalRead(BUTTON_PIN) == LOW) {
  initialize(MEM_ADDR);
  delay(500); // debounce
}
```

Now that you can read and write a byte and initialize the chip, you also need to be able to read a sample in case you want to use the chip in another sketch to process the data. The following shows a method to read a sample:

```
void read_sample(int address, unsigned int index, byte *buffer) {
  Wire.beginTransmission(address);
  Wire.write((int)(index >> 8));   // MSB
  Wire.write((int)(index & 0xFF)); // LSB
  Wire.endTransmission();

  Wire.requestFrom(address, SAMPLE_BYTES);
  for (int i = 0; i < SAMPLE_BYTES; i++) {
    if (Wire.available()) {
      buffer[i] = Wire.read();
    }
  }
}
```

Notice that you form a sequence of events similar to `read_byte()`. But rather than read a single byte, you use a loop to read the number of bytes for a sample.

You also need a method to store (write) a sample to the chip:

```
void write_sample(int address, unsigned int index, byte *data) {
  Wire.beginTransmission(address);
  Wire.write((int)(index >> 8));   // MSB
  Wire.write((int)(index & 0xFF)); // LSB
  Serial.print("START: ");
  Serial.println(index);
  for (int i = 0; i < SAMPLE_BYTES; i++) {
    Wire.write(data[i]);
  }
  Wire.endTransmission();

  delay(5); // wait for chip to write data
}
```

Once again, the method is similar to the write_byte() method, but you use a loop to write the bytes for a sample. Notice that you include a debug statement to show the starting index used. You do this so that you can see the value increase if you run the sketch multiple times.

■ **Note** You may have noticed that I duplicated the code among the *_byte() and *_sample() methods. I did so for clarity of the code, but it isn't strictly necessary. For example, you could consolidate the code if you changed the *_sample() methods to use an additional parameter indicating how many bytes to read/write. I leave this optimization to you as an exercise.

There is one more method to consider. Recall that you use a counter stored in index 0 to record the number of samples written. The write_sample() method simply writes a sample at a specific index. What you need is a method that manages the sample counter and stores the sample. Thus, you create a record_sample() method to handle the higher-level operation:

```
void record_sample(int address, int data) {
  byte sample[SAMPLE_BYTES];

  sample[0] = data >> 8;
  sample[1] = (byte)data;
  write_sample(address, next_index, sample);
  next_index += SAMPLE_BYTES;
  write_byte(address, 0, next_index);
}
```

Notice how you keep track of the number of samples and the next index for the next sample. You use the variable you created earlier and increment it by the number of bytes in the sample. This way, you always know what the next address is without reading the number of samples first and calculating the index. The last method updates the number of samples value.

Now that you have all the building blocks, Listing 5-1 shows the completed code for this sketch. Save the sketch as external_eeprom. Notice that in the sketch you do not include any code to read from sensors. I left this out for brevity and included some debug statements (shown in bold) in the setup() method instead to show how you record samples. Be sure to remove these statements when you modify the sketch for use with a sensor.

Listing 5-1. Storing and Retrieving Data on an External EEPROM

```
/**
  Sensor Networks Example Arduino External EEPROM data store

  This project demonstrates how to save and retrieve sensor data
  to/from an external EEPROM chip.
*/

#include <Wire.h>

#define FIRST_SAMPLE 0x02 // Index of first sample
#define MEM_ADDR 0x50      // EEPROM address
#define BUTTON_PIN 0x02    // Button pin
```

```
#define EEPROM_SIZE 32768 // Size of 24LC256
#define SAMPLE_BYTES 2     // Size of sample in bytes

int next_index = 0;        // Index of next sample

/* Initialize the chip erasing data */
void initialize(int address) {
  // Clear memory
  // NOTE: replace '10' with EEPROM_SIZE to erase all data
  for (int i = 0; i < 10; i++) {
    write_byte(address, i, 0xFF);
  }
  write_byte(address, 0, FIRST_SAMPLE);
  write_byte(address, 1, SAMPLE_BYTES);
  Serial.print("EEPROM at address 0x");
  Serial.print(address, HEX);
  Serial.println(" has been initialized.");
}

/* Write a sample to the chip. */
void write_sample(int address, unsigned int index, byte *data) {
  Wire.beginTransmission(address);
  Wire.write((int)(index >> 8));   // MSB
  Wire.write((int)(index & 0xFF)); // LSB
  Serial.print("START: ");
  Serial.println(index);
  for (int i = 0; i < SAMPLE_BYTES; i++) {
    Wire.write(data[i]);
  }
  Wire.endTransmission();

  delay(5); // wait for chip to write data
}

/* Write a byte to the chip at specific index (offset). */
void write_byte(int address, unsigned int index, byte data) {
  Wire.beginTransmission(address);
  Wire.write((int)(index >> 8));   // MSB
  Wire.write((int)(index & 0xFF)); // LSB
  Wire.write(data);
  Wire.endTransmission();

  delay(5);
}

/* Read a sample from an index (offset). */
void read_sample(int address, unsigned int index, byte *buffer) {
  Wire.beginTransmission(address);
  Wire.write((int)(index >> 8));   // MSB
  Wire.write((int)(index & 0xFF)); // LSB
  Wire.endTransmission();
```

154

```
    Wire.requestFrom(address, SAMPLE_BYTES);
    for (int i = 0; i < SAMPLE_BYTES; i++) {
      if (Wire.available()) {
        buffer[i] = Wire.read();
      }
    }
}

/* Read a byte from an index (offset). */
byte read_byte(int address, unsigned int index)  {
  byte data = 0xFF;

  Wire.beginTransmission(address);
  Wire.write((int)(index >> 8));    // MSB
  Wire.write((int)(index & 0xFF)); // LSB
  Wire.endTransmission();

  Wire.requestFrom(address,1);

  if (Wire.available()) {
    data = Wire.read();
  }
  return data;
}

/* Save a sample to the data chip and increment next address counter. */
void record_sample(int address, int data) {
  byte sample[SAMPLE_BYTES];

  sample[0] = data >> 8;
  sample[1] = (byte)data;
  write_sample(address, next_index, sample);
  next_index += SAMPLE_BYTES;
  write_byte(address, 0, next_index);
}

void setup(void) {
  int bytes_per_sample = SAMPLE_BYTES;
  byte buffer[SAMPLE_BYTES];
  delay(5000);
  Serial.begin(115200);
  Wire.begin();

  next_index = read_byte(MEM_ADDR, 0);
  bytes_per_sample = read_byte(MEM_ADDR, 1);
  Serial.println("Welcome to the Arduino external EEPROM project.");
  Serial.print("Byte pointer: ");
  Serial.println(next_index, DEC);
  Serial.print("Bytes per sample: ");
```

```
  Serial.println(bytes_per_sample, DEC);
  Serial.print("Number of samples:");
  Serial.println((next_index/bytes_per_sample)-1, DEC);

  // Add some sample data
  record_sample(MEM_ADDR, 6011);
  record_sample(MEM_ADDR, 8088);

  // Example of how to read sample data - read last 2 values
  read_sample(MEM_ADDR, next_index-(SAMPLE_BYTES * 2), buffer);
  Serial.print("First value: ");
  Serial.println((int)(buffer[0] << 8) + (int)buffer[1]);
  read_sample(MEM_ADDR, next_index-SAMPLE_BYTES, buffer);
  Serial.print("Second value: ");
  Serial.println((int)(buffer[0] << 8) + (int)buffer[1]);
}

void loop() {
  if (digitalRead(BUTTON_PIN) == LOW) {
    initialize(MEM_ADDR);
    delay(500); // debounce
  }
  //
  // Read sensor data and record sample here
  //
}
```

Notice that you include some additional statements for communicating the progress of the sketch via the serial monitor. Take some time to examine these so that you are familiar with what to expect when the sketch runs.

■ **TIP**   If you want to write protect the chip, disconnect the WP pin. Doing so makes the chip read only.

Testing the Sketch

To test the sketch, be sure the code compiles and you have your hardware set up correctly. When you have a sketch that compiles, upload it to your Arduino and launch a serial monitor.

When the sketch is loaded for the first time, you need to press the button to initialize the EEPROM. This is because the values on the chip are uninitialized for a new chip. You only have to do this the first time you run the sketch. Once you've done that, you should see output similar to that in Figure 5-4.

```
○ ○ ○                    /dev/tty.usbmodem1431

                                                        [ Send ]

Welcome to the Arduino external EEPROM project.
Byte pointer: 6
Bytes per sample: 2
Number of samples:2
START: 6
START: 8
First value: 6011
Second value: 8088
Welcome to the Arduino external EEPROM project.
Byte pointer: 10
Bytes per sample: 2
Number of samples:4
START: 10
START: 12
First value: 6011
Second value: 8088
EEPROM at address 0x50 has been initialized.
Welcome to the Arduino external EEPROM project.
Byte pointer: 2
Bytes per sample: 2
Number of samples:0
START: 2
START: 4
First value: 6011
Second value: 8088

☑ Autoscroll          [ No line ending ⬍ ]  [ 115200 baud ⬍ ]
```

Figure 5-4. *Example output*

Did you see something similar? If you run the sketch again (for example, by pressing the Reset button), you should see the value for the start index (from the `write_sample()` method) increase. Go ahead and give it a try.

Once you've done it a few times, press the pushbutton and notice what happens. As you can see in Figure 5-4, the start index is reset and the next samples are store at the beginning of memory.

For More Fun

The sketch for this project has a lot of promise. No doubt you can think of a number of things you could do with this code. The following are some suggestions for improving the code and experimenting with using an external EEPROM:

- Add some visual aids for use in embedded projects (cases with no serial monitor capability). You can add an LED that illuminates when there is data on the chip. You can also add a set of 7-segment LEDs to display the number of data samples stored.

- Improve the code for reuse. Begin by removing the redundancy described earlier in the read and write methods, and then move the code to a class to make it easier to use the EEPROM in other sketches.

- Add a second EEPROM chip to expand the amount of storage available. Hint: you need to set each chip to a different address, but the methods used are the same.

- Perhaps a bit easier and more in line with the hardware-hacking element of Arduino is moving the EEPROM to another Arduino and reading all the values stored. This demonstrates the nonvolatile nature of EEPROM chips.

■ **Caution**   Use appropriate grounding to avoid electrostatic discharge (ESD) damage to the chip.

Project: Writing Data to an SD Card

Aside from an EEPROM chip, you can also store data locally on an Arduino by writing the data to an SD drive. The SD drive is a good choice for storing data because the data is stored in files, which other devices can read (and write to).

For example, although writing data to an EEPROM chip is not difficult, reading that chip on a personal computer requires writing a sketch for the Arduino to transfer the data. However, the SD card can be removed from the Arduino (once files are closed) and inserted in an SD drive connected to a personal computer, allowing you to read the files directly. Thus, the SD card makes a better choice for sensor networks where your sensor nodes are not connected via a network or other wireless connections.

There are several choices for adding an SD card reader to an Arduino. Two of the most popular are the Arduino Ethernet shield and the microSD shield from SparkFun (`www.sparkfun.com/categories/240`). If you use the Arduino Ethernet shield, you can use the networking capabilities and the SD card together. A number of similar devices are available from a variety of vendors.

Adafruit also has a Data Logging shield for Arduino with an onboard SD drive (`www.adafruit.com/product/1141`). The Data Logging shield also includes an RTC, making it possible to store date and time along with the sample. I discuss using an RTC in the next project.

■ **Tip**   Both the microSD shield and the Data Logging shield offer a prototyping area that you can use to mount your sensor components or even an XBee module.

An SD drive allows you to create a hybrid node where you store data locally as well as transmit it to another node in the network. This redundancy is one of the ways you can build durability in to your sensor network. For example, if a node loses its connection to another node via the network, it can still record its data locally. Although it is a manual process to recover the data (you must go get the SD card), the fact that the data is recoverable at all means the network can survive network failures without losing data.

It is possible to use an EEPROM as a local storage backup option, but an EEPROM is harder to use, is not as durable as an SD card, does not have the same storage capacity, and is not as easy to use in other devices.

There is one other very important thing to consider concerning building a durable sensor node. Having a local backup of the data may not be helpful if you do not know when the data was stored. The Arduino does not have any time-keeping capability beyond a limited accuracy cycle time. Thus, if you store data locally without a timestamp of any kind that you can relate to other data, the samples taken may not be meaningful beyond the sequence itself (the order of the values).

To mitigate this, you can add an RTC module to the Arduino. The RTC allows you to store the date and time a sample was taken. This information may be critical if you are trying to plot values over time or want to know when a spurious or otherwise interesting event took place.

Hardware Setup

The hardware for this project uses the Arduino Ethernet shield, the microSD shield from SparkFun (with an SD card installed), or the Data Logging shield from Adafruit. For simplicity, I used the Arduino Ethernet shield and show the code changes necessary to use the microSD shield or the Data Logging shield (via #define statements).

You also need the RTC module. There is an excellent product from Adafruit that performs very well and includes an onboard battery that powers the clock even when the Arduino is powered down. Adafruit's DS1307 Real Time Clock breakout board kit (www.adafruit.com/products/264) is an outstanding module to add to your project. Figure 5-5 shows the Adafruit RTC module.

Figure 5-5. *DS1307 Real Time Clock breakout board (courtesy of Adafruit)*

SparkFun also has a product named Real Time Clock Module (www.sparkfun.com/products/99) that uses the same DS1307 chip and interface as the Adafruit offering. You can use either in this project.

■ **Note** The Adafruit RTC module requires assembly. The RTC module from SparkFun does not.

The RTC module uses an I2C interface that is easy to connect to the Arduino. Simply connect 5V power to the 5V pin, ground to the GND pin, the SDA pin to pin 4 on the Arduino, and the SCL pin to pin 5 on the Arduino. Figure 5-6 shows the wiring diagram for connecting the RTC module.

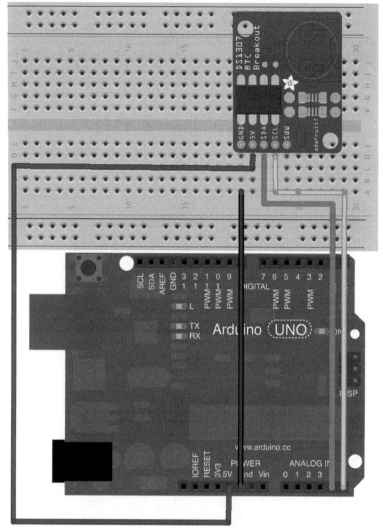

Made with 🗗 Fritzing.org

Figure 5-6. *Arduino with an Ethernet shield and RTC module*

■ **Note**   If you are using the Leonardo board, you have to use the new SCL/SCA pins located next to AREF, GND, and pin 13 nearest the USB connector.

Notice that the Ethernet shield is installed on the Arduino. Wiring connections would be the same if you were using the SparkFun microSD shield.

Software Setup

With the wiring in place, you are ready to start writing a sketch to write data to the SD card. But first, you must download and install the RTC library from Adafruit (`https://github.com/adafruit/RTClib`). Click the Download Zip button, extract the archive, rename the folder `RTClib`, and move it to your `Arduino/Library` folder.

Once the library is downloaded and installed (and you've restarted the Arduino IDE), you can begin a new sketch named `sd_file_example`. Enter the following code to specify the modules you need to use in the sketch. You need the Wire, RTC, SD, and String libraries:

```
#include <Wire.h>
#include <RTClib.h>
#include <SD.h>
#include <String.h>
```

Next, you need to define the pin to use to communicate with the SD drive. The following are the definitions for all three SD drive options described earlier. I use the Ethernet shield in this example; but if you are not using the Ethernet shield, you can comment out that line and uncomment out the line that corresponds with the shield you are using. You also include a definition for the name of the file you use to store samples:

```
// Pin assignment for Arduino Ethernet shield
#define SD_PIN 4
// Pin assignment for Sparkfun microSD shield
//#define SD_PIN 8
// Pin assignment for Adafruit Data Logging shield
//#define SD_PIN 10

// Sensor data file - require 8.3³ file name
#define SENSOR_DATA "sensdata.txt"
```

Now you declare some variables. You need one for the RTC module and one for the file you use on the SD drive:

```
RTC_DS1307 RTC;
File sensor_data;
```

With the preliminaries complete, you need a method to save a sensor sample to the SD card. The method must read the date and time from the RTC module, accept the sample as a parameter, and store the data. In this example, you place the date and time first, followed by the sample value. Name this method `record_sample()`.

Reading from the RTC module is easy with the RTC library. You simply use the library to get the current date and time with the now() method. From there, you can call methods to get the month, day, year, hour, and so on. Forming the string to write to the file can be done in a variety of ways. I used the string class to construct the string. Feel free to use any other method you favor instead:

```
// Capture the date and time
DateTime now = RTC.now();
```

Writing to the file is very easy. You simply open the file in write mode (`FILE_WRITE`) that automatically permits any writes to be written to the end of the file (append). This is nice because you don't have to worry about seeking or

---

³This refers to the old FAT file system requirements for file naming, where you can have a maximum of eight characters for the file name and three for the extension (`http://en.wikipedia.org/wiki/8.3_filename`). Do you remember those days?

finding out where a file pointer is in the file. Opening the file returns a file object instance, which you can use to write data. Writing to the file (once it is opened) requires only a single method call. The following shows a simplified set of calls to open a file using the SD library and write data. I leave the details of the record_sample() method for you to explore in Listing 5-2:

```
// Open the file
sensor_data = SD.open(SENSOR_DATA, FILE_WRITE);
// Save the data
sensor_data.write(1234);
sensor_data.write("\n");
// Close the file
sensor_data.close();
```

Of course, you need a few things to properly set up the components and libraries. The setup() method should contain, at a minimum, initialization for the Serial, Wire, and RTC libraries (by calling their begin() methods) and a call to the SD library to start communication with the SD drive. The following is an excerpt of the code needed for these steps. Notice that you also initialize the date and time for the RTC based on the last compiled date and time of the sketch (effectively, the date and time it was uploaded):

```
void setup () {
  Serial.begin(9600);
  delay(5000);  //Give time for user to connect serial monitor

  Wire.begin();
  RTC.begin();

  if (!RTC.isrunning()) {
    Serial.println("RTC is NOT running!");
    // Set time to date and time of compilation
    RTC.adjust(DateTime(__DATE__, __TIME__));
  }

  // disable w5100 SPI
  pinMode(10,OUTPUT);
  digitalWrite(10,HIGH);

  // Initialize the SD card.
  Serial.print("Initializing SD card...");
  if (!SD.begin(SD_PIN)) {
    Serial.println("initialization failed!");
    return;
  }
  Serial.println("initialization done.");
...
}
```

■ **Note** Notice that also you have code to turn off the Ethernet W5100 SPI interface. This is only necessary for the Ethernet shield and then only if you do not plan to use the networking capabilities.

There is one other thing you might want to add. You may want to check to see if you can read the file on the SD card. It is not enough to simply initialize the SD library. It is possible the SD drive will communicate properly but you cannot open or create files on the card itself. Add the following to the setup() method as an extra check. In this case, you check to see whether the file exists and, if it does not, attempt to create the file. You print a message if you get an error on the open call:

```
// Check for file. Create if not present
if (!SD.exists(SENSOR_DATA)) {
  Serial.print("Sensor data file does not exit. Creating file...");
  sensor_data = SD.open(SENSOR_DATA, FILE_WRITE);
  if (!sensor_data) {
    Serial.println("ERROR: Cannot create file.");
  }
  else {
    sensor_data.close();
    Serial.println("done.");
  }
}
```

The loop() method is where you place calls to the record_sample() method. In this case, leave the loop() method empty for brevity. Feel free to add your own code to read sensors here and call the record_sample() method for each.

Listing 5-2 shows the complete code for this project. Although the explanation thus far has been about the key parts of the sketch, notice that the listing adds additional error-handing code to make sure the SD drive is initialized properly and the file exists and can be written.

Listing 5-2. Storing Data on an SD Card

```
/**
  Sensor Networks Example Arduino SD card data store

  This project demonstrates how to save sensor data to a
  microSD card.
*/

#include <Wire.h>
#include <RTClib.h>
#include <SD.h>
#include <String.h>

// Pin assignment for Arduino Ethernet shield
#define SD_PIN 4
// Pin assignment for Sparkfun microSD shield
//#define SD_PIN 8
// Pin assignment for Adafruit Data Logging shield
//#define SD_PIN 10

// Sensor data file - require 8.3 file name
#define SENSOR_DATA "sensdata.txt"
```

```
RTC_DS1307 RTC;
File sensor_data;

void record_sample(int data) {
  // Open the file
  sensor_data = SD.open(SENSOR_DATA, FILE_WRITE);
  if (!sensor_data) {
    Serial.println("ERROR: Cannot open file. Data not saved!");
    return;
  }

  // Capture the date and time
  DateTime now = RTC.now();

  String timestamp(now.month(), DEC);
  timestamp += ("/");
  timestamp += now.day();
  timestamp += ("/");
  timestamp += now.year();
  timestamp += (" ");
  timestamp += now.hour();
  timestamp += (":");
  timestamp += now.minute();
  timestamp += (":");
  timestamp += now.second();
  timestamp += (" ");

  // Save the sensor data
  sensor_data.write(&timestamp[0]);

  String sample(data, DEC);
  sensor_data.write(&sample[0]);
  sensor_data.write("\n");

  // Echo the data
  Serial.print("Sample: ");
  Serial.print(timestamp);
  Serial.print(data, DEC);
  Serial.println();

  // Close the file
  sensor_data.close();
}

void setup () {
  Serial.begin(9600);
delay(5000);  //Give time for user to connect serial monitor
  Wire.begin();
  RTC.begin();
```

```
  if (!RTC.isrunning()) {
    Serial.println("RTC is NOT running!");
    // Set time to date and time of compilation
    RTC.adjust(DateTime(__DATE__, __TIME__));
  }

  // disable w5100 SPI
  pinMode(10,OUTPUT);
  digitalWrite(10,HIGH);

  // Initialize the SD card.
  Serial.print("Initializing SD card...");
  if (!SD.begin(SD_PIN)) {
    Serial.println("initialization failed!");
    return;
  }
  Serial.println("initialization done.");

  // Check for file. Create if not present
  if (!SD.exists(SENSOR_DATA)) {
    Serial.print("Sensor data file does not exit. Creating file...");
    sensor_data = SD.open(SENSOR_DATA, FILE_WRITE);
    if (!sensor_data) {
      Serial.println("ERROR: Cannot create file.");
    }
    else {
      sensor_data.close();
      Serial.println("done.");
    }
  }

  // Record some test samples.
  record_sample(1);
  record_sample(2);
  record_sample(3);
}

void loop () {
  // Read sensor data here and record with record_sample()
}
```

I added debug statements to the setup() method for illustration purposes and to make sure the sketch works. Placing these calls in the setup() method permits you to load the sketch (or reboot the Arduino) and check the contents of the SD card to see if the code worked. If you place the statements in the loop() method, then depending on when you turn off your Arduino (unplug it), you may not know how many lines were added or even if the file were closed properly. Placing the record_sample() statements in the setup() method means you have expected output to check.

■ **Tip** If you get SD drive initialization errors, check the pin assignment used in the definition section to make sure you are using the correct pin for your SD drive/shield.

If you encounter file-write or -open errors, make sure the SD card is formatted as a FAT partition, the SD card is not write protected, and you can create and read files on the drive using your personal computer.

Testing the Sketch

To test the sketch, be sure the code compiles and you have your hardware set up correctly. Once you have a sketch that compiles, upload it to your Arduino and launch a serial monitor. Figure 5-7 shows the expected output.

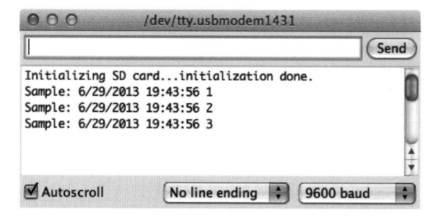

Figure 5-7. *Sample output for the SD card sketch*

■ **Note** The first time you run the sketch, you may see a message about initializing the SD card and creating the file. This is normal. Subsequent runs (restarts of the Arduino) will show the output like that in Figure 5-7.

If you run the sketch a number of times as it is written, it will insert three rows at the end of the file each time the sketch is initialized. This is because you placed sample calls to record_sample() in the setup() method for debugging purposes. These calls would naturally be placed in the loop() method after you read your sensors. Listing 5-3 shows an example of the file contents after running the sketch (starting the Arduino) four times.

Listing 5-3. Example Sensor File Contents

```
6/29/2013 19:43:56 1
6/29/2013 19:43:56 2
6/29/2013 19:43:56 3
6/29/2013 19:46:54 1
6/29/2013 19:46:54 2
6/29/2013 19:46:54 3
6/29/2013 19:47:18 1
6/29/2013 19:47:18 2
```

```
6/29/2013 19:47:18 3
6/29/2013 19:47:19 1
6/29/2013 19:47:19 2
6/29/2013 19:47:19 3
```

If you examine the file and find more sets of entries than you expect, try deleting the data from the file, starting your Arduino, and then pressing the Reset button twice. When you look at the contents, you should see exactly three sets of entries (one for the initial start because the sketch was in memory to begin with, and once for each time you restarted the Arduino).

If you see only partial sets (fewer than three rows for each set), check to ensure that you are allowing the Arduino to start before powering it off. It is best to use the serial monitor and wait until all three statements are echoed to the monitor before shutting down the Arduino.

Should the case arise that your sketch compiles and no errors are shown in the serial monitor but the data file is empty, check to make sure the card is usable and not corrupt. Try reformatting the card with the FAT file format.

HANDLE WITH CARE

MicroSD cards are very fragile. They can be damaged easily if handled improperly or subjected to ESD or magnetic fields. If your card does not work properly and you cannot reformat it, it is possible that it is damaged beyond use. You can try using a formatting program from `sdcard.org`, but if it fails, your card is no longer viable. So far, this has happened to me only once.

Now that you have examined two primary methods for storing data locally on an Arduino, let's look at the options available for the Raspberry Pi.

Local Storage Options for the Raspberry Pi

Because the Raspberry Pi is a personal computer, it has the capability to create, read, and write files. Although it may be possible to use an EEPROM connected via the GPIO header, why would you do that? Given the ease of programming and the convenience of using files, there is very little need for another form of storage.

You also know the Raspberry Pi can be programmed in a number of ways and with one of the most popular languages, Python.[4] Working with files in Python is very easy and is native to the default libraries. This means there is nothing that you need to add to use files.

The following project demonstrates the ease of working with files in Python. The online Python documentation explains reading and writing files in detail (`http://docs.python.org/2/tutorial/inputoutput.html#reading-and-writing-files`).

One thing you will notice is that it doesn't matters where the file is located—on the SD card or an attached USB drive. You only need know the path to the location (folder) where you want to store data and pass that to the `open()` method.

Savvy Python programmers[5] know that the Python library contains additional libraries and classes for manipulating folders, navigating paths, and much more. For more information, examine the Python documentation for the OS and Sys libraries. For example, look for `normpath()` and the `Path`[6] class.

---

[4]Ni! (With apologies to Monty Python.)
[5]Called Pythonistas.
[6]A path! A path! (More apologies to Monty Python.)

Project: Writing Data to Files

This project demonstrates how easy it is to use files on the Raspberry Pi with Python. Because no additional hardware or software libraries are needed, I can skip those sections and jump directly into the code.

Start your Raspberry Pi, and log in. Open a new file with the following command (or similar):

```
nano file_io_example.py
```

You name the file with a .py extension to indicate that it is a Python script. Enter the following code in the file:

```
import datetime

my_file = open("/home/pi/sample_data.txt", "a+")
my_file.write("%s %d\n" % (datetime.datetime.now(), 101))
my_file.close()
```

In this example, you first import the datetime. You use the datetime to capture the current date and time. Next, you open the file (notice that you are using the Pi users' home directory), write a row to the file, and then close the file.

Notice the open() method. It takes two parameters—the file path and name and a mode to open the file. You use "a+" to append to the file (a) and create the file if it does not exist (+). Other values include r for reading and w for writing. Some of these can be combined: for example "rw+" creates the file if it does not exist and allows for both reading and writing data.

■ **Note** Using write mode truncates the file. For most cases in which you want to store sensor samples, you use append mode.

For each execution, you should see one row with a slightly different time value corresponding to when the script was run. To execute the file, use the following command:

```
python ./file_io_example.py
```

Go ahead and try to run the script. If you get errors, check the code and correct any syntax errors. If you encounter problems opening the file (you see I/O errors when you run the script), try checking the permissions for the folder you are using. Try running the script a number of times, and then display the contents of the file. The following shows the complete sequence of commands for this project:

```
pi$ nano file_io_example.py
pi$ python ./file_io_example.py
pi$ python ./file_io_example.py
pi$ python ./file_io_example.py
pi$ more sample_data.txt
2013-07-07 21:35:08.794776 101
2013-07-07 21:35:09.641735 101
2013-07-07 21:35:10.304823 101
```

Did you get similar results? If not, correct any errors and try again until you do. As you can see from this simple example, it is very easy to write data to files using Python on the Raspberry Pi.

Remote Storage Options

Remote storage means the data is sent to another node or system for recording. This normally requires some form of communication or network connectivity to the remote system. Sensor networks by nature are connected and thus can take advantage of remote storage.

To give you an idea of what I am discussing, consider an Arduino sensor node with an XBee module connected to a Raspberry Pi–based node. Suppose also that you want to write your sample data to files. Rather than using an SD card on the Arduino node to store data, you could send that data to the Raspberry Pi–based node and store the data in a file there. The main motivation is that it is much easier to use files via Python on the Raspberry Pi. If you also factor in the possibility of having multiple Arduino sensor nodes with XBee modules, you can use the Raspberry Pi–based node as a data aggregate, storing all the data in a single file.

SINGLE FILE OR MULTIPLE FILES?

I sometimes get this question when discussing storing aggregate data. If your data is similar (for example, temperature), you can consider storing data from like sensors to the same file. However, if the data differs (such as temperature from one node and humidity from another), you should consider using different files. This makes reading the files easier because you don't have to write code (or use tools) to separate the data.

But are you really talking about only storing data in files? The answer is no. There are a number of mechanisms for storing data remotely. Although storing data in files is the easiest form, you can also store data in the cloud or even on a remote database server.

If you are experienced with using databases for storing and retrieving data, this method will appeal to you—especially if you plan to use other tools to process the data later. For example, you may want to perform statistical analyses or create charts that track the samples over time. Because working with databases is a complex topic, I examine this form of remote storage in the next couple of chapters.

You have already seen how easy it is to use files, but what about storing data in the cloud? What is that about? Simply stated, storing data in the cloud involves using a cloud-based data storage service to receive your data and host it in some way. The most popular form presents the data for others on the Internet to view or consume for their own use.

The following section discusses storing sample data in the cloud using a popular cloud-based data-hosting service named Xively (https://xively.com/). Storing data in this manner is a key element in the concept of the Internet of Things (http://en.wikipedia.org/wiki/Internet_of_Things). You see example projects for using Xively on both the Arduino and the Raspberry Pi.

Storing Data in the Cloud

Unless you live in a very isolated location, you have likely been bombarded with talk about the cloud. Perhaps you've seen advertisements in magazines and on television, or read about it in other books, or attended a seminar or conference. Unless you've spent time learning what *cloud* means, you are probably wondering what all the fuss is about.

Simply stated,[7] the *cloud* is a name tagged to services available via the Internet. These can be servers you can access (running as a virtual machine on a larger server), systems that provide access to a specific software or environment, or resources such as disks or IP addresses that you can attach to other resources. The technologies behind the cloud include grid computing (distributed processing), virtualization, and networking. The correct scientific term is *cloud computing*. Although a deep dive into cloud computing is beyond the scope of this book, it is enough to understand that you can use cloud computing services to store your sensor data. In this case, you can use Xively.

---

[7]Experienced cloud researchers will tell you there is a lot more to learn about the cloud.

▪ **Tip** Don't believe all the hype or sales talk about any product that includes "cloud" in its name. Cloud computing services and resources should be accessible via the Internet from anywhere, available to you via subscription (fee or for free), and permit you to consume or produce and share the data involved. Also, consider the fact that you must have access to the cloud to get to your data. Thus, you have no alternative if the service is unreachable (or down).

Xively provides a host of *platform as a service* products for use with Internet of Things projects. One of those products is the ability to store data and provide trend views of the data. That is, you can upload data to Xively and see a graph that plots the values over time. For sensor networks, this means you can see changes in samples visually. For example, if you were to plot temperature readings taken over the course of a week, you could spot a shift in the values by seeing a dip or spike in the line graph.

Although Xively offers a number of products available via paid subscription, there is a free access level (called a developer account) that permits users to store data for a limited time. Currently, data is saved for a maximum of 30 days, and you can connect up to 5 devices. Complete details about a developer account are listed on the Xively account information page (`https://xively.com/pricing/#developer-account`).

WHAT ABOUT PACHUBE OR COSM?

If you have read about a product and service called Pachube (pronounced patch bay) or one called Cosm that sounds a lot like Xively, there is a good reason for this. Xively is the new name for Cosm, which was once named Pachube. In the fast-paced world of startups and Internet technology, name and ownership or custodial changes are not uncommon.

Any books or references to these earlier names are not entirely out of date and may still be useful to read to get ideas on what type of data to host and present. For example, the latest Arduino IDE has example projects for Pachube that are still relevant.

Xively works via an application programming interface (API). Xively provides API libraries for a wide range of platforms including the Arduino and Python. You use the Python library for your Raspberry Pi.

The API permits you to connect to your Xively account via a special access (called an *API key*—discussed shortly) and save data to a specific location (called a *channel*). You can then log in to your Xively account and view the stored data.

The following section provides a quick walkthrough for getting up and running with Xively. Xively also provides a guided tour of using its services with greater detail about the concepts and things you can access. After you complete the next section, it may be helpful to view the 10-minute test drive (`https://xively.com/testdrive/`) to reinforce the concepts.

Getting Started with Xively

To use Xively, you must first sign up for a developer's account. Go to `https://xively.com/signup/` and fill in the form, including a desired username and your e-mail address; choose a password; and complete a short questionnaire (your name and zip code are mandatory). Then click Sign Up.

You must wait to log in until you have received an e-mail from Xively to activate your account. Click the link in the e-mail and log in, and you are taken to the developer home page and asked to add a device. Click Add Device. The form is shown in Figure 5-8.

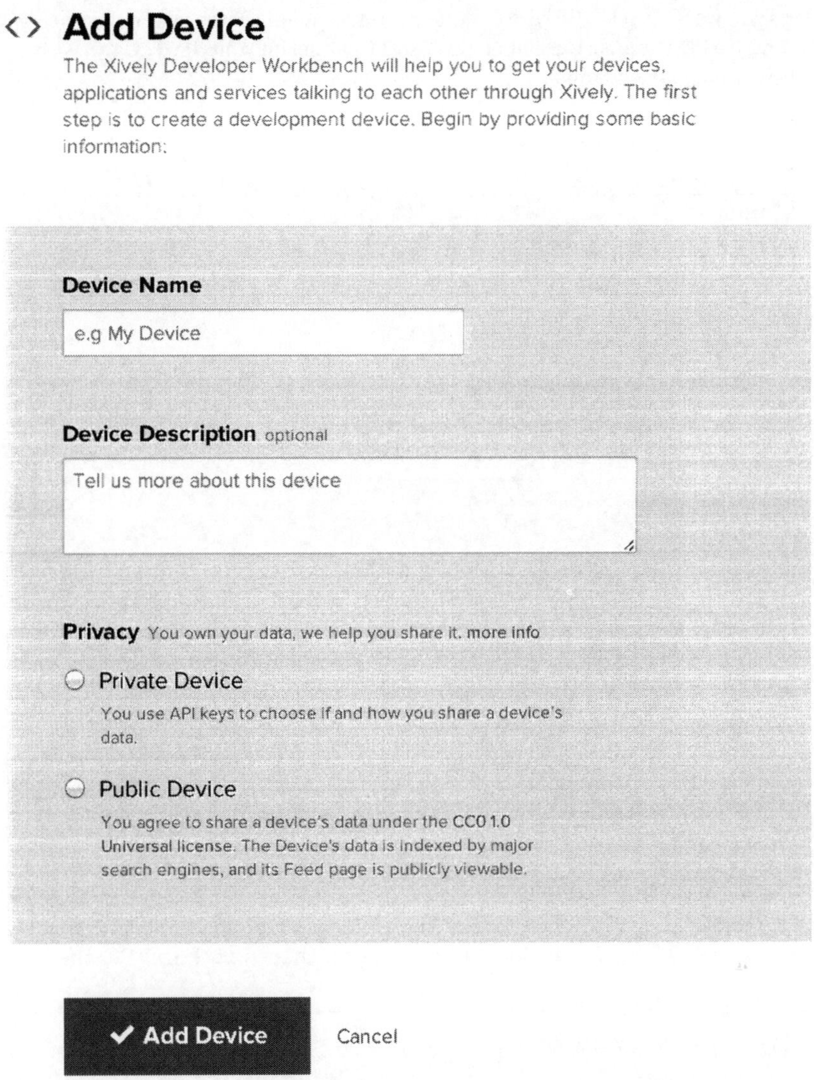

‹› **Add Device**

The Xively Developer Workbench will help you to get your devices, applications and services talking to each other through Xively. The first step is to create a development device. Begin by providing some basic information:

Device Name

```
e.g My Device
```

Device Description optional

```
Tell us more about this device
```

Privacy You own your data, we help you share it. more info

○ Private Device
   You use API keys to choose if and how you share a device's data.

○ Public Device
   You agree to share a device's data under the CC0 1.0 Universal license. The Device's data is indexed by major search engines, and its Feed page is publicly viewable.

✔ Add Device   Cancel

Figure 5-8. Adding a device for Xively

Enter a name for the device (for example, Arduino Sensor #1) and a description, and choose whether to make the device public (viewable by all) or private, which requires the use of special API keys. You should choose the private option for use with the projects in this book. API keys are created automatically, as you see after you enter the data for the device. When you have finished entering the data and choosing the access level, click Add Device. Go ahead and set up another device for a Raspberry Pi. Hint: click Develop on the menu at the top, and then click Add Device.

You also have a specific feed number for each device you create. This number is located near the top of the device home page. You need this number together with your API key to send data to the specific device on your account. Take a moment to note both the feed number and API key for your device. You use these in the example projects that follow.

When you create a device, you see options for creating channels. *Channels* are containers for the data you will upload. Each channel is a set of data plotted on a line graph. For sensor networks and the example projects that follow, you use one channel for each sensor sample. For example, you use one channel to record temperature in Celsius and another to record temperature in Fahrenheit.

You can create as many channels as you want or need. Be sure to note the exact spelling of the channel name, because you need it when you use the Xively API. To create a channel, click Add Channel on your device page. Figure 5-9 shows the small form for entering data for a channel.

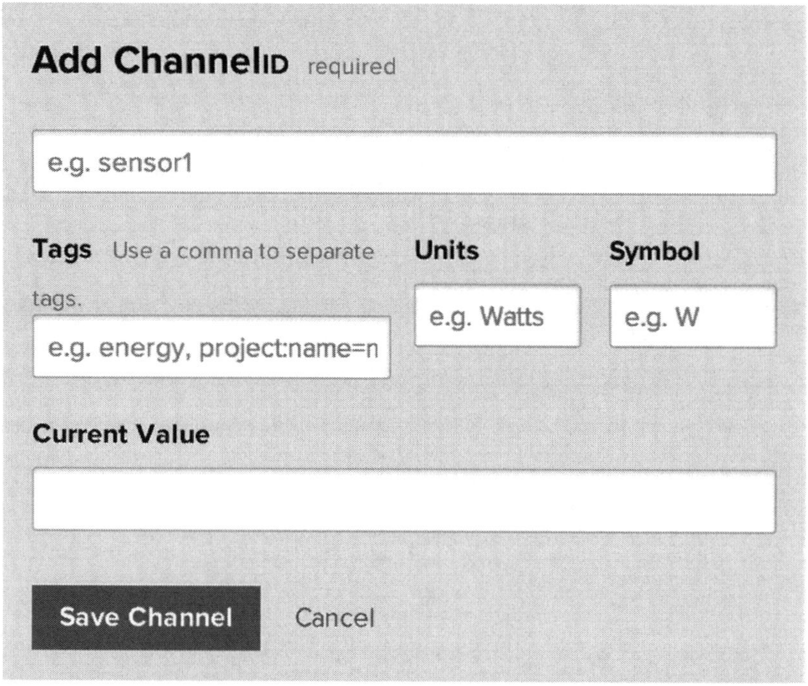

Figure 5-9. *Adding a channel to a device*

Enter a name for the channel, one or more tags separated by a comma (used for searching), and an optional unit of measure and symbol. You can also set a baseline value for the channel. Once this data is entered, click Save Channel.

■ **Note**   A device hosted on Xively is called a *feed*. The Xively API also refers to a feed's channel as a *datastream*.

That's all you need to do to get started with Xively (at least, the barest of steps), but there is much more to Xively than setting up devices and channels. Be sure to view the 10-minute tour of Xively if you haven't already.

Now that you have a Xively developer's account and have set up your Arduino and Raspberry Pi devices, let's explore how to use the Xively API.

Using the Xively API

Writing data to Xively is accomplished using a platform-specific library. Fortunately, there are libraries for the Arduino and the Raspberry Pi (via Python). Although it is possible to read and write data to and from a Xively feed, this section explores how to write (store) data. You can learn how to read data as an exercise, should you desire to use Xively as a temporary data store for later processing of the data.

The steps to write data to a Xively feed include the following. Although each of these is done slightly differently for each platform-specific library API, the flow is the same:

1. Store your feed ID and API key. You store these as either constants or strings for use in connecting to Xively.

2. Create an array of datastreams, and name each one. These identify the channels for the feed to which you write data. You store each datastream (channel) as a separate element.

3. Make a connection to Xively for a specific feed. Connect to the Xively service, and prepare a protocol connection for communicating with the server.

4. Write data to the feed. Send the data for storing and presenting the trend graph(s).

The code to do these steps for the Arduino for the first Xively project is as follows. I left out some of the finer details for brevity:

```
#include <Xively.h>

char xivelyKey[] = "<YOUR_KEY_HERE>";
#define FEED_NUMBER <YOUR_FEED_HERE>
char sensor1_name[] = "celsius";
char sensor2_name[] = "fahrenheit";
XivelyDatastream datastreams[] = {
  XivelyDatastream(sensor1_name, strlen(sensor1_name), DATASTREAM_FLOAT),
  XivelyDatastream(sensor2_name, strlen(sensor2_name), DATASTREAM_FLOAT),
};
XivelyFeed feed(FEED_NUMBER, datastreams, 2 /* number of datastreams */);
XivelyClient xivelyclient(...);
int ret = xivelyclient.put(feed, xivelyKey);
```

The code to do these steps in Python for the Raspberry Pi example project is as follows:

```
import xively

XIVELY_API_KEY = "<YOUR_KEY_HERE>"
XIVELY_FEED_ID = <YOUR_FEED_HERE>
api = xively.XivelyAPIClient(XIVELY_API_KEY)
feed = api.feeds.get(XIVELY_FEED_ID)
feed.datastreams = [
    xively.Datastream(id='celsius', current_value=tempc, ...),
    xively.Datastream(id='fahrenheit', current_value=tempf, ...),
]
feed.update()
```

Now that you understand the basics of writing data to Xively, let's take a look at how to do it in more detail for the Arduino. This is followed by an example for the Raspberry Pi.

Project: Writing Data to Xively with an Arduino

This project demonstrates how to write sensor data to a Xively device. Unlike the previous projects in this chapter, you use a sensor and generate some samples. In this case, you monitor temperature and save the Celsius and Fahrenheit values to channels on your Xively Arduino device. If you have not yet created a Xively device for the Arduino, do that now and record the feed ID and API key generated.

Hardware Setup

The hardware for this project is an Arduino with an Arduino Ethernet shield (or compatible), a network cable, a breadboard, breadboard wires, a TMP36 temperature sensor, and a 0.10uF capacitor. Wire the sensor and the capacitor as shown in Figure 5-10. Attach pin 1 of the sensor to the 5V pin on the Arduino, pin 2 of the sensor to the A0 pin on the Arduino, and pin 3 to ground on the Arduino. The capacitor is also attached to pins 1 and 3 of the sensor (orientation does not matter).

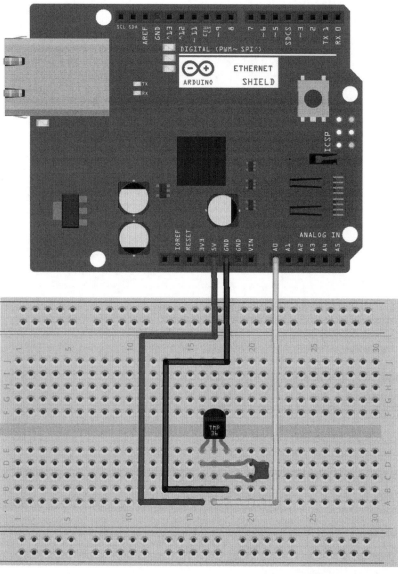

Made with **Fritzing.org**

Figure 5-10. *Wiring setup for the Xively temperature feed for the Arduino*

To use the Ethernet shield, you need to connect it via a network cable to a viable network connection via a router or switch. Check the link indicators on the networking device to make sure the device detects the Ethernet shield (you may need to turn on the Arduino, because some networking devices require the end device to be powered).

▪ **Tip**   If you are not certain that the networking device is working or your cable is viable, try connecting a laptop or similar device. If you can establish connectivity with your laptop, the Arduino Ethernet shield will also work correctly (once set up in the sketch).

Software Setup

The software needed for this project consists of the Xively library for the Arduino and a special HTTP client. You see how to obtain these libraries and take a short walkthrough of the code needed to communicate and store your sensor data in Xively. You saw a TMP36 sensor used with an Arduino in Chapter 3, and the code needed to read samples is the same. I leave the explanation of this code for you to explore in Listing 5-4.

You can download the Xively API Arduino library from `https://github.com/xively/xively_arduino`. Uncompress this folder, rename it `Xively` (or similar), and place it in your `Arduino/Libraries` folder. You can download the HTTP client from `https://github.com/amcewen/HttpClient`. Uncompress this folder, rename it `HttpClient` (or similar), and place it in your `Arduino/Libraries` folder.

▪ **Tip**   Be sure to restart the Arduino IDE if it was running when you copied the folders.

Now that you have the necessary libraries downloaded and copied, open a new Arduino project and name it Arduino_Xively. Start the file with the following `includes`. You need the SPI and Ethernet headers for the Ethernet card. The Xively library uses the HTTPClient header. Finally, you include the Xively header:

```
#include <SPI.h>
#include <Ethernet.h>
#include <HttpClient.h>
#include <Xively.h>
```

To use the Ethernet shield, you must also declare a MAC address. The IP address for the Ethernet shield is requested via DHCP. You define the MAC address as an array. This can be a random set of values, provided they are in the range 0x00–0xFF. You can use what is shown here:

```
byte mac_addr[] = { 0xDE, 0xAD, 0xBE, 0xEF, 0xFE, 0xED };
```

Next you define your Xively API key and feed ID. You also define the pin number for your TMP36 sensor. This example uses pin 0. You can choose whatever pin you want to use—just change this `define`, and the rest of the code will point to the correct pin:

```
char xivelyKey[] = "<YOUR_KEY_HERE>";
#define FEED_NUMBER <YOUR_FEED_HERE>
#define SENSOR_PIN 0
```

Recall that when I discussed how to use the Xively library, I said that you need to set up an array for your feed with each channel (also called a datastream) in its own element. In this project, you need two elements: one for temperature values in Celsius and another in Fahrenheit. Notice the names used in the following code. These names must match those defined as channels for your device on Xively. Spelling counts, so make sure they match what you defined in Xively:

```
char sensor1_name[] = "celsius";
char sensor2_name[] = "fahrenheit";
XivelyDatastream datastreams[] = {
  XivelyDatastream(sensor1_name, strlen(sensor1_name), DATASTREAM_FLOAT),
  XivelyDatastream(sensor2_name, strlen(sensor2_name), DATASTREAM_FLOAT),
};
```

Recall also that you must define an instance of the feed class initializing the class with your feed number, the array of datastreams (channels), and the number of datastreams. Following that, you need to create an instance of the EthernetClient class from the HTTPClient library and pass that to a new instance of the XivelyClient class. The following statements effect these implementations:

```
XivelyFeed feed(FEED_NUMBER, datastreams, 2 /* number of datastreams */);
EthernetClient client;
XivelyClient xivelyclient(client);
```

You create a method to read the sensor and return the temperature in Celsius and Fahrenheit. Name the method get_temperature(), and use the code from Chapter 3 to complete it. I leave this as an exercise for you but include the correct solution in a moment.

As in the previous projects, you also need a record_sample() method that writes the samples to Xively. Create a new method, and complete it as follows. Notice that here you call the put() method for the Xively client to send the samples to Xively. You need only pass an instance of your feed and your API key. That's it—it's that easy:

```
void record_sample(float tempc, float tempf) {
  datastreams[0].setFloat(tempc);
  datastreams[1].setFloat(tempf);

  Serial.print("Uploading to Xively ... ");
  int ret = xivelyclient.put(feed, xivelyKey);
  Serial.print("done. Return code = ");
  Serial.println(ret);

  // Wait for data upload
  delay(15000);
}
```

Two important steps are needed for the setup() method. You must initialize the serial class (so you can use the serial monitor) and initialize the Ethernet client. You use the begin() method for each of these operations. The Ethernet client class accepts a number of parameters, but in this case you need only the MAC address. See the Arduino documentation for additional parameters you can use, including passing a static IP address.

For the Ethernet class, you place the call to initialize the client in a loop with a one-second delay. If the call fails, it prints a warning and waits one second before trying again. If you encounter a situation where this occurs more than a couple of times or it never exits the loop, check to make sure you have plugged your Ethernet shield into a working network connection (connected to a router or switch).

The complete setup() method is as follows:

```
void setup() {
  Serial.begin(9600);
  delay (5000); // Give time to connect to serial monitor
  Serial.println("Starting cloud data upload.");

  while (!Ethernet.begin(mac_addr)) {
    Serial.println("Error starting Ethernet, trying again.");
    delay(1000);
  }
}
```

Finally, the loop() method contains a simplified set of operations as shown next. You merely call your get_temperature() method to get the temperature values and then call the record_sample() method to write the values to Xively. Keeping the loop() method short and high-level makes it easier to debug or add new samples:

```
void loop() {
  float temp_celsius;
  float temp_fahrenheit;

  // read and record sensor data
  get_temperature(&temp_celsius, &temp_fahrenheit);
  record_sample(temp_celsius, temp_fahrenheit);
}
```

Now that you understand the flow and contents of the sketch, you can complete the missing pieces and start testing. Listing 5-4 shows the complete sketch for this project.

Listing 5-4. Arduino-Based Xively Feed

```
/**
  Sensor Networks Example Arduino Xively Cloud Storage

  This project demonstrates how to save sensor data to an Xively feed.
*/

#include <SPI.h>
#include <Ethernet.h>
#include <HttpClient.h>
#include <Xively.h>

// Ethernet shield Mac address
byte mac_addr[] = { 0xDE, 0xAD, 0xBE, 0xEF, 0xFE, 0xED };

// Your Xively key
char xivelyKey[] = "<YOUR_KEY_HERE>";

// Your feed number
#define FEED_NUMBER <YOUR_FEED_HERE>

// Pin number for TMP36
#define SENSOR_PIN 0
```

```
// Define the strings for your datastream IDs
char sensor1_name[] = "celsius";
char sensor2_name[] = "fahrenheit";
XivelyDatastream datastreams[] = {
  XivelyDatastream(sensor1_name, strlen(sensor1_name), DATASTREAM_FLOAT),
  XivelyDatastream(sensor2_name, strlen(sensor2_name), DATASTREAM_FLOAT),
};

// Finally, wrap the datastreams into a feed
XivelyFeed feed(FEED_NUMBER, datastreams, 2 /* number of datastreams */);

EthernetClient client;
XivelyClient xivelyclient(client);

void get_temperature(float *tempc, float *tempf) {
  int adc_data = analogRead(SENSOR_PIN);

  Serial.print("Temperature is ");
  *tempc = ((adc_data * 1200.0 / 1024.0) - 500.0) / 10.0;
  Serial.print(*tempc);
  Serial.print("c, ");
  *tempf = ((*tempc * 9.0)/5.0) + 32.0;
  Serial.print(*tempf);
  Serial.println("f");

  // wait for 1 second
  delay(1000);
}

void record_sample(float tempc, float tempf) {
  datastreams[0].setFloat(tempc);
  datastreams[1].setFloat(tempf);

  Serial.print("Uploading to Xively ... ");
  int ret = xivelyclient.put(feed, xivelyKey);
  Serial.print("done. Return code = ");
  Serial.println(ret);

  // Wait for data upload
  delay(15000);
}

void setup() {
  Serial.begin(9600);
  delay (5000); // Give time to connect to serial monitor

  Serial.println("Starting cloud data upload.");

  while (!Ethernet.begin(mac_addr)) {
    Serial.println("Error starting Ethernet, trying again.");
    delay(1000);
  }
}
```

```
void loop() {
  float temp_celsius;
  float temp_fahrenheit;

  // read and record sensor data
  get_temperature(&temp_celsius, &temp_fahrenheit);
  record_sample(temp_celsius, temp_fahrenheit);
}
```

■ **Note**   Be sure to substitute your API key and feed number in the locations marked. Failure to do so will result in compilation errors.

Take some time to make sure you have all the code entered correctly and that the sketch compiles without errors. Once you reach this stage, you can upload the sketch and try it out.

Testing the Sketch

To test the sketch, be sure the code compiles and you have your hardware set up correctly. Once you have a sketch that compiles, upload it to your Arduino and launch a serial monitor. Figure 5-11 shows an example of the output you should see.

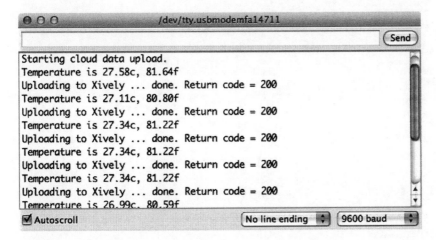

Figure 5-11. Sample serial monitor output

Did you see similar output? If you did not, check the return code as displayed in the serial monitor. You should be seeing a return code of 200 (meaning success). If the return code was a single digit (1, 2, 3, and so on), you are likely encountering issues connecting to Xively. If this occurs, connect your laptop to the same network cable, and try to access Xively.

■ **Tip**   You can find a complete list of Xively return codes at https://xively.com/dev/docs/api/communicating/http/http_status_codes/.

If the connection is very slow, you could encounter a situation in which you get an error code other than 200 every other or every N attempts. If this is the case, you can increase the timeout in the loop() method to delay processing further. This may help for some very slow connections, but it is not a cure for a bad or intermittent connection.

Let the sketch run for 15–30 minutes before you visit Xively. Once the sketch has run for some time, navigate to Xively, log in, and click your device page. You should see results similar to those shown in Figure 5-12. Notice the peak near the end of the graph. I simulated a drop and spike in the data by pressing a cold object (a spoon that had been in the freezer) on the sensor, followed by a warm device (my finger).

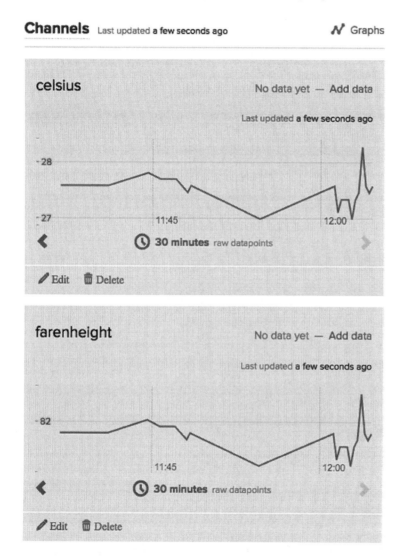

Figure 5-12. *Sample Xively feed for an Arduino*

If all is working for you and you see output similar to that shown in Figures 5-11 and 5-12, congratulations: you've just created data in the cloud!

For More Fun

You can have a lot of fun with this script. Try connecting other sensors and creating other channels for them on your device in Xively. You can also experiment with reading the data you saved in Xively.

Now that you know how to save data to Xively on the Arduino, let's explore how to do the same on the Raspberry Pi.

Project: Writing Data to Xively with a Raspberry Pi

This project demonstrates the ease of using the Xively Python library on the Raspberry Pi. You create the same sensor node as in the last project, but on a Raspberry Pi instead of an Arduino. If you have not completed the last project, take some time to read through it so the concepts introduced are familiar in this project.

You will use a Python script to read data from an analog temperature sensor (TMP36) and record it to your Xively feed. Recall that the Raspberry Pi does not have any analog to digital converters (ADCs), so you have to use a special module to add that functionality. In this case, you use an I2C module that provides 12-bit precision for reading values. You can use a more precise module (for example, 16-bit precision) if you cannot obtain the ADC module mentioned in the next section or have a different version already.

Hardware Setup

The hardware for this project consists of a Raspberry Pi, a Raspberry Pi breakout connector, a breadboard, the TMP36 sensor, a 0.10uF capacitor, jumper wires, and an ADC module.

I mentioned the Raspberry Pi does not include any ADCs, so you cannot use an analog sensor. In this project, you explore how to use a multichannel ADC with the Raspberry Pi to enable the use of the TMP36 analog temperature sensor. Figure 5-13 shows the 12-bit ADC from Adafruit (www.adafruit.com/products/1083). This module supports up to four sensors (channels). In the figure, you can see pins A0–A3; these are the pins used for each of the channels supported.

Figure 5-13. 12-Bit ADC module (courtesy of Adafruit)

■ **Tip**   You are exploring the use of the ADC module with a Raspberry Pi, because it supports the I2C protocol, but you can use the module with the Arduino too. See `http://learn.adafruit.com/adafruit-4-channel-adc-breakouts` for more details.

You also require connectivity to the Internet via a network connection on the Raspberry Pi. The Internet connection can be via a wired Ethernet connection or via a wireless connection. There are no specific requirements for connectivity as there are with an Arduino.

The ADC module is wired as follows (see Figure 5-14). Connect the VDD pin on the ADC module to the 5V pin on the Raspberry Pi breakout connector. Connect the GND pin on the ADC module to the GND pin on the Raspberry Pi breakout connector. Connect the SCL pin on the ADC module to the SCL pin on the Raspberry Pi breakout connector. Connect the SDA pin on the ADC module to the SDA pin on the Raspberry Pi breakout connector.

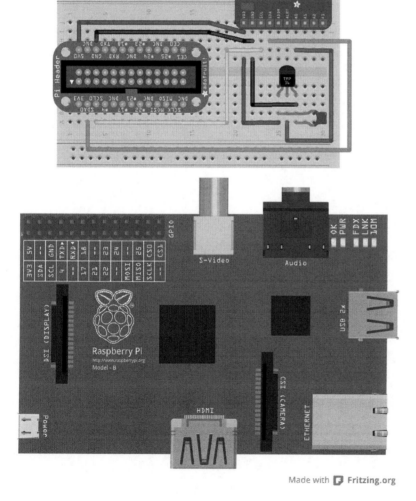

Figure 5-14.   *Wiring the TMP36 and ADC to the Raspberry Pi*

Connect the TMP36 sensor as follows (again, see Figure 5-14). Connect pin 1 to the same 5V connection as the ADC module and pin 3 to the GND connection on the ADC module. Pin 2 on the sensor connects to the A0 pin on the ADC module. Finally, connect the 0.10uF capacitor to pins 1 and 3 on the sensor. Orientation does not matter.

■ **Caution**   Be sure to double-check your connections and compare them to Figure 5-14. Failure to connect things properly on the Raspberry Pi can lead to a damaged board.

Once you have made these connections, power on your Raspberry Pi and issue the following command

```
$ sudo i2cdetect -y 0
```

You should see the ADC module appear as address 0x48 in the output, as shown in Figure 5-15.

```
pi@raspberrypi ~ $ sudo i2cdetect -y 0
     0  1  2  3  4  5  6  7  8  9  a  b  c  d  e  f
00:          -- -- -- -- -- -- -- -- -- -- -- -- --
10: -- -- -- -- -- -- -- -- -- -- -- -- -- -- -- --
20: -- -- -- -- -- -- -- -- -- -- -- -- -- -- -- --
30: -- -- -- -- -- -- -- -- -- -- -- -- -- -- -- --
40: -- -- -- -- -- -- -- -- 48 -- -- -- -- -- -- --
50: -- -- -- -- -- -- -- -- -- -- -- -- -- -- -- --
60: -- -- -- -- -- -- -- -- -- -- -- -- -- -- -- --
70: -- -- -- -- -- -- -- --
pi@raspberrypi ~ $
```

Figure 5-15. *Verifying the ADC module*

Software Setup

The software needed for this project includes the Xively Python library, the Python setup tools library, and the Adafruit Python library that you used in Chapter 04. Issue the following commands to install the Xively library for Raspberry Pi (https://github.com/xively/xively-python) and install it so that it is accessible via any Python script:

```
wget https://github.com/xively/xively-python/archive/master.zip
unzip master.zip
cd xively-python-master
sudo python ./setup.py install
```

You can also download the library by using a web browser, navigating to https://github.com/xively/xively-python, and clicking the Download Zip button.

Although several blogs and tutorials on using the Python Xively library do not mention it, I found that I needed to install the Python setup tools library before I could use the Xively library. To do this (if you haven't already), issue the following command:

```
sudo apt-get install python-setuptools
```

Recall from Chapter 4 that the Python library from Adafruit is available from GitHub. To download the module and install it, see the section entitled "Project: Building a Raspberry Barometric Pressure Sensor Node." I assume this library is placed in your home folder.

Now that you have the libraries you need, it is time to write a script to read samples from a TMP36 sensor (via the ADC module) and save data to Xively. To make things easier, you will create the Python script in the same folder as the Python library from Adafruit. If you have installed this library on your system and it is accessible via the Python path environment variable, you can place the new script anywhere you like. The following commands navigate to the desired folder and open an editor to enter the statements for the script:

```
cd ~/Adafruit-Raspberry-Pi-Python-Code
cd Adafruit_ADS1x15
nano raspi_xively.py
```

Because the code for this project is logically the same as the previous project (other than the fact that one is for the Arduino and the other is for Python), I focus only on the specific differences: the use of the ADC module and the handling of the main method for the script. I leave the exploration of the common elements as an exercise. These include connecting to Xively, reading samples from the sensor, and outputting diagnostic statements.

You begin by adding the statements to import the libraries you need. In this case, you need the datetime, sys, time, and Xively libraries. You also import the ADS1x15 library code from the Adafruit Python code:

```
import datetime
import sys
import time
import xively

from Adafruit_ADS1x15 import ADS1x15
```

Next, you need to work with the ADS module. The following statements identify the address of the module (0x00 by default) and create an instance of the ADS1x15 class:

```
ADS1015 = 0x00  # 12-bit A/D Converter
adc = ADS1x15(ic=ADS1015)
```

To read a value from the ADC module, you use the following method. Here you read a single element (value) on pin 0 with a maximum value of 5 volts and a sample rate (accuracy) of 500. You use this method in the get_temperature() method to read the sensor samples:

```
volts = adc.readADCSingleEnded(0, 5000, 500)
```

The last thing you need is a special construct of Python scripts. The following code defines a main() method. Up until this point in the script, nothing has been defined as code to run when the script is loaded. The main() method is analogous to the loop() method in an Arduino sketch. In this case, you do the same operations—read samples and record them in Xively:

```
def main():
    print "Starting cloud data upload."
    while True:
        tempc, tempf = get_temperature()
        record_samples(tempc, tempf)
```

The next section of code defines a gate (if statement) that runs if the script file is loaded via the Python interpreter. It wraps the call to main() in an exception loop that you can exit using the Ctrl+C key sequence. In this case, the exception KeyboardInterrupt is captured and the script ends (pass is executed as the last statement):

```python
if __name__ == '__main__':
    try:
        args = sys.argv[1:]
        main(*args)
    except KeyboardInterrupt:
        pass
```

This is a good trick to know because it has a second purpose. It permits other scripts to include the script (import it) and reuse its methods but does not execute the main() method. This is because the __name__ would be something other than __main__. In this way, you can make the code reusable without having the main method execute.

Listing 5-5 shows the complete code for the script for this project. Be sure to double-check all the code you've entered thus far and compare your solutions for record_sample() and get_temperature() to ensure that they both will work.

Listing 5-5. Complete Code for the **raspi_xively.py** Script

```python
#
# Sensor Networks Example Raspberry Pi Xively Cloud Storage
#
# This project demonstrates how to save sensor data to an Xively feed.
# Requires the use of a A/D converter. Specifically, the ADC1015 from
# Adafruit (http://www.adafruit.com/products/1083).
#
import datetime
import sys
import time
import xively

from Adafruit_ADS1x15 import ADS1x15

XIVELY_API_KEY = "<YOUR_KEY_HERE>"
XIVELY_FEED_ID = <YOUR_FEED_HERE>

ADS1015 = 0x00  # 12-bit A/D Converter

# Set the ADC using the default mode (use default I2C address)
adc = ADS1x15(ic=ADS1015)

def get_temperature():
    # Read channel 0 in single-ended mode, +/- 5V, 500 sps
    volts = adc.readADCSingleEnded(0, 5000, 500)

    tempc = (((float(volts)*1200.0)/1024.0)-500.0)/10.0
    tempf = ((tempc *9.0)/5.0)+32.0

    print "Samples generated: celsius: %f" % tempc,
    print "fahrenheit: %f" % tempf

    return (tempc, tempf)
```

185

```python
def record_samples(tempc, tempf):
    api = xively.XivelyAPIClient(XIVELY_API_KEY)
    feed = api.feeds.get(XIVELY_FEED_ID)
    now = datetime.datetime.now()
    print "Uploading to Xively ...",
    feed.datastreams = [
        xively.Datastream(id='celsius', current_value=tempc, at=now),
        xively.Datastream(id='fahrenheit', current_value=tempf, at=now),
    ]
    feed.update()
    print "done."
    time.sleep(5)

def main():
    print "Starting cloud data upload."
    while True:
        tempc, tempf = get_temperature()
        record_samples(tempc, tempf)

if __name__ == '__main__':
    try:
        args = sys.argv[1:]
        main(*args)
    except KeyboardInterrupt:
        pass
```

■ **Note**   Be sure to substitute your API key and feed number in the locations marked. Failure to do so will result in runtime errors.

Now that you have all the code entered, let's test the script and see if it works.

Testing the Script

Python scripts are interpreted programs. Although there is a fair amount of syntax checking at the start of a script, logic errors are not discovered until the statement is executed. Thus, you may encounter errors or exceptions if the script was not entered correctly (for example, if you misspelled a method or variable name). This may also happen if you failed to replace the placeholder for the API key and feed number.

To run the script, enter the following command. Let the script run for several iterations before using Ctrl+C to break the main loop. Figure 5-16 shows an example of the output you should see:

```
python ./raspi_xively.py
```

```
pi@raspberrypi ~/Adafruit-Raspberry-Pi-Python-Code/Adafruit_ADS1x15 $ python ./raspi_xively.py
Starting cloud data upload.
Samples generated: celsius: 21.239471 farenheight: 70.231049
Uploading to Xively ... done.
Samples generated: celsius: 22.383881 farenheight: 72.290985
Uploading to Xively ... done.
Samples generated: celsius: 22.097778 farenheight: 71.776001
Uploading to Xively ... done.
Samples generated: celsius: 21.811676 farenheight: 71.261017
-
```

Figure 5-16. *Sample output from the **raspi_xively.py** script*

Let the script run for 15–30 seconds, and then navigate to your Raspberry Pi device page on Xively. You should see your sensor data displayed, similar to that shown in Figure 5-17.

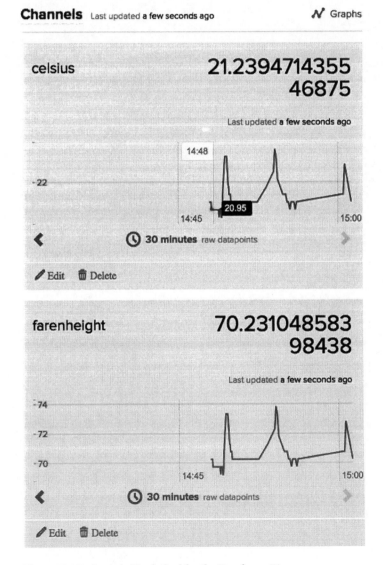

Figure 5-17. *Sample Xively feed for the Raspberry Pi*

If you do not see similar data, go back and check the return codes as discussed in the last project. You should see return codes of 200 (success). Check and correct any errors in network connectivity or syntax or logic errors in your script until it runs successfully for several iterations (all samples stored return code 200). If there are no errors but your data is still not displaying in the graph, check your time zone in your Xively profile. If the time zone is not set or is set incorrectly, the time in the chart will not match your local time, and thus the data will not be visible.

If you see similar data, congratulations! You now know how to generate data and save it to the cloud using two different platforms.

For More Fun

You can have a lot of fun with this script. Try connecting other sensors and creating other channels for them on your device in Xively. You can also experiment with reading the data you saved in Xively.

Storing Sensor Data in a Database

As you may have surmised, it is possible to store sensor data to a database on a Raspberry Pi. You can use MySQL as your database server and the Connector/Python library to write Python scripts that read sensor data and store the data in tables for later processing. Because there is a lot more involved than a few dozen lines of code (like setting up MySQL on the Raspberry Pi), you explore this topic in greater detail in Chapters 6 and 7.

Component Shopping List

A number of components are needed to complete the projects in this chapter, as listed in Table 5-2. Some of them, like the XBee modules and supporting hardware, are also included in the shopping list from other chapters. These are shown in Table 5-3.

Table 5-2. *Components Needed*

Tem	Vendors	Est. Cost USD	Qty Needed
I2C EEPROM	www.sparkfun.com/products/525	$1.95	1
Arduino Ethernet Shield	www.sparkfun.com/products/9026	$45.95	1*
	www.adafruit.com/products/201	$45.00	*
microSD Shield	www.sparkfun.com/products/9802	$14.95	*
Data Logging shield for Arduino	www.adafruit.com/products/1141	$19.95	*
DS1307 Real Time Clock breakout board kit	www.adafruit.com/products/264	$9.00	1**
Real Time Clock module	www.sparkfun.com/products/99	$14.95	**
12-bit ADC module	www.adafruit.com/products/1083	$9.95	1

* *You need only one of these options.*
** *Either of these will work.*

Table 5-3. *Components Reused from Previous Chapters*

Item	Vendors	Est. Cost USD	Qty Needed
Pushbutton (breadboard mount)	www.sparkfun.com/products/97	$0.35	1
Breadboard (not mini)	www.sparkfun.com/products/9567	$5.95	1
Breadboard jumper wires	www.sparkfun.com/products/8431	$3.95	1
TMP36 sensor	www.sparkfun.com/products/10988	$1.50	1
	www.adafruit.com/products/165		
0.10uF capacitor	www.sparkfun.com/products/8375	$0.25	1
Raspberry Pi Model B		$35 and up	1
HDMI or HDMI to DVI cable	Most online and retail stores	varies	1
HDMI or DVI monitor	Most online and retail stores	varies	1
USB keyboard	Most online and retail stores	varies	1
USB power supply	Most online and retail stores	varies	1
USB Type A to USB micro male	Most online and retail stores	varies	1
SD card, 2GB or more	Most online and retail stores	varies	1
Raspberry Pi breakout board	www.adafruit.com/products/914	$7.95	1
Resistor (as used in EPROM project)			

Summary

This chapter explored the local storage options for the Arduino and Raspberry Pi. You completed a number of small projects demonstrating each of the possible storage options. I also discussed storing sensor data on remote systems, including how to store data using a cloud computing service named Xively.

In the next chapter, I take a break from this exploration of sensor projects and begin discussing another form of remote storage: a database server. Chapter 6 focuses on setting up a MySQL server, and Chapter 7 focuses on using the MySQL server with the Arduino via a special connector (library) written for the Arduino.

CHAPTER 6

■ ■ ■

Turning Your Raspberry Pi into a Database Server

Now that you know what sensor networks are and even how to build sensor nodes using an Arduino and a Raspberry Pi, it's time to do something really cool with your Raspberry Pi. The last chapter discussed the various ways you can store data from your sensors. One of the most reliable and the most versatile is storing your sensor data in a database. This chapter explores using a Raspberry Pi as a database server.

You begin with a short introduction to MySQL and then jump in to getting MySQL up and running on a Raspberry Pi.[1] If you have experience with installing and using MySQL, you may want to skip ahead to the "Building a Raspberry Pi MySQL Server" section.

What Is MySQL?

MySQL is the world's most popular open source database system for many excellent reasons. First and foremost, it is open source, which means anyone can use it for a wide variety of tasks for free.[2] Best of all, MySQL is included in many platform repositories, making it easy to get and install. If your platform doesn't include MySQL in the repository (such as aptitude), you can download it from the MySQL web site (http://dev.mysql.com).

Oracle Corporation owns MySQL. Oracle obtained MySQL through an acquisition of Sun Microsystems, which acquired MySQL from its original owners, MySQL AB. Despite fears to the contrary, Oracle has shown excellent stewardship of MySQL by continuing to invest in the evolution and development of new features as well as faithfully maintaining its open source heritage. Although Oracle also offers commercial licenses of MySQL—just as its prior owners did in the past—MySQL is still open source and available to everyone.

---

[1]Note that the Raspberry Pi (which uses the ARM architecture rather that x86 or SPARC) is not a supported platform for MySQL at the time of writing—but you can make it work!

[2]According to GNU (www.gnu.org/philosophy/free-sw.html), "free software is a matter of liberty, not price. To understand the concept, you should think of 'free' as in 'free speech,' not as in 'free beer.' "

```
┌─────────────────────────────────────────────────────────────────────────┐
│              WHAT IS OPEN SOURCE? IS IT REALLY FREE?                       │
└─────────────────────────────────────────────────────────────────────────┘
```

Open source software grew from a conscious resistance to the corporate-property mindset. While working for MIT, Richard Stallman, the father of the free software movement, resisted the trend of making software private (closed) and left MIT to start the GNU (GNU Not Unix) project and the Free Software Foundation (FSF).

Stallman's goal was to reestablish a cooperating community of developers. He had the foresight, however, to realize that the system needed a copyright license that guaranteed certain freedoms. (Some have called Stallman's take on copyright "copyleft," because it guarantees freedom rather than restricts it.) To solve this, Stallman created the GNU Public License (GPL). The GPL, a clever work of legal permissions that permits the code to be copied and modified without restriction, states that derivative works (the modified copies) must be distributed under the same license as the original version without any additional restrictions.

There was one problem with the free software movement. The term *free* was intended to guarantee freedom to use, modify, and distribute; it was not intended to mean "no cost" or "free to a good home." To counter this misconception, the Open Source Initiative (OSI) formed and later adopted and promoted the phrase *open source* to describe the freedoms guaranteed by the GPL license. For more information about open source software, visit www.opensource.org.

MySQL runs as a background process (or as a foreground process if you launch it from the command line[3]) on your system. Like most database systems, MySQL supports Structured Query Language (SQL). You can use SQL to create databases and objects (using data definition language [DDL]), write or change data (using data manipulation language [DML]), and execute various commands for managing the server.

To issue these commands, you must first connect to the database server. MySQL provides a client application that enables you to connect to and run commands on the server. The application is named mysql and is known as the mysql *client* (previously the mysql monitor). Note that Oracle has stopped using the older name so that it will not be confused with the MySQL Enterprise Monitor, which is a premium product provided to customers who purchase an enterprise license.

Listing 6-1 shows examples of each type of command in action using the mysql client:

Listing 6-1. Commands Using the mysql Client

```
$ mysql -uroot -pXXXX
Welcome to the MySQL monitor.  Commands end with ; or \g.
Your MySQL connection id is 4
Server version: 5.5.23-log MySQL Community Server (GPL)

Copyright (c) 2000, 2011, Oracle and/or its affiliates. All rights reserved.

Oracle is a registered trademark of Oracle Corporation and/or its
affiliates. Other names may be trademarks of their respective
owners.

Type 'help;' or '\h' for help. Type '\c' to clear the current input statement.

mysql> CREATE DATABASE testme;
Query OK, 1 row affected (0.00 sec)
```

---

[3]And use the --console command-line option on Windows systems.

```
mysql> CREATE TABLE testme.table1 (sensor_node char(30), sensor_value int, sensor_event timestamp);
Query OK, 0 rows affected (0.00 sec)

mysql> INSERT INTO testme.table1 VALUES ('living room', 23, NULL);
Query OK, 1 row affected (0.00 sec)

mysql> SELECT * FROM testme.table1;
+-------------+--------------+---------------------+
| sensor_node | sensor_value | sensor_event        |
+-------------+--------------+---------------------+
| living room |           23 | 2013-02-04 20:30:13 |
+-------------+--------------+---------------------+
1 row in set (0.00 sec)

mysql> SET @@global.server_id = 111;
Query OK, 0 rows affected (0.00 sec)

mysql>
```

In this example, you see DML in the form of the CREATE DATABASE and CREATE TABLE statements, DDL in the form of the INSERT and SELECT statements, and a simple administrative command to set a global server variable. Next you see the creation of a database and a table to store the data, the addition of a row in the table, and finally retrieval of the data in the table.

A great many commands are available in MySQL. Fortunately, you need master only a few of the more common ones. The following are the commands you will use most often. The portions enclosed in <> indicate user-supplied components of the command, and [. . .] indicates that additional options are needed:

■ **Tip** If you use the mysql client, you must terminate each command with a semicolon (;) or \G..

- CREATE DATABASE <database_name>: Creates a database

- USE <database>: Sets the default database

- CREATE TABLE <table_name> [...]: Creates a table or structure to store data

- INSERT INTO <table_name> [...]: Adds data to a table

- UPDATE [...]: Changes one or more values for a specific row

- DELETE FROM <table_name> [...]: Removes data from a table

- SELECT [...]: Retrieves data (rows) from the table

Although this list is only a short introduction and nothing like a complete syntax guide, there is an excellent online reference manual that explains each and every command (and much more) in great detail. You should refer to the online reference manual whenever you have a question about anything in MySQL. You can find it at http://dev.mysql.com/doc/.

If you are thinking that there is a lot more to MySQL than a few simple commands, you are absolutely correct. Despite its ease of use and fast startup time, MySQL is a full-fledged relational database management system (RDBMS). There is much more to it than you've seen here. For more information about MySQL, including all the advanced features, see the reference manual.

MYSQL—WHAT DOES IT MEAN?

The name MySQL is a combination of a proper name and an acronym. SQL is Structured Query Language. The *My* part isn't the possessive form—it is a name. In this case, My is the name of the founder's daughter. As for pronunciation, MySQL experts pronounce it "My-S-Q-L" and not "my sequel." Indeed, the mark of a savvy MySQL user is in their pronunciation of the product. There is a corollary with Mac OS X.: is it "Mac O-S Ex" or "Mac O-S Ten"? Check it and see.

Getting Started with MySQL

Now that you know what MySQL is and how it is used, you need to know a bit more about RDBMSs and MySQL in particular before you start building your first database server. This section discusses how MySQL stores data (and where it is stored), how it communicates with other systems, and some basic administration tasks required in order to manage your new MySQL server.

■ **Note**   I present this information as a tutorial or primer on MySQL. You install MySQL on the Raspberry Pi in a later section.

WHAT'S A RELATIONAL DATABASE MANAGEMENT SYSTEM?

An RDBMS is a data storage-and-retrieval service based on the Relational Model of Data as proposed by E. F. Codd in 1970. These systems are the standard storage mechanism for structured data. A great deal of research is devoted to refining the essential model proposed by Codd, as discussed by C. J. Date in *The Database Relational Model: A Retrospective Review and Analysis*.[4] This evolution of theory and practice is best documented in *The Third Manifesto*.[5]

The relational model is an intuitive concept of a storage repository (database) that can be easily queried by using a mechanism called a *query language* to retrieve, update, and insert data. The relational model has been implemented by many vendors because it has a sound systematic theory, a firm mathematical foundation, and a simple structure. The most commonly used query mechanism is SQL, which resembles natural language. Although SQL is not included in the relational model, it provides an integral part of the practical application of the relational model in RDBMSs.

The data are represented as related pieces of information (attributes or *columns*) about a certain event or entity. The set of values for the attributes is formed as a *tuple* (sometimes called a *record* or *row*). Tuples are stored in tables that have the same set of attributes. Tables can then be related to other tables through constraints on keys, attributes, and tuples.

Tables can have special mappings of columns called *indexes* that permit you to read the data in a specific order. Indexes are also very useful for fast retrieval of rows that match the value(s) of the indexed columns.

---

[4]C. J. Date, *The Database Relational Model: A Retrospective Review and Analysis* (Reading, MA: Addison-Wesley, 2001).
[5]C. J. Date and H. Darwen, *Foundation for Future Database Systems: The Third Manifesto* (Reading, MA: Addison-Wesley, 2000).

How and Where MySQL Stores Data

The MySQL database system stores data via an interesting mechanism of programmatic isolation called a *storage engine* that is governed by the handler interface. The handler interface permits the use of interchangeable storage components in the MySQL server so that the parser, the optimizer, and all manner of components can interact in storing data on disk using a common mechanism. This is also referred to as a *pluggable storage engine.*[6]

■ **Note** MySQL supports several storage engines. Most are designed to write data to disk by default.[7] However, the MEMORY storage engine stores data in memory but is not persistent. That is, when the computer is rebooted, the data is lost. You can use the MEMORY storage engine for fast lookup tables. Indeed, one optimization technique is to create copies of lookup tables at startup using the MEMORY storage engine.

What does this mean to you? It means you have the choice of different mechanisms for storing data. You can specify the storage engine in the table CREATE statement shown in the following code sample. Notice the last line in the command: this is how a storage engine is specified. Leaving off this clause results in MySQL using the default storage engine. For the examples in this book, MySQL 5.5 uses the MyISAM storage engine by default:

■ **Tip** The default storage engine was changed from MyISAM to InnoDB in MySQL version 5.6. At the time of this writing, version MySQL 5.5 was available from the default repositories on Raspbian. You can download and install the latest version of MySQL if you prefer.

Create Table:

```
CREATE TABLE `books` (
  `ISBN` varchar(15) DEFAULT NULL,
  `Title` varchar(125) DEFAULT NULL,
  `Authors` varchar(100) DEFAULT NULL,
  `Quantity` int(11) DEFAULT NULL,
  `Slot` int(11) DEFAULT NULL,
  `Thumbnail` varchar(100) DEFAULT NULL,
  `Description` text
) ENGINE=MyISAM;
```

---

[6]If you would like to know more about storage engines and what makes them tick, see my book, *Expert MySQL* 2nd Ed. (Apress).
[7]MySQL also offers the NDB storage engine, which stores data in memory and supports very fast primary key writes. See the MySQL Cluster online documentation for more information.

Great! Now, what storage engines exist on MySQL? You can discover which storage engines are supported by issuing the following command. As you see, there are a lot to choose from. I cover a few that may be pertinent to planning sensor networks:

```
mysql> SHOW STORAGE ENGINES \G
*************************** 1. row ***************************
      Engine: InnoDB
     Support: YES
     Comment: Supports transactions, row-level locking, and foreign keys
Transactions: YES
          XA: YES
  Savepoints: YES
*************************** 2. row ***************************
      Engine: MRG_MYISAM
     Support: YES
     Comment: Collection of identical MyISAM tables
Transactions: NO
          XA: NO
  Savepoints: NO
*************************** 3. row ***************************
      Engine: BLACKHOLE
     Support: YES
     Comment: /dev/null storage engine (anything you write to it disappears)
Transactions: NO
          XA: NO
  Savepoints: NO
*************************** 4. row ***************************
      Engine: CSV
     Support: YES
     Comment: CSV storage engine
Transactions: NO
          XA: NO
  Savepoints: NO
*************************** 5. row ***************************
      Engine: MEMORY
     Support: YES
     Comment: Hash based, stored in memory, useful for temporary tables
Transactions: NO
          XA: NO
  Savepoints: NO
*************************** 6. row ***************************
      Engine: FEDERATED
     Support: NO
     Comment: Federated MySQL storage engine
Transactions: NULL
          XA: NULL
  Savepoints: NULL
*************************** 7. row ***************************
      Engine: ARCHIVE
     Support: YES
     Comment: Archive storage engine
```

```
      Transactions: NO
                XA: NO
        Savepoints: NO
*************************** 8. row ***************************
            Engine: MyISAM
           Support: DEFAULT
           Comment: Default engine as of MySQL 3.23 with great performance
      Transactions: NO
                XA: NO
        Savepoints: NO
8 rows in set (0.00 sec)
```

As of version 5.6, MySQL uses the InnoDB storage engine by default. Previous versions used MyISAM as the default. InnoDB is a fully transactional, ACID[8] storage engine. A *transaction* is a batch of statements that must all succeed before any changes are written to disk. The classic example is a bank transfer. If you consider a system that requires deducting an amount from one account and then crediting that amount to another account to complete the act of moving funds, you would not want the first to succeed and the second to fail or vice versa!

Wrapping the statements in a transaction ensures that no data is written to disk until and unless all statements are completed without errors. Transactions in this case are designated with a BEGIN statement and concluded with either a COMMIT to save the changes or a ROLLBACK to undo the changes. InnoDB stores its data in a single file (with some additional files for managing indexes and transactions).

The MyISAM storage engine is optimized for reads. MyISAM has been the default for some time and was one of the first storage engines available. In fact, a large portion of the server is dedicated to supporting MyISAM. It differs from InnoDB in that it does not support transactions and stores its data in an indexed sequential access method format. This means it supports fast indexing. You would choose MyISAM over InnoDB if you did not need transactions and you wanted to be able to move or back up individual tables.

Another storage engine that you may want to consider, especially for sensor networks, is Archive. This engine does not support deletes (but you can drop entire tables) and is optimized for minimal storage on disk. Clearly, if you are running MySQL on a small system like a Raspberry Pi, small is almost always better! The inability to delete data may limit more advanced applications, but most sensor networks merely store data and rarely delete it. In this case, you can consider using the Archive storage engine.

There is also the CSV storage engine (where CSV stands for *comma-separated values*). This storage engine creates text files to store the data in plain text that can be read by other applications such as a spreadsheet application. If you use your sensor data for statistical analysis, the CSV storage engine may make the process of ingesting the data easier.

So where is all this data? If you query the MySQL server and issue the command SHOW VARIABLES LIKE "datadir";, you see the path to the location on disk that all storage engines use to store data. In the case of InnoDB, this is a single file on disk located in the data directory. InnoDB also creates a few administrative files, but the data is stored in the single file. For most other storage engines except NDB and MEMORY, the data for the tables is stored in a folder with the name of the database under the data directory. Listing 6-2 shows an example:

Listing 6-2. Finding Where Your Data Is Located

```
mysql> SHOW VARIABLES LIKE 'datadir';
+---------------+------------------------+
| Variable_name | Value                  |
+---------------+------------------------+
| datadir       | /usr/local/mysql/data/ |
+---------------+------------------------+
1 row in set (0.00 sec)
```

---

[8]http://en.wikipedia.org/wiki/ACID

```
mysql> quit;
bye

$ sudo ls -lsa /usr/local/mysql/data
rwxr-x---    58 _mysql  wheel        1972 Feb  6 15:05 .
drwxr-xr-x   17 root    wheel         578 Jan 20 16:38 ..
-rw-rw----    1 _mysql  wheel           0 Feb  6 15:04 Chucks-iMac.local.err
-rw-rw----    1 _mysql  wheel           5 Feb  6 15:00 Chucks-iMac.local.pid
drwx------    6 _mysql  wheel         204 Oct 17 15:16 bvm
-rw-rw----    1 _mysql  wheel     5242880 Feb  6 15:00 ib_logfile0
-rw-rw----    1 _mysql  wheel     5242880 Feb  6 15:00 ib_logfile1
-rw-rw----    1 _mysql  wheel   815792128 Feb  1 17:16 ibdata1
-rw-rw----    1 _mysql  wheel    52428800 Feb  1 17:16 ibdata2
drwxr-x---   77 _mysql  wheel        2618 Jan  8 15:24 mysql
drwx------   38 _mysql  wheel        1292 Nov 27 08:46 sakila
drwx------  192 _mysql  wheel        6528 Oct 22 12:17 test
drwx------    6 _mysql  wheel         204 Dec 18 17:05 world_innodb

$ sudo ls -lsa /usr/local/mysql/data/bvm
drwx------    6 _mysql  wheel   204 Oct 17 15:16 .
drwxr-x---   58 _mysql  wheel  1972 Feb  6 15:05 ..
-rw-rw----    1 _mysql  wheel  5056 Oct 17 15:24 books.MYD
-rw-rw----    1 _mysql  wheel  1024 Oct 17 15:25 books.MYI
-rw-rw----    1 _mysql  wheel  8780 Oct 17 15:16 books.frm
-rw-rw----    1 _mysql  wheel    65 Oct 17 15:15 db.opt
```

■ **Tip**   When you use sudo for the first time, you are required to enter the password for the root user.

This example first queries the database server for the location of the data directory (it is in a protected folder on this machine). If you issue a listing command, you can see the InnoDB files identified by the ib and ibd prefixes. You also see a number of directories, all of which are the databases on this server. Below that is a listing of one of the database folders. Notice the files with the extension .MY?: these are MyISAM files (data and index). The .frm files are the configuration files created and maintained by the server.

■ **Tip**   If you want to copy data from one server to another by copying files, be sure to copy the .frm files as well! This is easy for MyISAM and Archive but much harder with InnoDB. In the case of InnoDB, you have to copy all the database folders and the InnoDB files to make sure you get everything.

Although it is unlikely that you would require a transactional storage engine for your Raspberry Pi MySQL Server, MySQL 5.6 has one, and it's turned on by default. A more likely scenario is that you would use the MyISAM or Archive engine for your tables.

For more information about storage engines and the choices and features of each, please see the online MySQL Reference Manual section "Storage Engines" (http://dev.mysql.com/doc/).

The MySQL Configuration File

The MySQL server can be configured using a configuration file, similar to the way you configure the Raspberry Pi. On the Raspberry Pi, the MySQL configuration file is located in the /etc/mysql folder and is named my.cnf. This file contains several sections, one of which is labeled [mysqld]. The items in this list are key-value pairs: the name on the left of the equal sign is the option, and its value on the right. The following is a typical configuration file (with many lines suppressed for brevity):

```
[mysqld]
port = 3306
basedir = /usr/local/mysql
datadir = /usr/local/mysql/data
server_id = 5
general_log
```

As you can see, this is a simple way to configure a system. This example sets the TCP port, base directory (the root of the MySQL installation including the data as well as binary and auxiliary files), data directory, and server ID (used for replication, as discussed shortly) and turns on the general log (when the Boolean switch is included, it turns on the log). There are many such variables you can set for MySQL. See the online MySQL reference manual for details concerning using the configuration file. You will change this file when you set up MySQL on the Raspberry Pi.

How to Start, Stop, and Restart MySQL

While working with your databases and configuring MySQL on your Raspberry Pi, you may need to control the startup and shutdown of the MySQL server. The default mode for installing MySQL is to automatically start on boot and stop on shutdown, but you may want to change that, or you may need to stop and start the server after changing a parameter. In addition, when you change the configuration file, you need to restart the server to see the effect of your changes.

You can start, stop, and restart the MySQL server with the script located in /etc/init.d/mysql. Here is a list of its options:

```
$ /etc/init.d/mysql --help
Usage: mysql.server  {start|stop|restart|reload|force-reload|status}  [ MySQL server options ]
```

The script can start, stop, and restart the server as well as get its status. You can also pass configuration (such as startup) options to the server. This can be useful for turning on a feature for temporary use as an alternative to modifying the configuration file. For example, if you want to turn on the general log for a period of time, you can use these commands:

```
/etc/init.d/mysql restart --general-log
/etc/init.d/mysql restart
```

The first restart restarts the server with the general log on, and the second restarts the server without the log enabled (assuming it isn't in the configuration file). It's probably a good idea to make sure no one is using the server when you restart it.

SHUTTING DOWN CORRECTLY

You may be tempted to just power down your Raspberry Pi database server like you do your Arduino sensor nodes, but you should avoid that temptation. The Raspberry Pi is a real computer with active file systems that require a synchronized shutdown. You should always execute a controlled shutdown before powering down.

To shut down the Raspberry Pi, recall that you issue the `sudo shutdown -h now` command. To reboot, you can use the `sudo shutdown -r now` command.

Creating Users and Granting Access

You need to know about two additional administrative operations before working with MySQL: creating user accounts and granting access to databases. MySQL can perform both of these with the GRANT statement, which automatically creates a user if one does not exist. But the more pedantic method is first to issue a CREATE USER command followed by one or more GRANT commands. For example, the following shows the creation of a user named sensor1 and grants the user access to the database room_temp:

```
CREATE USER 'sensor1'@'%' IDENTIFIED BY 'secret';
GRANT SELECT, INSERT, UPDATE ON room_temp.* TO 'sensor1'@'%';
```

The first command creates the user named sensor1, but the name also has an @ followed by another string. This second string is the host name of the machine with which the user is associated. That is, each user in MySQL has both a user name and a host name, in the form user@host, to uniquely identify them. That means the user and host sensor1@10.0.1.16 and the user and host sensor1@10.0.1.17 are not the same. However, the % symbol can be used as a wildcard to associate the user with any host. The IDENTIFIED BY clause sets the password for the user.

A NOTE ABOUT SECURITY

It is always a good idea to create a user for your application that does not have full access to the MySQL system. This is so you can minimize any accidental changes and also to prevent exploitation. For sensor networks, it is recommended that you create a user with access only to those databases where you store (or retrieve) data. You can change MySQL user passwords with the following command:

```
SET PASSWORD FOR sensor1@"%" = PASSWORD("secret");
```

Also be careful about using the wildcard % for the host. Although it makes it easier to create a single user and let the user access the database server from any host, it also makes it much easier for someone bent on malice to access your server (once they discover the password).

Another consideration is connectivity. As with the Raspberry Pi if you connect a database to your network and the network is in turn connected to the Internet, it may be possible for other users on your network or the Internet to gain access to the database. Don't make it easy for them—change your root user password, and create users for your applications.

The second command allows access to databases. There are many privileges that you can give a user. The example shows the most likely set that you would want to give a user of a sensor network database: read (SELECT),[9] add data (INSERT), and change data (UPDATE). See the online reference manual for more about security and account access privileges.

The command also specifies a database and objects to which to grant the privilege. Thus, it is possible to give a user read (SELECT) privileges to some tables and write (INSERT, UPDATE) privileges to other tables. This example gives the user access to all objects (tables, views, and so on) in the room_temp database.

As mentioned, you can combine these two commands into a single command. You are likely to see this form more often in the literature. The following shows the combined syntax. In this case, all you need to do is add the IDENTIFIED BY clause to the GRANT statement. Cool!

```
GRANT SELECT, INSERT, UPDATE ON room_temp.* TO  "sensor1 "@'%" IDENTIFIED BY "secret ";
```

MySQL and Python—MySQL Utilities

The Raspberry Pi was designed for Python, and most OS images include it. Wouldn't it be cool if you could work with the MySQL server using Python? Well, you can! Oracle provides two components you need to use MySQL in Python: the MySQL Connector/Python and MySQL Utilities.

First you need the Connector/Python database connector. This is a pure Python implementation of a common database connector for MySQL. Many other connectors are available. You can find Connector/Python at http://dev.mysql.com/downloads/connector/python/. Because it is Python, all you need to do is download it, untar it, and install it using commands similar to the following:

```
$ tar -xvf mysql-connector-python-1.0.8.tar.gz
$ cd mysql-connector-python-1.0.8/
$ python ./setup.py build
$ sudo python ./setup.py install
```

Next, you need MySQL Utilities, available for download from http://dev.mysql.com. The following are the steps necessary to install MySQL Utilities:

```
$ tar -xf mysql-utilities*
$ cd mysql-utilities*
$ python ./setup.py build
$ sudo python ./setup.py install
```

To use the utilities, you can simply execute them. You can find out which utilities are present by looking in the /scripts folder of the source you branched, as shown here:

```
pi@raspberrypi ~/source/lp/mysql-utilities/scripts $ ls *.py
mysqlauditadmin.py   mysqldbexport.py    mysqlfailover.py     mysqlreplicate.py    mysqlserverclone.py
mysqlauditgrep.py    mysqldbimport.py    mysqlindexcheck.py   mysqlrpladmin.py     mysqlserverinfo.py
mysqldbcompare.py    mysqldiff.py        mysqlmetagrep.py     mysqlrplcheck.py     mysqluc.py
mysqldbcopy.py       mysqldiskusage.py   mysqlprocgrep.py     mysqlrplshow.py      mysqluserclone.py
```

---

[9]Although most sensor nodes only write data, it is possible that some sensor data might need to be combined with other, known data (via a lookup table) to be relevant.

As you can see, there are 20 (or more) utilities for things like copying databases, cloning users, exporting and importing data, and much more. Listing 6-3 shows an example of running the `mysqlserverinfo` utility on a MySQL server installed on a Raspberry Pi. You can find more information about MySQL Utilities from the MySQL Workbench online manual (http://dev.mysql.com/doc/workbench/en/mysql-utilities.html) or by using the `--help` option for each utility.

Listing 6-3. Running MySQL Utilities on a Raspberry Pi

```
$ mysqlserverinfo --server=root:secret@localhost --format=vertical
# Source on localhost: ... connected.
*************************      1. row ************************
        server: localhost:3306
       version: 5.5.28-1
       datadir: /var/lib/mysql/
       basedir: /usr
    plugin_dir: /usr/lib/mysql/plugin/
   config_file: /etc/mysql/my.cnf
    binary_log: None
binary_log_pos: None
     relay_log: None
 relay_log_pos: None
1 rows.
#...done.
```

But wait, there's more! A utility named `mysqluc` provides a special console for working with all the utilities. If you launch the console and then issue `help` followed by `help utilities`, you see an overview of each utility as well as some useful commands for the console itself, as shown in Listing 6-4.

Listing 6-4. The MySQL Utilities User Console

```
Welcome to the MySQL Utilities Client (mysqluc) version 1.3.5 - MySQL Workbench Distribution 5.2.46
Copyright (c) 2000, 2013, Oracle and/or its affiliates. All rights reserved.

Oracle is a registered trademark of Oracle Corporation and/or its affiliates.
Other names may be trademarks of their respective owners.

Type 'help' for a list of commands or press TAB twice for list of utilities.

mysqluc> help
Command                   Description
---------------------     ----------------------------------------------------
help utilities            Display list of all utilities supported.
help <utility>            Display help for a specific utility.
help | help commands      Show this list.
exit | quit               Exit the console.
set <variable>=<value>    Store a variable for recall in commands.
show options              Display list of options specified by the user on
                          launch.
show variables            Display list of variables.
<ENTER>                   Press ENTER to execute command.
<ESCAPE>                  Press ESCAPE to clear the command entry.
<DOWN>                    Press DOWN to retrieve the previous command.
```

```
<UP>                    Press UP to retrieve the next command in history.
<TAB>                   Press TAB for type completion of utility, option,
                        or variable names.
<TAB><TAB>              Press TAB twice for list of matching type
                        completion (context sensitive).


mysqluc> help utilities
Utility            Description
----------------   ---------------------------------------------------------
mysqlauditadmin    audit log maintenance utility
mysqlauditgrep     audit log search utility
mysqldbcompare     compare databases for consistency
mysqldbcopy        copy databases from one server to another
mysqldbexport      export metadata and data from databases
mysqldbimport      import metadata and data from files
mysqldiff          compare object definitions among objects where the
                   difference is how db1.obj1 differs from db2.obj2
mysqldiskusage     show disk usage for databases
mysqlfailover      automatic replication health monitoring and failover
mysqlindexcheck    check for duplicate or redundant indexes
mysqlmetagrep      search metadata
mysqlprocgrep      search process information
mysqlreplicate     establish replication with a master
mysqlrpladmin      administration utility for MySQL replication
mysqlrplcheck      check replication
mysqlrplshow       show slaves attached to a master
mysqlserverclone   start another instance of a running server
mysqlserverinfo    show server information
mysqluserclone     clone a MySQL user account to one or more new users


mysqluc>
```

Great, now you have a set of Python utilities for MySQL—so what? The utilities are built using a well-defined library, which you can use yourself to create your own utilities. If you want to see the library, simply navigate to the location where you extracted the file you downloaded from http://dev.mysql.com, and look in the /mysql/utilities folder. There you see two folders: command and common. The command folder contains macro-level operations for each of the utilities provided. For example, the copy-database utility (mysqldbcopy) has a module named dbcopy.py. The common folder contains all the classes and modules that implement the lower-level methods of accessing and manipulating MySQL resources. For example, there are modules for server-level operations (server.py), database-level operations (database.py), and many more.

A detailed explanation of MySQL Utilities and its growing Python library would consume a volume in and of itself. If you are thinking about using Python to write applications to work with sensor data, you should consider looking at MySQL Utilities for retrieving and manipulating that data. You may find that building a sophisticated sensor monitoring system just got a lot easier!

Now that you've had a short (and perhaps a bit terse) introduction to MySQL, let's get started on your MySQL Raspberry Pi database server.

Building a Raspberry Pi MySQL Server

It is time to get your hands dirty and work some magic on your unsuspecting Raspberry Pi! Let's begin by adding a USB hard drive to it. Depending on the size of your data, you may want to seriously consider doing this.

If your data will be small (never more than a few megabytes), you may be fine using MySQL from your boot image SD card. However, if you want to ensure that you do not run out of space and keep your data separate from your boot image, you should mount a USB drive that automatically connects on boot. This section explains how to do this in detail.

■ **Tip**   Be sure you use a good-quality powered USB hub to host your external drive. This is especially important if you are using a traditional spindle drive, because it consumes a lot more power. Connecting your external drive directly to the Raspberry Pi may rob it of power and cause untold frustration. Symptoms include random reboot (always a pleasant surprise), failed commands, data loss, and so on. Always be sure you have plenty of power for your peripherals as well as your Raspberry Pi.

The choice of what disk to use is up to you. You can use a USB flash drive, which should work fine if it has plenty of space and is of sufficient speed (most newer models are fast). You can also use a solid-state drive (SSD) if you have an extra one or want to keep power usage and heat to a minimum. On the other hand, you may have an extra hard drive lying around that can be pressed into service. This section's example uses a surplus 250GB laptop hard drive mounted in a typical USB hard drive enclosure.

■ **Tip**   Using an external hard drive—either an SSD or traditional spindle drive—is much faster than accessing data on a flash drive. It is also typically cheaper per unit (gigabyte) or, as I mentioned, can be easily obtained from surplus.

Partitioning and Formatting the Drive

Before you can use a new or an existing drive with a file system incompatible with the Raspberry Pi, you must partition and format the drive. Because the surplus drive in this example had an old Mac partition on it, I had to follow these steps. Your Raspberry OS may be able to read the format of your old drive, but you should use the ext4 file system for optimal performance. This section shows you how to partition and format your drive.

Begin by connecting the drive to the Raspberry Pi. Then determine what drives are attached by using the fdisk command as shown:

```
pi@raspberrypi ~ $ sudo fdisk -l

Disk /dev/mmcblk0: 7948 MB, 7948206080 bytes
4 heads, 16 sectors/track, 242560 cylinders, total 15523840 sectors
Units = sectors of 1 * 512 = 512 bytes
Sector size (logical/physical): 512 bytes / 512 bytes
I/O size (minimum/optimal): 512 bytes / 512 bytes
Disk identifier: 0x000108cb

        Device Boot      Start         End      Blocks   Id  System
/dev/mmcblk0p1            8192      122879       57344    c  W95 FAT32 (LBA)
/dev/mmcblk0p2          122880    15523839     7700480   83  Linux
```

```
WARNING: GPT (GUID Partition Table) detected on '/dev/sda'! The util fdisk doesn't support GPT. Use
GNU Parted.
```

Disk /dev/sda: 120.0 GB, 120034123776 bytes
255 heads, 63 sectors/track, 14593 cylinders, total 234441648 sectors
Units = sectors of 1 * 512 = 512 bytes
Sector size (logical/physical): 512 bytes / 512 bytes
I/O size (minimum/optimal): 512 bytes / 512 bytes
Disk identifier: 0x00002d4a

Device Boot	Start	End	Blocks	Id	System
/dev/sda1	**1**	**234441647**	**117220823+**	**ee**	**GPT**

What you see here are all the devices attached to the Raspberry Pi. If you are new to Linux or partitioning drives, this may look like a lot of nonsense. I've highlighted the interesting rows in bold. Notice that the output identifies a 120GB drive located on a device designated as /dev/sda. All the interesting data about the drive is shown as well.

As I mentioned, there is already a partition on this drive, indicated by the row with the name of the device plus the number of the partition. Thus, /dev/sda1 is the one and only partition on this drive. Let's delete that partition and create a new one. You execute both operations using the fdisk application:

■ **Caution**　If you have a partition on your drive that has data you want to keep, abort now and copy the data to another drive first. The following steps erase all data on the drive!

```
pi@raspberrypi ~ $ sudo fdisk /dev/sda

WARNING: GPT (GUID Partition Table) detected on '/dev/sda'! The util fdisk doesn't support GPT.
Use GNU Parted.

Command (m for help): d
Selected partition 1

Command (m for help): n
Partition type:
   p   primary (0 primary, 0 extended, 4 free)
   e   extended
Select (default p): p
Partition number (1-4, default 1):
Using default value 1
First sector (2048-234441647, default 2048):
Using default value 2048
Last sector, +sectors or +size{K,M,G} (2048-234441647, default 234441647):
Using default value 234441647

Command (m for help): p

Disk /dev/sda: 120.0 GB, 120034123776 bytes
255 heads, 63 sectors/track, 14593 cylinders, total 234441648 sectors
Units = sectors of 1 * 512 = 512 bytes
Sector size (logical/physical): 512 bytes / 512 bytes
```

```
I/O size (minimum/optimal): 512 bytes / 512 bytes
Disk identifier: 0x00002d4a

   Device Boot      Start        End      Blocks   Id  System
/dev/sda1                2048   234441647   117219800   83  Linux

Command (m for help): w
The partition table has been altered!

Calling ioctl() to re-read partition table.
Syncing disks.
```

The first command, d, deletes a partition. In this case, there was only one partition, so you select it by entering 1. You then create a new partition using the command n and accept the defaults to use all the free space. To check your work, you can use the p command to print the device partition table and metadata. It shows (and confirms) the new partition.

If you are worried that you may have made a mistake, do not panic! The great thing about fdisk is that it doesn't write or change the disk until you tell it to with the w or write command. In the example, you issue the w command to write the partition table. To see a full list of the commands available, you can use the h command or run man fdisk.

■ **Tip**   For all Linux commands, you can view the manual file by using the command man <application>.

The next step is to format the drive with the ext4 file system. This is easy and requires only one command: mkfs (make file system). You pass it the device name. If you recall, this is /dev/sda1. Even though you created a new partition, it is still the first partition because there is only one on the drive. If you are attempting to use a different partition, be sure to use the correct number! The command may take a few minutes to run, depending on the size of your drive. The following example shows the command in action:

```
pi@raspberrypi ~ $ sudo mkfs.ext4 /dev/sda1
mke2fs 1.42.5 (29-Jul-2012)
Filesystem label=
OS type: Linux
Block size=4096 (log=2)
Fragment size=4096 (log=2)
Stride=0 blocks, Stripe width=0 blocks
7331840 inodes, 29304950 blocks
1465247 blocks (5.00%) reserved for the super user
First data block=0
Maximum filesystem blocks=0
895 block groups
32768 blocks per group, 32768 fragments per group
8192 inodes per group
Superblock backups stored on blocks:
        32768, 98304, 163840, 229376, 294912, 819200, 884736, 1605632, 2654208,
        4096000, 7962624, 11239424, 20480000, 23887872

Allocating group tables: done
```

```
Writing inode tables: done
Creating journal (32768 blocks): done
Writing superblocks and filesystem accounting information: done
```

Now you have a new partition, and it has been properly formatted. The next step is associating the drive with a mount point on the boot image and then connecting that drive on boot so you don't have to do anything to use the drive each time you start your Raspberry Pi.

Setting Up Automatic Drive Mounting

External drives in Linux are connected (mounted) with mount and disconnected (unmounted) with umount. Unlike with some operating systems, it is generally a bad idea to unplug your USB drive without unmounting it first. Likewise, you must mount the drive before you can use it. This section shows the steps needed to mount the drive and to make the drive mount automatically on each boot.

I begin with a discussion of the preliminary steps to get the drive mounted and ready for automatic mounting. These include creating a folder under the /media folder to mount the drive (called a *mount point*), changing permissions to the folder to allow access, and executing some optional steps to tune the drive:

```
pi@raspberrypi ~ $ sudo mkdir -p /media/HDD
pi@raspberrypi ~ $ sudo chmod 755 /media/HDD
pi@raspberrypi ~ $ sudo tune2fs -m 0 /dev/sda1
tune2fs 1.42.5 (29-Jul-2012)
Setting reserved blocks percentage to 0% (0 blocks)
pi@raspberrypi ~ $ sudo tune2fs -L MYSQL /dev/sda1
tune2fs 1.42.5 (29-Jul-2012)
pi@raspberrypi ~ $ sudo mount /dev/sda1 /media/HDD
```

These commands are easy to discern and are basic file and folder commands. However, the tuning steps using tune2fs (tune file system) are used to first reset the number of blocks used for privileged access (which saves a bit of space) and then label the drive as MYSQL. Again, these are optional, and you may skip them if you like.

■ **Tip** You can unmount the drive with sudo umount /dev/sda1.

At this point, the drive is accessible and ready to be used. You can change to the /media/HDD folder and create files or do whatever you'd like. Now let's complete the task of setting up the drive for automatic mounting.

The best way to do this is to refer to the drive by its universally unique identifier (UUID). This is assigned to this drive and only this drive. You can tell the operating system to mount the drive with a specific UUID to a specific mount point (/media/HDD).

Remember the /dev/sda device name from earlier? If you plugged your drive in to another hub port—or, better still, if there are other drives connected to your device and you unmount and then mount them—the device name may not be the same the next time you boot! The UUID helps you determine which drive is your data drive, frees you from having to keep the drive plugged in to a specific port, and allows you to use other drives without fear of breaking your MySQL installation if the drive is given a different device name.

To get the UUID, use the blkid (block ID) application:

```
pi@raspberrypi ~ $ sudo blkid
/dev/mmcblk0p1: SEC_TYPE="msdos" UUID="A1B1-918F" TYPE="vfat"
/dev/mmcblk0p2: UUID="10b4c001-2137-4418-b29e-57b7d15a6cbc" TYPE="ext4"
/dev/sda1: UUID="15ce7bf9-4a42-445f-86d6-2451ea6aa4f7" TYPE="ext4" LABEL="MYSQL"
```

Notice the line in bold. Wow! That's a big string. A UUID is a 128-byte (character) string. Copy it for the next step.

To set up automatic drive mapping, you use a feature called *static information* about the file system (fstab). This consists of a file located in the /etc folder on your system. You can edit the file however you like. If you are from the old school of Linux or Unix, you may choose to use vi.[10] The resulting file is as follows:

```
pi@raspberrypi ~ $ sudo nano /etc/fstab
proc            /proc        proc      defaults        0       0
/dev/mmcblk0p1  /boot        vfat      defaults        0       0
/dev/mmcblk0p2  /            ext4      defaults,noatime 0      0
UUID=15ce7bf9-4a42-445f-86d6-2451ea6aa4f7 /media/HDD    ext4    defaults,noatime   0   0
```

The line you add is shown in bold. Here you simply add the UUID, mount point, file system, and options. That's it! You can reboot your Raspberry Pi using the following command and watch the screen as the messages scroll. Eventually, you see that the drive is mounted. If there is ever an error, you can see it in the boot-up sequence:

```
$ sudo shutdown -r now
```

Now you are ready to build a MySQL database server! The following section details the steps needed to do this using your Raspberry Pi.

Project: Installing MySQL Server on a Raspberry Pi

Turning a Raspberry Pi into a MySQL database server is easy. This section shows you how to install MySQL and then how to move its default data directory from your boot image to the new external drive you connected in the previous section.

The steps involved include updating your aptitude base (the package manager) and then installing MySQL. Although the process is rather lengthy, I felt it best to show you the entire thing in case your base image is different or you encounter errors.

Installing MySQL

To install MySQL or any software not already in your base image, you must be connected to the Internet. If you have not already done so, connect your Raspberry Pi to the Internet using the Ethernet port (for Model B) or a wireless networking device.

As you may recall, you are using the Raspbian wheezy distribution, which is Debian-based. If you use some other distribution, it may have a different package manager, and the commands in this section may not work. In that case, you should be able to find similar commands for your distribution.

---

[10]What does *vi* mean? If you've ever had the pleasure of trying to learn it for the first time, you may think it means "virtually impossible," because the commands are terse (by design) and difficult to remember. But seriously, *vi* is short for *vim* or *Vi Improved* text editor. The name suggests that the original editor may very well have been *completely* impossible to use!

Let's begin with updating the package manager package headers. This is always a good idea, especially if you are using a distribution that was released more than a few months ago. The command apt-get update tells the system to download the latest headers from known host distributions. This ensures that you get the latest version of whatever software you are installing.

After that, installing the software is as simple as telling aptitude to install it. The trick is knowing the correct name. In this case, you're looking for mysql-server. Listing 6-5 shows the steps for updating aptitude and installing MySQL. (I have omitted some lines for brevity.) In addition to entering the commands, you are asked to reply to the prompt asking if it is OK to download MySQL and its prerequisites and to enter a password for the root user for MySQL.

■ **Note** When you see the password *secret* in the examples, it is used as a placeholder for whatever password you have chosen—it is not explicitly the word *secret*.

Listing 6-5. Installing MySQL on a Raspberry Pi

```
pi@raspberrypi ~ $ sudo apt-get update
Hit http://archive.raspberrypi.org wheezy InRelease
Get:1 http://mirrordirector.raspbian.org wheezy InRelease [12.5 kB]
Get:2 http://mirrordirector.raspbian.org wheezy/main armhf Packages [7,403 kB]
Hit http://archive.raspberrypi.org wheezy/main armhf Packages
Ign http://archive.raspberrypi.org wheezy/main Translation-en_GB
Ign http://archive.raspberrypi.org wheezy/main Translation-en
[...]
Reading package lists... Done

pi@raspberrypi ~ $ sudo apt-get install mysql-server
Reading package lists... Done
Building dependency tree
Reading state information... Done
The following extra packages will be installed:
  heirloom-mailx libaio1 libdbd-mysql-perl libdbi-perl libhtml-template-perl
  libmysqlclient16 libnet-daemon-perl libplrpc-perl mysql-client-5.5
  mysql-common mysql-server-5.5 mysql-server-core-5.5
Suggested packages:
  exim4 mail-transport-agent libipc-sharedcache-perl libterm-readkey-perl
  tinyca
Recommended packages:
  mailx
The following NEW packages will be installed:
  heirloom-mailx libaio1 libdbd-mysql-perl libdbi-perl libhtml-template-perl
  libmysqlclient16 libnet-daemon-perl libplrpc-perl mysql-client-5.5
  mysql-common mysql-server mysql-server-5.5 mysql-server-core-5.5
0 upgraded, 13 newly installed, 0 to remove and 246 not upgraded.
Need to get 9,859 kB/9,950 kB of archives.
After this operation, 91.1 MB of additional disk space will be used.
Do you want to continue [Y/n]? y
Get:1 http://mirrordirector.raspbian.org/raspbian/ wheezy/main mysql-common all 5.5.28+dfsg-1 [89.1 kB]
  [...]
Setting up libmysqlclient16 (5.1.62-1) ...
Setting up libdbd-mysql-perl (4.021-1) ...
```

```
Setting up mysql-client-5.5 (5.5.28+dfsg-1) ...
Setting up mysql-server-core-5.5 (5.5.28+dfsg-1) ...
Setting up mysql-server-5.5 (5.5.28+dfsg-1) ...
[ ok ] Stopping MySQL database server: mysqld.
130204 16:07:35 [Note] Plugin 'FEDERATED' is disabled.
130204 16:07:35 InnoDB: The InnoDB memory heap is disabled
130204 16:07:35 InnoDB: Mutexes and rw_locks use GCC atomic builtins
130204 16:07:35 InnoDB: Compressed tables use zlib 1.2.7
130204 16:07:35 InnoDB: Using Linux native AIO
130204 16:07:35 InnoDB: Initializing buffer pool, size = 128.0M
130204 16:07:35 InnoDB: Completed initialization of buffer pool
130204 16:07:35 InnoDB: highest supported file format is Barracuda.
130204 16:07:35 InnoDB: Waiting for the background threads to start
130204 16:07:36 InnoDB: 1.1.8 started; log sequence number 1595675
130204 16:07:36 InnoDB: Starting shutdown...
130204 16:07:38 InnoDB: Shutdown completed; log sequence number 1595675
[ ok ] Starting MySQL database server: mysqld . . . . ..
[info] Checking for tables which need an upgrade, are corrupt or were
not closed cleanly..
Setting up heirloom-mailx (12.5-2) ...
update-alternatives: using /usr/bin/heirloom-mailx to provide /usr/bin/mailx (mailx) in auto mode.
Setting up libhtml-template-perl (2.91-1) ...
Setting up mysql-server (5.5.28+dfsg-1) ...
```

You know that MySQL is installed by observing the line near the bottom stating that MySQL has started (highlighted in bold). If all goes well, you should see a status of [ok]. Although highly unlikely, if it all goes completely wonky,[11] you can remove the MySQL installation bundle with the following commands. They uninstall every package and remove any files created by the installation:

```
sudo apt-get autoremove mysql-server mysql-server-5.5
sudo apt-get purge mysql-server mysql-server-5.5
```

Once you've done this, you can try the install steps again and correcting your mistake.

Now that MySQL is installed, let's use the MySQL console and try to connect to the server. The command is `mysql -uroot -p<password>`, where `<password>` is the password you supplied when you installed MySQL. Listing 6-6 shows a successful connection to the new MySQL server. I executed some commands to test things and to gather information for the next step. Notice that the MySQL console displays the version of the MySQL server as well as a short name for the platform. In this case, I was connected to a MySQL 5.5.28-1 server on a Debian platform.

Listing 6-6. Connecting to MySQL

```
pi@raspberrypi ~ $ mysql -uroot -psecret
Welcome to the MySQL monitor.  Commands end with ; or \g.
Your MySQL connection id is 42
Server version: 5.5.28-1 (Debian)

Copyright (c) 2000, 2012, Oracle and/or its affiliates. All rights reserved.
```

---

[11] A highly technical term for when computers don't do what you think they should.

Oracle is a registered trademark of Oracle Corporation and/or its
affiliates. Other names may be trademarks of their respective
owners.

Type 'help;' or '\h' for help. Type '\c' to clear the current input statement.

```
mysql> show databases;
+--------------------+
| Database           |
+--------------------+
| information_schema |
| mysql              |
| performance_schema |
| test               |
+--------------------+
4 rows in set (0.00 sec)

mysql> show variables like '%dir%';
+-------------------------------------------+---------------------------+
| Variable_name                             | Value                     |
+-------------------------------------------+---------------------------+
| basedir                                   | /usr                      |
| binlog_direct_non_transactional_updates   | OFF                       |
| character_sets_dir                        | /usr/share/mysql/charsets/ |
| datadir                                   | /var/lib/mysql/           |
| innodb_data_home_dir                      |                           |
| innodb_log_group_home_dir                 | ./                        |
| innodb_max_dirty_pages_pct                | 75                        |
| lc_messages_dir                           | /usr/share/mysql/         |
| plugin_dir                                | /usr/lib/mysql/plugin/    |
| slave_load_tmpdir                         | /tmp                      |
| tmpdir                                    | /tmp                      |
+-------------------------------------------+---------------------------+
11 rows in set (0.00 sec)

mysql>
```

In the example, I issued the SHOW DATABASES command to see the list of databases and the SHOW VARIABLES command to show all variables containing the name dir. Notice the datadir output from the last command: this is the location of your data.

In the next section, you tell MySQL to use the external drive instead for storing your databases and data.

Moving the Data Directory to the External Drive

Recall that you want to use MySQL to store your sensor data. As such, the sensor data may grow in volume and over time may consume a lot of space. Rather than risk filling up your boot image SD, which is normally only a few gigabytes, you can use an external drive to save the data. This section shows you how to tell MySQL to change its default location for saving data.

The steps involved require stopping the MySQL server, changing its configuration, and then restarting the server. Finally, you test the change to ensure that all new data is being saved in the new location. Begin by stopping the MySQL server:

```
$ sudo /etc/init.d/mysql stop
```

You must create a folder for the new data directory:

```
$ sudo mkdir /media/HDD/mysql
```

Now you copy the existing data directory and its contents to the new folder. Notice that you copy only the data and not the entire MySQL installation which is unnecessary:

```
$ sudo cp -R /var/lib/mysql/*   /media/HDD/mysql
$ chown -R mysql mysql /media/HDD/mysql/
```

Next you edit the configuration file for MySQL. In this case, you change the datadir line to read datadir = /media/HDD/mysql. It is also a good idea to comment out the bind-address line to permit access to MySQL from other systems on the network:

```
$ sudo vi /etc/mysql/my.cnf
```

There is one last step. You must change the owner and group to the MySQL user that was created on installation. Here is the correct command:

```
$ sudo chown -R mysql:mysql /media/HDD/mysql
```

Now you restart MySQL:

```
$ sudo /etc/init.d/mysql start
```

You can determine whether the changes worked by connecting to MySQL, creating a new database, and then checking to see if the new folder was created on the external drive, as shown in Listing 6-7.

Listing 6-7. Testing the New Data Directory

```
pi@raspberrypi /etc $ mysql -uroot -psecret
Welcome to the MySQL monitor.  Commands end with ; or \g.
Your MySQL connection id is 41
Server version: 5.5.28-1 (Debian)

Copyright (c) 2000, 2012, Oracle and/or its affiliates. All rights reserved.

Oracle is a registered trademark of Oracle Corporation and/or its
affiliates. Other names may be trademarks of their respective
owners.
```

```
Type 'help;' or '\h' for help. Type '\c' to clear the current input statement.

mysql> create database testme;
Query OK, 1 row affected (0.00 sec)

mysql> show databases;
+--------------------+
| Database           |
+--------------------+
| information_schema |
| mysql              |
| performance_schema |
| test               |
| testme             |
+--------------------+
5 rows in set (0.00 sec)

mysql> quit

pi@raspberrypi /etc $ sudo ls -lsa /media/HDD/mysql
total 28732
    4 drwx------ 6 mysql mysql     4096 Feb  4 18:40 .
    4 drwxr-xr-x 3 root  root      4096 Feb  4 18:27 ..
    0 -rw-r--r-- 1 mysql mysql        0 Feb  4 18:27 debian-5.5.flag
18432 -rw-r----- 1 mysql mysql 18874368 Feb  4 18:40 ibdata1
 5120 -rw-r----- 1 mysql mysql  5242880 Feb  4 18:40 ib_logfile0
 5120 -rw-r----- 1 mysql mysql  5242880 Feb  4 18:27 ib_logfile1
    4 drwx------ 2 mysql mysql     4096 Feb  4 18:27 mysql
    4 -rw------- 1 mysql mysql        6 Feb  4 18:27 mysql_upgrade_info
    4 drwx------ 2 mysql mysql     4096 Feb  4 18:27 performance_schema
   32 -rw-r----- 1 mysql mysql    31544 Feb  4 18:27 raspberrypi.err
    4 drwx------ 2 mysql mysql     4096 Feb  4 18:27 test
    4 drwx------ 2 mysql mysql     4096 Feb  4 18:40 testme
pi@raspberrypi /etc $
```

In the output, the new database name is represented as the folder testme.

Well, there you have it—a new MySQL database server running on a Raspberry Pi! If you have followed the examples, your Raspberry Pi server looks something like Figure 6-1.

Figure 6-1. *Raspberry Pi database server with an external drive*[12]

If you are curious about what more you can do with your new database server, read on. In the next section, you tackle a very popular feature of MySQL called replication. It permits two or more servers to have copies of databases. For your purposes, it may be handy to use the copies as a backup so you don't have to do any manual file copying from your Raspberry Pi.

WHAT ABOUT OVERHEATING?

Concerns about overheating a Raspberry Pi are mainly for those who attempt overclocking and other risky modifications; you should worry if your Raspberry Pi is run continuously. Typically you run a database server 24x7, shutting it down only for maintenance.

If you are concerned about overheating, you can add heat sinks to your Raspberry Pi's major components for a reasonable cost (about $15). However, I have not seen any issues with running a Raspberry Pi indefinitely if it is housed in an enclosure that permits heat dissipation and it is placed in a climate-controlled environment. A definitive answer to this question has been provided by one of the founders himself (see www.youtube.com/watch?v=Sz8NMp4MgGO).

Advanced Project: Using MySQL Replication to Back Up Your Sensor Data

One of the nicest things about using an external drive to save your MySQL data is that at any point you can shut down your server, disconnect the drive, plug it in to another system, and copy the data. That may sound great if your Raspberry Pi database server is in a location that makes it easy to get to (physically) and if there are periods when it is OK to shut down the server.

---

[12]Raspberry Pi enclosure from Adafruit: www.adafruit.com/products/859. External drive enclosure from Other World Computing: http://eshop.macsales.com/shop/USB2/OWC_Express.

However, this may not be the case for some sensor networks. One of the benefits of using a Raspberry Pi for a database server is that the server can reside in close proximity to the sensor nodes. If the sensor network is in an isolated area, you can collect and store data by putting the Raspberry Pi in the same location. But this may mean trudging out to a barn or pond or walking several football field lengths into the bowels of a factory to get to the hardware if there is no network to connect to your database server.

But if your Raspberry Pi is connected to a network, you can use an advanced feature of MySQL called *replication* to make a live, up-to-the-minute copy of your data. Not only does this mean you can have a backup, but it also means you can query the server that maintains the copy and therefore unburden your Raspberry Pi of complex or long-running queries. The Raspberry Pi is a very cool small-footprint computer, but a data warehouse it is not.

What Is Replication, and How Does It Work?

MySQL replication is an easy-to-use feature and yet a very complex and major component of the MySQL server. This section presents a bird's-eye view of replication for the purpose of explaining how it works and how to set up a simple replication topology. For more information about replication and its many features and commands, see the online MySQL reference manual (http://dev.mysql.com/doc/refman/5.5/en/replication.html).

Replication requires two or more servers. One server must be designated as the origin or master. The master role means all data changes (writes) to the data are sent to the master and only the master. All other servers in the topology maintain a copy of the master data and are by design and requirement read-only servers. Thus, when your sensors send data for storage, they send it to the master. Applications you write to use the sensor data can read it from the slaves.

MOBILE DATABASE CLIENTS

If your sensor network is connected to the Internet—or, more precisely, your slave is connected to the Internet—you can use your mobile phone to read the data from anywhere. Several applications that you can download for your smartphone and tablet allow you to access MySQL servers.

For example, the MySQL Lite app for iPhone provides a basic point-and-click (tap) interface for navigating databases and executing simple queries.

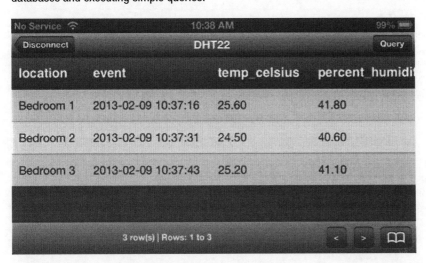

This figure shows a simple query from a sensor database that uses a DHT22 sensor to read temperature and humidity. Just because your sensor network is in the basement of an office building many miles (or hours, for commuters) away doesn't mean you can't get to the data.

The copy mechanism works using a technology called the *binary log* that stores the changes in a special format, thereby keeping a record of all the changes. These changes are then shipped to the slaves and re-executed there. Thus, once the slave re-executes the changes (called *events*), the slave has an exact copy of the data.

The master maintains a binary log of the changes, and the slave maintains a copy of that binary log called the *relay log*. When a slave requests data changes from the master, it reads the events from the master and writes them to its relay log; then another thread in the slave executes those events from the relay log. As you can imagine, there is a slight delay from the time a change is made on the master to the time it is made on the slave. Fortunately, this delay is almost unnoticeable except in topologies with very high traffic (lots of changes). For your purposes, it is likely when you read the data from the slave, it is up to date. You can check the slave's progress using the command SHOW SLAVE STATUS; among many other things, it shows you how far behind the master the slave is. You see this command in action in a later section.

Now that you have a little knowledge of replication and how it works, let's see how to set it up. The next section discusses how to set up replication with the Raspberry Pi as the master and a desktop computer as the slave.

How to Set Up Replication

This section demonstrates how to set up replication from a Raspberry Pi (master) to a desktop computer (slave). The steps include preparing the master by enabling binary logging and creating a user account for reading the binary log, preparing the slave by connecting it to the master, and starting the slave processes. You conclude with a test of the replication system.

Preparing the Master

Replication requires the master to have binary logging enabled. It is not turned on by default, so you must edit the configuration file and turn it on. Edit the configuration file with sudo vi /etc/mysql/my.cnf, and turn on binary logging by uncommenting and changing the following lines:

```
server-id         = 1
log_bin           = /media/HDD/mysql/mysql-bin.log
```

The first line sets the server ID of the master. In basic replication (what you have for version 5.5), each server must have a unique server ID. In this case, you assign 1 to the master; the slave will have some other value, such as 2. Imaginative, yes?

The next line sets the location and name of the binary log file. You save it to your external drive because, like the data itself, the binary log can grow over time. Fortunately, MySQL is designed to keep the file to a reasonable size and has commands that allow you to truncate it and start a new file (a process called *rotating*). See the online reference manual (http://dev.mysql.com/doc/refman/5.5/en/slave-logs-relaylog.html) for more information about managing binary log files.

Once the edits are saved, you can restart the MySQL server with the following command:

```
pi@raspberrypi /etc $ sudo /etc/init.d/mysql restart
[ ok ] Stopping MySQL database server: mysqld.
[ ok ] Starting MySQL database server: mysqld . . ..
[info] Checking for tables which need an upgrade, are corrupt or were
not closed cleanly..
```

To test the change, issue the following command in a MySQL console. You should see that the new variable has been set to ON:

```
mysql> show variables like 'log_bin';
+---------------+-------+
| Variable_name | Value |
+---------------+-------+
| log_bin       | ON    |
+---------------+-------+
1 row in set (0.01 sec)
```

After binary logging is turned on, you must create a user to be used by the slave to connect to the master and read the binary log. There is a special privilege for this named REPLICATION SLAVE. The following shows the correct GRANT statement to create the user and add the privilege. Remember the user name and password you use here—you need it for the slave:

```
mysql> GRANT REPLICATION SLAVE ON *.* TO 'rpl'@'%' IDENTIFIED BY 'secret';
Query OK, 0 rows affected (0.01 sec)
```

But one more piece of information is needed for the slave. The slave needs to know the name of the binary log to read and what position in the file to start reading events. You can determine this with the SHOW MASTER STATUS command:

```
mysql> show master status;
+------------------+----------+--------------+------------------+
| File             | Position | Binlog_Do_DB | Binlog_Ignore_DB |
+------------------+----------+--------------+------------------+
| mysql-bin.000001 |      245 |              |                  |
+------------------+----------+--------------+------------------+
1 row in set (0.00 sec)

mysql>
```

Now that you have the master's binary log file name and position as well as the replication user and password, you can visit your slave and connect it to the master. You also need to know the hostname or IP address of the Raspberry Pi as well as the port on which MySQL is running. By default, the port is 3306; but if you changed that, you should note the new value. Jot down all that information in Table 6-1.

Table 6-1. *Information Needed from the Master for Replication*

Item from Master	Value
IP Address or Hostname	
Port	
Binary log file	
Binary log file position	
Replication user ID	
Replication user password	

Preparing the Slave

The MySQL server you want to use as a slave should be the same version as the server on the Raspberry Pi, or at least a server that is compatible. The online reference manual specifies which MySQL versions work well together. Fortunately, the list of versions with issues is very short. In this section, you should have a server installed on your desktop or server computer and ensure that it is configured correctly.

The steps needed to connect a slave to a master include issuing a CHANGE MASTER command to connect to the master and a START SLAVE command to initiate the slave role on the server. Yes, it is that easy! Recall that you need the information from the master to complete these commands. The following commands show a slave being connected to a master running on a Raspberry Pi. Let's begin with the CHANGE MASTER command:

```
Chucks-iMac:~ cbell$ mysql -uroot -psecret -h 127.0.0.1 --port=13003
Welcome to the MySQL monitor.  Commands end with ; or \g.
Your MySQL connection id is 3
Server version: 5.5.21 Source distribution

Copyright (c) 2000, 2010, Oracle and/or its affiliates. All rights reserved.
This software comes with ABSOLUTELY NO WARRANTY. This is free software,
and you are welcome to modify and redistribute it under the GPL v2 license

Type 'help;' or '\h' for help. Type '\c' to clear the current input statement.

mysql> CHANGE MASTER TO MASTER_HOST='10.0.1.17', MASTER_PORT=3306,
MASTER_LOG_FILE='mysql-bin.000001', MASTER_LOG_POS=245, MASTER_USER='rpl', MASTER_PASSWORD='secret';
Query OK, 0 rows affected (0.22 sec)
```

This example uses the IP address of the Raspberry Pi, the port number (3306 is the default), the log file and position from the SHOW MASTER STATUS command, and the user name and password for the replication user. If you typed the command correctly, it should return without errors. If there are errors or warnings, use the SHOW WARNINGS command to read the warnings and correct any problems.

The next step is to start the slave processes. This command is simply START SLAVE. It normally does not report any errors; you must use SHOW SLAVE STATUS to see them. Here are both of these commands in action:

■ **Tip** For wide results, use the \G option to see the columns as rows (called *vertical format*).

```
mysql> start slave;
Query OK, 0 rows affected (0.00 sec)

mysql> show slave status \G
*************************** 1. row ***************************
               Slave_IO_State: Waiting for master to send event
                  Master_Host: 10.0.1.17
                  Master_User: rpl
                  Master_Port: 3306
                Connect_Retry: 60
              Master_Log_File: mysql-bin.000001
          Read_Master_Log_Pos: 107
               Relay_Log_File: clone-relay-bin.000003
                Relay_Log_Pos: 4
```

```
          Relay_Master_Log_File: mysql-bin.000001
               Slave_IO_Running: Yes
              Slave_SQL_Running: Yes
               Replicate_Do_DB:
           Replicate_Ignore_DB:
            Replicate_Do_Table:
        Replicate_Ignore_Table:
       Replicate_Wild_Do_Table:
   Replicate_Wild_Ignore_Table:
                     Last_Errno: 0
                     Last_Error:
                   Skip_Counter: 0
            Exec_Master_Log_Pos: 107
                 Relay_Log_Space: 555
                Until_Condition: None
                 Until_Log_File:
                  Until_Log_Pos: 0
              Master_SSL_Allowed: No
              Master_SSL_CA_File:
              Master_SSL_CA_Path:
                Master_SSL_Cert:
              Master_SSL_Cipher:
                 Master_SSL_Key:
          Seconds_Behind_Master: 0
Master_SSL_Verify_Server_Cert: No
                  Last_IO_Errno: 0
                  Last_IO_Error:
                 Last_SQL_Errno: 0
                 Last_SQL_Error:
     Replicate_Ignore_Server_Ids:
                Master_Server_Id: 1
1 row in set (0.00 sec)

mysql>
```

Take a moment to slog through all these rows. There are several key fields you need to pay attention to. These include anything with error in the name, and the state columns. For example, the first row (Slave_IO_State) shows the textual message indicating the state of the slave's I/O thread. The I/O thread is responsible for reading events from the master's binary log. There is also a SQL thread that is responsible for reading events from the relay log and executing them.

For this example, you just need to ensure that both threads are running (YES) and there are no errors. For detailed explanations of all the fields in the SHOW SLAVE STATUS command, see the online MySQL reference manual (http://dev.mysqlcom/doc) in the section "SQL Statements for Controlling Slave Servers."

Now that the slave is connected and running, let's check for that testme database on the slave.

```
mysql> show databases;
+--------------------+
| Database           |
+--------------------+
| information_schema |
| mysql              |
| performance_schema |
+--------------------+
3 rows in set (0.00 sec)

mysql>
```

Wait! Where did it go? Wasn't this example supposed to replicate everything? Well, yes and no. It is true that your slave is connected to the master and will replicate anything that changes on the master from this point on. Recall that you used the SHOW MASTER STATUS command to get the binary log file and position. These values are the coordinates for the location of the next event, not any previous events. Aha: you set up replication *after* the testme database was created.

How do you fix this? That depends. If you really wanted the testme database replicated, you would have to stop replication, fix the master, and then reconnect the slave. I won't go into these steps, but I list them here as an outline for you to experiment on your own:

1. Stop the slave.

2. Go to the master and drop the database.

3. Get the new SHOW MASTER STATUS data.

4. Reconnect the slave.

5. Start the slave.

Got that? Good. If not, it is a useful exercise to go back and try these steps on your own.

Once you get the master cleaned and replication restarted, go ahead and try to create a database on the master and observe the result on the slave. Following are the commands. I used a different database name in case you elected not to try the previous challenge:

```
pi@raspberrypi /etc $ mysql -uroot -psecret
Welcome to the MySQL monitor.  Commands end with ; or \g.
Your MySQL connection id is 38
Server version: 5.5.28-1-log (Debian)

Copyright (c) 2000, 2012, Oracle and/or its affiliates. All rights reserved.

Oracle is a registered trademark of Oracle Corporation and/or its
affiliates. Other names may be trademarks of their respective
owners.

Type 'help;' or '\h' for help. Type '\c' to clear the current input statement.

mysql> create database testme_again;
Query OK, 1 row affected (0.00 sec)
```

```
mysql> show databases;
+--------------------+
| Database           |
+--------------------+
| information_schema |
| mysql              |
| performance_schema |
| testme             |
| testme_again       |
+--------------------+
4 rows in set (0.01 sec)

mysql>
```

Returning to the slave, check to see what databases are listed there:

```
Chucks-iMac:mysql-5613 cbell$ mysql -uroot -psecret -h 127.0.0.1 --port=13003
Welcome to the MySQL monitor.  Commands end with ; or \g.
Your MySQL connection id is 14
Server version: 5.5.21 Source distribution

Copyright (c) 2000, 2010, Oracle and/or its affiliates. All rights reserved.
This software comes with ABSOLUTELY NO WARRANTY. This is free software,
and you are welcome to modify and redistribute it under the GPL v2 license

Type 'help;' or '\h' for help. Type '\c' to clear the current input statement.

mysql> show databases;
+--------------------+
| Database           |
+--------------------+
| information_schema |
| mysql              |
| performance_schema |
| testme_again       |
+--------------------+
4 rows in set (0.00 sec)

mysql>
```

Success! Now your Raspberry Pi database server is being backed up by your desktop computer.

IS THERE A BETTER WAY?

If you are wondering if there is an easier way to get replication working without fiddling around with commands on the slaves, then I have good news. There is a better way! See the `mysqlreplicate` utility in MySQL Utilities. This utility allows you to set up replication with a single command. For more information about `mysqlreplicate`, see the online MySQL Utilities documentation at `http://dev.mysql.com/doc/index-gui.html`.

Component Shopping List

The only new component you need for this chapter is a surplus USB hard drive, which is listed in Table 6-2. Table 6-3 shows a list of the supporting hardware that is included in the shopping list from other chapters.

Table 6-2. *Components Needed*

Item	Vendors	Est. Cost USD	Qty Needed
Surplus hard drive	Any USB hard drive (surplus or purchased)	Varies	1

Table 6-3. *Components Reused from Previous Chapters*

Item	Vendors	Est. Cost USD	Qty Needed
Raspberry Pi Model B		$35 and up	1
HDMI or HDMI to DVI cable	Most online and retail stores	Varies	1
HDMI or DVI monitor	Most online and retail stores	Varies	1
USB keyboard	Most online and retail stores	Varies	1
USB power supply	Most online and retail stores	Varies	1
USB Type A to USB micro male	Most online and retail stores	Varies	1
SD card, 2GB or more	Most online and retail stores	Varies	1

Summary

This chapter introduced MySQL and gave you a crash course on how to use it. You also installed MySQL on a Raspberry Pi and saw how to use more advanced features of MySQL, like replication.

Although it does not have nearly the sophistication of a high-availability, five-nines uptime (99.999%) database server, the low-cost Raspberry Pi with an attached USB hard drive makes for a very small-footprint database server that you can put just about anywhere.

This is great because sensor networks, by nature and often by necessity, need to be small and low cost. Having to build an expensive database server is not usually the level of investment desired.

Furthermore, depending on your choice of host for the sensor, saving data is difficult. If you choose an Arduino as the host, saving the data to a database requires a connection to the internet and reliance on another service to store your data. This is fine for cases where you can actually connect the sensor nodes to the Internet[13] (or the sensor network's aggregator node); but if you cannot or do not want to connect to the Internet, it is difficult to get data into a database server from the Arduino.

That is, it was until recently. As you will see, there is indeed a way to save sensor data from a sensor node. In the next chapter, you build a sensor node that saves its data in your new database server—directly from an Arduino!

---

[13]Having sensor nodes connected to the Internet is one of the building blocks for a new paradigm called the "internet of things".

■ ■ ■

MySQL and Arduino: United at Last!

In previous chapters, I discussed several methods you can use to store sensor data. One of those methods is storing the data in a database located on your network. If you recall, this has several advantages, not the least of which is that you do not have to connect your sensor network to the Internet to enable this capability.

This is not difficult to achieve if your sensor nodes are connected to a Raspberry Pi, but how do you do this if your sensor nodes are connected to an Arduino? The Arduino could be a sensor node itself, with one or more sensors connected directly to the Arduino I/O ports; or the Arduino could be a data aggregator, collecting data from other sensor nodes via a ZigBee wireless network using XBee modules as you saw in Chapter 3. But how do you insert data into MySQL without using a third-party service like Xively?

This chapter introduces a new database connector library that enables you to send sensor data from your Arduino to a MySQL database.

Introducing Connector/Arduino

Congratulations! You have just entered a new world of Arduino projects. With a new database connector made specifically for the Arduino, you can connect your Arduino project directly to a MySQL server without using an intermediate computer or a web-based service.

Having direct access to a database server means you can store data acquired from your project in a database. You can also check values stored in tables on the server. The connector allows you to keep your sensor network local to your facility—it can even be disconnected from the Internet or any other external network.

If you have used some of the other methods of storing data from an Arduino, such as writing data to flash memory (for example, a secure digital card) or an EEPROM device, you can eliminate the manual data copy and extraction methods altogether. Similarly, if your project is such that you cannot or do not want to connect to the Internet to save your data, the ability to write to a local database server solves that problem as well.

Saving your data in a database not only preserves the data for analysis at a later time, but also means your project can feed data to more complex applications. Better still, if you have projects that use large data volumes for calculations or lookups, you can store the data on the server and retrieve only the data you need for the calculation or operation—all without taking up large blocks of memory on your Arduino. Clearly, this opens a whole new avenue of Arduino projects!

The database connector is named Connector/Arduino. It implements the MySQL client communication protocol (called a *database connector*) in a library built for the Arduino platform. Henceforth I refer to Connector/Arduino when discussing general concepts and features and refer to the actual source code as the Connector/Arduino library, the connector, or simply the library.

Sketches (programs) written to use the library permit you to encode SQL statements to insert data and run small queries to return data from the database (for example, using a lookup table).

You may be wondering how a microcontroller with limited memory and processing power can possibly support the code to insert data into a MySQL server. You can do this because the protocol for communicating with a MySQL server is not only well known and documented, but also specifically designed to be lightweight. This is one of the small details that make MySQL attractive to embedded developers.

In order to communicate with MySQL, the Arduino must be connected to the MySQL server via a network. To do so, the Arduino must use an Ethernet or WiFi shield and be connected to a network or subnet that can connect to the database server (you can even connect across the Internet). The library is compatible with most new Arduino Ethernet, WiFi, and compatible clone shields that support the standard Ethernet library.

■ **Note**   Earlier versions of Connector/Arduino did not directly support the WiFi shield and required a lot of minor changes to get it to work. The latest beta version of the connector does support the WiFi shield. See the sidebar "What About the WiFi Shield?" for details on how to enable the WiFi code changes.

Hardware Requirements

Connector/Arduino requires an Arduino or Arduino clone with at least 32KB of memory. If you are using an older Arduino like the Duemilanove, be sure you have the version that uses the ATmega328p processor. Figures 7-1 and 7-2 depict two of the most common Arduino boards.

Figure 7-1. *Arduino Uno (courtesy of arduino.cc)*

Figure 7-2. *Arduino Leonardo (courtesy of arduino.cc)*

Notice that the headers are different on the Leonardo as compared to the Uno. You may not see the subtle differences in the boards, but the Leonardo has built-in USB communication capabilities that enable the use of a mouse and keyboard, four additional digital pins, six more analog pins, and one more pulse-width modulation (PWM) pin. For more information about the differences and new features, see http://arduino.cc/en/Guide/ArduinoLeonardo.

Connector/Arduino also requires the Arduino Ethernet shield or equivalent. This is because the library references the Ethernet library written for the Ethernet shield. If you have some other form of Ethernet shield, or if the Ethernet shield you are using requires a different library, you have to make a slight modification to the library to use it. You see this in a later section. Figure 7-3 shows the Arduino Ethernet shield, and Figure 7-4 shows the Arduino WiFi shield.

Figure 7-3. *Arduino Ethernet shield (courtesy of arduino.cc)*

Figure 7-4. Arduino WiFi shield (courtesy of arduino.cc)

WHAT ABOUT THE DUE OR YÚN?

The connector has been tested and works with both of the latest Arduino boards—the Due and Yún.

If you have a Due, you can use an Arduino Ethernet shield[1] with the connector. The only difference is that you must use the latest beta version of the Arduino IDE (currently version 1.5.4).

If you have a Yún, you can use the connector but not through the onboard Ethernet or WiFi adapter. Several modifications—some of which are non-trivial—are needed to make the connector work through the bridge. These modifications are beyond the scope of this book.

The good news is, you can use an Arduino Ethernet or WiFi shield on your Yún! Be sure to install the latest beta for the Arduino IDE and follow all the tips concerning working with a Leonardo board where applicable.

Finally, for both boards, if you are converting floating-point numbers using `dtostrf`, you must use the `#include <avr/dtostrf.h>` include in order for the compiler to find it.

---

[1] I was unable to get the WiFi shield to work with the Due. The WiFi library needs some work in this area, because it results in compilation errors. Check the WiFi guide page for the latest concerning using the WiFi shield with the Due.

What About Memory?

Connector/Arduino is implemented as an Arduino library. Although the protocol is lightweight, the library does consume some memory. In fact, the library requires about 20KB of flash memory to load. Thus, it requires the ATmega328 or similar processor with 32KB of flash memory.

That may seem like there isn't a lot of space for programming your sensor node, but as it turns out you really don't need that much for most sensors. If you do, you can always step up to a new Arduino with more memory. For example, the latest Arduino, the Due, has 512KB of memory for program code. Based on that, a mere 20KB is an insignificant amount of overhead.

How to Get MySQL Connector/Arduino

To start using the library, you simply download it from the Launchpad site (`https://launchpad.net/mysql-arduino`), uncompress the file, and copy the folders to your Arduino libraries folder. I describe each of these steps in more detail shortly.

The library is open source, licensed as GPLv2, and owned by Oracle Corporation. Thus, any modifications to the library that you intend to share must meet the GPLv2 license. Although it is not an officially supported product of Oracle or MySQL, you can use the library under the GPLv2.

■ **Note**   If you do plan to modify Connector/Arduino for distribution, please contact an Oracle MySQL Sales specialist for more information about your responsibilities under the GPLv2 license.

DATABASE CONNECTORS FOR MYSQL

There are many database connectors for MySQL. Oracle supplies a number of database connectors for a variety of languages. The following are the current database connectors available for download from `http://dev.mysql.com/downloads/connector/`:

- *Connector/ODBC*: Standard ODBC compliant

- *Connector/Net*: Windows .Net platforms

- *Connector/J*: Java applications

- *Connector/Python*: Python applications

- *Connector/C++*: Standardized C++ applications

- *Connector/C* (`libmysql`): C applications

- *MySQL native driver for PHP* (`mysqlnd`): PHP 5.3 or newer connector

As you can see, there is a connector for just about any programming language you are likely to encounter—and now there is even one for the Arduino!

■ **Tip**   There is a MySQL Forum for discussing the connector. See `http://forums.mysql.com/list.php?175`. If you get stuck and need some help, check the forum for possible answers.

Downloading the Library

Begin by navigating to the Connector/Arduino page on Launchpad (`https://launchpad.net/mysql-arduino`). The latest version is 1.0.0 Beta, and the file is named `mysql_connector_arduino-1.0.0b.zip`. Look on the right side of the page, and click the file to download and save it to your computer. Once it is downloaded, uncompress the file. You see two new folders in the location where you extracted the file.

You need to copy or move the two folders to your `Arduino/Libraries` folder. Place the entire folders named `mysql_connector` and `sha1` in your Arduino library folder. You can find where this is by examining the preferences for the Arduino environment, as shown in Figure 7-5.

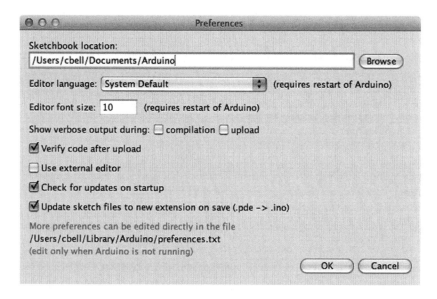

Figure 7-5. *Arduino Preferences dialog*

For example, the sketches folder on my Mac is /Users/cbell/Documents/Arduino. Thus, I copied the Connector/Arduino source code to folders named /Users/cbell/Documents/Arduino/Libraries/mysql_connector and /Users/cbell/Documents/Arduino/Libraries/sha1.

■ **Tip** If you copy a library to your `Libraries` folder while the Arduino application is running, you must restart it to detect the new library.

WHAT IS THE SHA1 LIBRARY?

The connector requires a special encryption library written by Peter Knight. The SHA1 library can be downloaded directly from Google at `http://code.google.com/p/cryptosuite/downloads/list`.

The files require minor modifications to use them. These modifications have already been made in the download file for the connector, so there is nothing you need to do.

However, if you want to see what has changed, examine the contents of the `sha1.diff` file. This file is a difference file; which can be applied with the `patch` program.

Now that you have the Connector/Arduino library installed, you are ready to start writing database-enabled sketches! Before you jump into to the library source code, let's first examine some of the limitations of using the library.

Limitations

Given the target platform—a small microcontroller with limited memory—there are some limitations to using a complex library on the Arduino platform. The first thing you should know about Connector/Arduino is that it isn't a small library: it can consume a lot of memory. Although the library uses dynamic memory to keep memory use to a minimum, how much memory is required depends on how you use the connector.

More specifically, you need to limit how many string constants you create. If you are issuing simple data-insertion commands (INSERT INTO), an easy way to calculate this is that the connector uses a bit more than the sum of the length of all of your strings. If you are querying the server for data, the connector uses a bit more than the cumulative size of a row of data returned.

If you are using the latest Arduino Due, this may not be an issue. But there are other considerations. The following are the known limitations of the Connector/Arduino:

- Query strings (the SQL statements) must fit into memory. This is because the class uses an internal buffer for building data packets to send to the server. It is suggested that long strings be stored in program memory using PROGMEM (see cmd_query_P). See http://arduino.cc/en/Reference/PROGMEM for more information.

- Result sets are read one row at a time and one field at a time.

- The combined length of a row in a result set must fit into memory.

- Server error responses are processed immediately. The connector prints the error code and message to the serial monitor.

Now that you know how the connector works on a high level, what hardware is required, and how to download and install the connector, let's dive in to using the connector to write sketches that insert data into a MySQL server.

Building Connector/Arduino-Enabled Sketches

Let's begin with a simple sketch designed to insert a single row into a table in MySQL. You are creating a "hello, world!" sketch (but saved in a database table). All database-enabled sketches share the same common building blocks. These include setting up a database to use, creating a sketch with a specific set of include files, connecting to the database server, and executing queries. This section walks through the basic steps needed to create and execute a database-enabled sketch.

Database Setup

The first thing you need is a database server! You can use your desktop or laptop computer if you'd prefer to limit the unknowns (always a good practice when experimenting with embedded systems). I used a laptop running MySQL to keep the example simple. However, if you built a Raspberry Pi MySQL database server in the previous chapter, feel free to use your shiny Raspberry Pi database server instead.

I also keep the example simple by using only the setup() method to connect to the MySQL server and issue the query. This simplifies things because the setup() method is called only once. Feel free to move the INSERT statement to the loop() method if you want to see what happens when multiple INSERTs are issued. Be sure to include the delay() call to allow the library sufficient time to execute and negotiate the protocol. Attempting to issue too many queries too quickly can be a source of strange errors or missing rows.

You begin by creating a database and a table to use to store the data. For this experiment, you create a simple table with two columns: a text column (char) to store a message and a TIMESTAMP column to record the date and time the row was saved. I find the TIMESTAMP data type to be an excellent choice for storing sensor data. It is rare that you

229

would not want to know when the sample was taken! Best of all, MySQL makes it very easy to use. In fact, you need pass only a token NULL value to the server, and it generates and stores the current timestamp itself.

Listing 7-1 shows a MySQL client (named mysql) session that creates the database and the table and inserts a row into the table manually. The sketch will execute a similar INSERT statement from your Arduino. By issuing a SELECT command, you can see each time the table was updated.

Listing 7-1. Creating the Test Database

```
$ mysql -uroot -psecret
Welcome to the MySQL monitor.  Commands end with ; or \g.
Your MySQL connection id is 102
Server version: 5.6.14-log Source distribution

Copyright (c) 2000, 2011, Oracle and/or its affiliates. All rights reserved.

Oracle is a registered trademark of Oracle Corporation and/or its
affiliates. Other names may be trademarks of their respective
owners.

Type 'help;' or '\h' for help. Type '\c' to clear the current input statement.

mysql> CREATE DATABASE test_arduino;
Query OK, 1 row affected (0.00 sec)

mysql> USE test_arduino;
Database changed
mysql> CREATE TABLE hello (source char(20), event_date timestamp);
Query OK, 0 rows affected (0.01 sec)

mysql> GRANT ALL ON *.* to 'root'@'%' IDENTIFIED BY 'secret';

mysql> INSERT INTO hello VALUES ('From Laptop', NULL);
Query OK, 1 row affected (0.00 sec)

mysql> SELECT * FROM hello;
+-------------+---------------------+
| source      | event_date          |
+-------------+---------------------+
| From Laptop | 2013-02-16 20:40:12 |
+-------------+---------------------+
1 row in set (0.00 sec)

mysql>
```

DESIGNING TABLES FOR STORING SENSOR DATA

When designing tables for your sensor networks, be sure to select the correct data type and length (if applicable) carefully. It would be a tragedy to learn months later that your painstakingly constructed sensor network has had its data truncated as a consequence of choosing the wrong data type. Similarly, if you run into problems with your sensor nodes or aggregate nodes failing when saving data, check the length of your character and other fields to ensure that you are not overrunning the allocated size (length).

Setting Up the Arduino

The hardware you need for this example is one Arduino or shield-compatible clone and an Arduino Ethernet shield. There are various forms of the Ethernet shield, but I prefer the Arduino-branded shields because they tend to be more reliable.

BUYER BEWARE: CHECK COMPATIBILITY

For the most part, Arduino clones described as "shield compatible" are safe to use. As with most things in life, sometimes get what you pay for, and it is always good practice to ask the vendor if there are any known limitations.

I failed to do this once, thinking I had found a great deal on an Ethernet shield that was "100% compatible," only to discover it had an annoying flaw that required me to remove the shield in order to upload sketches. Although the shield works and I use it regularly, it is *not* 100% compatible.

I like to mount my Arduino on a platform in order to make it easier to handle and less likely that I will accidentally set it down on a surface or object that conducts electricity—or, perhaps worse, that it will accidentally scratch my desk! Go ahead and mount the Ethernet shield to your Arduino. Be sure all the pins are seated. Figure 7-6 shows my Arduino and Ethernet shield mounted on a platform with a handy small breadboard nearby.

Figure 7-6. *Arduino with Ethernet shield*[2]

---

[2]Breadboard and mounting plate by Adafruit (www.adafruit.com/products/275).

Starting a New Sketch

It is time to start writing your sketch. Open your Arduino environment, and create a new sketch named `hello_mysql`. The following sections detail the parts of a typical MySQL database-enabled sketch. You begin with the required include files.

Include Files

To use the Connector/Arduino library, recall that it requires an Ethernet shield and therefore the Ethernet library. The Ethernet library also requires the SPI library. Recall also that Connector/Arduino requires the SHA1 library. Thus, you must include each of these in order. The following shows all the library header files you need to include at a bare minimum for a MySQL database-enabled sketch. Go ahead and enter these now:

```
#include <SPI.h>
#include <Ethernet.h>
#include <sha1.h>
#include <mysql.h>
```

Preliminary Setup

With the include files set up, you next must take care of some preliminary declarations. These include declarations for the Ethernet library and Connector/Arduino.

The Ethernet library requires you to set up a MAC address and the IP address of the server. The MAC address is a string of hexadecimal digits and need not be anything special, but it should be unique among the machines on your network. It uses Dynamic Host Control Protocol (DHCP) to get an IP address, DNS, and gateway information. The IP address of the server is defined using the `IPAddress` class (which stores the value as an array of four integers, just as you would expect).

On the other hand, the Ethernet class also permits you to supply an IP address for the Arduino. If you assign an IP address for the Arduino, it must be unique for the network segment to which it is attached. Be sure to use an IP scanner to make sure your choice of IP address isn't already in use.

The following shows what these statements would look like for a node on a 10.0.1.X network:

```
/* Setup for Ethernet Library */
byte mac_addr[] = { 0xDE, 0xAD, 0xBE, 0xEF, 0xFE, 0xED };
IPAddress server_addr(10, 0, 1, 23);
```

Next, you need to set up some variables for Connector/Arduino. You need to define a reference to the library and some strings to use for the data you use in the sketch. At a minimum, these include a string for the user ID, another for the password, and one for the query you use. This last string is optional because you can just use the literal string directly in the query call, but it is good practice to make strings for the query statements. It is also the best way to make queries parameterized for reuse.

The following is an example of the statements needed to complete the declarations for your sketch:

```
/* Setup for the Connector/Arduino */
Connector my_conn;          // The Connector/Arduino reference

char user[] = "root";
char password[] = "secret";
char INSERT_SQL[] = "INSERT INTO test_arduino.hello VALUES ('Hello from Arduino!', NULL)";
```

Notice the INSERT statement. You include a string to indicate that you are running the query from your Arduino. You also include the NULL value so that the server will create the timestamp for the row as shown in the manual execution previously.

Connecting to a MySQL Server

That concludes the preliminaries; let's get some code written! Next, you change the setup() method. This is where the code for connecting to the MySQL server should be placed. Recall that this method is called only once each time the Arduino is booted. Listing 7-2 shows the code needed.

Listing 7-2. Setup() Method

```
void setup() {
  Ethernet.begin(mac_addr);
  Serial.begin(115200);
  delay(1000);
  Serial.println("Connecting...");
  if (my_conn.mysql_connect(server_addr, 3306, user, password))
    delay(500);
  else
    Serial.println("Connection failed.");
}
```

The code begins with a call to the Ethernet library to initialize the network connection. Recall that when you use the Ethernet.begin() method, passing only the MAC address as shown in the example, it causes the Ethernet library to use DHCP to obtain an IP address. If you want to assign an IP address manually, see the Ethernet.begin() method documentation at http://arduino.cc/en/Reference/EthernetBegin.

Next is a call to serial monitor. Although not completely necessary, it is a good idea to include it so you can see the messages written by Connector/Arduino. If you have problems with connecting or running queries, be sure to use the serial monitor so you can see the messages sent by the library.

Now comes a call to the delay() method. You issue this wait of one second to ensure that you have time to start the serial monitor and not miss the debug statements. Feel free to experiment with changing this value if you need more time to start the serial monitor.

After the delay, you print a statement to the serial monitor to indicate that you are attempting to connect to the server. Connecting to the server is a single call to the Connector/Arduino library named mysql_connect(). You pass the IP address of the MySQL database server, the port the server is listening on, and the user name and password. If this call passes, the code drops to the next delay() method call.

This delay is needed to slow execution before issuing additional MySQL commands. Like the previous delay, depending on your hardware and network latency, you may not need this delay. You should experiment if you have strong feelings against using delays to avoid latency issues. On the other hand, should the connection fail, the code falls through to the print statement to tell you the connection has failed.

Running a Query

Now it is time to run the query. Place this code in the branch that is executed after a successful connection. Listing 7-3 shows the previous conditional statement rewritten to include the method call to run the insert query.

Listing 7-3. Connecting and Running a Query

```
if (my_conn.mysql_connect(server_addr, 3306, user, password))
  {
    delay(500);
    /* Write Hello to MySQL table test_arduino.hello */
    my_conn.cmd_query(INSERT_SQL);
  }
  else
    Serial.println("Connection failed.");
}
```

Notice that you simply invoke a method named cmd_query() and pass it the query you defined earlier. Yes, it is that easy!

Testing the Sketch

You now have all the code needed to complete the sketch except for the loop() method. In this case, you make it an empty method because you are not doing anything repetitive. Listing 7-4 shows the completed sketch.

■ **Tip** If you are having problems getting the connector working, see the "Troubleshooting Connector/Arduino" section and then return to this project.

Listing 7-4. "Hello, MySQL!" Sketch

```
/**
 * Example: Hello, MySQL!
 *
 * This code module demonstrates how to create a simple database-enabled
 * sketch.
 */
#include <SPI.h>
#include <Ethernet.h>
#include <sha1.h>
#include <mysql.h>

/* Setup for Ethernet Library */
byte mac_addr[] = { 0xDE, 0xAD, 0xBE, 0xEF, 0xFE, 0xED };
IPAddress server_addr(10, 0, 1, 23);    // The IP address of your database server

/* Setup for the Connector/Arduino */
Connector my_conn;                       // The Connector/Arduino reference

char user[] = "root";
char password[] = "secret";
char INSERT_SQL[] = "INSERT INTO test_arduino.hello VALUES ('Hello from Arduino!', NULL)";
```

```
void setup() {
  Ethernet.begin(mac_addr);
  Serial.begin(115200);
  delay(5000);
  Serial.println("Connecting...");
  if (my_conn.mysql_connect(server_addr, 3306, user, password))
  {
    delay(500);
    /* Write Hello, World to MySQL table test_arduino.hello */
    my_conn.cmd_query(INSERT_SQL);
    Serial.println("Query Success!");
  }
  else
    Serial.println("Connection failed.");
}

void loop() {
}
```

Before you press the button to compile and upload the sketch, let's discuss a couple of errors that could occur. If you have the wrong IP address or the wrong user name and password for the MySQL server, you could see a connection failure in the serial monitor like that shown in Figure 7-7.

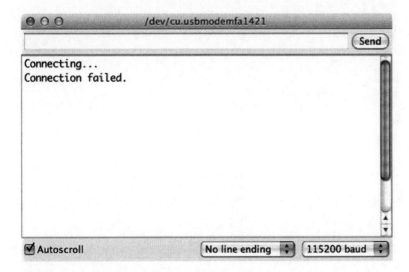

Figure 7-7. *Failed connection*

If your Arduino connects to the MySQL server but the query fails, you see an error in the serial monitor like the one shown in Figure 7-8.

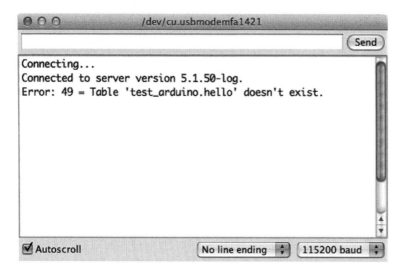

Figure 7-8. *Failed query*

Be sure to double-check the source code and the IP address of your MySQL server as well as the username and password chosen. If you are still encountering problems connecting, see the "Troubleshooting Connector/Arduino" section for a list of things to test to ensure that your MySQL server is configured correctly.

Once you have double-checked the server installation and the information in the sketch, compile and upload the sketch to your Arduino. Then start the serial monitor and observe the process of connecting to the MySQL server. Figure 7-9 shows a completed and successful execution of the code.

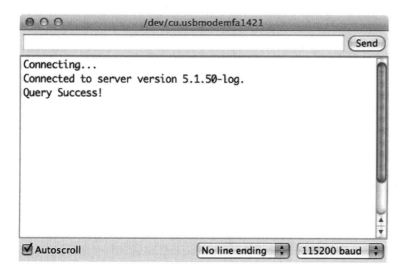

Figure 7-9. *Correct serial monitor output*

Wow, is that it? Not very interesting, is it? If you see the statements in your serial monitor as shown in Figure 7-9, rest assured that the Arduino has connected to and issued a query to the MySQL server. To check, simply return to the mysql client and issue a select on the table. But first, run the sketch a number of times to issue several inserts in the table.

You can do this in two ways. First, you can press RESET on your Arduino. If you leave your serial monitor running, the Arduino presents the messages in order, as shown in Figure 7-10. Second, you can upload the sketch again. In this case, the serial monitor closes, and you have to reopen it. The advantage of this method is you can change the query statement each time, thereby inserting different rows into the database. Go ahead and try that now, and check your database for the changes.

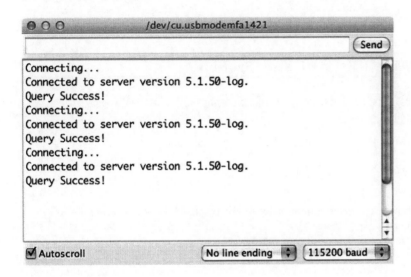

Figure 7-10. *Results of running the sketch several times*

Let's check the results of the test runs. To do so, you connect to the database server with the mysql client and issue a SELECT query. Listing 7-5 shows the results of the three runs from the example. Notice the different timestamp for each run. As you can see, I ran it once, then waited a few minutes and ran it again (I used the RESET button on my Arduino Ethernet shield), and then ran it again right away. Very cool, isn't it?

Listing 7-5. Verifying the Connection with the Serial Monitor

```
$ mysql -uroot -psecret
Welcome to the MySQL monitor.  Commands end with ; or \g.
Your MySQL connection id is 33
Server version: 5.6.14-log Source distribution

Copyright (c) 2000, 2010, Oracle and/or its affiliates. All rights reserved.
This software comes with ABSOLUTELY NO WARRANTY. This is free software,
and you are welcome to modify and redistribute it under the GPL v2 license

Type 'help;' or '\h' for help. Type '\c' to clear the current input statement.
```

```
mysql> select * from test_arduino.hello;
+-----------------+---------------------+
| source          | event_date          |
+-----------------+---------------------+
| From laptop     | 2013-02-19 15:17:38 |
| Hello from Arduino! | 2013-02-19 15:18:12 |
| Hello from Arduino! | 2013-02-19 15:28:39 |
| Hello from Arduino! | 2013-02-19 15:29:16 |
+-----------------+---------------------+
4 rows in set (0.01 sec)

mysql>
```

WHAT ABOUT THE WIFI SHIELD?

If you are planning to use the WiFi shield, you need to make a few minor changes to enable the WiFi-specific code in the connector.[3] Fortunately, it is very easy.

Begin by including the WiFi library prior to the connector include in your sketch, as follows:

```
#include <WiFi.h>          // Use this for WiFi
#include <mysql.h>
```

Next, you need to use one of the available WiFi connection mechanisms and comment out the Ethernet.begin() call. An example setup() method with changes is shown here:

```
// WiFi card example
char ssid[] = "my_lonely_ssid";
char pass[] = "horse_with_silly_name";

Connector my_conn;          // The Connector/Arduino reference

void setup() {
  Serial.begin(115200);
  while (!Serial);          // wait for serial port to connect. Needed for Leonardo only

  //Ethernet.begin(mac_addr);

  // WiFi section
  int status = WiFi.begin(ssid, pass);
  // if you're not connected, stop here:
  if ( status != WL_CONNECTED) {
    Serial.println("Couldn't get a WiF connection!");
    while(true);
  }
  // if you are connected, print out info about the connection:
  else {
    Serial.println("Connected to network");
    IPAddress ip = WiFi.localIP();
```

---

[3]Assuming you have downloaded and installed the WiFi shield library from https://github.com/arduino/wifishield.

```
      Serial.print("My IP address is: ");
      Serial.println(ip);
   }

   delay(1000);
   Serial.println("Connecting...");
   if (my_conn.mysql_connect(server_addr, 3306, user, password)) {
      delay(1000);
   }
   else
      Serial.println("Connection failed.");
}
```

Next, uncomment-out the WiFi-specific directives in the mysql.h file:

```
#define WIFI        // Uncomment out this for use with the WiFi shield
#include <WiFi.h>   // Uncomment out this for use with the WiFi shield
```

See (http://arduino.cc/en/Guide/ArduinoWiFiShield) for more examples of how to use a connection method to connect your WiFi shield to your access point.

If you plan to use the WiFi shield with an Arduino that is older than an Arduino Uno Revision 3, you need to use a jumper on the IOREF pin, as shown here (courtesy of arduino.cc) for the WiFi shield to work properly.

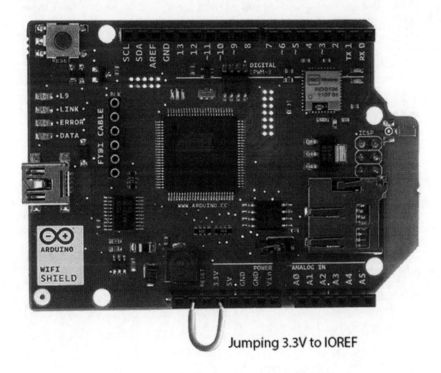

Jumping 3.3V to IOREF

The WiFi shield page has this and a host of other very important information for using the WiFi shield in your project.

Troubleshooting Connector/Arduino

Setting up and using Connector/Arduino as described usually results in success. However, there are cases when the setup does not go quite right and the examples in this chapter simply won't work. Many problems can be attributed to your choice of Arduino hardware, networking environment setup, and even MySQL server configuration. For example, if your Arduino hardware is not an official Arduino product, if it is newer than the examples used in the book, or if your Ethernet shield is a clone or something other than a wired network shield, you may encounter problems getting everything to work.

If this happens to you, don't give up![4] This section is designed to give you tips and techniques for figuring out what is wrong with your hardware, software, network, and operating system that may be preventing the connector from working.

Rather than include an exhaustive description of all the procedures needed for all cases,[5] I present a taxonomy that you can use to diagnose and solve your issues. There are several categories of problem areas. I discuss each of these in turn:

- MySQL server configuration
- MySQL user account problems
- Networking configuration
- Connector installation
- Other

The following sections explain the issue and suggest a cause and solution. It may be that one or more of these issues are causing your sketch to fail. The best way to use this section is to read through it from start to finish, checking your system along the way. Each section builds on the previous section, ensuring that all possible issues are solved in an orderly manner. I am certain you can get your sketch working using this technique.

■ **Tip** The Arduino site has a very good troubleshooting section for general Arduino help. You should consult this page in addition to following the advice in this section. See `http://arduino.cc/en/Guide/troubleshooting`.

MySQL Server Configuration

One of the most common issues that can cause your MySQL sketch to fail or not work properly has to do with how the MySQL server is configured. In general, you are likely to see errors connecting to the server in the serial monitor. This section contains a number of causes for this problem.

Server Is Not Using Networking

The MySQL server can be configured to disable networking with the `--skip-networking` option. In this case, you may be able to connect to your MySQL server on your local machine (on the machine where MySQL is installed) by using the `mysql` client, but accessing the machine from another host fails.

---

[4]As satisfying as it may be, please refrain from giving your tiny Arduino skeet-shooting lessons. All is not lost, and most issues can be resolved with a little patience and the techniques described here.

[5]An impossible feat for mere mortals.

The best way to check this without using a second computer (which is also a viable test) is to use the `mysql` client as follows. To test local connection to the server, run this command (substituting your username and password):

```
$ mysql -uroot -psecret
```

If this works, then your server is alive and accepting connections. If this does not work, refer to the MySQL online reference manual to check your configuration and other ways to ensure that MySQL is running properly.

Now, let's attempt to connect via the network. This is triggered whenever you use the host option as shown next. Notice that it is almost the same command, but in this case you supply the IP address of the server (your machine) and the port for MySQL:

```
$ mysql -uroot -psecret -h 10.0.1.23 --port 3306
```

This simulates how the Arduino connects to the MySQL server. If it works, it verifies that your MySQL server is alive and accepting network connections using the IP and port supplied. Be sure to use these settings in your sketch.

If the command fails, locate your `mysql.cnf` file (`mysql.ini` for some Windows installations), and remove the `skip-networking` option. You can disable it by placing a # in the first column of the line. Once you have done this, be sure to restart your MySQL server to make the changes take effect, and then try the previous test again.

Cannot Connect, and Correct IP Address Is Used

Another issue that is closely related to the `--skip-networking` option is the `--bind-address` option. This option ensures that MySQL listens and communicates on a specific IP address. It is used mainly for multi-homed systems (computers with multiple network adapters). If this option is enabled, and it is not set to the same IP address as the host on which it is installed, the MySQL server will exhibit behavior similar to the previous problem.

Testing this problem uses the same test as the previous example. The resolution is simply to comment-out the `bind-address` option in the MySQL configuration file. Remember to restart your MySQL server if you change the configuration file.

I Can Connect Locally but Not Remotely

If the previous issues do not resolve the problem or if your MySQL server is configured correctly and you still cannot connect, it is possible that your computer is running a firewall or similar port-blocking application. The best way to test this is to use a second computer and the `mysql` client application to try to connect to the server. If you get errors related to the server not responding or similar, the server could be blocking connections. Again, the command to use from the remote computer is

```
$ mysql -uroot -psecret -- 10.0.1.23 --port 3306
```

To resolve the issue, you must change your firewall or port-blocking application. MySQL uses port 3306 by default. Be sure to check your firewall application to ensure that it permits connections (inbound and outbound) through port 3306. If it does not, enable this port and try your sketch again.

■ **Tip** For more information about setting up the MySQL server for network access and platform-specific installation steps, see the online MySQL reference manual.

MySQL User Account Problems

Another very common source of issues concerns how the MySQL user is created. More specifically, it has to do with the choice of host name in the CREATE USER or GRANT statement. For example, if you issued the following commands, you could have problems connecting from your Arduino or a second computer:

```
mysql> CREATE USER 'joe'@'10.0.1.23' IDENTIFIED BY 'secret';
Query OK, 0 rows affected (0.01 sec)

mysql> GRANT SELECT ON test_arduino.* TO 'joe'@'10.0.1.24';
Query OK, 0 rows affected (0.01 sec)
```

Do you see the problems (there are three)? First, you created a user with a specific host (10.0.1.23), but later you granted SELECT privileges to the test_arduino database to the same user—or did you?

This is the second problem. In the GRANT statement, you used the host 10.0.1.24, which means when user joe connects from 10.0.1.24, he can see the test_arduino database.

The third problem arises from the second. Because you did not reference an existing user and host combination, MySQL does not require joe to use a password when connecting from host 10.0.1.24. You can see that this is the case by querying the mysql.user table:

```
mysql> SELECT user, host, password from mysql.user WHERE user = 'joe';
+------+-----------+-------------------------------------------+
| user | host      | password                                  |
+------+-----------+-------------------------------------------+
| joe  | 10.0.1.23 | *14E65567ABDB5135D0CFD9A70B3032C179A49EE7 |
| joe  | 10.0.1.24 |                                           |
+------+-----------+-------------------------------------------+
2 rows in set (0.00 sec)
```

Aha, you say. Aha indeed. The lesson here is always, always make sure your choice of user and host match the IP (or hostname) of the machine from which you want to connect.

But you may be thinking, "What about DHCP?" If you use DHCP, as do most sketches and examples, then you may not know what IP address your Arduino has been assigned. What do you do then?

One of the ways to reduce host-name and permissions problems is to use wildcards. Consider this alternative to the previous commands:

```
mysql> CREATE USER 'joe'@'10.0.1.%' IDENTIFIED BY 'secret';
Query OK, 0 rows affected (0.00 sec)

mysql> GRANT SELECT ON test_arduino.* TO 'joe'@'10.0.1.%';
Query OK, 0 rows affected (0.00 sec)

mysql> SELECT user, host, password from mysql.user WHERE user = 'joe';
+------+----------+-------------------------------------------+
| user | host     | password                                  |
+------+----------+-------------------------------------------+
| joe  | 10.0.1.% | *14E65567ABDB5135D0CFD9A70B3032C179A49EE7 |
+------+----------+-------------------------------------------+
1 row in set (0.00 sec)
```

Notice that here you use a % for the last portion of the IP address. This effectively permits the user to connect from any computer on that subnet. Cool! Notice also that your problem of two user accounts has been resolved.

Other issues related to user accounts are cases where you've forgotten the password, misspelled it, or used caps (or not caps) when you assigned the password. All these user account issues can be tested with the mysql client application. I recommend trying the connection locally and remotely from a second computer. If it works remotely, you know the account is set up correctly. Be sure to do a SELECT or two when you are connected with your Arduino user account, just to make sure the permissions are set correctly.

Networking Configuration

When networking problems occur, it isn't always obvious what is wrong. Rather than listing a number of common error conditions or specific examples, I discuss things you need to check to make sure things are working.

When there are networking issues, you are likely to encounter or observe an inability to connect to your MySQL server. Yes, you probably see the same problems as described previously in almost the same ways.

The best way to check whether you are having networking issues is to connect a second computer to the same network cable that you are using for your Arduino and try to connect with your friend the mysql client. Be sure to check that the computer is set up to get its IP address from DHCP and all other networking settings are the same as your Arduino (no static DNS, and so on).

This is very important because if your computer is configured with a static IP and the Arduino sketch is using DHCP (or vice versa), this can mask the problem! For example, if no DHCP server is available, Arduino sketches configured to get the IP address dynamically will fail.

If you connect a second computer to your network using the same cable as the Arduino, and it works but the sketch still does not work, you should consider the possibility that your Ethernet shield is faulty or incompatible with your hardware. Check the vendor' or manufacturer's web site for any limitations or compatibility workarounds. I have seen this on at least one occasion. Another possibility is that the shield has malfunctioned (rare, but it does happen).

Now, if your computer fails to connect to your MySQL server, check the following items to ensure that your networking is configured correctly. Some of these may seem a little dumb, but I can assure you that I've personally encountered each of these at least once:

- Is the router/switch turned on?[6]

- Are you using the correct subnet?

- Are you using the correct options *in the proper order* for Ethernet.begin()? See the online Arduino library reference page (http://arduino.cc/en/Reference/EthernetBegin) for more details.

- If you are trying to use DHCP, is there a DHCP server on your network?

- Is the network cable plugged in to the switch/router?[7]

- Check the lights on the switch/router. Does it show that the cable is connected? If not, you may have a bad cable.

Once again, check and fix all of these issues, go back to the second computer, and try the connection. When it is working, your sketch should connect to the MySQL server.

---

[6]You will be surprised how often this happens—and how humble you feel when you discover that it works great once it has proper power supplied.

[7]Been there, done that. Twice. You know it's got two ends, right?

■ **Note** A complete tutorial or overview of networking is beyond the scope of this book. However, a few well-typed key phrases in a Google search will net you a host of good advice for diagnosing networking problems.

Another thing to try is to load one of the example sketches for the Ethernet shield. For example, load, compile, and run the WebClient sketch. What you should see is a mass of data returned from a search request to google.com. If this works, you can be sure that your Ethernet shield is working properly and that you still have issues with either your database server or your sketch.

Connector Installation

The last major area of potential issues has to do with how the connector is installed. If you have gotten this far and your sketch compiles and uploads correctly, you do not have any problems related to the connector installation. I describe the most common installation problems in the following sections.

Compilation Errors Related to "No Module Named"

If you encounter compilation errors complaining that there is no module named Connector or similar errors, you do not have the libraries installed in the proper location. Go back to the "Downloading the Library" section earlier in this chapter, and ensure that you have downloaded the correct file, extracted the zip file, copied the folders to your Arduino libraries folder, and restarted the IDE.

■ **Tip** It is possible that your libraries folder is not where you think it is. Be sure to check the Preferences dialog to find the default location. The libraries folder should be a subfolder of the sketchbook location.

The best indicator that you have the connecter copied correctly is that you can see the mysql_connector example in the File ➤ Examples menu.

Compilation Errors Related to Include File

Errors like this can be caused by the use of quotes versus brackets in the #include <mysql.h> statement. If you are using quotes, and the mysql.cpp and mysql.h files are not copied to your project folder or a subfolder thereof, you may see compilation errors. The correct method is to use brackets with the connector files located in the libraries folder.

I Copied the mysql.* Files to My Project Folder but Still Get Errors

There are a few reasons to place the connector files in your project folder, but I must discourage this practice. If you encounter errors when trying to use the files local to your project, you should remove them and place them in the libraries folder according to the earlier instructions.

Other

There are also some other issues you could encounter that do not fall into the previous categories.

Strange Characters Appear in the Serial Monitor

If you see garbage or strange characters in your serial monitor output, it could be that your setting for the `Serial.begin()` method does not match the serial monitor setting. Choose the appropriate speed from the drop-down list in the serial monitor, and try your sketch again.

No Output in the Serial Monitor

This one is a lot harder to diagnose. Sometimes the Arduino is hung, or there is a hardware issue like a shield not being fully seated, insufficient power, or even a sketch that is too big to fit in memory (see the next section). When this occurs, check your hardware carefully for proper seating of all components, and make sure your Arduino IDE settings for the serial port and board are correct.

My Sketch Is Too Big

Because the connector uses a lot of program memory, it is possible to run out of space when compiling your sketch. When this occurs, you may get an error like the following:

```
Binary sketch size: 32510 bytes (of a 32256 byte maximum).
```

If this happens, try removing all the unnecessary variables, strings, include files, and code that you can. The troubleshooting section on the Arduino site has several entries for suggestions on reducing sketch size.

In the extreme case, you can edit the `mysql.cpp` and `mysql.h` files for the connector itself and remove unneeded features. In this case, you want to remove any methods you are not using by commenting them out.

For example, if you do not need to return any result sets, you can eliminate the methods for performing result-set processing. You can do this easily by commenting-out the following line of code in the `mysql.h` file and recompiling. If you get errors for missing methods, make sure you are not trying to use any result-set-related methods:

```
#ifndef mysql_h
#define mysql_h

#include "Arduino.h"
#include <SPI.h>
#include <Ethernet.h>

//#define WITH_SELECT  // Comment out this for use without SELECT capability
                       // to save space.
...
```

■ **Note** In some versions of the IDE, modifying the files may require reloading your sketch to activate the changes in the IDE.

None of These Solved My Problem—What Next?

If you have tried the suggestions in the previous sections and you are still having issues, go back to the top and work through the solutions again. If that does not solve the problem, try a different Arduino (such as an Uno) and a different Ethernet shield. The tests and diagnoses should have eliminated all other issues, leaving only the Arduino hardware as the suspect.

Now that you know the basics of what a MySQL database-enabled sketch requires, let's take a short tour of the Connector/Arduino library to learn what methods are available for your use.

A Tour of the MySQL Connector/Arduino Code

Before you embark on a project, let's take a moment to tour the source code for the library. This section examines the library and its supporting methods in more detail. If you never intend to extend or otherwise modify the library, you can skip ahead to the project section.

Library Files

The mysql_connector folder contains a number of files and a directory. The following list describes each of the files:

- examples: A directory containing example code for using the library.

- keywords.txt: The list of keywords reserved for the library.

- mysql.cpp: The core library source code.

- mysql.h: The header file for the library.

- Readme.txt: Getting-started documentation.

- sha1.diff: A difference file for changing the original sha1.h/.cpp files. If you are curious as to what was needed to use the SHA1 library, you can look at this file.

- sha1_no256.diff: A difference file for saving some space in the SHA1 library (see the sidebar "Saving Some Bytes").

SAVING SOME BYTES

If you are using an older Arduino or a clone that has 32KB of flash memory and need or want to save as much space as possible, you can trim the SHA1 library. The connector does not need some of the features in the SHA1 library; and because they take up space, you can eliminate them. If you would like to remove the unneeded code from the SHA1 library, apply the difference file (sha1_no256.diff) using patch as shown in Listing 7-6, and delete the sha1256.h and sh1256.cpp files. This will save you about 2KB of program space.

Listing 7-6. Difference File

```
--- ./sha1.cpp    2012-05-25 10:10:20.000000000 -0400
+++ /Volumes/Macintosh_Data/cbell/Documents/Arduino/libraries/sha1/sha1.cpp    2012-05-25
10:07:38.000000000 -0400
@@ -126,38 +126,4 @@
 #define HMAC_IPAD 0x36
 #define HMAC_OPAD 0x5c

-
-
-void Sha1Class::initHmac(const uint8_t* key, int keyLength) {
-  uint8_t i;
-  memset(keyBuffer,0,BLOCK_LENGTH);
-  if (keyLength > BLOCK_LENGTH) {
-    // Hash long keys
-    init();
```

```
-    for (;keyLength--;) write(*key++);
-    memcpy(keyBuffer,result(),HASH_LENGTH);
-  } else {
-    // Block length keys are used as is
-    memcpy(keyBuffer,key,keyLength);
-  }
-  //for (i=0; i<BLOCK_LENGTH; i++) debugHH(keyBuffer[i]);
-  // Start inner hash
-  init();
-  for (i=0; i<BLOCK_LENGTH; i++) {
-    write(keyBuffer[i] ^ HMAC_IPAD);
-  }
-}
-
-uint8_t* Sha1Class::resultHmac(void) {
-  uint8_t i;
-    // Complete inner hash
-  memcpy(innerHash,result(),HASH_LENGTH);
-  // now innerHash[] contains H((K0 xor ipad)||text)
-
-  // Calculate outer hash
-  init();
-  for (i=0; i<BLOCK_LENGTH; i++) write(keyBuffer[i] ^ HMAC_OPAD);
-  for (i=0; i<HASH_LENGTH; i++) write(innerHash[i]);
-  return result();
-}
 Sha1Class Sha1;
--- ./sha1.h     2012-05-25 10:10:20.000000000 -0400
+++ /Volumes/Macintosh_Data/cbell/Documents/Arduino/libraries/sha1/sha1.h     2012-05-25
10:07:06.000000000 -0400
@@ -22,7 +22,6 @@
     void init(void);
     void initHmac(const uint8_t* secret, int secretLength);
     uint8_t* result(void);
-    uint8_t* resultHmac(void);
     virtual size_t write(uint8_t);
     virtual size_t write(uint8_t* data, int length);
     using Print::write;
```

You can find the difference file in the source repository for this book on the Apress web site (http://www.apress.com).

Field Structure

The library uses a number of structures when communicating with the server. There is one structure that you use frequently when returning result sets. It is called field_struct and is shown in Listing 7-7.

Listing 7-7. Field Structure

```
// Structure for retrieving a field (minimal implementation).
typedef struct {
  char *db;
  char *table;
  char *name;
} field_struct;
```

The field structure is used to retrieve the metadata for a field. Notice that you get the database, table, and field name. This permits you to determine which table a field is derived from in the case of queries involving joins. The method used to populate this field structure, get_field(), creates the strings in memory. It is your responsibility to free this memory—the strings—when you are finished reading or operating on the data.

There are also two structures for working with result sets: column_names and row_values. I discuss these in more detail in the next section but include them here for completeness. Use column_names for getting column information and row_values for getting row values in a result set:

```
// Structure for storing result set metadata.
typedef struct {
  int num_fields;      // actual number of fields
  field_struct *fields[MAX_FIELDS];
} column_names;
```

```
// Structure for storing row data.
typedef struct {
  char *values[MAX_FIELDS];
} row_values;
```

Now that you understand the structures involved with working with the library methods, let's examine the methods available to you for communicating with a MySQL server.

Public Methods

Libraries—or, more specifically, classes—typically have one or more public methods that can be used by any caller (program) via an instantiation of the class. Classes also have some parts that are private, which are typically helper methods to do something internal for the class. The methods can abstract portions of the class or simply hide data and operations that do not need to be accessed by the caller (think abstract data types). The public methods and attributes are therefore the things the designer permits the caller to access.

The Connector/Arduino library has a number of public methods that define the library's capabilities. There are methods for connecting, executing queries, and returning results (rows) from the database. Listing 7-8 shows the method declarations for the public methods. I discuss the details of each in the following paragraphs.

Listing 7-8. Public Methods

```
boolean mysql_connect(IPAddress server, int port,
                      char *user, char *password);
boolean cmd_query(const char *query);
boolean cmd_query_P(const char *query);
void show_results();
int get_field(field_struct *fs);
int get_row();
int is_connected () { return client.connected(); }
```

The `mysql_connect()` method, as you have seen, is the method you must call to connect to a MySQL database server. This method must be called after the initialization of the Ethernet class and before any other method from the library. It requires the IP address of the server, the port for the server, and the username and password to use to connect. It returns a Boolean, where true indicates success and false means there was some error in connecting to the server. If you encounter problems connecting to the server, you should attempt to connect from another machine on your network using the `mysql` client and the IP, port, user, and password defined in your sketch, to ensure connectivity and that there are no user or password issues.

The `cmd_query()` method is one of two methods you can use to execute a query (SQL statement). This version of the method takes a constant string reference that contains the query you wish to execute. It return true for success or false for failure. If there is a failure and the MySQL server returns an error, this method displays the error in the serial monitor.

The other method to run queries, `cmd_query_P()`, works the same as `cmd_query()`, except that the string passed is defined using program space. For more information about using program space (called PROGMEM), see the Arduino online reference (`www.arduino.cc/en/Reference/PROGMEM`). Basically, if you need more space for data but can afford to use program space for data, you should use this method to execute strings from program space.

The `show_results()` method is both an example of how to retrieve data from the database for SELECT queries and a method you can use as is to execute after issuing the `cmd_query()` call. The method reads one row at a time and sends it to the serial monitor. It can be handy for testing queries and for experimenting with new sketches.

On the other hand, if you want to read rows from a database and process the data, you can write your own method to do this. You must first execute the query with `cmd_query()`; then, if there is a result set, read the column headers (the server always sends the column headers first) using `get_columns()` and read the rows with the iterator `get_next_row()`. I demonstrate how to use these methods in the next section.

The `is_connected()` method returns true if the Arduino is connected to the server or false if not. You can use this method to test connectivity if or when there are long periods of inactivity or errors.

Example Uses

Besides connecting to a database server, the two uses of the library are issuing queries that do not return results (like INSERT) and returning rows from queries that return result sets (like SELECT or SHOW VARIABLES). The following sections demonstrate each of these options.

Queries without Results

You have seen how to issue queries without result sets in the "Hello, MySQL!" example. Recall that this is simply a call to `cmd_query()` with the query passed as a string. The following shows an example of a query that returns no results:

```
char INSERT_SQL[] = "INSERT INTO test_arduino.hello VALUES ('Hello, MySQL!', NULL)";
my_conn.cmd_query(INSERT_SQL);
```

You may be wondering about how to handle errors. The good news is the Connector/Arduino library is designed to read the error from the server and display the error. See Figure 7-4 for an example of this feature in action.

Queries Returning Results

Returning results (rows) from the server is a bit more complicated but not overly so. To read a result set from the server, you must first read the result set header and the field packets, and then the data rows. Specifically, you must anticipate, read, and parse the following packets:

- *Result-set header packet*: Number of columns
- *Field packets*: Column descriptors
- *EOF packet*: Marker: end-of-field packets

- *Row data packets*: Row contents

- *EOF packet*: marker: End-of-data packets

This means the MySQL server first sends the number of fields and a list of the fields (columns) that you must read, and then the row data appears in one or more packets until there are no more rows. The algorithm for reading a result set is as follows:

1. Read result set header for number of columns.

2. Read fields until EOF.

3. Read rows until EOF.

Let's take a look at the contents of the show_results() method; see Listing 7-9.

Listing 7-9. Displaying Result Sets

```
void Connector::show_results() {
  column_names *cols;
  int rows = 0;

  // Get the columns
  cols = get_columns();
  if (cols == NULL) {
    return;
  }

  for (int f = 0; f < columns.num_fields; f++) {
    Serial.print(columns.fields[f]->name);
    if (f < columns.num_fields-1)
      Serial.print(',');
  }
  Serial.println();

  // Read the rows
  while (get_next_row()) {
    rows++;
    for (int f = 0; f < columns.num_fields; f++) {
      Serial.print(row.values[f]);
      if (f < columns.num_fields-1)
        Serial.print(',');
    }
    free_row_buffer();
    Serial.println();
  }

  // Report how many rows were read
  Serial.print(rows);
  Serial.println(" rows in result.");
  free_columns_buffer();
}
```

So what's going on here? Notice how the code is structured to execute the query; if there are results (cmd_query() does not return NULL), you read the column headers. The return from the get_columns() method is a structure that contains an array of field structures. The structure is shown next:

```
// Structure for retrieving a field (minimal implementation).
Typedef struct {
  char *db;
  char *table;
  char *name;
} field_struct;

// Structure for storing result set metadata.
Typedef struct {
  int num_fields;      // actual number of fields
  field_struct *fields[MAX_FIELDS];
} column_names;
```

Notice that the column_names structure has a fields array. Use that array to get information about each field in the form of the field_struct (shown earlier). In that structure, you can get the database name, table name, and column name. In the code you simply print out the column names and a comma after each.

Next, you read the rows using a special iterator named get_next_row(), which returns a pointer to a row structure that contains an array of the field values:

```
// Structure for storing row data.
typedef struct {
  char *values[MAX_FIELDS];
} row_values;
```

In this case, while get_next_row() returns a valid pointer (not NULL), you read each field and print out the values.

You may be wondering what MAX_FIELDS is. Well, it is an easy way to make sure you limit your array of columns (fields). This is defined in mysql.h and is set to 32. If you want to save a few bytes, you can change that value to something lower, but beware: if you exceed that value, your code will wander off into wonkyville[8] (unreferenced pointer). So tread lightly.

Notice also the calls to free_row_buffer() and free_columns_buffer(). These are memory-cleanup methods needed to free any memory allocated when reading columns and row values (hey—you have to put it somewhere!). You call the free_row_buffer() after you are finished processing the row and the free_columns_buffer() at the end of the method. If you fail to add these to your own query handler method, you will run out of memory quickly.

Why is it manual? Well, like the MAX_FIELDS setting, I wanted to keep it simple and therefore save as much space as possible. Automatic garbage collection would have added a significant amount of code.

You can use this method as a template to build your own custom query handler. For example, instead of printing the data to the serial monitor, you could display it in an LCD or perhaps use the information in another part of your sketch.

As an exercise, you can change the library to display the bar and dash output (called a *grid*). This isn't especially difficult but requires more than a few bytes of code (which is why I left it out of the library). If you'd like a hint for how to know how many dashes to print for each field, recall that you read the fields first (which includes the size of each field). The challenge is to print the bar and dashes so that they line up in the display area.

Now that you are more familiar with the Connector/Arduino library, let's reexamine the Arduino sensor node from Chapter 3—but this time, you add the code to save the sensor data to a MySQL server.

---

[8]A state of wonkiness where wonky is the norm.

ADJUSTING THE SPEED OF QUERY RESULTS

The library contains a delay in the `wait_for_client()` method (in `mysql.cpp`) that can be adjusted to improve the speed of query results returned. It is currently set at a modest delay. Depending on your network latency and proximity to the database server (as in, no network hops), you can reduce this value considerably. It was originally added to help prevent issues with slower wireless networks.

Project: Building a MySQL Arduino Client

In the previous sections, you learned what Connector/Arduino is and how to use it to make an Arduino MySQL client update a table in a MySQL database server. In this section, you revisit the sensor node example from an earlier chapter and make it save the data to the database instead of the serial monitor.

You proceed at a faster pace because all examples of using the Connector/Arduino library are the same. Also, rather than use the XBee modules, you wire the sensor to the Arduino to further simplify the example. Let's begin with the hardware setup.

■ **Note**   I repeat the steps from Chapter 3 to provide a complete explanation and walkthrough. I skip the details of the code for reading the DHT22 because that part is the same.

Hardware Setup

The hardware required for this project includes an Arduino, an Ethernet Shield, a DHT22 humidity and temperature sensor, a breadboard, a 4.7K Ohm resistor (colors: yellow, purple, red, gold), and breadboard jumper wires. With the exception of the Ethernet shield, this is the same setup as the project from Chapter 3.

■ **Tip**   If you get stuck or want more information, there is an excellent tutorial on Adafruit's web site. See `http://learn.adafruit.com/dht`.

Begin by placing your Arduino next to a breadboard. If you have not already done so, install the Ethernet shield on your Arduino. Be sure that all pins are seated in their sockets before proceeding.

Plug the DHT22 sensor into one side of the breadboard, as shown in Figure 7-11. Please refer to this often and double-check your connections before powering on your Arduino (or connecting it to your laptop). You want to avoid accidental experiments in electrical chaos theory.

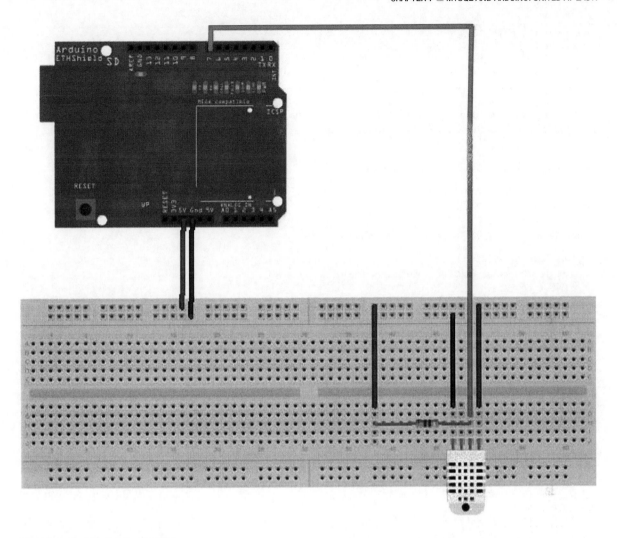

Figure 7-11. *Wiring the DHT22*

Next, connect the power from the Arduino to the breadboard. Use one jumper wire to connect the 5V pin on the Arduino to the breadboard power rail and another to connect the ground (GND) pin on the Arduino to the ground rail on the breadboard. With these wires in place, you are ready to wire the sensor. You use three of the four pins, as shown in Table 7-1.

Table 7-1. *DHT22 Connections*

Pin	Connected To
1	+5V
2	Pin 7 on Arduino, 4.7K resistor between VCC and the data pin (strong pullup)
3	No connection
4	Ground

Software Setup

To use the DHT22 with an Arduino, you need to have the latest DHT22 library. You can find the library at `https://github.com/ringerc/Arduino-DHT22`. You must download it and place it in your `Arduino/Libraries` folder.

To download the library, click the Zip button, save the file, and then unzip it. The folder created has an unusual name: `Arduino-DHT22-master`. You must rename it to something like `DHT22` to remove the dashes so the Arduino environment won't complain. Recall that if your Arduino environment is running when you copy the folder, you need to restart it in order for the Arduino environment to read the new library.

Setting Up the Sensor Database

You also need to create a table on your MySQL server. Listing 7-10 shows the steps needed to create the test database and the table.

Listing 7-10. Creating the DHT22 Database Table

```
$ mysql -uroot -psecret
Welcome to the MySQL monitor.  Commands end with ; or \g.
Your MySQL connection id is 3
Server version: 5.6.14-log Source distribution

Copyright (c) 2000, 2011, Oracle and/or its affiliates. All rights reserved.

Oracle is a registered trademark of Oracle Corporation and/or its
affiliates. Other names may be trademarks of their respective
owners.

Type 'help;' or '\h' for help. Type '\c' to clear the current input statement.

mysql> CREATE DATABASE dht22_test;
Query OK, 1 row affected (0.00 sec)

mysql> use dht22_test;
Database changed
mysql> CREATE TABLE dht22_test.temp_humid (
    ->     `id` int(11) NOT NULL AUTO_INCREMENT,
    ->     `temp_c` float DEFAULT NULL,
    ->     `rel_humid` float DEFAULT NULL,
    ->     PRIMARY KEY (`id`)
    -> ) ENGINE=MyISAM DEFAULT CHARSET=latin1;
    -> ;
Query OK, 0 rows affected (0.01 sec)

mysql>
```

Now that you have the hardware configured and the database set up, let's write some code!

Writing the Code

The code is very similar to the project from Chapter 3, except that you add the code needed to connect to the MySQL server and insert the sensor data. This code module demonstrates a basic data-collection node in the form of a temperature and humidity sensor node. It uses the common DHT22 sensor connected to an Arduino with an Ethernet shield.

Listing 7-11 shows the complete source code. Because it is a file included with Connector/Arduino, you see the license banner at the top of the file.

Listing 7-11. Reading a DHT22 Sensor

```
/*
  Sensor Networks Example Arduino DHT22 Sensor

  This project demonstrates how to receive sensor data from
  a DHT22 sensor saving the samples in a MySQL
  database.

  It uses an Arduino with an Ethernet shield installed.
*/
#include <SPI.h>
#include <Ethernet.h>
#include <sha1.h>
#include "mysql.h"
#include <DHT22.h>

byte mac_addr[] = { 0xDE, 0xAD, 0xBE, 0xEF, 0xFE, 0xED };
IPAddress server_addr(10, 0, 0, 24);
char user[] = "root";
char password[] = "secret";

Connector my_conn;         // The Connector/Arduino reference

#define DHT22_PIN 7        // DHT22 data is on pin 7
#define read_delay 5000    // 5 seconds
DHT22 myDHT22(DHT22_PIN); // DHT22 instance

void read_data() {
  DHT22_ERROR_t errorCode;

  errorCode = myDHT22.readData();
  switch(errorCode)
  {
    case DHT_ERROR_NONE:
      char buf[128];
      sprintf(buf, "INSERT INTO dht22_test.temp_humid VALUES (NULL, %hi.%01hi, %i.%01i)",
                   myDHT22.getTemperatureCInt()/10,
                   abs(myDHT22.getTemperatureCInt()%10),
                   myDHT22.getHumidityInt()/10,
                   myDHT22.getHumidityInt()%10);
      my_conn.cmd_query(buf);
      Serial.println("Data read and recorded.");
      break;
    case DHT_ERROR_CHECKSUM:
      Serial.print("check sum error ");
      Serial.print(myDHT22.getTemperatureC());
      Serial.print("C ");
```

```
      Serial.print(myDHT22.getHumidity());
      Serial.println("%");
      break;
    case DHT_BUS_HUNG:
      Serial.println("BUS Hung ");
      break;
    case DHT_ERROR_NOT_PRESENT:
      Serial.println("Not Present ");
      break;
    case DHT_ERROR_ACK_TOO_LONG:
      Serial.println("ACK time out ");
      break;
    case DHT_ERROR_SYNC_TIMEOUT:
      Serial.println("Sync Timeout ");
      break;
    case DHT_ERROR_DATA_TIMEOUT:
      Serial.println("Data Timeout ");
      break;
    case DHT_ERROR_TOOQUICK:
      Serial.println("Polled too quick ");
      break;
  }
}

void setup() {
  Ethernet.begin(mac_addr);
  Serial.begin(115200);
  delay(1000);
  Serial.println("Connecting...");
  if (my_conn.mysql_connect(server_addr, 3306, user, password))
    delay(500);
  else
    Serial.println("Connection failed.");
}

void loop() {
  delay(read_delay);
  read_data();
}
```

Notice that the setup() method has the same code as in the previous example, except that in this case you just connect to the server and exit. The code to insert the data into the MySQL database is added to the read_data() method, replacing the code for the serial output from the example in Chapter 3. I repeat the code here for clarity:

```
char buf[128];
sprintf(buf, "INSERT INTO dht22_test.temp_humid VALUES (NULL, %hi.%01hi, %i.%01i)",
            myDHT22.getTemperatureCInt()/10,
            abs(myDHT22.getTemperatureCInt()%10),
            myDHT22.getHumidityInt()/10,
            myDHT22.getHumidityInt()%10);
my_conn.cmd_query(buf);
```

You simply build a string from a static buffer of size 128 using the sprintf()[9] method to format and populate the values for the table. Notice also that the first value is NULL. Recall that this tells the database server to use the next value for the auto-increment column.

■ **Caution** Watch out for array sizes! If you intend to save character string data returned by sensor nodes, be sure your query will fit into memory.

The next method simply calls the cmd_query() method of Connector/Arduino and executes the query held in the buffer.

If you have a different network than what is depicted here, you can change the IPAddress variable accordingly. Likewise, if your user and password are different, be sure to change those values as well. Finally, if you want to slow the sample rate, you can adjust read_delay accordingly.

Once you have all the code entered into your Arduino environment and your Arduino is ready to go, it is time to try it out. If you have problems, refer to the earlier sections and Figures 7-8 through 7-10 for common errors.

Test Execution

Executing the sketch means uploading it to your Arduino and watching it run. If you haven't connected your Arduino, you can do that now. Be sure to connect an Ethernet cable to the Ethernet shield as well as the USB cable between the Arduino and your laptop (or desktop).

I like to begin by compiling the sketch. Click the checkmark on the left side of the Arduino application, and observe the output in the message screen at the bottom. If you see errors, fix them and retry the compile. Common errors include missing the DHT22 library (which may require restarting the Arduino application), typing errors, syntax errors, and the like. Once everything compiles correctly, you are ready to upload your sketch by clicking the Upload button on the toolbar.

As soon as the upload completes, open the serial monitor by clicking the button at right on the toolbar. Observe the Arduino connecting to the MySQL server and the message printed each time the sensor data is recorded. Let this run a few times to generate some data. Figure 7-12 shows the typical output you should see.

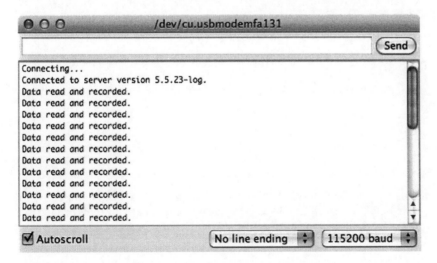

Figure 7-12. Serial monitor output for the DHT22 sensor project

---

[9]See the sprintf() documentation at www.cplusplus.com/reference/cstdio/sprintf/ for more details.

■ **Tip**   If you get "ACK Timeout" errors, try unplugging the sensor and plugging it back in, or disconnect and reconnect the power lead while the sketch is running. Be very careful to avoid ESD!

Once the thrill of watching your Arduino spin is over, stop the Arduino by disconnecting the USB cable. You can now check the database to ensure that the sensor data was recorded. Listing 7-12 shows the steps needed. All you do here is issue a SELECT command on the table. You should see one row for each time your Arduino recorded its data.

Listing 7-12. Checking the Database

```
$ mysql -uroot -psecret
Welcome to the MySQL monitor.  Commands end with ; or \g.
Your MySQL connection id is 188
Server version: 5.6.14-log Source distribution

Copyright (c) 2000, 2011, Oracle and/or its affiliates. All rights reserved.

Oracle is a registered trademark of Oracle Corporation and/or its
affiliates. Other names may be trademarks of their respective
owners.

Type 'help;' or '\h' for help. Type '\c' to clear the current input statement.

mysql> SELECT * FROM dht22_test.temp_humid;
+----+--------+-----------+
| id | temp_c | rel_humid |
+----+--------+-----------+
| 12 |   22.6 |      39.9 |
| 13 |   22.5 |        39 |
| 14 |   22.5 |      38.7 |
| 15 |   22.4 |      38.6 |
| 16 |   22.4 |      38.5 |
| 17 |   22.4 |      38.5 |
| 18 |   22.4 |      38.5 |
| 19 |   22.3 |      38.4 |
| 20 |   22.3 |      38.4 |
| 21 |   22.3 |      38.3 |
+----+--------+-----------+
10 rows in set (0.00 sec)

mysql>
```

If you see similar output, congratulations! You have just built your first database-enabled Arduino-based sensor node. This is an important step in building your sensor network, because you now have the tools needed to start building more sophisticated wireless sensor nodes and aggregate nodes for inserting sensor data into the database.

For More Fun

Once you are comfortable testing and experimenting with the project, if you have an inquisitive mind like me, you will probably start to see things that you can do to improve the code and the project. I list a few here for you to consider on your own. Don't be afraid to tweak and modify—that's one of the greatest joys of working with the Arduino!

- Change the code to store the temperature in Fahrenheit.

- Change the sampling rate to once every 15 minutes or once every hour.

- Change the table to add a new column, and use a trigger to automatically convert the temperature to Fahrenheit. Hint: `ALTER TABLE dht22_test.temp_humid ADD COLUMN temp_f float AFTER temp_c`.

- For experts: rather than split the data from the DHT22 and store two values in the database, store the raw value in the database and use a view to split the values.

Do you see a trend here? The last two bullets suggest moving some of the logic from the Arduino to the database. This is a very good practice and one you should hone by learning more about features such as views, functions, triggers, and events provided by the MySQL server.

Because the Arduino platform is a small device with limited capability, moving data manipulation to the database server not only saves on processing power but also save memory usage. Having the database server do the heavy work of data conversion may also permit you to take more frequent sensor readings.

To read more about triggers, views, and events, see the online MySQL reference manual.

The next two sections present some examples of how to use the connector in your sketches. These are not complete projects; rather, they are intended to be used as templates for writing your own sketches using the connector.

Project Example: Inserting Data from Variables

When writing the connector, I discovered a number of posts on my blog from people unfamiliar with C programming or those new to programming in general. This is great because it means the Arduino is reaching some of its target audience!

One of the questions that kept arising was how to do an INSERT query supplying values from sensors, or how to construct an INSERT statement with values stored in variables. The following code shows how to take a value (presumably read from a sensor or such) and insert the value into the database:

```
const char INSERT_DATA[] = "INSERT INTO test_arduino.temps VALUES (%s, NULL)";

// Inserting real time data into a table.
// Here we want to insert a row into a table but in this case we are
// simulating reading the data from a sensor or some other component.
// In this case, we 'simulate' reading temperature in Celsius.
float value_read = 26.9;

// To use the value in an INSERT statement, we must construct a string
// that has the value inserted in it. For example, what we want is:
// 'INSERT INTO test_arduino.temps VALUES (26.9, NULL)' but the 26.9 is
// held in the variable 'value_read'. So, we use a character string
// formatting operation sprintf(). Notice here we must convert the float
// to a string first and we use the %s specifier in the INSERT_DATA
// string.
```

```
char query[64];
char temperature[10];
dtostrf(value_read, 1, 1, temperature);
sprintf(query, INSERT_DATA, temperature);
my_conn.cmd_query(query);
```

Notice that you create a string with a special character sequence (%s). This sequence is called a *format specifier* and is used by the sprintf() method to instruct the method how to interpret (format) the data. There are many such specifiers for all manner of data types. For more information about format specifiers and the sprintf() method, see www.tutorialspoint.com/c_standard_library/c_function_sprintf.htm.

Notice also that you create a buffer to hold the formatted string. This is because the sprintf() method combines the string with the format specifier and the data from a variable into a new string.

In this example, I also show you how to deal with floating-point values. Floating-point values are not supported by the Arduino sprintf() method, so you have to first convert the floating-point value to a string and then use that string in your sprintf() method. The method you use to convert the floating-point value is dtostrf().

If you read through the code example, you see how this new string is formed. This resulting string is sent to the database, and the value is inserted into the database.

Project Example: How to Perform SELECT Queries

There are times when you need to get information out of your database server to be used in calculations or for displaying (or transmitting) labels. For example, suppose you have a sensor that requires calibration or conversion using a formula that depends on other data. Rather than code all of those things (there could be dozens or hundreds), consuming a lot of memory in the process, why not store that information in a database table and query it when you need to look up the value?

Similarly, suppose you have text strings that you would like to display in an LCD or perhaps even in the serial monitor, but the strings depend on the sensor being read. That is, you could have sensors located in different locations. Rather than code all of those strings and thereby consume a lot of space, you can save that space by putting those strings in a table and getting them when needed.

In this section, I demonstrate several examples of how to use the connector to return data from the database.

■ **Note** The library contains a number of methods useful for querying a database and consuming the data in your sketch. It also includes helpful methods for displaying the data, should you wish to see it in the serial monitor. Note that this code does add about 2KB more to your compiled sketch size. Depending on the memory size of your Arduino, if you add more than a few queries to your sketch, you could run out of space. See the troubleshooting section "My Sketch Is Too Big" for suggestions on reducing the size of your sketch.

Displaying a Result Set in the Serial Monitor

If you want to run a query and display the results in the serial monitor, you can use the built-in method show_results(). This method prints the column names separated by commas and then iterates over the result set and prints the values separated by commas.

The code is very simple. You need only call cmd_query(), passing it the query string, and then call the show_results() method. Of course, the serial monitor must be open for you to see the results:

```
// SELECT query returning rows (built-in methods)
// Here we simply read the columns, print the names, then loop through
// the rows printing the values read. We limit the result set to 10 rows to make this something
// that executes in a reasonable timeframe.
const char TEST_SELECT_QUERY[] = "SELECT * FROM world.city LIMIT 10";
my_conn.cmd_query(TEST_SELECT_QUERY);
my_conn.show_results();
```

Writing Your Own Display Method

There are cases where you may want to build your own iterator to read the result set from a query. For example, you may want to display the results in an LCD or send them to another node in your network. Fortunately, you can do so by writing your own version of show_results() using a number of helper methods. I discussed the show_results() method in a previous section, but I discuss the methods used again in the context of writing your own method.

These include get_columns() for retrieving the column names; get_next_row(), which is an iterator to read rows; and memory-cleanup methods free_columns_buffer() and free_row_buffer(). You call the free_row_buffer() method after processing the data for the row and the free_columns_buffer() once all the rows are read. Listing 7-13 shows all the steps you need to put into your own method to execute a query and process the results.

Listing 7-13. Custom Query Results Method

```
/**
 * do_query - execute a query and display results
 *
 * This method demonstrates how to execute a query, get the column
 * names and print them, then read rows printing the values. It
 * is a mirror of the show_results() example in the connector class.
 *
 * You can use this method as a template for writing methods that
 * must iterate over rows from a SELECT and operate on the values read.
 *
 */
/*
void do_query(const char *q) {
  column_names *c; // pointer to column values
  row_values *r;   // pointer to row values

  // First, execute query. If it returns a value pointer,
  // we have a result set to process. If not, we exit.
  if (!my_conn.cmd_query(q)) {
    return;
  }

  // Next, we read the column names and display them.
  //
  // NOTICE: You must *always* read the column names even if
  //         you do not use them. This is so the connector can
  //         read the data out of the buffer. Row data follows the
```

```
//           column data and thus must be read first.
c = my_conn.get_columns();
for (int i = 0; i < c->num_fields; i++) {
  Serial.print(c->fields[i]->name);
  if (i < c->num_fields - 1) {
    Serial.print(",");
  }
}
Serial.println();

// Next, we use the get_next_row() iterator and read rows printing
// the values returned until the get_next_row() returns NULL.
int num_cols = c->num_fields;
int rows = 0;
do {
  r = my_conn.get_next_row();
  if (r) {
    rows++;
    for (int i = 0; i < num_cols; i++) {
      Serial.print(r->values[i]);
      if (i < num_cols - 1) {
        Serial.print(", ");
      }
    }
    Serial.println();
    // Note: we free the row read to free the memory allocated for it.
    // You should do this after you've processed the row.
    my_conn.free_row_buffer();
  }
} while (r);
Serial.print(rows);
Serial.println(" rows in result.");

// Finally, we are done so we free the column buffers
my_conn.free_columns_buffer();
}
```

Notice that you first must read the columns. This is because MySQL always sends the column names before any rows. Once you have read the columns, you can then read the rows using the iterator helper method until there are no rows returned.

The get_columns() method returns a pointer to a special structure that contains the number of fields and an array of fields that is also a special structure. Both structures are shown next; you can see how they are used in Listing 7-13:

```
// Structure for retrieving a field (minimal implementation).
typedef struct {
  char *db;
  char *table;
  char *name;
} field_struct;
```

```
// Structure for storing result set metadata.
typedef struct {
  int num_fields;      // actual number of fields
  field_struct *fields[MAX_FIELDS];
} column_names;
```

get_next_row() returns a pointer to a similar structure that contains an array of strings. This is because all data (rows) returned from the server are returned as character strings. It is up to you to convert the values to other data types if you need to do so.

Here is the second structure:

```
// Structure for storing row data.
typedef struct {
  char *values[MAX_FIELDS];
} row_values;
```

You may be wondering why you have to do the memory-cleanup bits. Simply put, in order to make the connector as lightweight as possible, some of the convenience routines have been intentionally omitted. A case in point is clearing (freeing) memory allocated during the reads of the columns and row data. The previous example shows the proper location for these calls.

■ **Caution**   Failure to free the memory as shown will result in a rapid deterioration of your sketch's execution and an eventual freeze when memory is exhausted (no more memory is left to allocate).

Once you have created a method like this, you can use it elsewhere in your sketch to execute and process query results as follows:

```
// SELECT query returning rows (custom method)
// Here we execute the same query as above but use a custom method for reading
// and displaying the results. See the do_query() method above for more
// information about how it works.
const char TEST_SELECT_QUERY[] = "SELECT * FROM world.city LIMIT 10";
do_query(TEST_SELECT_QUERY);
```

If you plan to write a method like this to send the data elsewhere, take care in the amount of code you use and eliminate any unnecessary strings and conversions (floating-point conversion requires a library named dtostf that can add up to 2KB to your compiled sketch size).

Example: Getting a Lookup Value from the Database

Although the previous examples show you how to process result sets of multiple rows for displaying lots of data, the more common reason to query a database is to return a specific value or set of values for use in the sketch. Typically, this is done using a query that is designed to return a single row. For example, it could return a specific value from a lookup table.

As in the previous example, you must process the result set in order starting with the column data. You don't need it for this type of query, so you simply ignore it. You also still need to iterate over the rows, because the result set terminates with a special packet and the get_next_row() method reads that packet and returns NULL if it is encountered (signaling no more rows). Listing 7-14 shows the code you need to read a single value from the database and use it. This example can be made into a separate method if it will be called multiple times or from several places in your sketch.

Listing 7-14. Getting a Lookup Value

```
const char QUERY_POP[] =
  "SELECT population FROM world.city WHERE name = 'New York'";

// SELECT query for lookup value (1 row returned)
// Here we get a value from the database and use it.
long head_count = 0;
my_conn.cmd_query(QUERY_POP);

// We ignore the columns but we have to read them to get
// that data out of the queue.
my_conn.get_columns();

// Now we read the rows.
row_values *row = NULL;
do {
  row = my_conn.get_next_row();
  // We use the first value returned in the row - population of NYC!
  if (row != NULL) {
    head_count = atol(row->values[0]);
  }
} while (row != NULL);

// We're done with the buffers so Ok to clear them (and save precious memory).
my_conn.free_columns_buffer();
my_conn.free_row_buffer();

// Now, let's do something with the data.
Serial.print("NYC pop = ");
Serial.println(head_count);
```

As you can see, the library supports the capability to process queries that return result sets. These include SELECT, SHOW, and similar commands.

However, note (again) that the Arduino platform is very limited in the amount of memory available. Constructing a sketch with several complex queries that return large result sets is likely to exhaust the memory on Arduino boards such as the Uno and Leonardo. If your sketch is large, you may want to consider moving to the Due board.

Component Shopping List

A number of components are needed to complete the projects in this chapter. All of these components were used in previous chapters. They're listed in Table 7-2.

Table 7-2. Components Needed

Item	Vendors	Est. Cost USD	Qty Needed
Arduino Uno (any that supports shields)	Various	$25.00 and up	1
Arduino Ethernet shield	www.sparkfun.com/products/9026	$45.95	1
	www.adafruit.com/products/201	$45.00	
Breadboard (not mini)	www.sparkfun.com/products/9567	$5.95	1
Breadboard jumper wires	www.sparkfun.com/products/8431	$3.95	1
DHT22	www.sparkfun.com/products/10167	$9.95	1
	www.adafruit.com/products/385		
150 Ohm resistor	www.sparkfun.com/products/10969	$7.95	1

Summary

With the Connector/Arduino library, you can make your sensor nodes quite a bit more sophisticated. By enabling your sensor nodes to save data in a MySQL database, you also enhance your monitoring solutions by making the data much easier to access and stored in a very reliable place (a database server).

In this chapter, you discovered how to write database-enabled Arduino sketches and took a detailed tour of the Connector/Arduino library. Armed with this knowledge, you are ready to move on to creating a real sensor network. In the next chapter, you put the accumulated knowledge of the previous chapters to use in creating your first sensor network with a MySQL database server, an Arduino aggregate node, and wireless sensor nodes.

CHAPTER 8

■ ■ ■

Building Your Network: Arduino Wireless Aggregator + Wireless Sensor Node + Raspberry Pi Server

With the information you have learned thus far in the book, and especially in Chapters 6 and 7, it is time to put it all together and build your first sensor network with a MySQL database server.

In this chapter, you put all the components together and build a working sensor network that features your Raspberry Pi MySQL server as the data repository, a data aggregate node (you see examples of both Arduino and Raspberry Pi), and a number of sensor nodes connected via XBee modules. These are the building blocks you built in previous chapters, now combined to demonstrate how you can build low-cost sensor networks.

Data-Aggregate Nodes

Recall that a *data aggregator* is a special node designed to receive information from multiple sources (sensors) and store the results. The source data can originate from multiple sensors on the node itself, but more often the data-aggregate node receives information from multiple sensor nodes that are not attached directly to the aggregate node (they connect via XBee modules).

Most often, these sensors are hosted by other nodes and placed in other locations, and the data-aggregate node is connected to the sensor nodes via a wired or wireless connection. For example, you may have a sensor hosted on a low-power Arduino in one location and another sensor hosted on a Raspberry Pi in another location, both connected to your data-aggregate node using XBee modules. Except for the limitations of the network medium chosen, you can have dozens of nodes feeding sensor data to a data-aggregate node.

The use of data-aggregate nodes has several advantages. If you are using a wireless technology such as ZigBee with XBee modules, data-aggregate nodes can permit you to extend the range of the network by placing the data-aggregate nodes nearest the sensors. The data-aggregate nodes can then transmit the data to another node such as a database server via a more reliable medium.

For example, you may want to place a data-aggregate node in an outbuilding that has power and an Ethernet connection to collect data from remote sensor nodes located in various other buildings. A case to consider is monitoring temperature in one or more rooms or even external storage buildings. These buildings may or may not have power but most likely are not wired for Ethernet. The data-aggregate node therefore could be placed in the closest building that has power and an Ethernet port.

■ **Note**   In this case, I mean the closest point to the sensor nodes that is still within range of the wireless transmission media (such as XBee).

Data-aggregate nodes can also permit you to move the logic to process a set of sensors to a more powerful node. For example, if you use sensors that require code to process the values (such as the TMP36), you can use a data-aggregate node to receive the raw data from those sensors, store it, and calculate the values at a later time. Not only does this ensure that you have code in only one location, but it also allows you to use less sophisticated (less powerful) hosts for the remote sensors. That is, you could use less expensive or older Arduino boards for the sensors and a more powerful Arduino for the data-aggregate node. This has the added advantage that if a remote sensor is destroyed, it is not costly to replace.

Recall also that you have to decide where you want to store your sensor data. Data-aggregate nodes either can store the data locally on removable media or an onboard storage device (local storage) or can transmit the data to another node for storage (remote storage). The choice of which to use is often based on how the data will be consumed or viewed.

For example, if you want to store only the last values read from the sensors, you may want to consider some form of visual display or remote-access mechanism. In this case, it may be more cost effective and less complicated to use local storage storing only the latest values.

On the other hand, if you require data values recorded over time for later processing, you should consider storing the data on another node so that the data can be accessed without affecting the sensor network. That is, you can store the data on a more robust system (say, a personal computer, server, or cloud-based service) and further reduce the risk of losing data should the aggregate node fail.

The following sections explore examples of each form of data aggregator based on the examples from previous chapters. I keep these sections brief to provide a frame of reference and to help you build knowledge for the projects discussed later in this chapter.

Local-Storage Data Aggregator

A *local-storage data aggregator* is a node designed to receive sensor data from one or more sensors or sensor nodes and store the data on a device that is built in to or attached to the node. Recall that for Arduino-based nodes this is typically EEPROM (memory) or an SD drive via either the Arduino Ethernet Shield or another SD card shield. Recall that for the Raspberry Pi this could be the SD boot drive, a USB drive, or an EEPROM connected via the general-purpose input/output (GPIO) pins.

The nature of the local storage is a limiting factor in what you can do with a local-storage data-aggregate node. That is, if you want to process the data at a later time, you would choose a medium that permits you to retrieve the data and move it another computer. As mentioned in Chapter 5, the EEPROM is an unlikely choice due to its volatility and difficulty in connecting to a personal computer. This leaves the SD card or a removable drive as the only reasonable alternatives. But if the sensor data is used primarily for displaying data, you can use the EEPROM to store the latest values or a short list of values for display on demand.

This does not mean the local-storage data aggregator is a useless concept. Let's consider the case where you want to monitor temperature in several outbuildings. You are not using the data for any analysis but merely want to be able to read the values when it is convenient (or required).

One possible solution is to design the local-storage data-aggregate node with a visual display. For example, you can use an LCD to display the sensor data. Of course, this means the data-aggregate node must be in a location where you can get to it easily.

But let's consider the case where your data-aggregate node is also in a remote location. Perhaps it too is in another outbuilding, but you spend the majority of your time in a different location. In this case, a remote-access solution would be best.

Fortunately, you can provide such a mechanism with very little work. Consider the Ethernet library for the Arduino. There are sample sketches that show you how to host a lightweight web server on the Arduino. For the case where you simply want to access the sensor data for viewing from a remote location, a web server is the perfect solution. You point your browser to your data-aggregate node and view the data.

The design of such a data-aggregate node would require storing the latest values locally, say in memory or EEPROM, and, when a client connects, displaying the data. This is a simple and elegant solution for a local-storage data-aggregate node. The following project demonstrates these techniques.

Project: Data-Aggregate Node with Local Storage

If you have not built the components from the previous projects or had problems getting one or more to work, you may want to go back and revisit those chapters. I discuss each of the components needed, but not to the level of detail in the previous chapters. If you find you need a refresher for some of the components, please refer to those chapters cited.

With that stated, it's time to build your first sensor network with a local-storage data-aggregate node. Savvy readers will realize you've already built examples of all the sensor components in the previous chapters. What is new is the choice of local storage and the mechanism for displaying the data.

In this project, you build a data-aggregate node that can be accessed via an Ethernet network and that supports a lightweight web server to display the last values read from each of several sensors. The sensor nodes are networked with XBee modules to the data-aggregate node. Except for the web server portion and the choice of using the onboard EEPROM for storing data, the code for the data-aggregate node is similar to code you have used in previous projects.

Hardware

The hardware for this project consists of several XBee-based temperature sensor nodes communicating to an Arduino-based node that will be your data-aggregate node. I discussed XBee modules in Chapter 2 and the XBee temperature sensor node in Chapter 3.

Data-Aggregate Node

Because you want to use a web server, the data-aggregate node requires an Arduino Ethernet shield as well as an XBee shield (or equivalent). If you use both shields with your Arduino, you may need to use a stackable header kit (www.sparkfun.com/products/11417) to ensure that the Ethernet shield does not prohibit the pins from the XBee shield to seat properly.

Figure 8-1 shows the data-aggregate node I used for the project. The Arduino shield is mounted on the Arduino board, and headers are used to raise the height of the connections so that the XBee shield can be mounted securely. Although this makes for a rather tall stack of boards, it is still a compact form.

Figure 8-1. *Arduino-based data-aggregate node*

If you are using XBee modules that have an on-chip antenna or another form of antenna that does not protrude from the top of the XBee module, you may be able to place the XBee shield on the Arduino first and the Ethernet shield on top. In this case, you would not need the additional risers.

The stackable headers kit is a handy accessory to have because it permits you to raise the height of shields so that you can access or in some cases view components on the Arduino board (like the LEDs and various buttons or switches common to some shields). You can find stackable header kits at SparkFun, Adafruit, and most vendors that stock Arduino boards and shields.

You also need a way to power your data-aggregate node. If you plan to execute the project as an experiment and leave the node connected to your laptop via a USB cable, then you are fine and need nothing more. But if you plan to deploy the node, you need to power the Arduino via a typical wall wart power supply. A 9V power supply should be sufficient, or you can use a 9V battery connected via a barrel connector. Figure 8-2 shows a wall wart power supply from SparkFun. Figure 8-3 shows a 9V battery carrier from SparkFun.

Figure 8-2. *Wall wart power supply (courtesy of SparkFun)*

Figure 8-3. *9V battery carrier (courtesy of SparkFun)*

Be sure to use an XBee module configured with the COORDINATOR API firmware for the data-aggregate node. Please refer to Chapter 2 for details on how to configure your XBee modules.

Sensor Nodes

Recall from Chapter 3 that the hardware for the XBee sensor node consists of a breadboard, some jumper wires, a breadboard power supply, a power supply (a typical 5–9V wall wart will do nicely), a TMP36 temperature sensor, and a 0.10uF capacitor. You also need an XBee breakout board with male headers (0.1" spacing for breadboards) like those available from Adafruit or SparkFun. Power for the temperature sensor nodes can be via a 9V battery or, if power is available, a 9V wall wart power supply.

I repeat the wiring diagram from Chapter 3 in Figure 8-4 for convenience. You need to build at least two of these temperature sensor nodes, but three would make for a better test project.

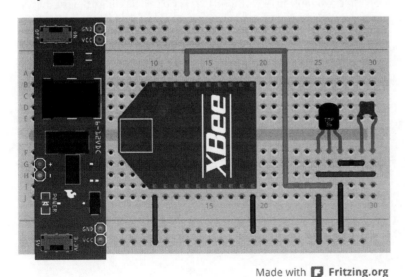

Made with ▢ **Fritzing.org**

Figure 8-4. *Wiring the TMP sensor node*

■ **Note**   It may be possible to use lower voltage power supplies. Consult the documentation for your breadboard power supply for more information.

Be sure to use an XBee module configured with the ROUTER API firmware for each sensor node. Please refer to Chapter 2 for details on how to configure your XBee modules.

Go ahead and build your temperature sensor nodes. Wire them up, and double-check the power settings for your breadboard power supply. Be sure it is set to 3.3V. Once you have all of your temperature sensor nodes wired, don't power them on yet. You need to wait until you have finished writing and uploading the sketch to the data-aggregate node before powering on the sensor nodes. I discuss the sketch in the next section.

■ **Tip**   While you are working with this project—and, indeed, the first few times you power up the network—you should test everything at the same location. For example, set up the sensor nodes and the data-aggregate node on the same table or workbench, and debug the network until everything works correctly. Only then can you safely deploy the sensor nodes to their remote locations.[1]

Software

The software for this project does not require any additional special libraries or similar downloads. All the libraries needed are included in the latest release of the Arduino IDE. I present an overview of the sketch first and then discuss the new portions in more detail. I skip some of the code used in previous projects, for brevity. Please refer to the complete code in Listing 8-4 for more details, and be sure you understand how the code works.

Overview

The sketch you use is a combination of the web server example in the Arduino IDE as well as the code from previous projects. You rearrange things a bit because there is less need for writing data to the serial monitor. In fact, you don't really need to write anything to the serial monitor. But you do leave in a few statements for debugging purposes.

If you have not experimented with the web server examples in the Arduino IDE (see Examples ➤ Ethernet), you may want to do so if you find the code for this sketch challenging (or if you want to just have fun with your Arduino and its Ethernet shield).

■ **Tip**   If the sketch does not work as you expect, feel free to add additional print statements to print debug information to the serial monitor. This is a very common practice for writing and debugging large or complex sketches.

The web server portion of this sketch is very close to the BarometricPressureWebServer example in the Arduino IDE. You modify the code slightly to make it more readable because you need a few more statements than the example provides. Essentially, you use the EthernetServer library to listen for a connection; and once a connection is made, you write HTML code back to the client via an instance of EthernetClient. You explore this code in more detail shortly.

---

[1]Within XBee range, of course.

As stated previously, you're storing the last values from each sensor node for display in the web server. Storing these values presents a problem when using the Arduino, as described in Chapter 5. Your choices are limited to using the SD drive on the Arduino Ethernet shield or the onboard EEPROM.

Although you experimented with an external EEPROM in Chapter 5, you use the onboard EEPROM instead for simplicity. The onboard EEPROM varies in size among the choices of Arduino boards, but in most cases it is large enough to store a dozen or so bytes for each sensor node. In the case of this project, you store only 10 bytes per sensor node, and 512 bytes are available for use[2] on an Arduino Duemilanove board.

To use the onboard EEPROM, simply include the EEPROM.h file in your sketch. Reading from and writing to the onboard EEPROM is very easy and is done one byte at a time. You call EEPROM.read(), passing in the address for the byte you want to read. Writing to EEPROM is similar. You call EEPROM.write(), passing in the address where you want to store the byte and the value of the data (byte) you want to store. Examples of using this library can be found in the Arduino IDE.

Now let's get into the code! The following sections present the major components of the sketch—web server, local storage, and reading from the sensor nodes. I omit the code for manipulating the sensor data because that is a direct copy of the code from Chapter 3. Open a new sketch in the Arduino IDE, and name it Arduino_Web_Aggregate.

Lightweight Web Server

The code for the lightweight web server was taken from an example in the Arduino IDE. You modify the example by moving into a separate function the code to send the data to the client.

To build a web server, you first must include the correct library and declare a few variables. The following excerpt shows the code needed (with code from other components omitted for clarity):

```
#include <Ethernet.h>
#include <SPI.h>
...
byte mac[] = {
  0xDE, 0xAD, 0xBE, 0xEF, 0xFE, 0xED};
IPAddress ip(10, 0, 1, 111);

// Start Ethernet Server class with port 80 (default for HTTP)
EthernetServer server(80);
...
```

Notice that you include the Ethernet and SPI headers. You also declare two variables: a MAC address and an IP address. In previous projects, you allowed the Ethernet library to use DHCP to assign the IP address; but in this case you need to know the IP address, and therefore you must use a static IP address. Be sure to choose one that is valid for the network segment where your data-aggregate node will be attached.

Finally, you initialize an instance of the EthernetServer class, passing it in port 80 (which is the default for an HTTP service). You can choose another port number, but it may require adding it to your URL in order to access the web server. For example, if you choose 3303, you would use http://10.0.1.111:3303.

Now comes the really fun part. The web server you build is a simplified service that returns only a small amount of HTTP code to the client. Aside from the include files and variables, you also need to initialize the Ethernet classes in the setup() method. The following shows what is needed. Essentially, you initialize the SPI library, then the

---

[2]If you plan to use this project as a model for your custom sensor network, you may want to consider writing code to check for memory overruns.

Ethernet library, and finally the server instance. Notice that you pass the IP address as the second parameter to the `Ethernet.begin()` method:

```
void setup() {
  // start the SPI library:
  SPI.begin();

  // start the Ethernet connection and the server:
  Ethernet.begin(mac, ip);
  server.begin();
...
}
```

To make the web server respond when a client attaches, you add a new method named `listener()` to the sketch. The following shows where this method is called—from the `loop()` method. In this case, you first check for a response from the sensors; and if no sensor data is available, you check to see if a client has attached and respond to the call:

```
void loop() {
  if [...]

  } else {
    // Listen for client and respond.
    listener();
  }
}
```

As for the listener portion, what you need to do is check to see if a client has connected via the `server.available()` method. The return of this method is an instance of the `EthernetClient` class. If the variable is not `NULL` (a client has connected), you then check to see whether the client is available via the `client.available()` method. If so, you send the data for each response requested until a newline is detected.

You begin by sending HTTP headers via the `client.print()` and `client.println()` methods. You also send a banner welcoming the user. If sensor data is stored locally, you send the data for each sensor node stored (via a loop); otherwise, you send a status banner stating there is no data.

The sending of the sensor data is via a new method named `send_sensor_data()`. This method uses the `client.print()` and `client.println()` methods[3] of the client instance to write the data in text form and the ending HTTP tags for each block of data. In this case, you send the address of the sensor node, the temperature in Celsius, the temperature again in Fahrenheit, and the reference voltage from the sensor node.

Listing 8-1 shows the code needed to listen for a client and send the response. I show an excerpt of the client code to send data: the `setup()` and `loop()` code, for brevity. Refer to Listing 8-4 for the complete code needed.

Listing 8-1. The Web Server Code

```
...
void send_sensor_data(EthernetClient *client, int num_sample) {
  unsigned int address;
  float temp_c;
  float temp_f;
  float volts;
```

---

[3]Since you pass the client variable by reference, you dereference the pointer using –> instead of a period.

```
    // Read sensor data from memory and display it.
    read_sample(num_sample, &address, &temp_c, &temp_f, &volts);

    client->println("<br />");
    client->print("Node Address: ");
    client->print(address, HEX);
    client->print(".");
...
}

void listener() {
  // listen for incoming clients
  EthernetClient client = server.available();
  if (client) {
    Serial.println("Got a connection!");
    // an http request ends with a blank line
    boolean currentLineIsBlank = true;
    while (client.connected()) {
      if (client.available()) {
        char c = client.read();
        // if you've gotten to the end of the line (received a newline
        // character) and the line is blank, the http request has ended,
        // so you can send a reply
        if (c == '\n' && currentLineIsBlank) {
          // send a standard http response header
          client.println("HTTP/1.1 200 OK");
          client.println("Content-Type: text/html");
          client.println();

          // Print header
          client.println("Welcome to the Arduino Data Aggregate Node!");
          client.println("<br />");

          // read sensor data
          byte num_samples = EEPROM.read(0);
          for (int i = 0; i < num_samples; i++) {
            send_sensor_data(&client, i);
          }
          // if no data, say so!
          if (num_samples == 0) {
            client.print("No samples to display.");
            client.println("<br />");
          }
          break;
        }
```

```
      if (c == '\n') {
        currentLineIsBlank = true;
      }
      else if (c != '\r') {
        currentLineIsBlank = false;
      }
    }
  }
}
    // give the web browser time to receive the data
    delay(1);
    // close the connection:
    client.stop();
  }
}
...
```

Now that you understand how the web server component works, let's examine the local-storage component.

Local Storage Using the Onboard EEPROM

The local-storage component uses the onboard EEPROM to store and retrieve the sensor data. In the overview section, I discussed how easy it is to use the library. In this section, I discuss the specifics of how you store and retrieve the sensor data.

Because you're storing only the last values (samples) from each sensor node and you may have more than one sensor node communicating, you need a simple mechanism to keep the data organized. You use something similar to the external EEPROM project from Chapter 5.

You use the first byte of EEPROM memory (address 0) to store the number of samples present and a block of 10 bytes for each sample. Rather than store the entire 64-bit address for each sensor node (the XBee 64-bit network address), you store the last 2 bytes, which will display 4 hexadecimal digits when converted to hexadecimal and displayed as text.[4] You also store only the raw sensor data, which is a float (4 bytes), and the reference voltage, which is also a float (4 bytes), Thus, you need 10 bytes to store a sample.

Because you store only the raw data from the sensor, you must perform the temperature calculations as you did in Chapter 3 at a later time. I leave this for you to explore in Listing 8-4.

You also add code to the setup() method to initialize the EEPROM on the initial start. In this case, writing a 0 to address 0 means there are no samples stored. This ensures that you can restart from scratch simply by resetting (or powering off then on) the data-aggregate node. If you find you need to make the values persistent, take the following code out of the setup() method after it has executed at least once:

```
void setup() {
  ...
  // Initialize the EEPROM
  EEPROM.write(0, 0);
}
```

---

[4]Why only four digits (characters)? Won't there be collisions? No, not necessarily. Most XBee modules you can purchase do not have 64-bit addresses where the last four digits are the same. It is possible, but unlikely. If you find this is the case for your XBee modules, consider using the last eight characters instead.

To make things a bit easier, you create four new methods for reading and writing from and to the EEPROM. Listing 8-2 shows the complete methods. Notice that you have two sets of methods, one for integers (2 bytes) and one for float variables (4 bytes):

Listing 8-2. EEPROM Helper Methods

```
...
// Read an integer from EEPROM
int read_int(byte position) {
  int value = 0;
  byte* p = (byte*)(void*)&value;
  for (int i = 0; i < sizeof(value); i++)
      *p++ = EEPROM.read(position++);
  return value;
}

// Read a float from EEPROM
float read_float(byte position) {
  float value = 0;
  byte* p = (byte*)(void*)&value;
  for (int i = 0; i < sizeof(value); i++)
      *p++ = EEPROM.read(position++);
  return value;
}

// Write an integer to EEPROM
void write_int(byte position, int value) {
  const byte *p = (const byte *)(const void *)&value;
  for (int i = 0; i < sizeof(value); i++)
      EEPROM.write(position++, *p++);
}

// Write a float to EEPROM
void write_float(byte position, float value) {
  const byte *p = (const byte *)(const void *)&value;
  for (int i = 0; i < sizeof(value); i++)
      EEPROM.write(position++, *p++);
}
...
```

Notice that in the code you use some pointer trickery to turn the integer and float into an array of bytes. This is not uncommon for code written by advanced C and C++ programmers. Although it is possible to use other methods (such as shifting bytes) to break the values into bytes, I wanted to include this advanced technique to get you thinking about how pointers work. Much of what you are likely to encounter in more complex sketches will involve manipulating pointer in similar ways.

■ **Tip**   For those of you who simply cannot leave things alone (you know who you are), no doubt you can see some room for optimization here. Notice that the methods are very similar. The only thing that really changes is the type. So how would you optimize this code even further? Hint: consider a template[5]
(http://playground.arduino.cc/Code/EEPROMWriteAnything).

Now that you understand how to store and retrieve samples to and from the EEPROM, let's examine how this fits into the code for reading data from the sensor nodes.

Reading Data from Sensor Nodes via XBee

The code for reading data from multiple XBee modules is unchanged from the project in Chapter 3. Indeed, the code you wrote for that sketch can and does support connections to multiple sensor nodes. Recall that this is possible because your data-aggregate node uses an XBee module configured as the coordinator, and your sensor nodes use XBee modules configured as routers.

Because the initialization code is unchanged from the project in Chapter 3, I omit those details here. But the code for storing the sensor data is different. In this case, you need to store the sample in memory (EEPROM). Because you want to store only the latest value, you must look for the sample in memory first by address. If you find a match, you save the data in the same location. If you do not find a match among the samples stored, you add it to the end and increment the number of samples stored. You name this method the same as before—record_sample().

But you do not end there. You also need methods to read and write the sample data. You break these into separate methods so that you can make the record_sample() method smaller and easier to read. Thus, you create read_sample() and write_sample() methods that uses the EEPROM helper methods described previously to store and retrieve the samples.

Listing 8-3 shows the major portions of the new code for storing sensor data and the completed code for the loop() method. Notice how it precludes the listener() call.

Listing 8-3. Reading from XBee Sensor Nodes

```
// Read a sample from EEPROM
void read_sample(byte index, unsigned int *address, float *temp_f,
                 float *temp_c, float *volts) {
  float temp;
  byte position =  (index * bytes_per_sample) + 1;

  *address = read_int(position);

  temp = read_float(position + 2);

  *temp_c = ((temp * 1200.0 / 1024.0) - 500.0) / 10.0;
  *temp_f = ((*temp_c * 9.0)/5.0) + 32.0;

  *volts = read_float(position + 6);
}
```

---

[5]I did not use templates here because I do not want to make the code too complex. As it is, unless you are familiar with pointers, you may think this code is illegible and won't compile or that it mysteriously "just works." In that case, you have to take my word that it does. How much more mysterious can someone make their code for those new to Arduino programming than by using templates? I know some very good C++ programmers who find using templates a challenge.

```
// Write sample to EEPROM
void write_sample(byte index) {
  byte position =  (index * bytes_per_sample) + 1;

  write_int(position, address);
  write_float(position + 2, temperature);
  write_float(position + 6, voltage);
}

void record_sample(ZBRxIoSampleResponse *ioSample) {
  int saved_addr;

  // Get sample data from XBee
  get_sample_data(ioSample);

  // See if already in memory. If not, add it.
  byte num_samples = EEPROM.read(0);
  boolean found = false;
  for (byte i = 0; i < num_samples; i++) {
    byte position = (i * bytes_per_sample) + 1;

    // get address
    saved_addr = read_int(position);
    if (saved_addr == address) {
      write_sample(i);
      found = true;
    }
  }
  if (!found) {
    // Save sample
    write_sample(num_samples);

    // Update number of sensors
    num_samples++;
    EEPROM.write(0, num_samples);
  }
}

...

void loop() {
  //attempt to read a packet
  xbee.readPacket();

  if (xbee.getResponse().isAvailable()) {
    // got something

    if (xbee.getResponse().getApiId() == ZB_IO_SAMPLE_RESPONSE) {

      // Get the packet
      xbee.getResponse().getZBRxIoSampleResponse(ioSample);
```

```
        // Get and store the data locally (in memory)
        record_sample(&ioSample);
      }
      else {
        Serial.print("Expected I/O Sample, but got ");
        Serial.print(xbee.getResponse().getApiId(), HEX);
      }
    } else if (xbee.getResponse().isError()) {
      Serial.print("Error reading packet.  Error code: ");
      Serial.println(xbee.getResponse().getErrorCode());
    } else {
      // Listen for client and respond.
      listener();
    }
  }
}
```

This completes the discussion of the new components for this sketch. The following section includes the entire sketch with all of these components in their proper context. Be sure to take your time reading through the code. It is by far the largest sketch (code) you have worked with in this book.

Putting It All Together

Now that you understand the workings of the major components of the sketch, let's examine the completed sketch in more detail. Listing 8-4 shows the completed code for the sketch.

■ **Tip** If you are using a Leonardo, check the notes in the code regarding the pins for the XBee shield. Depending on which shield you are using with your Leonardo, you may need to change these.

Listing 8-4. Local-Storage Data-Aggregate Node

```
/**
  Sensor Networks Example Arduino Data Aggregate Node

  This project demonstrates how to receive sensor data from
  multiple XBee sensor nodes, save the samples in the onboard
  EEPROM and present them as a web page. It uses an Arduino
  with an XBee shield with an XBee coordinator installed.

  Note: This sketch was adapted from the examples in the XBee
  library created by Andrew Rapp.
*/

#include <XBee.h>
#include <SoftwareSerial.h>
#include <Ethernet.h>
#include <SPI.h>
#include <EEPROM.h>
```

```
byte bytes_per_sample = 10; // address (2), temp (4), volts (4)

// Setup pin definitions for XBee shield
uint8_t recv = 2;  // or 8 if using a Leonardo
uint8_t trans = 3; // or 9 if using a Leonardo
SoftwareSerial soft_serial(recv, trans);

// assign a MAC address and IP address for the Arduino
byte mac[] = {
  0xDE, 0xAD, 0xBE, 0xEF, 0xFE, 0xED};
IPAddress ip(10, 0, 1, 111);

// Start Ethernet Server class with port 80 (default for HTTP)
EthernetServer server(80);

// Instantiate an instance of the XBee library
XBee xbee = XBee();

// Instantiate an instance of the IO sample class
ZBRxIoSampleResponse ioSample = ZBRxIoSampleResponse();

// Sample data values
unsigned int address;        // Last 4 digits of XBee address
float temperature;           // Raw temperature value
float voltage;               // Reference voltage

// Get sample data
void get_sample_data(ZBRxIoSampleResponse *ioSample) {
  Serial.print("Received data from address: ");
  address = (ioSample->getRemoteAddress64().getMsb() << 8) +
              ioSample->getRemoteAddress64().getLsb();
  Serial.print(ioSample->getRemoteAddress64().getMsb(), HEX);
  Serial.println(ioSample->getRemoteAddress64().getLsb(), HEX);
  temperature = ioSample->getAnalog(3);
  int ref = xbee.getResponse().getFrameData()[17] << 8;
  ref += xbee.getResponse().getFrameData()[18];
  voltage = (float(ref) * float(1200.0 / 1024.0))/1000.0;
}

// Read an integer from EEPROM
int read_int(byte position) {
  int value = 0;
  byte* p = (byte*)(void*)&value;
  for (int i = 0; i < sizeof(value); i++)
      *p++ = EEPROM.read(position++);
  return value;
}
```

```
// Read a float from EEPROM
float read_float(byte position) {
  float value = 0;
  byte* p = (byte*)(void*)&value;
  for (int i = 0; i < sizeof(value); i++)
      *p++ = EEPROM.read(position++);
  return value;
}

// Write an integer to EEPROM
void write_int(byte position, int value) {
  const byte *p = (const byte *)(const void *)&value;
  for (int i = 0; i < sizeof(value); i++)
      EEPROM.write(position++, *p++);
}

// Write a float to EEPROM
void write_float(byte position, float value) {
  const byte *p = (const byte *)(const void *)&value;
  for (int i = 0; i < sizeof(value); i++)
      EEPROM.write(position++, *p++);
}

// Read a sample from EEPROM
void read_sample(byte index, unsigned int *address, float *temp_f,
                 float *temp_c, float *volts) {
  float temp;
  byte position =  (index * bytes_per_sample) + 1;

  *address = read_int(position);

  temp = read_float(position + 2);

  *temp_c = ((temp * 1200.0 / 1024.0) - 500.0) / 10.0;
  *temp_f = ((*temp_c * 9.0)/5.0) + 32.0;

  *volts = read_float(position + 6);
}

// Write sample to EEPROM
void write_sample(byte index) {
  byte position =  (index * bytes_per_sample) + 1;

  write_int(position, address);
  write_float(position + 2, temperature);
  write_float(position + 6, voltage);
}

// Record a sample
void record_sample(ZBRxIoSampleResponse *ioSample) {
  int saved_addr;
```

```
  // Get sample data from XBee
  get_sample_data(ioSample);

  // See if already in memory. If not, add it.
  byte num_samples = EEPROM.read(0);
  boolean found = false;
  for (byte i = 0; i < num_samples; i++) {
    byte position = (i * bytes_per_sample) + 1;

    // get address
    saved_addr = read_int(position);
    if (saved_addr == address) {
      write_sample(i);
      found = true;
    }
  }
  if (!found) {
    // Save sample
    write_sample(num_samples);

    // Update number of sensors
    num_samples++;
    EEPROM.write(0, num_samples);
  }
}

void send_sensor_data(EthernetClient *client, int num_sample) {
  unsigned int address;
  float temp_c;
  float temp_f;
  float volts;

  // Read sensor data from memory and display it.
  read_sample(num_sample, &address, &temp_c, &temp_f, &volts);

  client->println("<br />");
  client->print("Node Address: ");
  client->print(address, HEX);
  client->print(".");
  client->println("<br />");
  client->print("Temperature: ");
  client->print(temp_c);
  client->print(" degrees C");
  client->println("<br />");
  client->print("Temperature: ");
  client->print(temp_f);
  client->print(" degrees F");
  client->println("<br />");
  client->print("Voltage: ");
  client->print(volts);
  client->print(" volts.");
  client->println("<br />");
}
```

```
void listener() {
  // listen for incoming clients
  EthernetClient client = server.available();
  if (client) {
    Serial.println("Got a connection!");
    // an http request ends with a blank line
    boolean currentLineIsBlank = true;
    while (client.connected()) {
      if (client.available()) {
        char c = client.read();
        // if you've gotten to the end of the line (received a newline
        // character) and the line is blank, the http request has ended,
        // so you can send a reply
        if (c == '\n' && currentLineIsBlank) {
          // send a standard http response header
          client.println("HTTP/1.1 200 OK");
          client.println("Content-Type: text/html");
          client.println();

          // Print header
          client.println("Welcome to the Arduino Data Aggregate Node!");
          client.println("<br />");

          // read sensor data
          byte num_samples = EEPROM.read(0);
          for (int i = 0; i < num_samples; i++) {
            send_sensor_data(&client, i);
          }
          // if no data, say so!
          if (num_samples == 0) {
            client.print("No samples to display.");
            client.println("<br />");
          }
          break;
        }
        if (c == '\n') {
          currentLineIsBlank = true;
        }
        else if (c != '\r') {
          currentLineIsBlank = false;
        }
      }
    }
  }
  // give the web browser time to receive the data
  delay(1);
  // close the connection:
  client.stop();
  }
}
```

```
void setup() {
  // start the SPI library:
  SPI.begin();

  // start the Ethernet connection and the server:
  Ethernet.begin(mac, ip);
  server.begin();

  Serial.begin(9600);
  while (!Serial); // Wait until Serial is ready - Leonardo
  soft_serial.begin(9600);
  xbee.setSerial(soft_serial);

  // Initialize the EEPROM
  EEPROM.write(0, 0);
}

void loop() {
  //attempt to read a packet
  xbee.readPacket();

  if (xbee.getResponse().isAvailable()) {
    // got something

    if (xbee.getResponse().getApiId() == ZB_IO_SAMPLE_RESPONSE) {

      // Get the packet
      xbee.getResponse().getZBRxIoSampleResponse(ioSample);

      // Get and store the data locally (in memory)
      record_sample(&ioSample);
    }
    else {
      Serial.print("Expected I/O Sample, but got ");
      Serial.print(xbee.getResponse().getApiId(), HEX);
    }
  } else if (xbee.getResponse().isError()) {
    Serial.print("Error reading packet.  Error code: ");
    Serial.println(xbee.getResponse().getErrorCode());
  } else {
    // Listen for client and respond.
    listener();
  }
}
```

Take some time to go through the sketch until you are completely satisfied that you understand how everything works together. Once you are familiar and comfortable with the code, compile it and upload it to your Arduino.

Testing the Project

Once the code compiles and uploads successfully to your Arduino data-aggregate node, and before any sensor nodes are powered on, connect to your Arduino via a web browser. Be sure to use the IP address you put in your sketch. Figure 8-5 shows the correct response. You can also open the serial monitor at this time.

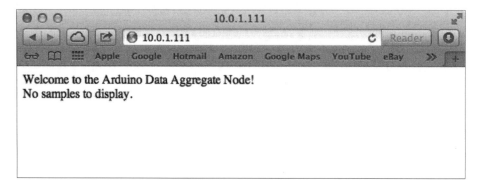

Figure 8-5. Example response from a data-aggregate node with no sensors attached

If you see this response, you have successfully written a very lightweight web server running on an Arduino! How cool is that? Now, power on one of your temperature sensor nodes and wait for 5–10 minutes. If you haven't opened the serial monitor, do so now, and then wait for the sensor node data to arrive. You should see the message "Received data from address: NNNNN" in the serial monitor. When this happens, refresh your browser and notice the changes.

If you get some data back in the web browser, go ahead and power on all of your sensor nodes and wait for a while for several samples to arrive. Figure 8-6 shows what your serial monitor should be printing if you have three temperature sensor nodes running. Note that the addresses will be different and should match your XBee modules.

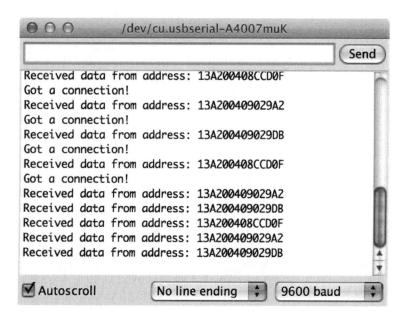

Figure 8-6. Sample output in the serial monitor

Wait until you see several iterations of samples arrive, and then refresh your browser. You should see only one entry containing the latest sample for each sensor connected. Figure 8-7 shows an example result where there are three sensor nodes supplying data.

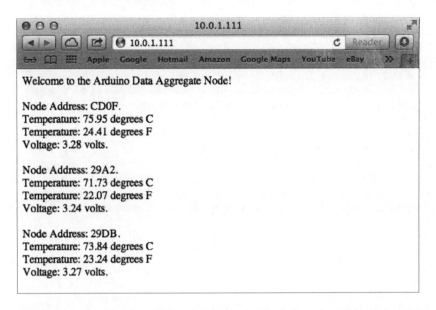

Figure 8-7. *Sample web page for a remote data-aggregate node with local storage*

Wait for a few minutes, and then refresh your browser. You should see the sample values change. If they do not (or you just want to have some fun), carefully affect the values of the sensors by locating them nearer to heat or cool sources.

■ **Note**   If you do not see any data from your sensor nodes and there is nothing in the serial monitor indicating any data was received, use the troubleshooting section in Chapter 2 to diagnose possible issues with your XBee modules. Remember, they all must have the same version of the API firmware, and the sensor nodes must have the ROUTER role and the data-aggregate node the COORDINATOR role. Also, be sure to allow at least 10 minutes for the XBee modules to connect and form a network.

Ok, that was a hoot, wasn't it? Yes indeed: you now have demonstrated mastery of the basic building blocks of a sensor network. Although you used only Arduino nodes to keep this easier to comprehend, the next project introduces the Raspberry Pi into the mix and further rounds out your cache of sensor networking tools.

■ **Note**   It is Ok if your output varies from what is shown. In some cases you may also notice a small discrepancy between what the sensor reports and measurements from more accurate devices. As long as you see values within tolerance for your particular sensor (check the vendor's data sheet for this), your sensor node is working properly.

For More Fun

There are a lot of really cool things you can do with this project. The most obvious to me is replacing the XBee address with meaningful labels. More specifically, label the sensor nodes by their location. For example, XBee node CD0F is located on my porch, whereas node 29DB is in my office. It would be more meaningful if the labels on the web page stated Dr. Bell's Office and Mrs. Bell's Porch. Hint: make a lookup table for this data so that you can substitute the values when displayed to the client.

Another area of exploration is to use the SD card rather than the onboard EEPROM to store the data. Rather than store only the last value for each sensor node, store a running list of values for each sensor in a separate file. When the client requests the data, display only the last values written to each file. This will demonstrate the minor changes needed to make the local-storage data-aggregate node into a node that permits storage of values over time. Be careful not to exceed the capacity of the SD card!

There is one thing that this project does not have that would be considered essential for cases where you want to know when a sample was taken: the date and time of the sample! The project stores the latest values for each sensor, but you don't know when the sample was taken. For example, what if you receive data from one sensor only once and something happens to cause the sensor to stop sending data? Without a date and time reference, you have no way to know this. To resolve this issue, you can modify the project to use a real-time clock module and store the date and time of each sample as you saw in Chapter 5. Hint: you need to extend the methods for storing the sample data by adding the real-time clock value.

If you are looking for a significant challenge, modify the code to send the data to Xively, and use Xively as your data-storage mechanism. This demonstrates the minor changes needed to change this node into a remote-storage node.

Remote-Storage Data Aggregator

A *remote-storage data aggregator* is a node designed to receive sensor data from one or more sensors or sensor nodes and store the data on a different node. Most often it is the case that the other node is a system with a more robust storage device. For example, it may be a computer that can store large files or a database server that permits you to store the data in tables.

Remote-storage data-aggregate nodes can be less sophisticated than local-storage data-aggregate nodes because there is no need to process the data for display or storage in a local device. Rather, you merely pass the raw data to the remote node (system) for storage.

Remote storage is also the first choice for cases where you want to store the data for later processing. Although it may be the case that the loss of some values may be acceptable, it is more likely that you want to collect all the data produced so that your analysis can be more accurate.[6] You therefore want the connection from the data-aggregate node to the remote-storage node to be reliable.

It may also be the case that there are multiple nodes to which you send the data. Consider a situation in which you are working with different sensors or sensors that produce data in different formats. In this case, you may want to send data from some sensors to one remote node and other data to other node(s). The reasons for doing such are less paramount than those for using different local-storage data-aggregate nodes, but it is still a concern. I consider this and similar topics for planning sensor networks in the next chapter.

You see a working example of this form of data-aggregate node for both the Arduino and Raspberry Pi in the following sections.

---

[6]Which reminds me of my advanced statistics professor, who opened the semester with the question, "How much data makes for a statistically relevant sample size?" He did not offer an answer, but he asked the question again at the end of the semester. To his delight, the answer presented by the students was, "It depends on what you're doing with the data." When pressed for a numerical answer, his response was unwaveringly, "42."

Project: Arduino Data-Aggregate Node with Database Storage

This project uses the previous project as its basis. You reuse the same hardware and software but with a slightly different sketch. If you have not built the components from the previous project or had problems getting it to work, you may want to go back and diagnose and correct the problem first.

You also use the MySQL database server you created in Chapter 6 and the connection mechanism from Chapter 7. If you have not built the database server, you need to go back to Chapter 6 and build it.

■ **Note** If you have problems getting your Raspberry Pi configured with MySQL or want to simplify the project, you can use a MySQL server running on another computer. However, you should get your Raspberry Pi database server running if you plan to install or use this project as a basis for your own sensor network.

With that stated, it's time to build your sensor network storing the samples in a database. Savvy readers will realize you've already built examples of all the components in the previous chapters.

Hardware

This project uses the same hardware as the previous project for the sensor nodes and the data-aggregate node. The difference is that you add a new node—the MySQL database server.

Recall from Chapter 6 that the MySQL database server is a Raspberry Pi with an external hard drive connected via a USB hub (the Raspberry Pi cannot power devices like hard drives via the USB bus). Please refer to the "Building a Raspberry Pi MySQL Server" section in Chapter 6 to build the MySQL database server if you have not done so already.

Go ahead and power on the database server and make sure it can accept connections. You can leave the server powered on and connected while working with the other nodes. It is best to leave the sensor nodes powered off until you get all the software changes completed for the data-aggregate node.

Software

As with the hardware, you use the same software as in the previous project, albeit with additional libraries for the MySQL connection and a few modifications to the sketch. Because you are using the same XBee configuration, all the code for reading data from the XBee modules is the same as in the previous project.

I omit the code for creating a web server and writing the data values to EEPROM. This removes a lot of the code, but the basic structure is the same. The new portions are the calls to the MySQL Connector Arduino library for connecting to the database server and issuing queries to save the data, as you saw in Chapter 7. You work through each of the new parts of the sketch in the following paragraphs. A later section looks at configuring the MySQL database.

Adding the MySQL Connector Code to the Sketch

Recall from Chapter 7 that you need to include the sha1 and mysql libraries to use the MySQL Connector Arduino library. Refer to Chapter 7 to install these libraries. Once you have the libraries installed, open a new sketch and name it Arduino_MySQL_Aggregate. The following shows the libraries needed for reading data from the XBee module as well as the new libraries sha1 and mysql:

```
#include <XBee.h>
#include <SoftwareSerial.h>
#include <Ethernet.h>
#include <SPI.h>
#include <sha1.h>
#include <mysql.h>
```

You reuse the variables for communicating with the XBee but add an instance of the Connector class from the mysql library and user and password strings as shown here:

```
Connector my_conn;

char user[] = "root";
char password[] = "secret";
```

You also need to store the IP address[7] of the MySQL database server. You do this via the following. Be sure to use the correct IP address for your MySQL server—failure to use the correct address will result in connection errors when the sketch first starts (because you connect to the server in the setup() method):

```
IPAddress server_addr(10, 0, 1, 24);
```

You keep the get_sample_data() method from the previous project but drop the listener(), send_sensor_data(), and EEPROM read and write methods. The record_sample() method requires rewriting, however. In this case, you still call get_sample_data(); but instead of calculating the temperature from the raw data and displaying it to the serial monitor, you build an INSERT SQL statement for saving the data in a table (I explain the database setup in the next section). This requires building the string to save the last four digits of the hexadecimal address, the raw temperature, and the voltage in the string. Once the string is built, you simply call the cmd_query() method of the MySQL Connector class instance (my_conn). The new method is shown next:

```
void record_sample(ZBRxIoSampleResponse *ioSample) {
  int saved_addr;

  // Get sample data from XBee
  get_sample_data(ioSample);

  // Send data to MySQL
  String query("INSERT INTO house.temperature VALUES(NULL, '");
  String addr(address, HEX);
  char buff[40];
  query += addr;
  query += ("', '");
  query += dtostrf(temperature, 4, 4, buff);
  query += ("', '");
  query += dtostrf(voltage, 4, 4, buff);
  query += ("', NULL, NULL)");

  Serial.println(&query[0]);
  my_conn.cmd_query(&query[0]);
}
```

---

[7]It must be a valid IP address for the network segment to which your server is connected.

The changes to the setup() method require adding the code to connect to the database server. You remove the calls to server.begin() and EEPROM.write(0, 0) because you are neither initiating a web server nor using the EEPROM to store the samples. Instead, add the following to the end of the setup() method:

```
Serial.println("Connecting to MySQL...");
if (my_conn.mysql_connect(server_addr, 3306, user, password))
{
  delay(500);
  Serial.println("Success!");
}
else
{
  Serial.println("Connection failed.");
}
```

Modifying the loop() method is much easier. All the calls are in place for reading from the XBee modules and calling the record_sample() method. The only thing left to do is to remove the last else statement that contains the call to the listener() method.

As you can see, the modifications to the sketch from the last project are very easy. In fact, if you want to save some time coding, you can copy the code from the previous project and remove the parts you do not need. Listing 8-5 shows the completed sketch, including all the parts reused from the last project.

■ **Tip** Remember, if you are using a Leonardo, check the notes in the code regarding the pins for the XBee shield.

Listing 8-5. Arduino Remote-Storage Data Aggregate

```
/**
  Sensor Networks Example Arduino Data Aggregate Node

  This project demonstrates how to receive sensor data from
  multiple XBee sensor nodes saving the samples in a MySQL
  database.

  It uses an Arduino with an XBee shield with an XBee
  coordinator installed.

*/

#include <XBee.h>
#include <SoftwareSerial.h>
#include <Ethernet.h>
#include <SPI.h>
#include <sha1.h>
#include <mysql.h>

// Setup pin definitions for XBee shield
uint8_t recv = 2;  // 8 if using a Leonardo
uint8_t trans = 3; // 9 if using a Leonardo
SoftwareSerial soft_serial(recv, trans);
```

```
// assign a MAC address and IP address for the Arduino
byte mac[] = {
  OxDE, OxAD, OxBE, OxEF, OxFE, OxED};
IPAddress ip(10, 0, 1, 111);
IPAddress server_addr(10, 0, 1, 24);

// Instantiate an instance of the XBee library
XBee xbee = XBee();

// Instantiate an instance of the IO sample class
ZBRxIoSampleResponse ioSample = ZBRxIoSampleResponse();

/* Setup for the Connector/Arduino */
Connector my_conn;              // The Connector/Arduino reference

char user[] = "root";
char password[] = "root";

// Sample data values
unsigned int address;           // Last 4 digits of XBee address
float temperature;              // Raw temperature value
float voltage;                  // Reference voltage

// Get sample data
void get_sample_data(ZBRxIoSampleResponse *ioSample) {
  Serial.print("Received data from address: ");
  address = (ioSample->getRemoteAddress64().getMsb() << 8) +
            ioSample->getRemoteAddress64().getLsb();
  Serial.print(ioSample->getRemoteAddress64().getMsb(), HEX);
  Serial.println(ioSample->getRemoteAddress64().getLsb(), HEX);
  temperature = ioSample->getAnalog(3);
  int ref = xbee.getResponse().getFrameData()[17] << 8;
  ref += xbee.getResponse().getFrameData()[18];
  voltage = (float(ref) * float(1200.0 / 1024.0))/1000.0;
}

// Record a sample
void record_sample(ZBRxIoSampleResponse *ioSample) {
  int saved_addr;

  // Get sample data from XBee
  get_sample_data(ioSample);

  // Send data to MySQL
  String query("INSERT INTO house.temperature VALUES(NULL, '");
  String addr(address, HEX);
  char buff[40];
  query += addr;
  query += ("', '");
  query += dtostrf(temperature, 4, 4, buff);
  query += ("', '");
  query += dtostrf(voltage, 4, 4, buff);
  query += ("', NULL, NULL)");
```

```
    Serial.println(&query[0]);
    my_conn.cmd_query(&query[0]);
}

void setup() {
  // start the SPI library:
  SPI.begin();

  // start the Ethernet connection and the server:
  Ethernet.begin(mac, ip);
  Serial.begin(9600);
  while (!Serial); // Wait until Serial is ready - Leonardo
  soft_serial.begin(9600);
  xbee.setSerial(soft_serial);

  Serial.println("Connecting to MySQL...");
  if (my_conn.mysql_connect(server_addr, 3306, user, password))
  {
    delay(500);
    Serial.println("Success!");
  }
  else
  {
    Serial.println("Connection failed.");
  }
}

void loop() {
  //attempt to read a packet
  xbee.readPacket();

  if (xbee.getResponse().isAvailable()) {
    // got something

    if (xbee.getResponse().getApiId() == ZB_IO_SAMPLE_RESPONSE) {

      // Get the packet
      xbee.getResponse().getZBRxIoSampleResponse(ioSample);

      // Get and store the data locally (in memory or on card?)
      record_sample(&ioSample);
    }
    else {
      Serial.print("Expected I/O Sample, but got ");
      Serial.print(xbee.getResponse().getApiId(), HEX);
    }
  } else if (xbee.getResponse().isError()) {
    Serial.print("Error reading packet.  Error code: ");
    Serial.println(xbee.getResponse().getErrorCode());
  }
}
```

You may be wondering why you remove the code for calculating the temperature in Fahrenheit and Celsius. You do this because you can move this functionality to the database server. Not only does this free up some processing power, but for platforms like the Arduino it also frees up a small amount of memory. The savings for this project may be minimal, but consider the case for a very complex sketch or an Arduino that is doing other things. Any savings in memory could allow for more room to store data or work with sensors.

For example, consider the need for building a node that not only serves as a data aggregate via an XBee network but also hosts a number of sensors on the Arduino connected via an I2C interface and displays data via some other hardware-specific interface such as an LCD panel or even a hard-copy printer.[8] All these components require the inclusion of libraries; and depending on the size of the Arduino, you may run low on memory. I have built sketches that have forced me to use an Arduino Mega not because of the size of my sketch but due to the sum of the memory needed for the libraries I needed to use.

Now that you have the sketch built, let's turn to the database server and see what needs to be done to support storing the samples in a table.

Setting Up the MySQL Database

This section discusses the work needed on the MySQL server to make a database for saving and reporting your sensor data. The first thing you need to do is create the database you want to use and populate it with the necessary objects. In this case, you need two tables and a trigger. I show you all the commands needed but omit most of the interaction with the server for brevity. Refer to Chapters 6 and 7 for a quick-start tutorial on MySQL if you have not read those chapters.

Connect to your MySQL database server. Recall that you can do this via the `mysql -uroot -p<password>` command if run on the database server itself. Go ahead and create the database and name it `house`, as shown:

```
CREATE DATABASE house;
USE house;
```

The data will be stored in a table. As mentioned previously, you want to store the address of the XBee sensor node (the last four hexadecimal digits of the 64-bit address), the raw temperature sample, and the voltage.

It is at this point you can consider adding some functionality to the database server that would otherwise require much more work on the data-aggregate node. For example, consider the fact that you want to know when the sample was taken. That is, you want to store the date and time of the sample. If you remember from earlier chapters, you must use a real-time clock module connected to the Arduino in order to display the date and time of the sample. Fortunately, you can avoid all that code and hardware by simply instructing the database server to store this data automatically by creating a column using the `timestamp` data type. This data type stores the current date and time when the row is inserted into the table. Very cool, eh?

But you may wonder how that works. The trick to making the server fill in the data for the field is to pass the value NULL in the INSERT statement. This is a special sentinel value that the server interprets to mean you want to calculate the timestamp and save it. Note that you can provide a specific timestamp for the column, should you need to store a specific value.

You can also move the code to calculate the temperature in Fahrenheit and Celsius to the database. This requires the use of a *trigger* (a special block of code that can be executed at specific moments when a row is inserted, updated, or deleted). You look at the trigger in a moment; for now, you can simply add a column for each temperature value.

Thus you need a total of six columns: date and time of the sample, address of the sensor node, raw temperature sample, voltage, temperature in Fahrenheit, and temperature in Celsius. The CREATE TABLE statement needed to realize this table is as follows. Name the table `temperature`:

```
CREATE TABLE `temperature` (
  `sample_date` timestamp NOT NULL DEFAULT CURRENT_TIMESTAMP ON UPDATE CURRENT_TIMESTAMP,
  `address` char(8) DEFAULT NULL,
```

---

[8]Yes, these exist! See www.sparkfun.com/products/10438.

```
  `raw_temp` float DEFAULT NULL,
  `voltage` float DEFAULT NULL,
  `fahrenheit` float DEFAULT '0',
  `celsius` float DEFAULT '0'
) ENGINE=InnoDB DEFAULT CHARSET=latin1⁹;
```

Notice that you do not use a primary key. I leave it to you to consider the implications, and I discuss considerations for database design in the next chapter.

WHAT ABOUT NODES WITHOUT XBEES? WHAT ADDRESS DO I USE?

The table you create here uses a short character string for the address of the XBee sensor node. What do you use if you add a sensor node that doesn't use XBees (it connects directly to the server for storing data) or if there are sensors connected to the data-aggregate node? In either case, you can simply create your own unique value for each sensor. You can use the convention of the last four digits of the XBee 64-bit address and store the hexadecimal value. You can just as easily number your sensor nodes and sensors with values starting from 0000 to FFFF. This leaves you plenty of values to work with. But be sure not to use the same value as one of your XBees.

Recall that one of the challenges from the last project is to use meaningful names for each of the sensor nodes. You can move this to the database server as well, in the form of a lookup table. In this case, you need a column that matches the values stored in the temperature table and another column for storing a more meaningful name. This allows you to add more human-friendly data while preserving the original form of the data. Later, you see how to retrieve this information when querying data on the server. The following statements create the new table named sensor_names and populate it with data. You conclude with a sample SELECT statement to retrieve the data entered:

```
CREATE TABLE `sensor_names` (
  `address` char(8) DEFAULT NULL,
  `name` char(30) DEFAULT NULL
) ENGINE=InnoDB DEFAULT CHARSET=latin1;

INSERT INTO sensor_names VALUES ('29a2', 'New Porch');
INSERT INTO sensor_names VALUES ('29db', 'Living Room');
INSERT INTO sensor_names VALUES ('cd0f', 'Office');

SELECT * FROM house.sensor_names;
+---------+-------------+
| address | name        |
+---------+-------------+
| 29a2    | New Porch   |
| 29db    | Living Room |
| cd0f    | Office      |
+---------+-------------+
3 rows in set (0.00 sec)
```

---

⁹What is missing here? Can you spot a potential problem with this table? I'll give you a hint: can it accept duplicate rows? What about ordering of the rows? Are these an issue?

> ■ **Tip** Use the addresses for your own XBee nodes in the following INSERT statements when you use them in your project.

Now let's consider the trigger. This is how you transplant the code to calculate the temperature in the Fahrenheit and Celsius scales to the database server. I encourage you to examine the syntax and use of triggers in the online MySQL Reference Manual (http://dev.mysql.com/doc/refman/5.6/en/create-trigger.html). In the meantime, I show you what statements are needed to add the trigger you need.

You need to detect when a new row is added to the table. When that happens, you want to perform the calculations and store the results in the appropriate columns. Thus, you need to create a trigger that operates before a new row is inserted. When that event occurs, you can perform the calculations. The following shows the trigger you need to create. The calculations should look very familiar, albeit with a different syntax. Notice the use of the new operator, which lets you reference the values from the incoming (new) row to either read or write:

```
DELIMITER //
CREATE TRIGGER calc_temp BEFORE INSERT ON temperature
FOR EACH ROW
BEGIN
  declare c float;
  set c = ((new.raw_temp * 1200.0 / 1024.0) - 500.0) / 10.0;
  set new.celsius = c;
  set new.fahrenheit = ((c * 9.0)/5.0) + 32.0;
END;
//
DELIMITER ;
```

The first thing you may notice is the use of the DELIMITER command. This is a special command that can be used to replace the ; character that determines the end of a statement in the mysql client. In this case, you use // instead of ;.

The DELIMITER change is needed because the body of your trigger contains SQL statements that end with a semicolon. If you had not changed the delimiter, the mysql client would detect an end of statement and attempt to execute the partially coded trigger. If you run into syntax errors when creating this trigger, check to make sure you use the DELIMITER command as shown. Notice that the last thing you do is change the delimiter back to a semicolon.

Notice also that you set up the trigger to execute before an insert and you have a loop to process each new row. Although you're issuing single INSERT statements, this syntax is required because there may be cases where more than one new row is added at a time. For example, if there are transactions involved, the changes may not be committed (permanently stored) until several rows have been processed. In this case, the trigger will fire once, and the body will be processed once for each of the new rows.

You also need to grant access to the user. You do this with a GRANT statement:

```
mysql> GRANT ALL ON *.* to 'root'@'%' IDENTIFIED BY 'secret';
```

Now that you have your MySQL database server set up and the necessary database objects created, let's put it all together and see how it runs. It is at this time that you can upload the sketch to your Arduino data-aggregate node (making sure it is plugged in to your network) and power on the sensor nodes. Wait 3–5 minutes before powering on the sensor nodes.

Testing the Project

Once your sketch is loaded, open the serial monitor and observe the statements about connecting to the MySQL database server. If all is well, you should see a success message. If you do not, check the IP address you used, and be sure to check that your MySQL server is running and is accepting connections.

When you see the connection success message, you can power on your sensor nodes. You should start seeing a message printed in the serial monitor for each sensor node. Recall from Listing 8-5 that you print an announcement of data read from an XBee (and show the address). You also display the completed INSERT statement for the sample data.

If you let the sketch run for some time and have several sensor nodes powered on and communicating, you will start to see the sketch recording samples from those sensor nodes too. Figure 8-8 shows an example of the statements printed for samples from several sensor nodes.

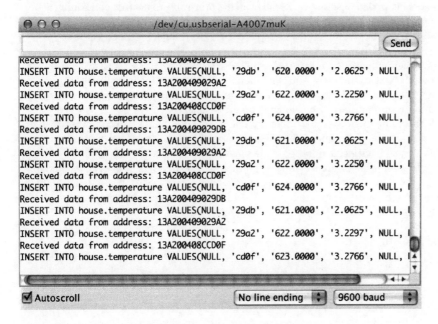

Figure 8-8. Sample sensor readings for multiple sensor nodes

If you see results similar to these examples, you've solved the project! But what about the data in the database? How do you see it? Once the sketch has run for some time, connect to your MySQL database server, issue the following command, and observe the results:

```
mysql> SELECT * FROM house.temperature;
+---------------------+---------+----------+---------+------------+---------+
| sample_date         | address | raw_temp | voltage | fahrenheit | celsius |
+---------------------+---------+----------+---------+------------+---------+
...
| 2013-07-29 01:31:26 | 29a2    |      622 |  3.2297 |    73.2031 | 22.8906 |
| 2013-07-29 01:31:33 | cd0f    |      623 |  3.2766 |    73.4141 | 23.0078 |
| 2013-07-29 01:31:37 | 29db    |      621 |  2.0625 |    72.9922 | 22.7734 |
| 2013-07-29 01:31:41 | 29a2    |      622 |  3.2297 |    73.2031 | 22.8906 |
| 2013-07-29 01:31:47 | cd0f    |      624 |  3.2766 |     73.625 |  23.125 |
| 2013-07-29 01:31:52 | 29db    |      621 |  2.0625 |    72.9922 | 22.7734 |
| 2013-07-29 01:31:56 | 29a2    |      622 |  3.2297 |    73.2031 | 22.8906 |
| 2013-07-29 01:32:02 | cd0f    |      624 |  3.2766 |     73.625 |  23.125 |
| 2013-07-29 01:32:06 | 29db    |      620 |  2.0578 |    72.7812 | 22.6562 |
| 2013-07-29 01:32:10 | 29a2    |      622 |  3.2297 |    73.2031 | 22.8906 |
| 2013-07-29 01:32:17 | cd0f    |      624 |  3.2719 |     73.625 |  23.125 |
+---------------------+---------+----------+---------+------------+---------+
165 rows in set (0.01 sec)
```

Notice that I had many rows to see! This is because I set my XBee modules sleep time to a very low value. In practice, you would set the sleep time for more than a few seconds. It is fine to leave it sampling frequently for this project.

Notice also that you have data populated for the sample date, Fahrenheit, and Celsius columns! This shows that the timestamp data type worked and your trigger fired on INSERT, creating the calculated values. Isn't that slick and easier than making your poor overworked Arduino crank out the values?

Now let's consider another feature of the database server. Recall from the previous project that you could easily see the last known samples for each sensor node. How can you reproduce this feature if you never store those values any place? It is unlikely you will need to have this feature, but let's explore it in case you need similar features.

The answer is that you do store those values! You store every value in a sample. The problem is, you don't know which row in the table is the latest for each sensor. But the answer is still there, isn't it?

This is where savvy SQL programmers earns their pay. You can indeed get to this data by using a bit of SQL magic called *grouping* and the MAX() function. In this case, you want the name of the sensor (not the address) and the temperature values in Fahrenheit and Celsius—just like what you had on the web server.

To get the name, you must *join* (combine the rows of two tables matching on a common set of columns) the temperature and sensor_names tables, matching on address. Recall that the values in each table will match—that is, one row in the sensor_names table will match a specific number of rows in the temperature table.

But what about the last values? To get this data, you use the MAX() function on a subquery (a query executed from within another query) to return the latest timestamp for each group of addresses. Notice the GROUP BY clause in the subquery. You can use the results in the subquery to limit the output of your SELECT to only those rows that match the latest value for each address. The following shows the complete SELECT statement and sample results:

```
mysql> SELECT name, fahrenheit, voltage
FROM temperature join sensor_names ON temperature.address = sensor_names.address
WHERE sample_date IN (
    SELECT MAX(sample_date)
    FROM temperature
    GROUP BY address
);
+-------------+------------+---------+
| name        | fahrenheit | voltage |
+-------------+------------+---------+
| New Porch   |    73.2031 |  3.2297 |
| Living Room |    72.7812 |  2.0578 |
| Office      |     73.625 |  3.2719 |
+-------------+------------+---------+
3 rows in set (2.48 sec)
```

If you are thinking that is a very complex query, don't feel bad. SQL can be quite a challenge when you start working with databases. If you find that you need to use such queries, it would be worth purchasing a book on learning SQL to become more familiar with the power and functionality available in SQL commands.

For More Fun

There are a number of things you can do with this project. In fact, all the challenges from the previous project apply. The only thing left to do is substitute a Raspberry Pi for one of the sensor nodes and substitute a Raspberry Pi for the data-aggregate node. You do the latter in the next project, but let's consider how to do the former.

Chapter 4 explores how to create a sensor node hosted by a Raspberry Pi. Consider taking this challenge one step further and combining it with what you learned in Chapter 5 regarding using the TMP36 sensor. Add such a node to your network.

For even more fun, you can add the web server components from the previous project to the sketch. Leaving these elements in place also introduces a form of the data-aggregate node discussed in Chapter 2—a hybrid data-aggregate node. Recall that the advantage here is that if the node loses connection to the server (or the server goes down), you can at least get the latest data from the data-aggregate node.

Now that you have mastered data-aggregate nodes with the Arduino, let's explore building data-aggregate nodes with the Raspberry Pi.

Project: Raspberry Pi Data-Aggregate Node with Database Storage

This project uses the sensor nodes from the previous project, but rather than use an Arduino as the host for the data-aggregate node, you use a Raspberry Pi. You also use the same MySQL database server from the previous project to store sensor data from the XBee sensor nodes via the Raspberry Pi data-aggregate node.

The goals of the project are to reproduce the functionality from the last project. That is, you want the Raspberry Pi to receive sensor samples from multiple sensor nodes via an XBee module (the coordinator) and save those results in your MySQL database.

The basis for this project is the Raspberry Pi XBee project from Chapter 4. It may be good to review that text to familiarize yourself with the task. I show the wiring diagram from Chapter 4 as a refresher.

Hardware

This project requires the XBee hosted sensor nodes from the previous projects, a Raspberry Pi, a GPIO breakout board and cable, a breadboard, an XBee adapter, and some breadboard jumpers.

The wiring is the same as in the section "Project: Creating a Raspberry Pi Data Collector for XBee Sensor Nodes" in Chapter 4. Figure 8-9 shows the breadboard and wiring from Chapter 4. Wire the XBee adapter as shown, connect the GPIO cable to your Raspberry Pi, and then power up! You don't have to install the XBee yet, but it is a good idea to do so. Remember, you need your coordinator node.

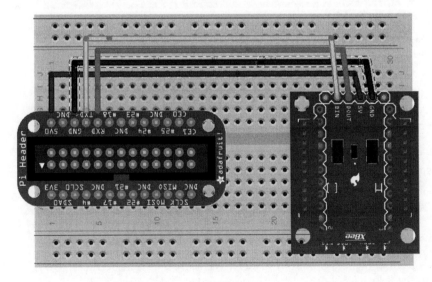

Figure 8-9. *Connecting an XBee to a Raspberry Pi*

Software

The software requirements for this project are the same as the project from Chapter 4. That is, you're using the Connector/Python library. Refer to Chapter 4 for information on how to download and install the library.

Now let's start writing your Python script. If you want to copy the script from Chapter 4, you can. Simply copy it to a file named `pi_xbee_mysql.py`. Or you can open a new file and enter the code from scratch.

The first statements you need to enter are those for including the libraries you need. Recall from Chapter 4 that these include the `serial` and `xbee` libraries. You also add the `mysql.connector` library, as shown here:

```
import serial
import xbee
import mysql.connector
```

Next, you define some variables. You use the same variables and definitions from the project in Chapter 4 but add two new ones for your MySQL code. In this case, you need to add a variable to store the instance of a database connector class.

You also need to expand the constants to include those required to communicate with the MySQL server. You add the username, host (or IP), port, and password. These are the same values you would use to connect to the MySQL server via the `mysql` client. The following shows all the constants and variables:

```
# Constants
SERIAL_PORT = '/dev/ttyAMA0'
BAUD_RATE = 9600
USER = 'root'
HOST_OR_IP = '10.0.1.24'
PORT = 3306
PASSWD = 'secret'

# Instantiate an instance for the serial port
ser_port = serial.Serial(SERIAL_PORT, BAUD_RATE)

# Instantiate an instance of the ZigBee class
# and pass it an instance of the Serial class
xbee1 = xbee.zigbee.ZigBee(ser_port)

# Variables for MySQL Connector/Python code
socket = None
db_conn = None
```

■ **Caution** Make sure all the constants match your XBee configuration and specifics for accessing your MySQL database server. If the script does not run correctly or you cannot connect to MySQL, double-check these settings.

Now you get to the meat of the script. Because you are writing the script using the same form as the project from Chapter 4 (one large while infinity loop[10] with a break exception), you refrain from making functions for each operation (connecting to the server, executing queries, and so on). Rather, you create a single function because this will be called once per iteration through the loop (while).

---

[10]I call it an infinity loop because the test condition is always true. In this case, unless you kill the script or press Ctrl+C, it will continue to run as long as the hardware remains powered on and working.

You name the method run_query() and pass it the database connection instance and a query string. The method creates a cursor, executes the query, and then checks for a result. If results are available, it returns them to the caller. The complete method is as follows:

```
def run_query(conn, query_str):
    results = None
    cur = conn.cursor(
        cursor_class=mysql.connector.cursor.MySQLCursorBufferedRaw)
    try:
        res = cur.execute(query_str)
    except mysql.connector.Error, e:
        cur.close()
        raise Exception("Query failed. " + e.__str__())
    try:
        results = cur.fetchall()
    except mysql.connector.errors.InterfaceError, e:
        if e.msg.lower() == "no result set to fetch from.":
            pass # This error means there were no results.
        else:    # otherwise, re-raise error
            raise e
    conn.commit()
    cur.close()
    return results
```

Next, you connect to the database server (remember, function declarations are not executed when encountered—only when called). You create a dictionary of values, setting them to the constants shown earlier. This is a technique you can use in any Python script to avoid passing a large set of parameters. The following code attempts to connect to the MySQL server and, if successful, returns an instance of the database connector class:

```
# Connect to database server
try:
    parameters = {
        'user': USER,
        'host': HOST_OR_IP,
        'port': PORT,
        'passwd': PASSWD,
        }
    db_conn = mysql.connector.connect(**parameters)
except mysql.connector.Error, e:
    raise Exception("ERROR: Cannot connect to MySQL Server!")
```

If the connection fails, you throw an exception. If this happens, be sure to check your constants for the correct values, and try connecting to the MySQL server using the mysql client application using the same parameters. Once you can connect successfully via the mysql client, try the script again.

The next portion is the while infinity loop. You alter the code from the project in Chapter 4 by stripping out all the code for calculating the temperature and instead replace it with code to build an INSERT query for saving the data in the database:

```
while True:
    try:
        # Read a data frame from the XBee
        data_samples = xbee1.wait_read_frame()
```

```
        # Get the address of the source XBee
        address = data_samples['source_addr_long']

        print("Reading from XBee:")
        samples = data_samples['samples'][0]

        # Save results in the table
        short_addr = "{0:02x}{1:02x}".format(ord(address[6]), ord(address[7]))
        volts = (float(samples['adc-7']) * (1200.0 / 1024.0)) / 1000.0
        query = ("INSERT INTO house.temperature VALUES(NULL, '{0}', "
                 "{1}, {2}, NULL, NULL)".format(short_addr,
                                                samples['adc-3'],
                                                volts))
        print (query)
        run_query(db_conn, query)

    # Catch keyboard interrupt (CTRL-C) keypress
    except KeyboardInterrupt:
        break
```

Notice the code you use to build the string. There is some trickery involved in capturing the last 4 hexadecimal digits of the address. Check the code lookup the methods used if you are not familiar with them.

Once the while infinity loop is terminated, you must disconnect from the server. The following code does that. In this case, you ignore any errors—you are disconnecting, and you don't care if you fail because the script will stop:

```
# Close the port
ser_port.close()

# Disconnect from the server
try:
    db_conn.disconnect()
except:
    pass
```

If you are thinking this isn't a lot of code, you are correct. The Connector/Python library makes working with MySQL in Python very easy. Listing 8-6 shows the complete code for this project. Take some time to make sure everything is entered correctly before you attempt to run the script.

Listing 8-6. Raspberry Pi Remote-Storage Data Aggregator

```
# RasPi XBee Remote Storage Data Aggregator - Beginning Sensor Networks
#
# For this script, we read data from an XBee coordinator
# node whenever data is received from an XBee sensor node.
# We also need a connection to a database server for saving
# the results in a table.
#
# The data read is from one sample (temperature from a
# XBee sensor node and the supply voltage at the source).
```

```python
import serial
import xbee
import mysql.connector

# Constants
SERIAL_PORT = '/dev/ttyAMA0'
BAUD_RATE = 9600
USER = 'root'
HOST_OR_IP = '10.0.1.24'
PORT = 3306
PASSWD = 'secret'

# Instantiate an instance for the serial port
ser_port = serial.Serial(SERIAL_PORT, BAUD_RATE)

# Instantiate an instance of the ZigBee class
# and pass it an instance of the Serial class
xbee1 = xbee.zigbee.ZigBee(ser_port)

# Variables for MySQL Connector/Python code
db_conn = None

def run_query(conn, query_str):
    results = None
    cur = conn.cursor(
        cursor_class=mysql.connector.cursor.MySQLCursorBufferedRaw)
    try:
        res = cur.execute(query_str)
    except mysql.connector.Error, e:
        cur.close()
        raise Exception("Query failed. " + e.__str__())
    try:
        results = cur.fetchall()
    except mysql.connector.errors.InterfaceError, e:
        if e.msg.lower() == "no result set to fetch from.":
            pass # This error means there were no results.
        else:    # otherwise, re-raise error
            raise e
    conn.commit()
    cur.close()
    return results

# Connect to database server
try:
    parameters = {
        'user': USER,
        'host': HOST_OR_IP,
        'port': PORT,
        'passwd': PASSWD,
        }
```

```
    db_conn = mysql.connector.connect(**parameters)
except mysql.connector.Error, e:
    raise Exception("ERROR: Cannot connect to MySQL Server!")

# Read and save temperature data
while True:
    try:
        # Read a data frame from the XBee
        data_samples = xbee1.wait_read_frame()

        # Get the address of the source XBee
        address = data_samples['source_addr_long']

        print("Reading from XBee:")
        samples = data_samples['samples'][0]

        # Save results in the table
        short_addr = "{0:02x}{1:02x}".format(ord(address[6]), ord(address[7]))
        volts = (float(samples['adc-7']) * (1200.0 / 1024.0)) / 1000.0
        query = ("INSERT INTO house.temperature VALUES(NULL, '{0}', "
                  "{1}, {2}, NULL, NULL)".format(short_addr,
                                                  samples['adc-3'],
                                                  volts))
        print (query)
        run_query(db_conn, query)

    # Catch keyboard interrupt (CTRL-C) keypress
    except KeyboardInterrupt:
        break

# Close the port
ser_port.close()

# Disconnect from the server
try:
    db_conn.disconnect()
except:
    pass
```

Testing the Project

To test the project, make sure your XBee coordinator node is installed in the XBee adapter. Wait a few moments before you turn on your XBee sensor nodes. Once all nodes are powered on, you're ready to go. Issue the following command to launch the script:

```
python ./pi_xbee_mysql.py
```

If you see syntax errors or exceptions, be sure to fix them and rerun the command. You know it is working (or at least doesn't have any errors) if the script starts and nothing happens. Recall that the code is waiting for a packet (sample) to be received from the XBee sensor nodes. When the nodes start to send data, you see output similar to what is shown in Figure 8-10. Remember, you can stop your script at any time by pressing Ctrl+C.

```
pi@raspberrypi ~ $ python ./pi_xbee_mysql.py
Reading from XBee:
INSERT INTO house.temperature VALUES(NULL, 'cd0f', 620, 3.2671875, NULL, NULL)
Reading from XBee:
INSERT INTO house.temperature VALUES(NULL, '29db', 617, 2.0484375, NULL, NULL)
Reading from XBee:
INSERT INTO house.temperature VALUES(NULL, '29a2', 618, 3.2390625, NULL, NULL)
Reading from XBee:
INSERT INTO house.temperature VALUES(NULL, 'cd0f', 619, 3.2671875, NULL, NULL)
Reading from XBee:
INSERT INTO house.temperature VALUES(NULL, '29db', 617, 2.0484375, NULL, NULL)
Reading from XBee:
INSERT INTO house.temperature VALUES(NULL, '29a2', 618, 3.2390625, NULL, NULL)
Reading from XBee:
INSERT INTO house.temperature VALUES(NULL, 'cd0f', 619, 3.2671875, NULL, NULL)
```

Figure 8-10. Sample output on the Raspberry Pi MySQL data-aggregate node

To check to see if your samples were saved in the database, connect to the server and execute the following query:

```
SELECT * FROM house.temperature;
```

You should see a number of rows in the result set and be able to match the rows to the output from your script. Once you've verified it is working, congratulate yourself: you have now mastered building remote-storage data-aggregate nodes using both an Arduino and a Raspberry Pi!

Furthermore, you have demonstrated how versatile the XBee modules are by using the same XBee sensor nodes in each project. Take some time and experiment with the script and the data that is being stored in the database.

ODD BEHAVIOR OR WEIRD SCIENCE?

If you watch your XBee modules—or, more precisely, the LEDs attached to the XBee shield and adapters—you may see a strange thing. Or, if you are curious, stop your script and observe the XBee modules. Notice that the XBee coordinator module LEDs blink momentarily. If you look closely at the sensor nodes (assuming they are in the same room), you may notice that their LEDs flicker, too. Why is this? The script isn't running, so what are they doing?

Recall from the discussion about XBee modules that they have a very limited onboard processor. When you program them to read a sensor and send the result to the coordinator, the sensor nodes will continue to do so, provided they have connected to a coordinator node. Also recall that the coordinator node is connected to the Raspberry Pi and is powered on. This is true even when the script isn't running. In fact, the coordinator node is happily receiving data from the other XBee nodes. Its basic programming (by default) defines this behavior.

This is a very nice feature because it means you do not have to power off all of your sensor nodes each time you want to rerun the script. As long as the XBee (ZigBee) network is running, the XBee modules will keep doing their thing. When you start your script, the XBee library simply catches the next data sample sent.

For More Fun

That was a lot of fun, wasn't it? You may be wondering what more you could do with such a solid bit of Python code. Well, there are some cool things you can do.

The biggest challenge I can suggest is taking this script and rewriting it slightly to get the data from a TMP36 sensor via an ADC module. In other words, change the Raspberry Pi data-aggregate node into a sensor node that stores its data directly into the database.

Aside from that, you may want to experiment with changing the script into a daemon so that you can run it in the background and still use your Raspberry Pi for other things.

Component Shopping List

There are no required components needed for the projects in this chapter. Table 8-1 shows a list of the optional components that you may need to complete the projects. The remaining components, such as XBee modules and supporting hardware, are included in the shopping lists from other chapters; these are shown in Table 8-2.

Table 8-1. *Components Needed*

Item	Vendors	Est. Cost USD	Qty Needed
Stackable header kit	www.sparkfun.com/products/11417	$1.50	1*
	www.adafruit.com/products/85	$1.95	

* Optional and may not be needed.

Table 8-2. *Components Reused from Previous Chapters*

Item	Vendors	Est. Cost USD	Qty Needed
Arduino (any that support shields)	Various	$25.00 & up	One for each node
XBee shield	www.sparkfun.com/products/10854	$24.95	1
TMP36 sensor	www.sparkfun.com/products/10988	$1.50	One for each sensor node
	www.adafruit.com/products/165		
0.10uF capacitor	www.sparkfun.com/products/8375	$0.25	One for each sensor node
Breadboard (not mini)	www.sparkfun.com/products/9567	$5.95	One for each sensor node + one for Raspberry Pi
Breadboard jumper wires	www.sparkfun.com/products/8431	$3.95	1
XBee-ZB (ZB) Series 2 or 2.5	www.sparkfun.com	$25.00	2–4 (one for each node)
	www.adafruit.com		
Raspberry Pi Model B		$35 and up	2
HDMI or HDMI to DVI cable	Most online and retail stores	Varies	1
HDMI or DVI monitor	Most online and retail stores	Varies	1
USB keyboard	Most online and retail stores	Varies	1
USB power supply	Most online and retail stores	Varies	1
USB type A to USB micro male	Most online and retail stores	Varies	1

(continued)

Table 8-2. (*continued*)

Item	Vendors	Est. Cost USD	Qty Needed
SD Card 2GB or more	Most online and retail stores	Varies	1
Surplus hard drive	Any USB hard drive (surplus or purchased)	varies	1
Raspberry Pi breakout board	www.adafruit.com/products/914	$7.95	1
Wall adapter 9V (optional)	www.sparkfun.com/products/298	$5.95	1 for each node**
9V Battery Holder (optional)	www.sparkfun.com/products/10512	$2.95	1 for each node**
	www.adafruit.com/products/67	$3.95	
XBee Regulated Explorer with headers[11]	www.sparkfun.com/products/11373	$9.95	One for each sensor node + 1 for the Raspberry Pi

*** You can mix and match these, provided you have enough to power all nodes.*

Summary

In this chapter, you explored how to build data-aggregate nodes and connect sensor nodes to them for building wireless sensor networks. You learned how to use local storage to store and display sensor data from sensors connected via a ZigBee (XBee) network, and you also discovered how to use the Raspberry Pi as a database server for storing and retrieving sensor data. You even explored how to build data-aggregate nodes with both an Arduino and a Raspberry Pi.

In the next chapter, I present considerations about planning sensor networks as well as more advanced sensor network topics. I discuss how to handle sensor data from multiple sensors, and you learn more about how to use the MySQL database to generate reports and views of the data for analysis.

---

[11]You have used some in previous chapters, but you may need a few more depending on how many sensor nodes you decide to add.

CHAPTER 9

■ ■ ■

Planning Wireless Sensor Networks

Now that you have learned the basic building blocks for constructing a wireless sensor network with the Arduino and Raspberry Pi, you can turn your attention to some of the more intricate details of designing and implementing sensor networks. This chapter explores considerations for planning sensor networks, discusses some advanced sensor network topics, and offer tips for designing databases.

Sensor Networks Best Practices

Let's begin with a discussion of some best practices[1] you can employ to make your sensor network projects more successful. In this section, I discuss practices for planning data-aggregate nodes, designing databases, and a number of tips and techniques for building sensor networks.

Considerations for Data-Aggregate Nodes

This section examines some important considerations for planning data-aggregate nodes. I discuss placement of the nodes in the network as well as design considerations for data storage.

Network Type and Node Placement

An important consideration is the type of network connection available for the data-aggregate node. This may be dictated by the node's use or physical placement.

If you plan to have a data-aggregate node that you want to have access to via your computer, you must consider placing that node where you can connect it to your Ethernet network. This may be via a wireless Ethernet (WiFi) connection or via a cabled connection.

On the other hand, if your data-aggregate node communicates with sensor nodes via XBee modules, the range of the modules may dictate where you place your data-aggregate node. For example, if your sensor nodes are located in outbuildings or in or near ponds that are some distance from a building with a network connection or even too far away for WiFi, you may not be able to connect to the node with your computer and therefore will have to periodically physically visit the node to retrieve the data.

That doesn't mean you have to jump on your ATV or golf cart to run down to the old chicken house to get your data every night! In fact, there are alternatives you can and should consider. First, you can use intermediate XBee router nodes placed in series until you reach a location with a network connection where your data-aggregate node can be placed.

---

[1]A cursory examination of professional and scholarly articles suggests there isn't a standard yet. However, I include some of the more commonly repeated practices as well as a few of my own.

How does this work? It is one of the advantages of the ZigBee protocols—to create networks on the fly and relay information from one router to another to extend the maximum range. It comes as a consequence of using the API mode, but you can also control this easily with the AT mode and send your data to a specific router, which then sends the data to another (and another) until you reach your data-aggregate node.

Another possibility is to use a directional WiFi connection that focuses the WiFi signal using a line-of-sight, point-to-point connection. You don't have to spend a fortune to do it! In fact, if you (or someone you know) likes Pringles, you can use a Pringles can to create a directional WiFi antenna (www.oreillynet.com/cs/weblog/view/wlg/448).

A more extreme solution involves using a cellular modem on the data-aggregate node to send data to another node via the Internet. Most cellular carriers frown on setting up web or database servers accessible from the Internet (some forbid it). Thus, you are limited to sending data from the data-aggregate node out of your home network to a web or database server. This option can incur recurring costs for the connection (you need a SIM card and a data plan from your carrier of choice).

■ **Note**   Although there is no pluggable cellular solution for the Raspberry Pi, you can use a cellular module with it. Doing so requires more work and perhaps building more complex software but should be possible.

For example, if you choose to use an Arduino for your data-aggregate node, you can use the cellular shield from SparkFun (www.sparkfun.com/products/9607) along with a SIM card to connect your node to the Internet. Figure 9-1 shows the cellular modem. A sample sketch is on the SparkFun product page for using the modem. If you dialup modem AT commands,[2] you will recognize many of the commands shown in the online documentation.

Figure 9-1. *Cellular modem shield (courtesy of SparkFun)*

---

[2]Ah, those were the days, eh? ATDT… screech, squawk, bleep, blurb, ding, ding, ding!

If you find that none of these solutions will work because your sensor nodes and data-aggregate nodes are just too far away for any practical (and affordable) networking alternative, you may have to consider leaving those data-aggregate nodes as local storage nodes and collecting the data periodically to use in your analysis.

Storing Data

One major consideration for designing a data-aggregate node is the type of data it will store: that is, what sensors the node will support. It is typically better to use a data-aggregate node to store data for the same sensors or sensor nodes that generate the same type of data.

For example, if you are collecting temperature data from several locations as well as water levels from several ponds, the data produced by these two events differs. Temperature is normally a floating-point value; water level is most often a Boolean value (1 = water level ok, 0 = water level low), which corresponds to the most common form of measuring water level: a float and switch.[3]

Clearly, storing these two sets of sensor data together would require more work because you would be mixing different data types. This might require choices such as storing the data in different files or even in different databases. Furthermore, consuming the data and detecting what the data represents (the type of sensor) would require more logic, because you would need some way to detect what sensor node went with what data type.

Although the problem of storing water level and temperature may be easy to code around, consider storing samples from two sensors that produce the same data type but are interpreted differently. Recall the examples of reading barometric pressure. It too is represented as a floating-point number. For example, how would you know which sensor generated a value of 65.71929—the barometric or temperature sensor? It may be possible to write code specific to the sensor itself, but what if the sensor data is being relayed to another node? How then would you know how to interpret the data?

One solution to this problem is to use a different data-aggregate node for each group of like sensor nodes. In the example of using temperature and water-level sensor nodes, you would have one data-aggregator for the temperature sensor nodes and another for the water-level sensors.

Another possibility for local storage on data-aggregate nodes is to store a special field that indicates from what sensor the data was read. You could include additional information as you saw in some of the example projects, such as date and time and a text string that represents a name you have given to the sensor. Listing 9-1 shows an example of a file format that employs a similar scheme. The first row is provided for documentation purposes and is not normally included in the file (but savvy programmers normally do include such things for documentation purposes).

Listing 9-1. Storing Additional Data with the Sample

```
# sensor_number, datetime, value, comment
3, 2013-09-02 14:25:21, 1, Water level Ok pond1
1, 2013-09-02 14:30:01, 65.90013, Water temp pond 1
3, 2013-09-02 14:37:04, 1, Water level Ok pond2
2, 2013-09-02 14:38:31, 65.81723, Water temp pond 2
1, 2013-09-02 14:45:23, 66.00123, Water temp pond 1
3, 2013-09-02 14:45:36, 0, Water level LOW! pond2
3, 2013-09-02 14:54:17, 1, Water level Ok pond1
2, 2013-09-02 14:59:54, 66.00011, Water temp pond 2
3, 2013-09-02 15:08:41, 1, Water level Ok pond1
1, 2013-09-02 15:10:22, 65.99913, Water temp pond 1
```

---

[3]There are more sophisticated sensors that can sense water level over a range and provide a means to calculate water volume. These sensors typically produce either an integer or a float representing the water level.

Notice in the listing that the data is formatted as a comma-separated-value (CSV) file. This is an implementation choice (you could have chosen to use tabs, semicolons, and so on) that makes reading the file easier on a computer. If you use Python, you can read the file using only a few library calls.

If you examine the data, you see that you have to know something about the sensor number to be able to interpret the data. If the sensor number is 1 or 2, you know it is temperature; but if it is 3 or 4, it is water level. Again, this may not be that big of an issue, but if you have a data-aggregate node receiving samples from dozens of sensors (or worse, from sensors that have been added to the network after the code was written for the data-aggregate node), you could end up with unknown values in the sensor number—that is, values you don't know how to interpret because you don't know what kind of sensor generated them. You can solve this by having a separate data-aggregate node for each type of sample (sensor).

Notice also how the data is arranged. Do you see anything that suggests conformity? If you have knowledge and experience with databases, no doubt you have already realized this, but consider for a moment what a table in a database is made of: rows and columns, where the columns are the fields and the rows are data. In this case, you can define two tables, each with four columns. The water temperature data could be in one table, because its value is an integer (or Boolean, perhaps), and the water temperature data is a floating-point number.

Clearly, storing this data in a database makes sense. That's what databases are for—storing logically related groups of data for a single row (in this case, an event or a sample). With that in mind, let's look at considerations for using databases to store sensor data.

Considerations for Sensor Network Databases

In-depth, full coverage of the topic of database design is well beyond the scope of this book. Indeed, entire tomes and even several sets of volumes have been written about database design. Rather than go into all the theory and then relate that to practice, let's look at the subject from a slightly different angle: how you can best design your databases for easy storage and retrieval.

■ **Note** I assume no prior knowledge of database design. If you have database design experience, you may want to skim this section.

As you saw in Chapter 6, you use the MySQL database system as the database server. Not only is it open source (it is free, as in free beer), but it is also the most popular choice for developers because it offers large database system features in a lightweight form that can run on just about any consumer computer hardware. MySQL is also very easy to use, and its popularity has given rise to many online and printed resources for learning and using the system. Despite this, the following examples and suggestions can be used with any relational database server (but may require slight changes to syntax for some).

How Data Is Organized

Let's begin by discussing how data is grouped in a database server. As you know, the server permits you to create any number of databases for storing data. Typically, you want to create a separate database for each of your sensor networks. This makes working with the data a logical whole so that data for one sensor network isn't intermixed with data from another.

The database itself is a container for a number of objects. You have seen examples of tables and even a trigger in Chapter 8. Here, you focus on the table. The table is a container that is designed specifically to hold instances of data described (or categorized) by its layout (the number of columns and their data types). For example, for the data shown in Listing 9-1, you can generate a table for the temperature sensors as follows:

```
CREATE TABLE `pond_water_temp` (
  `sensor_number` int(11) DEFAULT NULL,
  `sample_collected_on` timestamp,
  `temperature` float DEFAULT NULL
) ENGINE=InnoDB DEFAULT CHARSET=latin1;
```

Notice the `sample_collected_on` field. You define this as `timestamp`, which MySQL will fill in with the date and time when a row is inserted in the table. Unless you need absolute accuracy, setting this value shortly after the sample is collected will suffice to record the date and time at which the sample was taken.

As mentioned previously, the example in Listing 9-1 has data that is interleaved. You want to separate that data, and thus you generate a table to store the other samples as follows:

```
CREATE TABLE `pond_water_level` (
  `sensor_number` int(11) DEFAULT NULL,
  `sample_collected_on` timestamp,
  `water_level` boolean DEFAULT 1
) ENGINE=InnoDB DEFAULT CHARSET=latin1;
```

You may be wondering what happened to the comments. The `comments` field (column) is not really needed. Recall the discussion about storing a human-friendly name in Chapter 8. Here, you create a lookup table to store that data. For example, the lookup table allows you to equate a sensor number of 3 to a friendly name of Water Level Pond 1:

```
CREATE TABLE `sensor_names` (
  `sensor_number` int(11) DEFAULT NULL,
  `sensor_name` char(64) DEFAULT NULL
) ENGINE=InnoDB DEFAULT CHARSET=latin1;
```

So what have you done here? First, you designed two tables to store data from two different types of sensors (as defined by what data types are collected), and you added a lookup table to help eliminate duplicate data (storing Water Temp Pond 1 over and over again wastes space).

But what does this mean for the data-aggregate node? If you consider Listing 9-1 again, you see that the node has to write the sensor number, calculate and write the timestamp (perhaps from an onboard RTC or RTC module), write the value from the sensor, and (based on a lookup code) store a string for the comment (to make it easier for a human to read).

However, if you implement the previous tables, the data-aggregate node need only send the sensor number and the sample value to the database server. Sound familiar? That is exactly what you did in the project in Chapter 8.

Table Design Notes

Let's return to designing tables. When you design your tables, you should keep a few things in mind. First, consider what data types are needed for storing your samples. You should consider not only how many values each sample contains but also their format (data type). The basic data types available include integer, float, double, character, and Boolean. There are many others, including several for dates and times as well as binary large objects (blobs) for storing large blocks of data (like images), large texts (the same as blobs, but not interpreted as binary), and much more. See the online MySQL Reference Manual for a complete list and discussion of all data types (http://dev.mysql.com/doc/refman/5.6/en/).

You can also consider adding additional columns such as a timestamp field, the address of the sensor node, perhaps a reference voltage, and so on. Write all of these down, and consider the data type for each.

Once you have decided on your table columns, the next thing you should consider is whether to allow duplicates in the table—that is, two or more rows that contain the same data. To avoid this, you can define a *primary key* (a special index) by specifying one or more columns as the key. You want to choose a column (or columns) that ensures that no two rows will have the same data for that column(s).

For example, if you choose sensor_number from the previous example as a primary key, you most certainly have a problem. Indeed, the database server will complain the instant you try to save a second value for each sensor. Why? Because to become the primary key, the sensor_number column must contain a unique value for every row in the table!

But the layout of the tables does not contain any column that is guaranteed to be unique. You may be thinking the timestamp field can be unique, but although that may be true, you typically do not use timestamp fields for the primary key. So what do you do in this case?

You can use an automatically generated column as the primary key. It is called an auto_increment field property in MySQL. You can add this to any table, as shown here using the ALTER TABLE command:

```
ALTER TABLE pond_water_temp ADD COLUMN id INT AUTO_INCREMENT PRIMARY KEY FIRST;
```

Here you add a new column named id that is an auto-incrementing field and is the primary key. You add the first modifier because primary key columns should be the first column in a table (not that order matters normally, but here it does).

You can do the same for both tables. Once this is done, when a new row is inserted, you specify NULL as you do for the timestamp field, and MySQL fills in the data for you. Listing 9-2 shows this principle at work.

Listing 9-2. Auto-Increment Fields

```
mysql> INSERT INTO pond_water_temp VALUES (NULL, 3, NULL, 72.56);
Query OK, 1 row affected (0.00 sec)

mysql> SELECT * FROM pond_water_temp;
+----+---------------+---------------------+-------------+
| id | sensor_number | sample_collected_on | temperature |
+----+---------------+---------------------+-------------+
|  1 |             3 | 2013-08-10 16:55:14 |       72.56 |
+----+---------------+---------------------+-------------+
1 row in set (0.00 sec)

mysql> INSERT INTO pond_water_temp VALUES (NULL, 3, NULL, 82.01);
Query OK, 1 row affected (0.00 sec)

mysql> SELECT * FROM pond_water_temp;
+----+---------------+---------------------+-------------+
| id | sensor_number | sample_collected_on | temperature |
+----+---------------+---------------------+-------------+
|  1 |             3 | 2013-08-10 16:55:14 |       72.56 |
|  2 |             3 | 2013-08-10 16:55:34 |       82.01 |
+----+---------------+---------------------+-------------+
2 rows in set (0.00 sec)
```

```
┌──────────────────────────────────────────────────────────────┐
│                  DOES THAT REALLY DO ANYTHING?                 │
└──────────────────────────────────────────────────────────────┘
```

You may be thinking that this new field adds an artificial primary key to the table and doesn't really do anything. For the most part, you are correct.

This example is for illustration purposes and therefore teaches the concept of using a primary key as a practice you should consider whenever you design a table. The fact that the auto-increment key isn't used to reference another table or that it relates to the rows themselves is overlooked for the sake of practice.

Let's return to the lookup table. Although this table is unlikely to have many rows (it depends on the number of sensors), it is also true that one row in this table matches one and only one sensor. So you can use the sensor_number column here as a primary key. I leave the ALTER TABLE statement for you to consider.

■ **Note**   Database designers sometimes forego the use of primary keys on tables with only a few rows, citing the additional overhead needed to maintain indexes and so on. The truth is, it matters little either way because lookup tables are seldom modified (changed or data added) and if used frequently can result in the table being cached in its entirety. That being said, it does no harm to add a primary key.

Adding Indexes for Query Efficiency

A primary key is a special type of index. It is an index, but when used with auto-increment fields it is a nice way of identifying a given row and allowing duplicate rows (among the other columns). However, there is another aspect of indexes that can make your data access much easier (and possibly faster).

Consider for the moment a table with many thousands of rows.[4] Suppose you want to see all the sensor samples for sensor number 2. How does the database server find all of these rows using the tables you defined earlier? You issue the following query, but what happens inside the server?

```
SELECT * FROM pond_water_temp WHERE sensor_number = 2;
```

Because the table has an index (the primary key on the column id that you added), it uses this to systematically read each and every row in order, choosing (returning) those rows that match the WHERE clause (in this case, sensor_number = 2). This is bad because the server does not know if these rows appear in the first *N* rows or even if sensor_number = 2 is in the last row in the table. Thus, it must read each and every row. This is called a *table scan* and is best avoided when working with tables with a lot of rows.

How do you do that? By adding another index called a *secondary index*! If you have an index on the sensor_number column, the server can use that index to examine each of the rows in a different order. It will look through the table starting with sensor_number 1 and then 2, and so on. It knows to stop after reading the last row whose sensor_number is 2. In fact, MySQL has some extra trickery included that permits the server (the part called the *optimizer*) to further expedite the query and skip to the first row with sensor_number = 2. Here is how you do it. You use the CREATE INDEX command:

```
CREATE INDEX s_num ON pond_water_temp (sensor_number);
```

---

[4]It may take several hundreds of thousands of rows for you to see this in action.

The CREATE INDEX command allows you to name the index (s_num) and specify the table (ON pond_water_temp) and the column(s) you want to index in parentheses, (sensor_number). You can see a complete syntax explanation for this and all other commands supported by MySQL in the online MySQL Reference Manual.

Now when you issue the earlier SELECT, the server uses the new index to read the rows in a different order. Note that the rows are not reordered on disk; rather, the index creates an alternate map or access method to find the rows in a specific order.

You may be thinking, "But wait: can't I do all of these table design steps in one go?" The answer is, yes, you can! Let's look at the pond_water_temp table as a single CREATE statement:

```
CREATE TABLE `pond_water_temp` (
  `id` int(11) NOT NULL AUTO_INCREMENT,
  `sensor_number` int(11),
  `sample_collected_on` timestamp,
  `temperature` float DEFAULT NOT NULL,
  PRIMARY KEY (`id`),
  KEY `s_num` (`sensor_number`)
) ENGINE=InnoDB;
```

Notice that the auto-increment column is defined first, then your sensor number, the timestamp for when the sample was collected, the value (temperature), and the primary key and secondary index definitions. This statement replaces the three you just used—CREATE TABLE, ALTER TABLE, and CREATE INDEX. Cool, eh?

As you can see, creating tables in MySQL is easy once you understand the syntax (and know what you want to do). You can find all the syntax and many examples of each in the online MySQL Reference Manual.

Once again, there is far more to consider for designing tables, but these at least are the things you need to know to make the most of your database system and to store and retrieve your data effectively.

Other Considerations

This section explores some additional best practices that can be helpful in making your work with sensor networks more enjoyable.

Stay within Range of XBee Modules

XBee modules have an impressive range that belies their diminutive size. The specifications for the XBee series 2 modules you use in this book are

- *Indoor/Urban*: Up to 133 feet

- *Outdoor line-of-sight*: Up to 400 feet

However, these maximums are very much influenced by interference from devices on similar frequencies and the composition of the building you are in.[5] For example, suppose your house is very old and has plaster walls and a tin roof. Wireless of any kind in your home operates well below the specified ranges. You need to test your XBee range in your own location to find your maximum range. If that is impractical, I recommend that you cut the specification values in half when planning your network to ensure that you don't place XBee-based sensor nodes out of range.

---

[5]You should avoid placing your XBee modules near large metal objects or at the bottom of concrete wells.

You can test the maximum range of your XBee modules before you develop your sensor network. One way is to create the XBee temperature sensor node project and use a USB XBee adapter on your laptop computer connected via a terminal program, as you saw in Chapter 2. I include an unscientific method for determining a maximum reliable range next. For this to work, your sensor node should be set to deliver data every few seconds (say, every 10 seconds) and be running API firmware:

1. Connect the coordinator node to the laptop.

2. Connect to the coordinator via a terminal program.

3. Place the sensor node in its intended location.

4. Hold your laptop near the sensor node (within a few feet), and power on the sensor node.

5. Wait until the XBee network is formed and you start receiving data.

6. Move slowly away, watching the data as the coordinator receives it.

7. When the coordinator starts presenting error packets or stops receiving data, you've gone too far.

This method is hardly scientific, but it can give you a rough gauge as to whether your sensor nodes are close enough (within range) to your data-aggregate node.

Keep an Engineering Logbook

Many developers, engineers, and scientists keep notes about their projects in paper notebooks or digital notebooks using apps like Evernote (`http://evernote.com/`). A voice recorder can also be handy in catching those impromptu ideas when you don't have time or it is too dangerous to use pen and paper.[6] Some people are more detailed than others, but most take notes during meetings and phone conversations, thereby providing a written record of verbal communications.

The best note takers write down their ideas when they occur. Sometimes the mind works best when you are performing menial tasks and ideas come to you out of the blue. When this occurs, good engineers know to write down these ideas—even if they later turn to so much dirt—because the best ideas often start with a simple concept. Failure to write down these tidbits can often lead to more experimentation and even wasted time working on alternatives.

If you aren't in the habit of keeping an engineering logbook, you should consider doing so. I have found a logbook to be a vital tool in my work. Yes, it does require more effort to write things down, and the log can get messy if you try to include all the various drawings and emails you find important (my notebooks are often bulging with clippings from important documents taped in place like some sort of engineer's scrapbook). The payoff is potentially huge, however.

This is especially true when designing sensor networks and the myriad of sensors and electronic circuits involved. You may be at a trade show (or a Maker's Faire) and see something that really sparks an idea. Or maybe you see a circuit in a magazine or find a really cool sensor but need to design a circuit to host it. Writing down these ideas can enable you to achieve your goals.

It also helps you to remember concepts and critical information such as which way a sensor is wired, to avoid rework (or guesswork) that could lead to failed components and frustration. I am very thankful I keep a logbook of those times when I double-check my wiring only to discover a misplaced jumper or wire routing. It has saved me time and money (not having to replace fried components).

Naturally, you can use any type of notebook you desire; but if you want to class up your notes a bit, you can purchase a notebook made especially for keeping engineering notes. These typically have subdued gridlines and sometimes text areas for recording key information like the project name and page number. Two of my favorite notebooks include the small project-sized notebooks from SparkFun and the larger Maker's Notebook from Maker Shed.

---

[6]Like while driving. Sadly, I've seen drivers do this. Personal grooming seems to be the most popular form of activity people should never do while driving, after texting, email, tweeting, and so on.

The SparkFun notebooks come in red or grey and feature 52 pages of white grid on light grey pages. They are semi-flexible, lightweight, and just the right size (10" x 7.5") for recording your notes for all but the largest, world-domination-level projects.[7] Figure 9-2 shows the two options available. What isn't shown in the photos is the nifty embossed SparkFun logo. Classy. The links for these notebooks are as follows:

- Red: `www.sparkfun.com/products/11064`

- Grey: `www.sparkfun.com/products/11063`

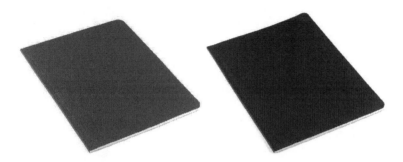

Figure 9-2. *Red SparkFun Notebook (courtesy of SparkFun)*

If you are looking for a notebook with more pages and more features—one specially designed for multiple small projects—you may be interested in looking at the Maker's Notebook from Maker Shed (`www.makershed.com/Maker_s_Notebook_p/9780596519414.htm`).

This notebook features 150 numbered pages of graph paper, each with a special header for noting the project name, date, and page reference pointers. It also includes such nice additions as a space for a table of contents, a pocket for those small notes you write to yourself but later cannot read due to your own handwriting,[8] and stickers with electronic components for making circuits.

This notebook is a bit more expensive than a run-of-the-mill lined or grid-filled notebook, but it is worth a look if you desire a good tool to help manage notes for multiple projects. Figure 9-3 shows the Maker's Notebook.

---

[7]Projects like those are strictly discouraged.

[8]Unless your penmanship is far superior to most, this will happen to you eventually. Writing down an idea while riding a bucking train can often lead to illegible text. Sometimes reading such notes in the same environment where they were written helps.

Figure 9-3. *Maker's Notebook (courtesy of Adafruit)*

HOW TO MANAGE PAGES FOR MULTIPLE PROJECTS

One of the challenges of keeping a single notebook for multiple projects underway is how to manage pages. That is, if you are working on project X and write down some really cool ideas in the middle of working on project Y, how do you keep track of what pages belong to each project?

The Maker's Notebook solves this by allowing you room to note which page number is next at the bottom of each page. This can be really helpful when your project notes start to interleave (and they will). Think of it as a sort of manual linked list.

Another solution is to keep a living index at the front of your notebook that lists the page numbers for each project. This is not as nice as the Maker Shed solution, but it works.

Putting It All Together: Testing and Deploying Your Sensor Network

The projects in this book are designed to teach you how to build sensor networks by breaking the tasks into smaller components that you can combine. With the exception of the projects in Chapter 8 (they are complete sensor network examples), you can implement each in relative isolation from the other projects. Some are alternative implementations, like the examples that show the same project first using an Arduino and then using a Raspberry Pi.

In some cases, especially in the "For More Fun" sections, I've suggested certain modifications and alternative solutions for you to experiment with. Experimentation is an excellent way to learn, but you should consider moving to a more formal evaluation of the solution when preparing your own sensor network.

In other words, test your network before deploying it. I cannot tell you have many times a well-planned hardware design has failed due to some unexpected consequence unrelated to the design. For example, you may find a physical obstruction that wasn't there or wasn't considered when you planned your network; or the cabling available or power in the area may be faulty; or you may find that the actual range of your radios in the target environment is shorter than anticipated. Whatever the case, usually bench-testing the solution prior to deploying it can help eliminate problems with the nodes themselves, allowing you to focus on what is different—the physical environment.

What I mean by *bench testing* is to assemble the components in one location and power everything on as if it were deployed in the field. Not only does this allow you to ensure that the sensor network is working, but it also permits you to monitor the nodes themselves for anomalies. For example, incorrectly wiring a component may destroy it, but sometimes you can salvage the component by cutting power quickly.

Let's consider the last project in Chapter 8—a sensor network comprising a database node, a data-aggregate node, and several sensor nodes. There are several excellent methods to test a network like this, but the following approach can help you diagnose problems you may encounter when you deploy your own sensor networks. In this case, I assume the software for each node is properly installed and working (that is, the XBee nodes are configured correctly, and the sketches and scripts are working properly):

1. Starting with the database node, power it on and test connectivity from your network. Ensure that you can connect to MySQL as the user account you plan to use (and from the machines—IP Addresses—that will need to access it) and that the user has privileges to update the databases you've designed. For more information about granting privileges to users, see the online MySQL Reference Manual.

2. Move to the data-aggregate node, and modify the sketch to insert dummy data into the database. Go back to the database, and ensure that the data has been inserted.

3. Power down your data-aggregate node, and move the coordinator XBee module to a USB XBee adapter. Connect it to your laptop, open a terminal application, and connect to the USB port with the XBee module.

4. Power on each of your sensor nodes, one at a time, and observe the terminal window. Ensure that each of the sensor nodes sends data and that the data is received (echoed in the terminal). Power down all XBee nodes, and remove the coordinator node from your laptop.

5. Return the data-aggregate node to its operational state (including running the final sketch or script), and power it up. Wait about 5 minutes, and then power on your sensor nodes. Connect to your database server, and ensure that data is being inserted into the table.

Once you have your sensor network assembled and running correctly, you can begin considering deployment. I prefer to deploy the sensor nodes first and (if possible) move my data-aggregate node and database server closer to the sensor nodes. I then power everything on, starting with the database server and then the data-aggregate node; then I wait 5 minutes and power on the sensor nodes.

Moving the data-aggregate node close to the actual location of the sensor nodes helps minimize any issues with ranges or obstructions. When I see that the network is operating correctly, I power everything off and deploy my data-aggregate node to its proper location and start the process again. Once that stage works, I deploy the database server and test the network one more time. When everything is working correctly, I power it all down again, erase (DELETE FROM ...) the sample data, and power everything up. At this point, my deployment is complete, and I can work on the next stage: consuming the accumulated data for analysis.

With these best practices and considerations in mind, let's look at a topic that can sometimes lead to impromptu tinkering.[9]

■ **Note** The projects in this chapter are intended for demonstration purposes and therefore do not include all the steps for building each project. However, given your knowledge level at this point, you can easily fill in the missing parts.

Choosing Sensor Nodes

When you consider how to host a sensor, you have some choices to make. Sometimes this decision is based on the type of sensor and the data it produces. For example, you can host almost any sensor with an Arduino. With some additional hardware, you can do so with the Raspberry Pi; and you can also host certain sensors with XBee modules (see Chapter 2).

But other things can determine the configuration of your sensor nodes and your data-aggregate nodes. These include the type of networking to use and whether the sensor node will use Ethernet or XBee (ZigBee) to communicate. There are also a number of alternative configurations for your sensor nodes that you have not explored thus far. I discuss each of these aspects in more detail in this section.

Wired Or Wireless?

I mentioned in Chapter 8 that I consider a wired Ethernet connection a requirement for a data-aggregate node. But that is just the most typical case. It may be that you have WiFi Ethernet instead.

The main reason is that the data-aggregate node is typically accessed much more frequently than the sensor nodes. You may include data-aggregate nodes that have web servers, as you saw in Chapter 8, or you may decide to have the data-aggregate nodes send the data to another node (such as a database) for storage. In these cases, having a fast and reliable network is a must.

Typically, you use XBee modules and the ZigBee protocols to connect a data-aggregate node to sensor nodes. However, you can use the API protocols in ZigBee to communicate with your data-aggregate nodes. The challenge is to build a set of routines to match how you intend to interact with the data-aggregate nodes. It is not impossible (and I have seen proof of people who have designed such networks), but it takes a lot more work and eliminates a number of possibilities for data access.

The main consideration is to place your data-aggregate nodes on the most reliable network medium. Wired Ethernet is the most robust, followed by WiFi and then ZigBee. If the data will be stored locally and retrieved manually, then the choice of network medium may not matter. However, if you need to access the data remotely or store it on a remote node (such as a database server), then wired Ethernet is definitely the right choice.

Arduino or Raspberry Pi?

Choosing an Arduino or a Raspberry Pi should be based on a number of factors. These include cost, security, functionality, expandability, and connectivity. Your choice will likely be based on one or more of these and may dictate (or limit) your implementation of your sensor or data-aggregate node.

---

[9]In other words, an emergency redesign of a failed implementation—fancy words for a poor design choice.

Cost

If you are planning a large network or have a limited budget, cost may be a primary concern. This is likely to be seen in the per-node cost. Sensors are typically commodities, and the prices normally don't vary much from one vendor to another. But the price of the host itself may make a difference. Let's look at each board with cost in mind.

The current average cost of the Raspberry Pi model B (in the US) is about $45. This is about $10.00 more than the MSRP should be for these boards, but given the high demand and somewhat limited supply, it is no surprise vendors are charging more.

The cost for an Arduino is a bit harder to pin down. Because the Raspberry Pi is closed source whereas the Arduino is open source, you can find a lot of different vendors selling a variety of Arduino-compatible boards. Although you can buy a Raspberry Pi from different vendors, there are no Raspberry Pi clones. As a consequence, you can find any number of varieties of Arduino-compatible boards starting from as low as $15.00. Currently, the average price (on eBay and Amazon) for a Uno or Duemilanove clone is about $21.00.

If you are planning 20 sensor nodes (and none are XBee-based), your cost savings through choosing an Arduino over a Raspberry Pi could be significant. For example, if you find Raspberry Pi boards for $45.00 each and Arduino-compatible boards for $21.00 each, it will cost you $480.00 more to use Raspberry Pi boards than Arduino boards.

However, if you must augment your Arduino boards with shields, the cost of the shield could bring your total outlay much closer to the cost of the Raspberry Pi. In some cases, it could even cost more to buy an Arduino and a shield than a Raspberry Pi. On the whole, the takeaway is that if cost is an issue, the Arduino is often the less expensive choice.

Security

I have not said much about security or securing your sensor and data-aggregate nodes in this book. Let's take a moment to briefly consider this topic.

We generally can agree that a database node should be secure with a modicum of password security and access restrictions,[10] what about the sensor nodes themselves? Theft may be less of a concern, but you should at least consider securing your sensor nodes against theft. The average thief looking for a target of opportunity is not likely to steal your sensor node.[11]

However, physical access to the nodes is a concern. Although it is possible for someone to exploit an Arduino node if they have direct access, it is much harder to do so with an Arduino than a Raspberry Pi. The primary reason is that the Arduino is loaded electronically; someone could reprogram the microcontroller, but there is little they can do without knowing how the sketch was written. But all that is needed to exploit a Raspberry Pi node is an SD card with a fresh OS loaded.[12] Thus, you should consider making it as difficult as possible for someone to get physical access to your Raspberry Pi nodes—especially if they are connected to your local network or the Internet.

Sadly, there is another concern—electronic intrusion. Because the Arduino is a microcontroller, it is not likely that someone will attempt to connect to it for nefarious activities. There is a much greater likelihood that someone will attempt to exploit a Raspberry Pi node. This means you have to be more careful when deploying Raspberry Pi-based nodes. Basic security practices go a long way, but if you don't take care and plan against intrusion, your Raspberry Pi nodes could be vulnerable.

If you are concerned about the security of your nodes, you should consider reading more about sensor network security. However, the bottom line here is that Raspberry Pi nodes tend to be easier to exploit than Arduino nodes.

---

[10]Don't mount it to the outside of your house and put a huge sticker on that says, "database server."
[11]Let's hope not, anyway.
[12]Scary, isn't it?

Functionality

The functionality provided by the host is another area where you may want to focus. If you are looking to add functionality such as a web server, a local database server, or remote access via SSH; or connectivity to peripherals such as hard disks, keyboard, display, and so on; there is really no choice. The Raspberry Pi is a fully functional personal computer (and mini server).

On the other hand, the Arduino is very easy to program and has a much wider hardware support base, making it possible to host a much wider array of sensor options and even electronic circuits. This is because the Arduino has a more robust hardware interface than the GPIO of the Raspberry Pi.

For example, consider that the Raspberry Pi requires an ADC to interface with analog sensors. Thus, if you plan to use only analog sensors but still need the features of the Raspberry Pi, the cost of your sensor will be a bit higher (for the price of the ADC module).

The decision rests on whether you need computer-like features or better hardware support options. If you require personal computer or server features for your node, you should choose a Raspberry Pi. If you need to support a more diverse set of sensors and related hardware, you should choose the Arduino.

Expandability

Expandability is closely related to functionality. I focus on this as a separate consideration because it has a bearing on sensor networks. There are two aspects of expandability that you should consider: the availability of pluggable modules and the ability to add more features to the node.

The clear winner in the availability of pluggable modules is the Arduino. There are dozens of shields that support all manner of hardware features. From simple sensor boards to XBee hosting to advanced motor control and robotics, there is a shield for just about anything you want to do for a sensor network.

That doesn't mean you should count the Raspberry Pi out. If you need to store a lot of data on a node, you are less likely to choose the Arduino because it is very easy to add a local hard disk to the Raspberry Pi. Similarly, if you need complex display capabilities, the Raspberry Pi requires no additional hardware (just use a monitor).

■ **Note** You can indeed use small to medium-sized LCD panels on the Arduino. There are many examples, including example sketches, in the Arduino IDE. However, it is a lot easier to write a Python script to produce screen output than it is to try to cram a lot of information on a small LCD.

Thus, if you need expandability from an electronics perspective, you should choose the Arduino. If you need more expandability for attaching storage devices or displaying a lot of data, you should choose the Raspberry Pi.

Connectivity

The last area to consider is connectivity. Once again, this depends on your perspective. If you want to connect your node to other nodes via XBee modules, the platforms are equally capable.

If you plan to connect your node to an Ethernet network, you must consider the fact that the Raspberry Pi (model B) comes Internet-ready with a LAN port (Ethernet), whereas the Arduino (excluding the Yun and Arduino Uno Ethernet variant) requires an Ethernet shield; therefore the cost may be much closer. For example, you can purchase a basic Arduino Ethernet clone shield for about $30.00. Given that the Arduino costs about $21.00 for an older clone board, your cost has exceeded that of the Raspberry Pi.

However, the Arduino currently has one advantage over the Raspberry Pi for when it comes to connectivity: it is much easier to interface specialized hardware. Recall the discussion earlier on the use of cellular modems to connect your nodes to the Internet for collecting data. Because there is no pluggable solution for the Raspberry Pi, the Arduino is the better choice in this case. This may also apply to other forms of connectivity provided by the use of specialized shields.

Thus the consideration of connectivity for Ethernet and Bluetooth gives the advantage to the Raspberry Pi, whereas specialized communication such as a cellular modem gives the advantage to the Arduino

---

■ **Tip** There may be cases where you want to have the power of a Raspberry Pi but the flexibility and expandability of an Arduino. I'll reveal one such solution in the next section.

Now that you have seen some considerations for choosing what host to use, let's look at a couple of alternative solutions that you may want to consider—starting with a purpose-built sensor node.

Alternative Hosts

This section considers two alternatives for basing your sensor and data-aggregate nodes. You see an Arduino-compatible board designed expressly for sensor networks and outdoor operation as well as a daughter board designed to create a hybrid node combining a Raspberry Pi with an Arduino.

Seeed Studio Wireless Sensor Kit

One of the best Arduino-compatible kits is the Seeed Studio Wireless Sensor kit—also called the Stalker Waterproof Solar Kit (www.seeedstudio.com/wiki/Seeeduino_Stalker_-_Waterproof_Solar_Kit). The kit consists of a Seeed Studio Stalker board, a solar panel, battery pack, case, XBee adapter, hardware and accessories. Figure 9-4 shows what is included in the kit.

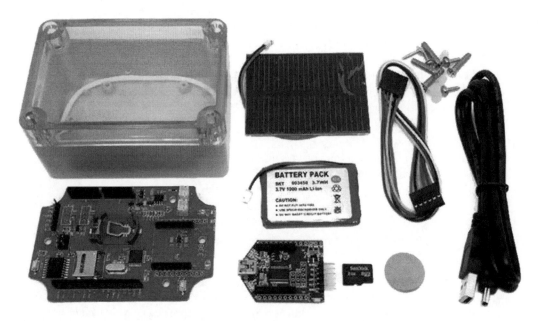

Figure 9-4. *Seeed Studio Stalker wireless sensor node (courtesy of Seeed Studio)*

The Seeed Studio Stalker board is a Seeedduino (Arduino-compatible) board and is the true gem in this kit. Not only is it fully compatible with Arduino (because it has the same processor), but it also has an onboard RTC, XBee headers, SD card, and more. The full specifications are listed next. Figure 9-5 shows a photo of the Stalker board in more detail:

- Based on the popular Seeeduino Arduino clone
- ATmega328P microcontroller
- Real-time clock
- MicroSD card drive
- I2C pin header
- Programmable switch and LED
- XBee-compatible headers

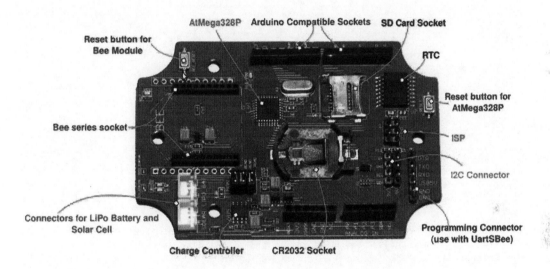

Figure 9-5. Seeeduino Stalker Arduino-compatible board (courtesy of Seeed Studio)

The Stalker is marketed as a wireless sensor node based on its onboard XBee support. You may be wondering why I have left the discussion of this board to the end of the book. Simply put, the Stalker is a specialized board that requires building your sensor nodes with very specific hardware and software. Although it can indeed make building sensor networks easier by taking away a lot of the harder work of connecting modules and interfacing with them, this very nature makes it less valuable for learning how sensor nodes are built.

It is better to learn the basic building blocks of putting together sensor nodes so that when you begin working with more advanced sensor networks or incorporating advanced sensors into your sensor nodes, you have the proper experience and knowledge to use them. Besides, it is a lot more fun to build something from scratch.[13]

---

[13]You can learn quite a lot about hardware by this approach. You haven't truly pushed yourself to learn until you've made a few mistakes. If you take the proper care and precautions, the end result of minor mistakes is nothing more than a fried component or two.

However, if the features of the board are what you need, then you should consider using as many of these as you require. The cost is a bit higher, as you can imagine. The cost of the kit is about $59.50, and the board itself is $39.00. If you consider that the board has an RTC as well as XBee headers, the $39.00 cost is less than buying an Arduino, separate XBee shield, and RTC module combined.

All the onboard features can be used in your sketches. For example, you can read temperature from the onboard RTC (the DS3231 chip has a temperature sensor) using only a single method call. To get this functionality, you must download and install the DS3231 library from (`https://github.com/wyolum/alamode/raw/master/bundles/alamode-setup.tar.gz`). Listing 9-3 shows the sketch to read temperature from the RTC.

▨ **Note**   Other example projects for the DS3231 are available via the Arduino IDE.

Listing 9-3. Reading Temperatures on the Seed Studio Stalker

```
// Date and time functions using DS3231 RTC connected via I2C and Wire lib

#include <Wire.h>
#include "DS3231.h"

DS3231 RTC; //Create the DS3231 object

void setup ()
{
    Serial.begin(57600);
    Wire.begin();
    RTC.begin();
}

void loop ()
{
    RTC.convertTemperature();              //convert current temperature into registers
    Serial.print(RTC.getTemperature()); //read registers and display the temperature
    Serial.println("deg C");
    delay(1000);
}
```

As you can see, the DS3231 library and the Stalker make building and deploying a temperature sensor node very easy. All you need to do is add the XBee code you've explored in previous projects, and you can quickly build a solar-powered wireless temperature sensor node. Cool.

▨ **Tip**   You can find a lot more information about programming the Seed Studio Stalker on the company wiki for this board (`www.seeedstudio.com/wiki/Seeeduino_Stalker_v2.1`).

Getting back to the solar part of the kit, the Stalker has a *lithium polymer* (LiPo) battery-charging circuit designed specifically for attaching a solar panel and a LiPo battery. The solar panel charges the battery during the day, providing adequate power for the node to run overnight (assuming your XBee is utilizing sleep mode and you don't have a lot of circuitry drawing power). This means you can build this kit and use it outdoors to communicate sensor data to your sensor network without worry of providing power or network connections. If you have a property with outbuildings without power (or ponds), this kit has the features you need to install a remote sensor.

The thing I like most about the Seeed Studio Stalker is that it is a fully compatible Arduino clone. If you do not use the Stalker in its waterproof case, you can use it in place of one your Arduino nodes (because it is an Arduino). With the onboard RTC, XBee headers, and microSD card drive, you may even be able to use this board for all of your sensor nodes—data aggregators included. Best of all, you can buy the Seeed Studio Stalker without the wireless kit for a much lower price (www.seeedstudio.com/depot/seeeduino-stalker-v2-p-727.html).

If you are planning a home temperature-monitoring sensor network, you should consider using this board for your remote sensors at the least. However, considering all the goodies you get in the wireless sensor kit, it is an excellent value.

Raspberry Pi Alamode

Another variant you may want to consider is the Raspberry Pi Alamode. This board is a very special piece of hardware designed to bridge the gap between the Arduino and the Raspberry Pi. The Alamode is a daughter board for the Raspberry Pi that plugs into the GPIO header and features a fully compatible Arduino clone.

This board is also available from Seeed Studio and has a lot of the same features. See www.seeedstudio.com/depot/alamode-arduino-compatible-raspberry-pi-plate-p-1285.html?cPath=6_7 for more details. Figure 9-6 shows a photo of the board.

Figure 9-6. *Raspberry Pi Alamode (courtesy of Seeed Studio)*

More specifically, the Alamode is an Arduino-compatible board that you can connect to your Raspberry Pi; and you can write sketches that you can interact with via another program on the Raspberry Pi. Like the Seeed Studio Stalker, it also supports Arduino shields so you can write sketches that take advantage of the shields and pass the functionality on to the Raspberry Pi via a sketch on the Alamode. You can also run the Arduino IDE on the Raspberry Pi to load sketches on the Alamode. Some of the best features of the Alamode include the following:

- Arduino compatible

- Connects to the Raspberry Pi via the GPIO header

- Automatically controls voltage on the GPIO header, providing 3.3V safe voltage on the GPIO but powering the Alamode with 5V

- Has a separate microUSB port for powering the Alamode

- Supports headers for controlling servos

- MicroSD drive

- Onboard RTC that can be used by the Raspberry Pi

- Supports additional headers for FTDI, ICSP, and a GPS module

The Alamode represents a unique hardware solution for sensor nodes. It permits you to use the best of both platforms on a single node. Let's say you need to use a special component or feature that is only available for the Arduino, but you also need computer resources such as a full-featured web server and lots of storage for your data-aggregate node. To solve this problem, you must find a way to connect the Arduino to your Raspberry Pi. The Alamode is that bridge. You can write sketches for the Alamode (even directly from the Raspberry Pi!) that provide the data from whatever shield, sensor, or other hardware you connect to the Alamode Arduino headers.

For example, you can access the RTC on the Alamode from the Raspberry Pi. To do this, you must have the I2C drivers on the Raspberry Pi. Fortunately, you achieved this earlier in the book. The setup is not overly complicated and involves adding a new module to the Raspberry Pi so that it can get its date and time from the RTC on the Alamode via the I2C interface. In fact, you access it as you would any I2C RTC module. A complete walkthrough of accessing an RTC via I2C is available from Adafruit (http://learn.adafruit.com/adding-a-real-time-clock-to-raspberry-pi).

As a consequence of its uniqueness and implementation, there are some limitations. First, although it is true that you can use the Arduino IDE from the Raspberry Pi, doing so requires installing a special patch for the IDE that changes the IDE slightly to recognize the Alamode. You can download the patch and apply it using the following commands on the Raspberry Pi:

```
$wget www.wyolum.com/downloads/alamode-setup.tar.gz
$ tar -xvzf alamode-setup.tar.gz
$ cd alamode-setup
$ sudo ./setup
```

Once you complete these steps and restart the IDE, you see the Alamode listed under the Board submenu. To set up the Alamode, select it from this menu and then select the /dev/ttyS0 serial port.

■ **Tip** A complete walkthrough of getting started with the Alamode can be found at http://wyolum.com/projects/alamode/alamode-getting-started/.

Communication between the Alamode and the Raspberry Pi can be accomplished using the Firmata library, which is built into the Arduino IDE. Fortunately, there are a number of examples you can explore in the Arduino IDE. There are also walkthroughs on the Alamode wiki (http://wyolum.com/projects/alamode/).

The Raspberry Pi Alamode is still a very new product and as yet has not been used (or at least reported or documented) enough to realize its full potential. However, I believe that if you need a special piece of hardware that is available for the Arduino, but you need to use it directly on a Raspberry Pi (like that cellular shield), this product may provide an excellent solution.

Project: Home Temperature-Monitoring Network

This chapter would not seem complete if I didn't have a project to discuss. By this point, though, you have all the knowledge you need to build sensor networks using Arduino boards, Raspberry Pi computers, and even dedicated XBee sensor nodes. Thus, rather than provide yet another step-by-step example, this section presents a walkthrough of the planning stages of creating a home temperature-monitoring network.

This project will seem a lot like the projects from Chapter 8. That is intentional. Everything you need to build this network was demonstrated in that project. What I am discussing here are the considerations for actually designing and deploying such a sensor network. The intent of the project is to provide one possible practical example for how to get started planning and implementing a sensor network.

Planning Considerations

The first question you need to ask when planning a sensor network is, "Why?" The second question is, "What do I expect to get from the data?" The reasons for creating a home temperature network are many and varied, but generally you expect to be able to track the ambient temperature of the home so that you can either plan changes to the heating and cooling systems or verify that they are working correctly (the thermostat settings match the actual temperatures measured).

As for why you would create the network, consider cases where the house is large, has several heating and air conditioning systems (HVAC), or was expanded over time to include rooms that are isolated or poorly supported by different HVAC systems. Or perhaps you have more personal reasons like differing opinions of hot/cold among family members or the need to protect sensitive medical equipment. Whatever the reasons, they should be considered a design element.

For this example, suppose the reason is that your home has multiple HVAC systems and has been expanded over the years in such a way that some rooms are noticeably warmer or cooler during different seasons of the year. In this case, you want to be able to predict the effects of outside climate (temperature) on the inside of the home.

Planning the Nodes

The next thing you should do is evaluate the resources available for a sensor network. Let's assume the home has two floors and only the first floor and one room on the second floor are wired for Ethernet, but there is a wireless Ethernet router (wireless access port) that can be accessed from anywhere in the home. There are four bedrooms, a den, a kitchen, a formal dining room, three bathrooms, and a sunroom (enclosed porch). The construction of the home limits radio signals to no more than 30–40 feet.

These criteria mean you must design the sensor network following a specific model. Namely, you need to collect data over time from multiple sensors. You could use as many as 12 (11 inside and 1 outside), but let's say you identify 5 zones in the home representing key areas where the temperature can differ from the rest of the home.

If you take sensor samples 6 times every 24 hours, you will be storing 36 samples per day (6 per sensor), more than 256 per week, and more than 91,000 per year. If you are measuring temperature, this could result in as much as a few megabytes of data per year. Although this isn't too much data to store on an SD card, if you want to compute averages over time compared to an outside variable (the outside climate), you must read the data and calculate the comparisons at some point (perhaps several times a month). Thus, you would be better suited to use a database server to store the data. Also, because you want to know when each sample was taken, you need to design the database table to store a timestamp for each sample.

If you consider the radio limitations of the home and the fact that it has multiple floors and a number of rooms, you can expect to require at least one data-aggregate node that is centrally located in the home. However, it is possible you could need more, depending on the placement of the sensors and the effects of the limited range.

For this project, assume that a centrally located data-aggregate node will suffice. In addition, you decide the data-aggregate nodes will connect to the database node via Ethernet but the sensor nodes will communicate with the data-aggregate node using XBee modules.

You will implement the five internal sensor nodes using XBee modules (to which you can connect the TMP36 directly), but for the outside node you will use the Seeed Studio Wireless Sensor Kit discussed earlier.

As for powering the nodes, you can use common 5V–9V wall wart power supplies for all sensor nodes. Also assume that the peripherals for the Raspberry Pi database node are gathered from on-hand surplus components.

Cost Considerations

Finally, you want to limit the cost of the network as much as possible. You also want to keep the samples relative in scale. The best way to do this is to use the same temperature sensor for each node. The most cost-effective solution is to use a sensor like the TMP36.

To sum up your node requirements, you need six sensor nodes (including one that can be installed outside), a database node, and a data-aggregate node. Taking all this into consideration, one possible hardware shopping list is shown in Table 9-1.

Table 9-1. *Sample Shopping List for the Home Temperature Sensor Network*

Description	Qty	Cost	Ext. Cost
Raspberry Pi (database server)	1	35.00	35.00
TMP36 sensors w/resistor	6	1.50	9.00
Seeed Studio Wireless Sensor Kit	1	59.50	59.50
XBee-ZB (ZB) Series 2 or 2.5	7	25.00	175.00
Arduino-compatible boards	1	21.00	21.00
Power adapters (one for each node)	8	6.95	55.60
Ethernet shields	1	45.00	45.00
Arduino XBee shield	1	24.95	24.95
		TOTAL	$425.10

I leave out some of the finer details for brevity, but the more costly items are listed. That is, I omit the cost of breadboards, cases, and so on for the sensor nodes because these are only one way to implement the circuitry. You could just as easily build a circuit on a preprinted circuit prototyping board and place each in a small enclosure (bits like this are called *vitamins* in the 3D printing world—an appropriate description I think). Examples of these are shown in Figures 9-7 and 9-8.

Figure 9-7. Prototyping circuit board (courtesy of SparkFun)

Figure 9-8. Small enclosure (courtesy of SparkFun)

What About Implementation?

Recall that at the start of this project, I said you have all the knowledge you need to implement this project. If you consider the nodes you need, you can find examples of how to build each one in previous chapters. The database node is found in Chapter 8, the Arduino data-aggregate node is also in Chapter 8, the XBee sensor nodes are in Chapter 3, and an example of the outdoor sensor node is included in this chapter (the Seeed Studio Wireless Sensor Kit).

I therefore leave the implementation to you; you can study those examples and implement them. Fortunately, little or no modification should be necessary. Other than perhaps substituting prototype circuit boards for the breadboards and sturdy enclosures for all the nodes, your implementation should be the same as the examples.

Conclusion

Once you have purchased all the components and assembled the sensor nodes in their final form, you can bench-test the entire network and then deploy the sensor nodes, testing for reliable connections between the sensor nodes and the data-aggregate node. Once all this checks out, you secure the sensor nodes in their locations, the data-aggregate node is installed in the central location, and the database node is installed in a secure area.

Returning to what you expect to get from the network, after it has run for some time—a week perhaps—without errors or problems, you can start issuing queries on the database to check for differences observed between the outside sensor values and the indoor sensor values. Once you have several months' worth of data, you can start to consider grouping the data by season (through a selection on the timestamp column).

I hope this example has reinforced the material in the book as way to validate your efforts in constructing all the projects and experimenting with them. I am fully confident that doing so will mean, should you follow this example to form a similar network, you succeed handily.

For More Fun

The total cost of these components is approximately $425.00, not including miscellaneous vitamins and shipping costs. This may sound like a lot, but consider substituting other components such as using fewer XBee sensor nodes and more Arduino sensor nodes with WiFi shields or the use of a Raspberry Pi for the data-aggregate node.

Optional Component Shopping List

No required components are needed for the examples in this chapter. Rather, the components and accessories listed in this chapter are optional—things you may want to consider purchasing if needed. Table 9-2 shows a list of the components mentioned in this chapter.

Table 9-2. *Optional Components*

Item	Vendors	Est. Cost USD
Engineering Notebook	www.sparkfun.com/products/11064 (red)	$4.95
	www.sparkfun.com/products/11063 (grey)	$4.95
	www.adafruit.com/products/295 (Maker's)	$19.99
Seeed Studio Stalker Wireless Sensor Kit	www.seeedstudio.com/depot/seeeduino-stalker-waterproof-solar-kit-p-911.html?cPath=84_13	$59.50
Seeed Studio Stalker Board	www.seeedstudio.com/depot/seeeduino-stalker-v2-p-727.html	$39.00
Raspberry Pi Alamode	www.seeedstudio.com/depot/alamode-arduino-compatible-raspberry-pi-plate-p-1285.html?cPath=6_7	$35.00
	www.makershed.com/AlaMode_for_Raspberry_Pi_p/mkwy1.htm	$49.99
Cellular shield	www.sparkfun.com/products/9607	$99.95
Prototyping circuit board	www.sparkfun.com/products/8815	$4.50
Small enclosure	www.sparkfun.com/products/11366	$7.95

Summary

This chapter explored some of the nuances of designing and implementing wireless sensor networks. I discussed some of the more popular best practices for sensor networks, considerations for planning databases to store the sensor data, how best to retrieve and use the data from a database, and how to choose what type of host to use for each sensor node. You also explored the design of a whole home temperature-monitoring system with special considerations for selecting hardware for the sensors.

Now that you have a basic (and some more advanced) understanding of wireless sensor networks, you can put down this book in triumph and start thinking of some really cool ways you can implement what you have learned. Perhaps you want to monitor the temperature in your house, workshop, or garage. Or perhaps you want to design a more complex network that monitors sound, movement, and ambient temperature changes (like a home security system).

An even more ambitious project would be to build your own weather station from discrete components, with a sensor node for each data sample (wind speed, temperature, gas readings, rain gauge, and so on). All that and more is possible with what you have learned in this book. Good luck, and happy sensor networks!

APPENDIX

■ ■ ■

Shopping List

This appendix contains the consolidated shopping list for all components required for building all the projects in Chapters 2–8 (Table A-1). Also contained is the optional shopping list for the projects in Chapter 9 (Table A-2). The lists have been sorted by item name for easier reference.

Table A-1. *Consolidated Component Shopping List*

Item	Vendors	Est. Cost USD	Qty Needed
12-bit ADC module	www.adafruit.com/products/1083	$9.95	1
Arduino (any that supports shields)	Various	$25.00 and up	1
Arduino Ethernet shield	www.sparkfun.com/products/9026	$45.95	1
	www.adafruit.com/products/201	$45.00	
Arduino XBee shield	www.sparkfun.com/products/10854	$24.95	1
Barometric pressure sensor	www.sparkfun.com/products/11282	$19.95	1
	www.adafruit.com/products/391		
Breadboard (not mini)	www.sparkfun.com/products/9567	$5.95	3+
Breadboard jumper wires	www.sparkfun.com/products/8431	$3.95	1
Breadboard power supply	www.sparkfun.com/products/10804	$14.95	3+
Breakaway male headers (set)	www.sparkfun.com/products/11239	$9.95	1
	www.adafruit.com/products/392		
Capacitor, 0.10uF	www.sparkfun.com/products/8375	$0.25	1
Data-logging shield for Arduino	www.adafruit.com/products/1141[1]	$19.95	
DHT22	www.sparkfun.com/products/10167	$9.95	1
	www.adafruit.com/products/385		
DS1307 real-time clock breakout board kit	www.adafruit.com/products/264	$9.00	1
DS18B20 digital temperature sensor	www.sparkfun.com/products/245	$4.95	1

(continued)

---

[1]Not needed if you have an Ethernet shield with a microSD reader.

Table A-1. (*continued*)

Item	Vendors	Est. Cost USD	Qty Needed
	www.adafruit.com/products/374		
Ethernet cable	Most online and retail stores		
FTDI cable for use with XBee Adapter Kit	www.adafruit.com/products/70	$20.00	1[2]
HDMI or DVI monitor	Most online and retail stores	varies	1
HDMI or HDMI-to-DVI cable	Most online and retail stores	varies	1
I2C EEPROM	www.sparkfun.com/products/525	$1.95	1
LED (any color)	www.sparkfun.com/products/9592	$0.35	1
microSD shield	www.sparkfun.com/products/9802[3]	$14.95	1
Pushbutton (breadboard mount)	www.sparkfun.com/products/97	$0.35	1
Raspberry Pi breakout board	www.adafruit.com/products/914	$7.95	1
Raspberry Pi Model B		$35 and up	1
Real-time clock module	www.sparkfun.com/products/99	$14.95	1[4]
Resistor, 150 Ohm	www.sparkfun.com/products/10969	7.95	1 kit
Resistor, 10K Ohm (from kit)			
Resistor, 4.7K Ohm (from kit)			
SDcard, 2GB or more	Most online and retail stores	varies	1
Soldering iron and solder	Most online and retail stores	varies	1
TMP36 sensor	www.sparkfun.com/products/10988	$1.50	3+
	www.adafruit.com/products/165		
USB keyboard	Most online and retail stores	varies	1
USB power supply	Most online and retail stores	varies	1
USB to mini-USB cable for use with XBee Explorer USB	www.sparkfun.com/products/11301	$3.95	1 for each USB explorer
USB type A to USB micro male	Most online and retail stores	varies	1
Wall power supply (6V–12V)	www.sparkfun.com/products/10273	$6.95	1
XBee adapter kit	www.adafruit.com/products/126	$10.00	1**
XBee Explorer Dongle	www.sparkfun.com/products/9819	$24.95	1**

(*continued*)

---

[2]You need one for each XBee adapter kit.
[3]Not needed if you have an Ethernet shield with a microSD reader.
[4]You do not need this if you have the DS1307 module.

Table A-1. (*continued*)

Item	Vendors	Est. Cost USD	Qty Needed
XBee Explorer USB	www.sparkfun.com/products/8687	$24.95	1**
XBee Explorer Regulated with headers	www.sparkfun.com/products/11373	$9.95	1
XBee shield	www.sparkfun.com/products/10854	$24.95	1
XBee-ZB (ZB) series 2 or 2.5	www.sparkfun.com	$25.00	3
	www.adafruit.com	$25.00	

** *You only need three total of any of these adapters*

Table A-2. *Optional Component Shopping List*

Item	Vendors	Est. Cost USD
Cellular shield with cellular module	www.sparkfun.com/products/9607	$99.95
Engineering notebook	www.sparkfun.com/products/11064 (red)	$4.95
	www.sparkfun.com/products/11063 (grey)	$4.95
	www.adafruit.com/products/295 (Maker's)	$19.99
Prototyping circuit board	www.sparkfun.com/products/8815	$4.50
Raspberry Pi Alamode	www.seeedstudio.com/depot/alamode-arduino-compatible-raspberry-pi-plate-p-1285.html?cPath=6_7	$35.00
	www.makershed.com/AlaMode_for_Raspberry_Pi_p/mkwy1.htm	$49.99
Seed Studio Stalker board	www.seeedstudio.com/depot/seeeduino-stalker-v2-p-727.html	$39.00
Seed Studio Stalker wireless sensor kit	www.seeedstudio.com/depot/seeeduino-stalker-waterproof-solar-kit-p-911.html?cPath=84_13	$59.50
Small enclosure	www.sparkfun.com/products/11366	$7.95
Stackable header kit Used to increase clearance between shields or the Arduino board	www.sparkfun.com/products/11417	$1.50
	www.adafruit.com/products/85	$1.95

Index

■ B

Barometric pressure sensor
    BMP085 I2C sensor, 131
    I2C feature, 131
    /etc/modules, 131
    getPiRevision() method, 136
    hardware, setup, 132
    output, 136
    software, setup
        Adafruit_BMP085 code, 134
        I2C protocol, 133
        git utility, 134
        i2cdetect utility, 134
        pi_bmp085.py script, 135

■ C

client.available() method, 274
client.print() method, 274
client.println() method, 274
Cloud computing services
    API, 172
    Arduino (writing data to Xively)
        fun, script, 181
        hardware setup, 174
        software, 175
        test the sketch, 179
    device/channel, 171
    meaning, 169
    Pachube/Cosm, 170
    Raspberry Pi (writing data to Xively)
        hardware, 181
        Python scripts, 186
        script format, 188
        software, 183
    Xively, 170
Component shopping list
    MySQL, 222
    storing sensor data, 188

■ D

Data-aggregate nodes
    advantages, 267
    components, 306
    local-storage (see Local-storage data aggregator)
    Raspberry pi server
        coding file, 302
        Connector/Python library, 300
        constants and variables, 300
        hardware, 299
        INSERT query, 301
        mysql client application, 301
        mysql.connector library, 300

        MySQL database server, 299
        run_query() method, 301
        testing, 304
        TMP36 sensor via ADC module, 306
    remote-storage data (see Remote-storage
        data aggregator)
Database connector library
    Arduino Preferences dialog, 228
    components, 264
    database-enabled sketch
        database setup, 229
        Ethernet.begin() method, 233
        Ethernet shield, 231
        header files, 232
        preliminary setup, 232
        query, 233
        setup() method, 233
        testing (see Testing)
    definition, 223
    flash memory, 227
    hardware requirements
        Arduino Ethernet shield, 225
        Arduino Leonardo, 225
        Arduino Uno, 224
        Arduino WiFi shield, 226
    inserting data, 259
    limitations, 229
    MySQL Arduino Client
        complete source code, 255
        features, 259
        hardware setup, 252
        sensor database, 254
        software setup, 254
        test execution, 257
    MySQL connector/Arduino code, 227
        cmd_query(), 249
        field structure, 247
        free_columns_buffer() method, 251
        free_row_buffer() method, 251
        get_columns() method, 251
        get_next_row() method, 251
        grid, 251
        library files, 246
        public methods, 248
        show_results() method, 250
    SELECT query
        custom query results method, 261
        get_columns() method, 261–262
        Lookup Value, 263
        show_results() method, 261
    SHA1 library, 228
    troubleshooting
        binary sketch size, 245
        connector installation, 244
        MySQL server configuration, 240

■ S

■ T

Get the eBook for only $10!

Now you can take the weightless companion with you anywhere, anytime. Your purchase of this book entitles you to 3 electronic versions for only $10.

This Apress title will prove so indispensible that you'll want to carry it with you everywhere, which is why we are offering the eBook in 3 formats for only $10 if you have already purchased the print book.

Convenient and fully searchable, the PDF version enables you to easily find and copy code—or perform examples by quickly toggling between instructions and applications. The MOBI format is ideal for your Kindle, while the ePUB can be utilized on a variety of mobile devices.

Go to www.apress.com/promo/tendollars to purchase your companion eBook.

Apress®
THE EXPERT'S VOICE™

Druck: KN Digital Printforce GmbH · Schockenriedstraße 37 · 70565 Stuttgart